Learning D

Leverage the modern convenience and modeling power
of the D programming language to develop software
with native efficiency

Michael Parker

open source✲
community experience distilled

PACKT PUBLISHING

BIRMINGHAM - MUMBAI

Learning D

First published: November 2015

Production reference: 1241115

Published by Packt Publishing Ltd.
Livery Place
35 Livery Street
Birmingham B3 2PB, UK.

ISBN 978-1-78355-248-1

www.packtpub.com

Credits

Author
Michael Parker

Reviewers
John Loughran Colvin
Jonathan M Davis
Kingsley Hendrickse
David Nadlinger
Steven Schveighoffer
Ilya Yaroshenko

Commissioning Editor
Akhram Hussain

Acquisition Editor
Reshma Raman

Content Development Editor
Merwyn D'souza

Technical Editor
Vivek Arora

Copy Editor
Imon Biswas

Project Coordinator
Neha Bhatnagar

Proofreader
Safis Editing

Indexer
Rekha Nair

Production Coordinator
Melwyn Dsa

Cover Work
Melwyn Dsa

Foreword

How far things have come! I started D in 1999. The odds of any new programming language endeavor succeeding were minimal.

But here we are with the latest book on D, *Learning D* by *Michael Parker*.

The arc of programming languages I've learned follows a consistent pattern – my first Fortran code looked a lot like Basic. My first C code looked similar to Fortran. C++ code looked similar to C, and my early D code looked similar to C++. It takes some time to get used to a language before learning its own idiomatic style, and this is what it takes before the source code starts to shine.

After all, if your D code looks similar to C++, what's the point?

Learning D fills the need to get up-to-speed quickly by explaining how to write code in a way that fits in perfectly with D's combination of characteristics. Far from being a dry technical specification, Michael writes about D from a more personal perspective, as you'd expect from someone tutoring you. He lists how to use the features, how they compare with other languages, and offers best practices. He offers background anecdotes and explanations for why some things are the way they are, and how D has evolved, which can be surprisingly helpful in using the language more effectively.

D has been characterized in many ways, but my favorite is that it is designed to be fun to program in. After all, programming being our profession, isn't it better when we enjoy our tools?

I know this book is a labor of love from Michael, as the language itself is a labor of love from myself and the rest of the D community. I hope this joy is successfully imparted to you, the reader and programmer. I'm sure that Michael and I would be well rewarded for our endeavors if this is the case.

Enjoy!

Walter Bright
Creator of the D Language and Engineer

About the Author

Michael Parker created the popular D library collection, Derelict, in 2004, and has been the primary maintainer ever since. He also blogs about the language at *The One with D*, and is a coauthor of the book *Learn to Tango with D, Apress*. He lives in Seoul, South Korea, with his wife, Mi Kyoung, and their dogs, Charlie, Happy, Joey, and Toby.

This is the first book on which I've been the sole author, but no author works alone. Without the professional assistance of my editors, Merwyn D'souza and Reshma Raman, I would have been lost at sea. I'd hate to admit how many errors would have persisted without the expert feedback of the technical reviewers, John Colvin, Jonathan Davis, Kingsley Hendrickse, David Nadlinger, Steven Schveighoffer, and Ilya Yaroshenko. They have all helped make this a much better book than it otherwise would have been; the blame for any remaining technical errors that may surface rests squarely on my shoulders.

I'd like to offer a great deal of gratitude to all of the active members of the D community who participate in the D forums, helping both newbies and old-timers alike in overcoming confusion and solving problems. I'd especially like to thank Ali Çehreli and Adam D. Ruppe, whose own writings and posts in the newsgroups helped to clarify some issues I had in exploring corners of D I had rarely touched before writing this book. Thanks also to Walter Bright and Andrei Alexandrescu, both of whom have made a number of sacrifices to further the development of this wonderful programming language.

Finally, I could never have expended the time and energy on this book that I did without the support of my wife, Mi Kyoung. I owe her a great many missed dinners and canceled events, along with my everlasting thanks and love.

About the Reviewers

John Loughran Colvin is an avid programmer and active member of the D community with multiple projects in flight, including a collaboration aiming to build a comprehensive base for scientific programming in D (`http://dlangscience.github.io/`).

> I would like to thank friends and family who keep me sane while I do all this!

Jonathan M Davis is the primary author of `std.datetime` in D's standard library, Phobos, and is one of Phobos' core contributors. He is a professional developer and has experience in a number of programming languages, including C++, Haskell, Java, and D. For better or worse, he's well known in the D community for answering questions and being long-winded. He currently resides in California.

Kingsley Hendrickse is a polyglot software developer who specializes in building software using agile principles. His career began in the late '90s where he focused primarily on functional and automated testing but gradually expanded into agile and software engineering while working at ThoughtWorks.

After many years programming in Ruby and Java, he was introduced to the D language while looking for new challenges. He has a wide range of development interests and is currently focusing on web development using Scala, D, and JavaScript using a functional programming style.

He has spent the last decade working for a wide range of prominent banking and financial companies.

Steven Schveighoffer has a bachelors degree in computer science from WPI, and has 16 years of experience working on various systems from small microcontrollers to enterprise servers. He has been active in the D community since 2007 and has made several major contributions to the D language and runtime.

Steve is a principal software engineer at National Resource Management Inc., an energy savings company (http://www.nrminc.com/).

www.PacktPub.com

Support files, eBooks, discount offers, and more

For support files and downloads related to your book, please visit www.PacktPub.com.

Did you know that Packt offers eBook versions of every book published, with PDF and ePub files available? You can upgrade to the eBook version at www.PacktPub.com and as a print book customer, you are entitled to a discount on the eBook copy. Get in touch with us at service@packtpub.com for more details.

At www.PacktPub.com, you can also read a collection of free technical articles, sign up for a range of free newsletters and receive exclusive discounts and offers on Packt books and eBooks.

https://www2.packtpub.com/books/subscription/packtlib

Do you need instant solutions to your IT questions? PacktLib is Packt's online digital book library. Here, you can search, access, and read Packt's entire library of books.

Why subscribe?

- Fully searchable across every book published by Packt
- Copy and paste, print, and bookmark content
- On demand and accessible via a web browser

Free access for Packt account holders

If you have an account with Packt at www.PacktPub.com, you can use this to access PacktLib today and view 9 entirely free books. Simply use your login credentials for immediate access.

Table of Contents

Preface

Walter Bright first released the D programming language into the wild on December 8, 2001. Three weeks later, seven more iterations of the compiler had been uploaded to the Digital Mars website, incorporating fixes for bugs reported by users who had already begun experimenting with this exciting new language. In the years since, enthusiasts have continued to actively participate in D's development, pushing the language through two major versions and numerous compiler releases. D is very much a community-driven programming language.

This book aims to bring you up to speed with D to the degree that you can be confident in developing your own D programs and, if you are so motivated, participate in activities that drive the language forward. It is assumed that you already have some familiarity with other languages similar to D, such as C++ or Java, and have some familiarity with working with the command line. With this in mind, fewer details will be given for the features of D that are similar to those of other C-family languages and no instructions will be given on how to perform basic command-line tasks, such as changing directories or setting the system path.

What this book covers

Chapter 1, How to Get a D in Programming, introduces you to the D programming language and provides instructions for setting up the DMD compiler and the DUB build tool and package manager.

Chapter 2, Building a Foundation with D Fundamentals, gives an overview of all of D's foundational features, such as basic types, loop constructs, flow control, and more.

Chapter 3, Programming Objects the D Way, discusses D's support for object-oriented programming, including aggregate types and interfaces.

Chapter 4, Running Code at Compile Time, provides a tutorial on the compile-time aspects of D, including its support for Generative Programming and CTFE (Compile-Time Function Evaluation).

Chapter 5, Generic Programming Made Easy, explores the basics of D's support for Generic Programming, including templates, template constraints, and mixins.

Chapter 6, Understanding Ranges, introduces the Range concept, which serves as the core of D's support for functional programming.

Chapter 7, Composing Functional Pipelines with Algorithms and Ranges, explores several range-based functions in the standard library that can be used to write functional-style code and reduce memory allocations.

Chapter 8, Exploring the Wide World of D, looks at the D ecosystem, highlighting specific websites, tools, and third-party libraries.

Chapter 9, Connecting D with C, references how to create D bindings for C libraries to take advantage of existing codebases.

Chapter 10, Taking D Online, introduces the asynchronous, event-driven networking and web app framework, vibe.d, through the development of a sample project.

Chapter 11, Taking D to the Next Level, provides a quick look at other language and library features that can serve as a starting point for further exploration of the D programming language.

What you need for this book

To compile the code examples in this book, you will need DMD 2.068 or a later version. To compile the sample projects, you will also need DUB 0.9.24 or a later version. Installation instructions for both are provided in the first chapter.

In order to download dependencies, the color example in *Chapter 8, Exploring the Wide World of D*, and the sample project in *Chapter 10, Taking D Online*, requires an Internet connection the first time they are compiled.

Who this book is for

This book is intended for those with some background in a C-family language who want to learn how to apply their knowledge and experience to D. Perhaps you're a college student looking to use D for hobby projects, or a career programmer interested in expanding your skillset. This book will help you get up to speed with the language and avoid common pitfalls that arise when translating C-family experience to D.

Conventions

In this book, you will find a number of text styles that distinguish between different kinds of information. Here are some examples of these styles and an explanation of their meaning.

Code words in text, database table names, folder names, filenames, file extensions, pathnames, dummy URLs, user input, and Twitter handles are shown as follows: "An anonymous enum declaration does not declare a new type."

A block of code is set as follows:

```
void healthBasedSwap(int[] squad1, int[] squad2) {
    import std.algorithm : sort, SwapStrategy;
    import std.range : chain;
    squad1.chain(squad2).sort!((a,b) => a > b,
    SwapStrategy.unstable)();
}
```

When we wish to draw your attention to a particular part of a code block, the relevant lines or items are set in bold:

```
void healthBasedSwap(int[] squad1, int[] squad2) {
    import std.algorithm : sort, SwapStrategy;
    import std.range : chain;
    squad1.chain(squad2).sort!((a,b) => a > b,
    SwapStrategy.unstable)();
}
```

Any command-line input or output is written as follows:

```
dmd hello.d
```

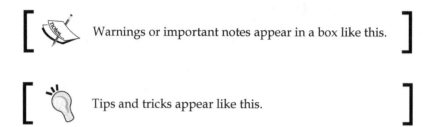

Warnings or important notes appear in a box like this.

Tips and tricks appear like this.

Reader feedback

Feedback from our readers is always welcome. Let us know what you think about this book—what you liked or disliked. Reader feedback is important for us as it helps us develop titles that you will really get the most out of.

To send us general feedback, simply e-mail feedback@packtpub.com, and mention the book's title in the subject of your message.

If there is a topic that you have expertise in and you are interested in either writing or contributing to a book, see our author guide at www.packtpub.com/authors.

Customer support

Now that you are the proud owner of a Packt book, we have a number of things to help you to get the most from your purchase.

Downloading the example code

You can download the example code files from your account at http://www. packtpub.com for all the Packt Publishing books you have purchased. If you purchased this book elsewhere, you can visit http://www.packtpub.com/support and register to have the files e-mailed directly to you.

Errata

Although we have taken every care to ensure the accuracy of our content, mistakes do happen. If you find a mistake in one of our books—maybe a mistake in the text or the code—we would be grateful if you could report this to us. By doing so, you can save other readers from frustration and help us improve subsequent versions of this book. If you find any errata, please report them by visiting http://www.packtpub.com/submit-errata, selecting your book, clicking on the **Errata Submission Form** link, and entering the details of your errata. Once your errata are verified, your submission will be accepted and the errata will be uploaded to our website or added to any list of existing errata under the Errata section of that title.

To view the previously submitted errata, go to https://www.packtpub.com/books/content/support and enter the name of the book in the search field. The required information will appear under the **Errata** section.

Piracy

Piracy of copyrighted material on the Internet is an ongoing problem across all media. At Packt, we take the protection of our copyright and licenses very seriously. If you come across any illegal copies of our works in any form on the Internet, please provide us with the location address or website name immediately so that we can pursue a remedy.

Please contact us at copyright@packtpub.com with a link to the suspected pirated material.

We appreciate your help in protecting our authors and our ability to bring you valuable content.

Questions

If you have a problem with any aspect of this book, you can contact us at questions@packtpub.com, and we will do our best to address the problem.

1
How to Get a D in Programming

Before diving into the core features of the D programming language, some laying of groundwork is in order. This first chapter serves as a gentle introduction to D and as a guide to installing the prerequisite tools of the trade we'll be using throughout the book. The example program shown here isn't anything earth-shatteringly amazing, but it does demonstrate a couple of features of D that do not exist in other languages. The sample project that is developed over the course of the book is also introduced here, with a look at the motivation behind it and the features that will be implemented. Here's what you can expect to see:

- Say hello to D: This examines a simple D program and gives you advice on where to go for help with D

- The Digital Mars D compiler: This covers how to install and run DMD

- Say hello to MovieMan: This is an introduction to the two versions of the sample project developed throughout the book

- DUB—the D build tool and package manager: This covers how to install DUB and configure it to build the first version of MovieMan

Say hello to D

The D programming language is a multi-paradigm language that belongs to the C family. Out of the box, it supports aspects of procedural, object-oriented, generic, generative, and functional programming. That's not to say that it's an OOP language or a functional programming language, or that it can accurately be pigeonholed into any specific paradigm. The philosophy of D is to provide a range of tools that allow the programmer to have efficiency, control, and modeling power while ensuring that all of the disparate parts work smoothly together. Use object orientation where you need it, but forgo it for procedural or functional programming in other areas of your code base and be assured that it will all work together as a cohesive whole. Many D programmers will tell you that there isn't one specific feature of D that, taken in isolation, makes the language a pleasure to use. Rather, it's the sum of all the parts that keeps them writing D code.

New users coming to D from other C-family languages will find a great deal that looks familiar. That can be reassuring and makes for a good head start on learning some of D's features; caution is warranted, however. It's tempting to take that familiarity for granted and try to write D as if it were a more familiar language. For the most part, things will work as expected. D is, after all, a member of the C family. But in some cases, this is certain to lead to unexpected compiler errors, or the realization that some blocks of code aren't behaving in the manner the new D user thinks they should. In other cases, there is a more idiomatic D approach that can improve readability or maintainability, particularly when working with the standard library.

To learn a new language effectively, it's necessary to come at it with as close to a blank slate as possible. Just because features look the same on the surface as they do in another language, doesn't mean they are the same underneath. Given that premise, a consistent theme in this book is that D is not C++, Java, C#, or any language other than D. When you are writing D code, you should be thinking in D. Several of the code snippets in the book are intended not just to introduce D features, but to demonstrate explicitly how certain features differ from other languages. You are encouraged to enter such snippets into an editor yourself, especially if C++ is already in your muscle memory. Implementing the snippets as you encounter them and seeing the differences in action makes it more likely that you'll think in D instead of C++ when working on your own D projects.

D started life as the Mars programming language, but Walter's friends kept calling it D. Eventually, he began to do so as well and the name stuck (see the D FAQ at `http://dlang.org/faq.html#q1` for background). Neither name lends itself to productive web searches, but search engines are able to recognize the keyword *dlang*. Use that in your list of search terms rather than simply using D and you should be rewarded with a number of relevant hits.

An introductory program

This section presents a simple D program demonstrating a handful of language and library features. A brief description of each feature is then given, along with a reference to the chapter in which it is explained in more detail. Anyone familiar with C should be able to follow the code rather easily, though there might be a couple of features that seem unusual. If you happen to find any of it confusing, don't worry about it for now. Each feature will be explained later in the book.

In preparation for implementing all of the code snippets and examples in this book, it's a good idea to create a directory somewhere that's easy to navigate to from the command line—for example `C:\LearningD` or `~/learningd`. However you choose to name this directory, it will be referred to as `$LEARNINGD` throughout the book. Each chapter should have its own subdirectory. The example in this section should be saved as `$LEARNINGD/Chapter01/hello.d`.

Note that I prefer to use forward slashes when I type source paths, unless I'm talking specifically about Windows, which means Windows users should convert them to backslashes as needed.

Let's look at the example now:

```
import core.thread;
import std.stdio;
void main() {
    import std.range : iota, retro;
    write("Greeting in ");
    foreach(num; iota(1, 4).retro) {
        writef("%s...", num);
        stdout.flush();
        Thread.sleep(1.seconds);
    }
    writeln();
    writeln("Hello world!");
}
```

The first thing to understand is that all D source files serve a purpose beyond just being text files on your computer. A D source file is also a D module. Most D users use the terms *source file* and *module* interchangeably. A **module** is one of several levels of encapsulation in a D program (we'll talk more about encapsulation in *Chapter 3, Programming Objects the D Way*). If you compile a D source file named `hello.d`, then the compiler will read it into memory and your program will contain a single module named `hello`. This is the default behavior. Since we are implementing a simple one-module program, we'll just accept the default and put off learning how to override it until *Chapter 2, Building a Foundation with D Fundamentals*.

The first two lines of the example look like this:

```
import core.thread;
import std.stdio;
```

An import declaration tells the compiler to look up a given module, specified by the name immediately following the `import` keyword, and then make some or all of its symbols available within a specific section of the current module. In the format we use here, in which no symbols are specified, all publicly visible symbols in the imported module are made available. The location of the declaration is what determines the section, or scope, in which the symbols will be available. In this case, since the declarations are in module scope and no specific symbols are listed, the net effect is that every publicly visible symbol in the `core.thread` and `std.stdio` modules is available for use throughout the entirety of our `hello` module.

Consider the module name `std.stdio`. Each part of the name has a defined meaning. Although the term **module name** is used to refer to the full name, the part to the right of the dot, `stdio`, is the actual module name. The part to the left of the dot, `std`, is the name of a **package**. Packages are used to group modules into hierarchies. A module can belong to only one package, but that package can be a subpackage of another package, which can be a subpackage of another package, and so on. This means you can have multiple package names on the left side of the dot, such as `mylib.data.formats.json`. Here, we have three packages and are referring to a module called `json`. The package named `formats` is a subpackage of `data`, which is a subpackage of the top-level, or root, package called `mylib`. There's more to say about modules and import declarations in *Chapter 2, Building a Foundation with D Fundamentals*.

The `std` and `core` packages are available with any D compiler; the former is part of Phobos, the D standard library, and the latter is part of the runtime library, DRuntime. `std.stdio` makes available everything needed for basic file I/O, including reading from standard input (`stdin`) and writing to standard output (`stdout`). The module `core.thread` provides facilities for creating new threads and affecting the execution of the current thread.

Now take a look at the next line:

```
void main() {
```

Every D program requires a function named `main`. When a program is first launched, control passes from the operating system to the C runtime and from there to the D runtime. Finally, `main` is called and the program takes control. We'll look at this in a little more detail in *Chapter 3, Programming Objects the D Way*, when we'll also see that it's possible to execute code before `main` is called.

There are four fundamental alternatives for declaring a `main` function. Which one to choose is entirely dependent on the requirements of the program:

```
void main() {}
void main(string[] args) {}
int main() { return 0; }
int main(string[] args) { return 0; }
```

The first two versions are ultimately equivalent to the latter two; the compiler will ensure that they actually return `0` upon successful execution. Execution is considered to fail when an exception is thrown (exceptions are introduced in *Chapter 3, Programming Objects the D Way*). For most of the examples in this book, the first signature is all we need. Except for a couple of snippets later on, we aren't going to parse any command line arguments, so we can dispense with forms that accept an array of `string`s. We also aren't writing any programs that need to pass a return value to the OS on exit, so we have no need of the versions with the `int` return.

Windows programmers might be wondering how D handles `WinMain`. DRuntime knows only of `main`, so if `WinMain` is used as the program entry point, then all of the initialization normally carried out by DRuntime must be handled manually. We'll learn more about DRuntime later.

Let's get back to the code. The next line is another import declaration, one which differs from the two declarations at the top of the module:

```
import std.range : iota, retro;
```

Because this declaration is inside a function, it is called a **scoped import**. Symbols made visible by scoped imports are only visible inside the scope in which the declaration is made. In this case, the symbols are visible only inside `main`. There's more to this declaration, though. Notice the colon, followed by `iota` and `retro`. In an import declaration, a colon followed by a comma-separated list of symbols means that only the listed symbols will be visible. In this case, no symbols from `std.range` are visible in `main` other than `iota` and `retro`. We'll see what they do shortly.

It's time for a line that actually puts something on the screen. For that, we're going to invoke a handy and very flexible function from the `std.stdio` module:

```
write("Greeting in ");
```

The `write` function is one of a handful of functions that print text strings to standard output. It's analogous to the C standard library function `puts`, but it differs in that it can take any number of arguments of any type. Each argument will be printed in the order they are given to the function, with no spaces added between them. For example:

```
write("Happy ", 100, "th birthday to", "you!")
```

This prints the text `Happy 100th birthday to you!`.

The next line introduces three items:

```
foreach(num; iota(1, 4).retro) {
```

The `foreach` loop is a loop construct that can be used to iterate over a range. `iota` is a function that returns a range of numbers, in this case from 1 to 3. `retro` is a function that takes a range as input and returns a new one containing the elements of the original range in reverse order. The ultimate result of this line is a loop iterating over the numbers 3, 2, 1. The `foreach` loop is described in *Chapter 2, Building a Foundation with D Fundamentals*. The entirety of *Chapter 6, Understanding Ranges*, is devoted to explaining ranges, an integral part of D. Both the `iota` and `retro` functions are described in *Chapter 7, Composing Functional Pipelines with Algorithms and Ranges*.

It's worth noting here that `iota(1, 4).retro` is the same as `retro(iota(1, 4))`. The former syntax is possible because of a feature called **Uniform Function Call Syntax (UFCS)**. Given a function `func` and a function argument `arg`, `func(arg)` can be written as `arg.func()`. You'll learn more about UFCS in *Chapter 2, Building a Foundation with D Fundamentals*.

Next up are the three lines of the `foreach` loop:

```
writef("%s...", num);
stdout.flush();
Thread.sleep(1.seconds);
```

The `writef` function is a variation of `write` that prints a formatted text string to standard output. It's analogous to the C standard library function `printf`; with `.stdout` is a global instance of a type called `File`, both of which are declared in `std.stdio`.

When writing to a file handle, the operating system buffers text internally for efficiency. Normally, when the handle belongs to a console or terminal, line buffering is enabled. This means that the buffer is flushed when a newline character is printed to the output stream. In this example, calling `flush` manually flushes the buffer in order to achieve the effect of having one number printed per second; otherwise, it would all be printed at once after the loop exits and the first call to `writeln` executes. This effect is regulated by the call to `Thread.sleep`, which causes execution of the process to pause for one second.

Note that the call to `Thread.sleep` is not using UFCS. `Thread` is a class, and `sleep` is a static member function. `1.seconds`, however, does use UFCS. The function `seconds` is declared in a runtime module named `core.time`. This module is imported indirectly by `core.thread` such that all of its symbols are visible. `1.seconds` is the same as `seconds(1)` (parentheses on function calls are sometimes optional). This function returns an instance of the `Duration` type, which `sleep` uses to determine how long to pause the current thread. Public imports and function call syntax are discussed in *Chapter 2, Building a Foundation with D Fundamentals*. Classes and member functions are introduced in *Chapter 3, Programming Objects the D Way*.

Finally, the last two lines of the example:

```
writeln();
writeln("Hello world!");
```

The `writeln` function is identical to `write`, but has one additional feature: it appends a newline character to the output. Here, we call it twice. The first call appends a newline to the text that was written in the loop, while the second prints the greeting. This could be condensed to one line as `writeln("\nHello world!")`. Note that there is also a formatting version of this function called `writefln`.

In order to verify that this program works as expected, it will need to be compiled and executed. Instructions on how to do so will be discussed later in the chapter.

Getting help

In your journey with D, you're inevitably going to need assistance. There are a couple of primary online locales where experienced D users can be found answering questions from not-so-experienced D users and having fierce debates about language features, as passionate programmers are known to do.

The first place any new D user should look is `http://forum.dlang.org/`. This isn't a self-contained forum as the URL implies, but rather a web interface to a newsgroup server maintained by Digital Mars. If you ever find yourself wondering why you can't edit or delete posts in the D forums, this is why. The forum targeting new users is `digitalmars.D.learn`, project and major news announcements are made in `digitalmars.D.announce`, while `digitalmars.D` is where you can go to witness or participate in discussions about the state of the language and its future direction. As you become more familiar with D and its ecosystem, some of the other forums might start to be of interest to you.

The web interface called DFeed was developed in D by an active community member named Vladimir Panteleev. You can find the source for DFeed at `https://github.com/CyberShadow/DFeed`.

If the web interface doesn't do it for you, there are other options to access the forums. Given that the primary backend is a newsgroup, you can set up an account in a newsgroup reader for `news.digitalmars.com` and select the newsgroups you're interested in following. Alternatively, you can point your browser at `http://lists.puremagic.com/mailman/listinfo` and subscribe to forums of interest via the mailing list interface. Again, the mailing lists are collectively an alternative interface to the newsgroups and not a completely independent entity.

The D community is generally helpful and friendly to those asking questions in the `digitalmars.D.learn` forum. You should never feel hesitant about asking questions in the D forums. Experienced users drop by regularly, willing to answer the most basic questions. You can also find a number of D users idling in the #D IRC channel. If you have an IRC client, #D is located at `http://freenode.net/`. Anyone there can answer your questions about D. I've never been much of an IRC user, but I do drop by #D now and again. Whenever I'm around, I'll be happy to answer questions about this book or any of my other D projects. I'm usually found under the handle `aldacron` in IRC and my real name in the forums.

The Digital Mars D compiler

DMD is the reference compiler for the D programming language. Created by Walter Bright, it is still maintained by him with the help of a handful of talented volunteers. It's not the only D compiler out there. GDC is built on top of the **GNU Compiler Collection** (**GCC**) and LDC uses the LLVM toolchain. Both compilers were created, and continue to be maintained, by members of the D community. As you write more D code, you'll find that DMD has blazingly fast compile times, while GDC and LDC produce highly optimized executables that tend to have better performance (though they are far from slow in terms of compilation speed). Because of this, it's not uncommon for D programmers to use DMD during development of a new project to take advantage of the faster compile times, then use one of the other compilers to build the final release and benefit from the more advanced optimizations. That said, we're going to be focused exclusively on DMD in this book. The code snippets and the sample project should compile with GDC or LDC just fine, but any compiler-specific instructions in the text will be for DMD.

There is nothing complex about installing DMD. Before we make that happen, it's important to understand a couple of things about how DMD works.

Frontends, backends, and linkers

One of the primary goals Walter established during D's early development was that it must be binary-compatible with C. Essentially, this means that it should be possible to compile a C source file with a C compiler and combine the output into a program that is written in D and compiled with a D compiler, or vice versa. To achieve this goal, output from a D compiler has to be in a format that C toolchains can understand. An in-depth discussion of compiler technology is quite a long way beyond the scope of this book, but it's necessary to have a minimal understanding of a small part of it in order to make DMD work for you more effectively.

Compilers typically have two major components that work together to create the final output: the frontend and the backend. The frontend is tied directly to a specific language. It takes source code as input and transforms it into an intermediate, language-agnostic format as output. The backend is tied to a specific platform. It takes the transformed code from the frontend as input and generates machine code as output, typically in the form of object files. Once the object files are created, ultimately one of two things will happen: either they are passed to a tool that links them into a final executable or they are passed to a tool that packs them into a library. The former tool is called a **linker** and the latter is called a **librarian** or **archiver**, though it's possible for one tool to perform both tasks.

For Walter to achieve his goal of binary compatibility with C, he opted to make use of existing toolchains where possible. This way, he could expend most of his effort on the frontend, the part that actually deals with D source code, and leave the rest to existing, tried-and-tested tools. He was already in the C and C++ compiler business—the company he owns, Digital Mars, distributes the Digital Mars C and C++ Compiler (DMC)—so he had his own existing backend and linker sitting on his hard drive. Appropriately, he began to implement a D frontend and hooked it up with the DMC backend to create DMD. Since the Digital Mars C(++) toolchain is Windows-specific, other options needed to be considered when it came time to port DMD to additional platforms. Walter's solution was to modify the backend to generate the appropriate output for each target platform, then have the compiler make use of each platform's system linker and librarian to generate the final binaries.

Running DMD on POSIX systems is a straightforward process. Since the compiler uses the system toolchain to create the final output on each system it supports, things tend to work smoothly without any conflicts. This includes support for both 32- and 64-bit output. The story on Windows isn't quite so rosy.

> In this book, POSIX is used to describe any non-Windows, Unix-like system supported by DMD, whether they are 100 percent POSIX-certified or not. That includes Linux, Mac OS X, and the various BSDs.

The problem is that the Digital Mars linker, OPTLINK, is ancient. It uses an object file format that is incompatible with most modern C and C++ toolchains. We'll explore this issue in more detail in *Chapter 9, Connecting D with C*, because it's an important thing to understand when interacting with C. Another point about OPTLINK is that it only supports 32-bit output. 64-bit support was implemented on Windows by giving DMD the ability to generate object files in a format understood by the Microsoft toolchain.

The major upside of this approach is that it eliminates the annoyances that come from conflicting object file formats on Windows, at least when compiling 64-bit binaries with the -m64 command line switch. The downside is that compiling 64-bit binaries with DMD now requires the installation either of a version of Windows SDK that includes the MS tools, or a non-Express version of Microsoft Visual Studio. DMD cannot be a completely self-contained distribution for 64-bit development on Windows. As of DMD 2.067, the Microsoft tools can also be used in place of the default Digital Mars toolchain to generate 32-bit binaries by passing a command line switch, -m32mscoff, to DMD.

Installing DMD

Installing the very latest release of DMD is always dead easy. Simply point your browser to http://dlang.org/download.html and pick your poison. Several options are available, including an installer for Windows, a DMG file for Mac OS X, deb packages for Ubuntu and Debian, RPM files for Fedora, CentOS and openSuse, and ZIP files for each of those platforms plus FreeBSD.

DMD is also available from the package repositories of most Linux systems, as well as through homebrew and macports for OS X users and the ports tree for BSD systems. If it isn't available in your platform's package repository, or if it's outdated, choose the appropriate package for your platform from the download page. The ZIP file is a good choice when you want more control over where the compiler is installed. Here, we're going to note a couple of specific points related to the Windows installer, then we'll see how to install from the ZIP file.

The Windows installer

Either a version of the Windows SDK that ships with the Microsoft linker or a non-Express version of Microsoft Visual Studio must be installed in order to compile 64-bit apps (or to use the -m32mscoff option) with DMD on Windows. It will help a great deal if one of these is installed *before* installing DMD. This way, the DMD installer can automatically find where the MS tools are located and configure the compiler to use them. If DMD is installed first, then its configuration file, sc.ini, must be manually edited for it to find them.

Older versions of the Windows SDK shipped with a complete compiler toolchain. Since the release of the Windows 8 SDK, that is no longer the case. The Express versions of Visual Studio include the toolchain, but do not ship with the system libraries needed by DMD. Installing the Windows 8, 8.1, or 10 SDKs with a version of Visual Studio Express will provide everything necessary. When using an older version of the SDK, no additional software needs to be installed.

A better option is to install a non-Express version of Visual Studio. The Community versions are available for free. These include everything DMD needs in one package. Support for VS 2015 was added in DMD 2.069.

The DMD installer will also ask if you want to install Visual D. This is a Visual Studio plugin developed by Rainer Schuetze. While I strongly recommend that you use a text editor and the command line to work through the code samples in this book in order to better familiarize yourself with DMD, you might find Visual D quite useful later on, especially if you enjoy using Visual Studio.

Installing from the ZIP

Installing from the ZIP file isn't difficult, but requires a bit of manual manipulation for things to work easily from the command line. The required steps differ across platforms. We'll start with how to install from the ZIP on Windows before looking at installation on the supported POSIX platforms.

The Windows ZIP

Unzip the files into any directory. I recommend something short and easy to remember, such as `C:\D` (this is the default location used by the installer). Optionally, add the `windows\bin` subdirectory to the system `PATH`. Assuming you've unzipped in `C:\D`, the full path would be `C:\D\dmd2\windows\bin`.

The Windows version of DMD is distributed as a 32-bit program and can compile both 32-bit and 64-bit binaries. By default, it is configured to compile 32-bit using OPTLINK. If you're happy with that, there's nothing else to do. 64-bit binaries can be compiled by passing `-m64` on the command line when invoking DMD but, as described, the MS toolchain will have to be installed for it to work. After the MS tools are installed, open the `C:\D\dmd2\windows\bin\sc.ini` file in a text editor. There, you'll find a block of instructions on how to configure DMD to use the Microsoft tools. Several of the standard Windows SDK and Visual Studio paths are already preconfigured, with most of them commented out. If the default, uncommented paths do not match your version of the Microsoft toolchain, it should be enough to comment out those lines by adding a semicolon, `;`, in front of each and uncommenting the lines that match your installation by deleting the existing semicolons from in front of them. At this point, I'd like to remind you that the DMD installer takes care of all of this for you.

On every supported platform except Windows, the DMD configuration file is called `dmd.conf`. On Windows, it's called `sc.ini` to maintain compatibility with the Digital Mars toolchain that DMD uses by default.

The POSIX ZIPs

On the three POSIX systems supported by DMD (Mac OS X, Linux, and FreeBSD), it's not uncommon to extract the ZIP in the home directory. This will result in a `~/dmd2` directory. The easiest thing to do with this is to leave the binaries where they are and add the appropriate subdirectory to the system `PATH` variable.

The Linux ZIP file contains both 32-bit and 64-bit versions of DMD; the Mac OS X ZIP file contains a 64-bit version of DMD; for FreeBSD, there are two ZIP files, one for 32-bit and one for 64-bit DMD. Choose the appropriate path from among the following to add to your system PATH variable:

- ~/dmd2/linux/bin32
- ~/dmd2/linux/bin64
- ~/dmd2/osx/bin
- ~/dmd2/freebsd/bin32
- ~/dmd2/freebsd/bin64

A 32-bit DMD will compile 32-bit apps by default, and a 64-bit DMD will compile 64-bit by default. For all versions of DMD, the command line flag -m32 will force 32-bit compilation and -m64 will force 64-bit compilation.

Compiling the example

With all of that background out of the way, it's time to get down to business. Open a command prompt and navigate to the directory where you saved the example. If you followed my advice, that should be $LEARNINGD/Chapter01. Now execute the following command:

```
dmd
```

If the PATH variable is properly configured, you should see the compiler print a header containing copyright information and the compiler version, followed by a list of supported command line options and a brief description of each (you might need to scroll up to see all of it). Now try this:

```
dmd hello.d
```

If you see errors or are unable to get DMD to run, head to the digitalmars.D.learn forum introduced earlier and ask for help. Otherwise, you should find yourself the proud parent of a brand new executable binary, called either hello or hello.exe, in the current directory. This is what its output looks like for me from the Windows Command Prompt:

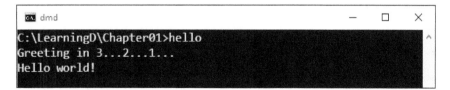

You've now successfully compiled and executed a D program. It took you two commands to do so, but it doesn't have to be that way. DMD has a number of useful command line options, some of which are tied closely to language features. Other options are independent of language features and instead control the location or format of the final output, or instruct the compiler to perform a specific task. One such option, -run, is useful for trying out short examples like the ones you'll see in this book.

When DMD is executed with the -run option, it creates an executable in the current directory as normal. The difference is that -run causes the compiler to immediately execute the program and then delete the executable after the program exits. Try it on the hello.d example and see. This will save you from the execution step every time you want to compile and run an example.

Documentation and source code

In addition to several useful tools, the DMD distribution ships with some HTML documentation and the source code for the compiler, DRuntime, and Phobos. Both docs and source can be beneficial even after becoming familiar with D, but especially so while learning it.

The documentation

In the root directory where you installed or unzipped DMD, you'll find a subdirectory called html. Open the html/d/index.html file in a web browser and you'll see the front page of the documentation for your version of the compiler. The documentation for the latest compiler release is also available online at http://dlang.org/. In the navigation bar on the left-hand side of the page, as seen in the following screenshot, look for the links named **D Reference** and **Standard Library**; the former is the place to look up information about language features, the latter is the documentation for the DRuntime and Phobos libraries:

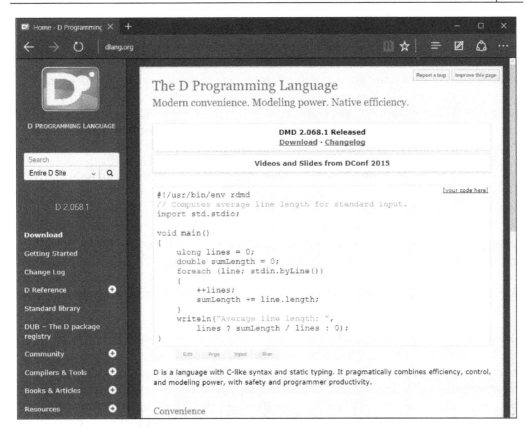

Now and again, you might find that the documentation for a function or a language feature isn't clear. Sometimes, it isn't as descriptive as it could be, or refers to functionality that has changed. Keep in mind that D is a community-driven language that relies on users to help by reporting problems or contributing fixes. If you'd like to contribute, documentation fixes can be submitted as pull requests at `https://github.com/D-Programming-Language/dlang.org`, and bug reports can be filed at `https://issues.dlang.org/` under the websites component. Once that's out of the way, you still need to solve the problem that caused you to look in the docs in the first place. You can do that by visiting the forums and asking for help, or often by going right to the source.

The source

At the same level as the `html` directory lives another directory labelled `src`. Open it up and you'll see subdirectories called `dmd`, `druntime`, and `phobos`. In each is the source code for the eponymous project. I don't expect readers of this book to start modifying the compiler just yet, but you might want to read the files `src/dmd/readme.txt` and `src/dmd/backendlicense.txt` to understand the licenses of the DMD frontend and backend source. More immediately useful is the source for DRuntime and Phobos, which is all released under the Boost Software License.

As you're learning D, taking a peek at a function's implementation can help clarify its usage if the documentation comes up short. Later, studying the Phobos source can be a great way to learn some D idioms and other useful tricks. At some point in your D career, you might be interested in exploring what DRuntime does under the hood to manage your program. In the beginning, you'll likely find more benefit from the source in the `core` package. `core` is the primary DRuntime package, the part of the runtime that users directly interact with. We won't spend a lot of time on `core` in this book, but there will be brief discussions about a few of the modules it exposes as the need arises.

The source that ships with each DMD release is the source for that specific version of the compiler. Once a new version is out the door, development continues toward the next release. All such development happens at GitHub, specifically in the D Programming Language organization at https://github.com/D-Programming-Language. Here, you can find projects for the compiler, Phobos, Druntime, the website, and several tools and utilities, including the Windows installer, Visual D, and DUB (which we'll look at shortly). If you enjoy contributing to open source projects and also enjoy using D, there are many ways to contribute aside from committing your own source modifications. The quickest way to get started is to report bugs at https://issues.dlang.org/, or to review contributions at GitHub. The more users contribute, the faster the language moves forward.

Say hello to MovieMan

Example code and snippets are quite suited to the role they play in a book such as this: highlighting the usage of a language feature in the context of an explanation about that feature. What they aren't ideal for is showing the big picture, or reinforcing how all the disparate language features work together. That role is best played by a sample project that is developed over the course of the book.

In deciding what sort of program to develop as the sample project, I had a few goals in mind. Most importantly, it should be easy for the reader to follow, shouldn't be too time-consuming to implement, shouldn't have any third-party library dependencies, and should serve as a demonstration of as many D features as possible. I finally settled on something that I think fits each requirement to some degree. Few readers will find it immediately useful in its final form, but that's no problem. A practical post-book D project is to modify or extend the sample to tailor it to a specific, customized use case.

The problem

A few months before I started on this book, my wife and I moved house. Though I rarely buy new DVDs these days, I've assembled a modest collection of them over the years. I was more than a little obsessive about keeping them in their original cases, so I kept them lined up on a number of shelves, loosely organized around genre or leading actor/actress. That is just untenable in the long run. They take up too much space and they're a pain to pack when relocating. Even so, I'm reluctant to rip them to cloud storage and throw them all out. Motivated by the move, I bought several multi-disc cases (the kind with a zipper on the outside and several CD/DVD sleeves on the inside) and transferred each disc from its original case into one of the new ones.

This was something I just wanted to get done, so I only made a meager effort to organize the cases. The result is that it's no easy thing to find a particular DVD. Since the move, I've had it in the back of my mind to whip up a program I can use to organize things, but I've continually put it off as it isn't a big priority. This book is the perfect excuse to get it done. So you and I are going to create a program that can allow me to organize my DVDs. I'm going to call it MovieMan (for Movie Manager) because that sounds much better to me than DVDMan.

The features

We're going to develop two versions of the program. In order to keep the size and complexity of the program manageable, the first version will be a command-line program with a limited number of features. The user will be able to:

- Enter a movie title, a case ID, and a page (sleeve) number
- Find and display movies by title
- List all movies in a given case
- List all movies on a given page of a given case
- List all movies

We'll implement this first version piece by piece, adding new functionality as we learn about the language features we'll use to implement it. We'll complete the program in *Chapter 7, Composing Functional Pipelines with Algorithms and Ranges*.

In *Chapter 10, Taking D Online*, we'll spend the entire chapter developing a different version of the program as a web application using a library called `vibe.d`. The purpose of this version isn't to demonstrate language features, but to show how to develop web apps with `vibe.d`. We'll relax our requirement about third-party libraries (`vibe.d` is a library, after all) and make use of a database API to store the movie data. We'll also add support for editing movies and deleting them from the database. By the end of the book, you'll have two fairly simple programs that illustrate how several D features work together.

DUB – the D build tool and package manager

There is nothing challenging about compiling simple D programs with DMD on the command line, but things can get a bit out of hand as a project grows. A complex D program will be composed of numerous modules and can be dependent on several third-party libraries. There are a number of approaches that users have taken to compile their D projects. Some use makefiles or existing tools that have some form of support for D, such as CMake or SCons, and a few have even created their own build tools from scratch. For several years, I used a custom build script written in D for most of my projects.

In the past, having so many different approaches for building D code could sometimes be a bit of an annoyance for users of D libraries, particularly when using multiple libraries that each had a different build system. Users of a library I maintain often asked me to add support for different build systems to better match their own workflow, something I was extremely reluctant to do since learning, implementing, and maintaining such support would cut into my already scarce free time. Thankfully, this is one growing pain that the D community has left behind. In this section, I'm going to introduce you to DUB, which has fast become a central part of the D ecosystem.

Created by Sönke Ludwig, DUB provides a unified approach to building D projects. To facilitate this, it also serves as a distribution platform. Anyone with a D library can share it with the world by creating a DUB configuration for it and registering it in the DUB registry. Subsequently, any DUB user can use the library by adding a single line to her project's DUB configuration file. It can also be used to easily distribute open source executables. Potential users can use one DUB command to download, compile, and run a D program.

In *Chapter 8, Exploring the Wide World of D*, we're going to look at the DUB registry and see how to use DUB-enabled libraries in your own projects as we take a tour of the D ecosystem. Now, we're going to set up a DUB configuration specifically for `MovieMan`, but the same steps can be applied to any new project you create.

Getting started

DUB is available in most of the common package repositories and the latest release can always be found at http://code.dlang.org/download. Download the appropriate tarball, installer, or ZIP file for your platform. Installing from ZIP or tarball generally requires no special steps beyond unzipping the files to a directory of your choice (such as `C:\dub` or `~\dub`) and ensuring the directory is on your `PATH`. POSIX systems will also need to have some prerequisites installed, so be sure to read the instructions on the download page. The Windows installer and ZIP both come bundled with all dependencies.

Once the program is installed and `PATH` is properly configured, open a command prompt and type the following command:

```
dub -h
```

If all goes well, you'll see a list of commands and command-line options (you will likely have to scroll up to see the whole thing). The command-line options are generic, meaning they can be passed to `dub` with any DUB command.

DUB usage revolves around commands. The default behavior when no commands are specified is to build and run any DUB project in the current directory. Unlike command-line options, DUB commands have no preceding dash. You can get help on any DUB command by passing its name to `dub` followed by `-h` or `--help` (the former is a synonym for the latter). For example, to get help with the `build` command, type the following:

```
dub build -h
```

This will print a brief description of the command, along with any command-specific arguments it accepts, followed by the same list of common command-line options you saw with `dub -h`. Much of what you need to know to get started with DUB on the command line can be gleaned from using the `-h` option. If you get stuck, you can ask for help in the DUB forums at http://forum.rejectedsoftware.com/groups/rejectedsoftware.dub/.

Configuring the MovieMan project

It's possible to set up a new project by hand, but DUB can set up a common directory structure and an initial configuration with a simple command called `init`. By default, with no arguments, `init` will create a new project using the current working directory as the project root and the name of that directory (not the full path) as the project name. If an argument is given to `init`, DUB will use it as the project name and create a new subdirectory of the same name in the current directory. Let's do that now for MovieMan.

Navigate to `$LEARNINGD/Chapter01` and execute the following command:

```
dub init MovieMan
```

Listing the contents of the `MovieMan` directory shows the following:

```
09/20/2015  12:31 PM    <DIR>          .
09/20/2015  12:31 PM    <DIR>          ..
09/20/2015  12:31 PM              38 .gitignore
09/20/2015  12:31 PM             120 dub.sdl
09/20/2015  12:31 PM    <DIR>          source
```

DUB has generated three files and one subdirectory in the project directory tree. You can see two of the files in the preceding output. The third file, `app.d`, is inside the `source` subdirectory.

DUB is tightly integrated with Git, a distributed source control system. The `.gitignore` file is used to tell Git to pay no attention to files whose names match certain patterns. DUB is helping out by generating this file and including some file types that aren't commonly included in source control, but that might be created as part of the build process. For our purposes, we can ignore `.gitignore`.

By default, when running DUB in a project directory, it searches for the project source files in the `source` subdirectory. Also by default, it expects to find the `source/app.d` file. If this file exists, an executable will be built; if not, DUB compiles a library. The `app.d` that `dub init` generates for us isn't empty. It contains a `main` function that prints a line of text to the screen.

Sometimes, you might want to add DUB support to an existing project where it might be problematic to change the directory structure or rename the main module to `app.d`, or perhaps you just don't want to follow the convention that DUB expects. No matter your reasons, all of the defaults in the preceding paragraph can be overridden in the configuration file, `dub.sdl`. As you gain more experience with DUB, you'll learn how to go beyond the simple configurations we use in this book.

Understanding dub.sdl

DUB supports two formats for its project configuration files: **Simple Declarative Language** (**SDLang**) and **JavaScript Object Notation** (**JSON**). The former is the default format output by the `init` command (the command `dub init -fjson` will create `dub.json` instead). Originally, JSON was the only format supported. As of DUB 0.9.24, SDLang is the preferred format, though JSON will be supported indefinitely. Go to `http://semitwist.com/sdl-mirror/Language+Guide.html` for more about SDLang and `http://json.org/` for JSON.

DUB requires a configuration file to be present in any project it is intended to manage. It supports a number of predefined fields for defining metadata that provide information about the project, such as its name and description, and instructions for DUB to follow when building the project. The documentation at `http://code.dlang.org/package-format` is the place to visit to keep informed on supported DUB configuration options.

 You've already seen the term **package** in reference to a hierarchical grouping of D modules. It's common to use the term **DUB package** to refer to a DUB project.

The configuration generated by the `init` command is entirely metadata. The metadata in a DUB package configuration comprises the first few lines by convention. None of the entries are required to be in any particular order. Take a look at the complete contents of the `dub.sdl` file generated by `dub init` for the `MovieMan` project:

```
name "movieman"
description "A minimal D application."
copyright "Copyright © 2015, Mike Parker" authors "Mike Parker"
```

Every DUB package must have a name that can be used as a unique identifier. The name should be comprised of lowercase alphanumeric characters. Dashes and underscores are also permitted. When generating a project, DUB will always use lowercase letters. If the configuration file is manually edited to include uppercase characters in the package name, DUB will internally convert them to lowercase when it loads the file.

The `name` field is the only one that is required. The other fields can be deleted and the project will build just fine. However, if there is any intention to register the package with the online DUB registry, then it's a good idea to always include the generated metadata fields at a minimum. There are other useful metadata fields that are not generated by default, such as `license` and `homepage`. The more metadata provided, the more potential users can learn about the project from the DUB registry.

Most of the metadata items are only visible from the package-specific page in the registry. The `name` and `description` fields are the only two that are displayed in the list of all registered packages. As such, the description shouldn't be very long or overly vague. What you want is a short, succinct summary of the package so that anyone browsing the registry can determine whether it's something he might be interested in. We aren't going to register `MovieMan` in the DUB registry, but if we were, then we might use something like the following to describe it:

```
description "A command-line DVD database."
```

The name used in the `copyright` and `authors` fields for a generated `dub.json` comes from the name of the user account under which `dub init` was executed. Multiple authors can be listed as follows:

```
authors "Bjarne Gosling" "Brian Pike"
```

Several configuration fields recognized by DUB require a list of values.

The majority of DUB directives are not simply metadata, but they directly influence the build process. There are directives for specifying library dependencies, compiler flags, which compiler to use, and more. We'll add one to the MovieMan configuration shortly.

Building and running MovieMan

DUB allows you to build a project and run the resulting executable in two separate steps, or to do it all at once. To build the project without running it, you use the aptly-named `build` command. To both build and execute the project, you can use the `run` command, which is the default behavior when invoking `dub` without specifying any commands (so both `dub` and `dub run` are the same thing).

Let's give DUB a go at building the project, first by specifying the `build` command. Here's what I see on my system:

```
C:\LearningD\Chapter01\MovieMan>dub build
Building movieman ~master configuration "application", build type debug.
Compiling using dmd...
Linking...
```

You can see that, by default, DUB isn't very verbose about what it's doing. It tells you which build configuration it's building and the build type, lets you know when it starts compiling and which compiler it's using, and then tells you that it's creating (linking) the executable. The build configuration, build type, and compiler can all be specified in the configuration file.

Now that the executable is built, it's just sitting there waiting to be executed. Let's make use of the `run` command to do so:

```
C:\LearningD\Chapter01\MovieMan>dub run
Target movieman ~master is up to date. Use --force to rebuild.
Running .\movieman.exe
Edit source/app.d to start your project.
```

If you haven't yet examined the generated `app.d` in your text editor, it might not be immediately obvious to you that the last line is the actual output of the generated code and the previous lines are from DUB itself. Look at the first line of output in particular. This is telling you that the executable is already built and that, if you want to build it again, you should use the `--force` option to do so. That might seem like an odd message to see when running the program. To understand it, try running the `build` command again:

```
C:\LearningD\Chapter01\MovieMan>dub build
Target movieman ~master is up to date. Use --force to rebuild.
```

As you can see, DUB refused to build the project and is telling you why and what to do. Try again, this time with the `--force` option and it will build successfully. Also, see what happens when you invoke `dub` and `dub --force`.

So the take away here is that DUB isn't going to rebuild your project if it is already up-to-date and it will always check whether a rebuild is needed before executing the program. We can define "up-to-date" to mean that the timestamp of the executable is more recent than the last modification time of any of the source files. If you edit any source file in the `source` directory, then trying to build again will succeed. To demonstrate that, let's edit `app.d` to look like the following:

```
import std.stdio;
void main() {
  writeln("Hi! My name is MovieMan.");
}
```

Now, executing either `dub` or `dub run` will cause DUB to notice that `app.d` has a more recent timestamp than the executable. In response, it will rebuild the application before executing it.

To build or not to build

The build command comes in handy when you invoke it as you add new code to a project. I like to do so after adding several new lines, or a new function, just to make sure everything still compiles. DMD is so fast that, even as a project gets larger, this does not impede development. Only when I've completed adding or modifying a feature do I invoke dub run to make sure the app is working as expected.

Changing the output directory

Executable programs often ship with a number of resources. These generally should be located either in the same directory as the executable or in subdirectories. By default, the binary that DUB builds, whether it is a library or an executable, is output to the same directory in which the dub.json file resides (which we can call the project or package root). When there are resources to worry about, this can look a little cluttered. Even without resources, I prefer my binaries to be written in their own directory. This can be accomplished with one simple addition to dub.sdl:

```
targetPath "bin"
```

targetPath is a build directive that tells DUB where to write the binary. It can be placed anywhere in the file, but convention dictates that it follow the metadata. Here, I've used a relative path that will cause DUB to create a subdirectory named bin (if it doesn't already exist) and write the binary there. Absolute paths, such as C:\dev\MovieMan or /~/bin/MovieMan, are also acceptable. However, you should prefer relative paths to keep your DUB packages completely self-contained if you are going to distribute them.

Summary

In this chapter, you've taken an introductory look at the D programming language, including a line-by-line breakdown of a simple D source file. You've learned how to install and run DMD, the Digital Mars D Compiler. You've become acquainted with the sample project you'll be working on throughout this book, called MovieMan, by looking at the feature requirements of the two different versions you'll create. Finally, you've had an overview of DUB and how you'll use it to manage the sample project.

Now that you know enough about the tools to get some work done, we can dig into the language and start using it in the next chapter. There, we'll look at the basic features that form the building blocks of any D program.

2
Building a Foundation with D Fundamentals

In this chapter and the next, we're going to look at the fundamental building blocks of D programming. There's a lot of information to cover, so our focus in both chapters will primarily be on the syntax, differences from other C-family languages, and how to avoid common beginner mistakes.

If you enter the code snippets into a text editor and try to compile them as you work through this chapter and the rest of the book, please keep the following in mind. Many of the snippets make use of one or more functions from `std.stdio`. In order to be successfully compiled, they all require a `main` function. However, both declarations are often missing from the snippets listed in the book in the interest of saving space. Use the following as a template to implement any such snippets yourself:

```
import std.stdio;
void main() {
    // Insert snippet here
}
```

Here's how this chapter is going to play out:

- The very basics: Identifiers, scope, modules, comments, variable declarations, and initialization
- Basic types: Integral and floating-point types, aliases, properties, and operators
- Derived data types: Pointers, arrays, strings, and associative arrays
- Control flow statements: Loops, conditionals, scope, and go to statements
- Type qualifiers: Immutable and const
- Functions: Everything to do with functions
- MovieMan: The first steps

The very basics

With the exception of source code comments, everything in this section is required knowledge for anyone who intends to successfully compile a D program.

Identifiers

The names of variables, functions, user-defined types, and so on, are all **identifiers**. Identifiers are *case-sensitive* and can consist of any combination and number of **Universal Character Names (UCN)**, underscores, and digits. D does not itself define what constitutes a valid UCN. Instead, it refers to the list of valid UCNs specified in Annex D of the C99 standard. Aside from the English alphabet, characters from several languages are valid UCNs. Henceforth, I will refer to UCNs as *letters*. Identifiers in this book will be constrained to the English alphabet.

There are a few rules to follow when choosing identifiers:

- The first character in an identifier can only be a letter or an underscore.
- The use of two leading underscores is reserved for the compiler implementation. This is currently not enforced by the compiler; barring any conflicts, it will happily compile any symbols that begin with two underscores. However, this raises the chance that such code will stop compiling with future compiler releases.
- Certain keywords are reserved by the language and attempting to use them as identifiers will cause compilation to fail. A list of all reserved identifiers can be found at `http://dlang.org/lex.html` under the **Keywords** section.
- The standard library defines several identifiers in the global namespace, which precludes using them as custom identifiers.

Source file encoding

D source files can be in any one of the ASCII, UTF-8, UTF-16, or UTF-32 encodings. Both big- and little-endian versions of the latter two are accepted.

A note about scope

As we work through this chapter and the next, we'll see several types of declaration. We saw one already in the first chapter: import declarations, where *module scope* was also mentioned. There are a couple of things to keep in mind about scope when making any declaration.

First, anything declared in module scope is visible anywhere in that module no matter at what point in the module it is declared. Consider the following:

```
void main() {
  writeln("Scope this!");
}
import std.stdio;
```

Putting the import declaration before or after `main` makes no difference. The `writeln` function is visible inside `main` either way. This also applies to type and variable declarations.

> Some with C or C++ experience may sometimes refer to D's module scope as **global scope**. Others will argue that this is inaccurate. A `myVar` variable declared in the `mymod` module can be accessed as `mymod.myVar`, so the module name (and package name) can serve as a namespace. However, this syntax is not generally enforced, so the variable can also be accessed simply as `myVar`. Just understand that, when you see someone use the term **global scope** in D, they are probably using it as a synonym for **module scope**.

Drilling down to a lower level, every function has an associated **function scope**. Then there are **block scopes**, which are automatically created by some statements, such as `foreach`, and can also be created manually inside a function scope or another block scope using braces: { and }. Almost any declaration that can be made in module scope can also be made in a local scope, but the declaration must come before the point of use.

```
void main() {
  writeln("Scope this!");
  import std.stdio;
}
```

Try to compile this and the compiler will complain that `writeln` is not defined. Declarations can be made at any point in a local scope—top, middle, or bottom—as long as they are not used before the point of declaration. We'll revisit scope when we go through aggregate types in *Chapter 3, Programming Objects the D Way*.

More on modules

D's module system is very simple to understand once you've taken the time to do so. Unfortunately, new D users often expect D modules to behave like C headers, or imports to be Java-like. The purpose of this section is to disabuse you of any such notions. This is not the last we'll see of modules. We'll revisit them in the next chapter.

Module declarations

In the first chapter, we saw that a D source file saved as `hello.d` automatically becomes a module named `hello` when the compiler parses it. We can explicitly name a module using a module declaration. If present, the module declaration must be the first declaration in the file. There can be only one module declaration per file. By convention, module names are all lowercase.

Module declarations are optional, but they become a necessity when packages are involved. Let's experiment with D's package feature now. Create a subdirectory in `$LEARNINGD/Chapter02` called `mypack`. Then save the following as `mypack/greeting.d`:

```
module mypack.greeting;
import std.stdio;
void sayHello() {
  writeln("Hello!");
}
```

Now save the following as `Chapter02/hello2.d`:

```
import mypack.greeting;
void main() {
  sayHello();
}
```

Open a command prompt, `cd` to `$LEARNINGD/Chapter02`, and try to compile `hello2.d`. Here's what it looks like for me on Windows:

```
C:\LearningD\Chapter02>dmd hello2
OPTLINK (R) for Win32  Release 8.00.17
Copyright (C) Digital Mars 1989-2013  All rights reserved.
http://www.digitalmars.com/ctg/optlink.html
hello2.obj(hello2)
 Error 42: Symbol Undefined _D6mypack8greeting8sayHelloFZv
hello2.obj(hello2)
 Error 42: Symbol Undefined _D6mypack8greeting12__ModuleInfoZ
--- errorlevel 2
```

The very first word of the output starts with OPTLINK, indicating a linker error. The phrase Symbol Undefined is another hint that it's a linker error. This tells us that the compile stage was successful; both hello2.d and, because it was imported, greeting.d, were parsed just fine, and then hello2.d was compiled into an object file. The compiler then passed the object file to the linker, but the linker could not find a symbol. Specifically, the missing symbol is sayHello, which is the function in greeting.d.

This is a common mistake made by many new D programmers, especially those who are well acquainted with Java. There's a misconception that simply importing a module will cause it to automatically be compiled and linked into the final executable. Import declarations are solely for the compiler to know which symbols are available for use in the module it is currently compiling. The compiler *does not* automatically compile imported modules. In order for imported modules to be compiled and linked, they should be passed to the compiler as well.

```
dmd hello2.d mypack/greeting.d
```

So how did the compiler find greeting.d when we didn't pass it on the command line? The compiler works on the assumption that package names correspond to directory names and module names are filenames. By default, it will search the current working directory for any packages and modules it encounters in import statements. Since the current working directory in our example is $LEARNINGD/ Chapter02 and it has a subdirectory, mypack, which matches the package name in the import declaration mypack.greeting, the compiler easily finds greeting.d in the mypack subdirectory. If you change the name of greeting.d to say.d and compile *only* hello2.d again, you'll get a compiler error instead of a linker error:

```
hello2.d(1): Error: module greeting is in file 'mypack\greeting.d' which
cannot be read
```

Again, passing both modules to the compiler will eliminate the error. Before checking the file system, the compiler will first check all of the modules passed on the command line to see if any of them match the name in an import declaration. In this case, as long as there is a module declaration, the name of the file plays no role. This breaks when you are compiling source files individually (with the -c command-line option), or using third-party libraries, so when using packages it's best to always put module declarations in every source file and match the module names to the filenames. It doesn't matter in which order source files are fed to the compiler, but by default the name of the first file will be used as the name of the executable. This can be overridden with the -of command line switch.

More about import declarations

We introduced standard import declarations, selective imports, and local imports in the first chapter. There are other options for import declarations. First up: **public imports**.

`hello2` imports `mypack.greeting`, which imports `std.stdio`. Imports are private by default, so nothing from `std.stdio` is visible inside `hello2`. You can verify this by adding a `writeln` function to `main` in `hello2.d`. Compiling will yield the following error:

```
hello2.d(4): Error: 'writeln' is not defined, perhaps you need to import
std.stdio; ?
```

 The compiler will often make recommendations for specific symbols when it encounters one that it doesn't know about—which is a good way to catch spelling errors—but it doesn't generally recommend imports. `writeln` and friends are a special case.

Make one small modification to `mypack/greeting.d`: put `public` in front of the import.

```
public import std.stdio;
```

Now, when `hello2` imports `mypack.greeting`, it also makes all the symbols from `std.stdio` visible in `hello2`. There are three syntax options for public imports, which are shown in the following code:

```
public import std.stdio;
public {
   import std.stdio;
}
public:
   import std.stdio;
```

In the first line, `public` applies only to that declaration. In the second line, it applies to everything between the braces. The last one applies to everything in the module until a new protection attribute is encountered. In any of those lines, you can replace `public` with `private` to explicitly replicate the default behavior. Note that public imports can only be declared in module scope.

Not just for protection

The three different syntaxes seen here with protection attributes can also be used with other D attributes that we will see later in this and subsequent chapters, even if it is not explicitly mentioned. Regarding the colon syntax, there is one key point to be aware of. If a `public:` is followed by a `private:`, all subsequent declarations will be `private`, that is, the `public` is "turned off." This is not the case with all attributes, as many are independent and do not have a counter attribute to "turn them off." In those cases, the colon syntax makes the attribute valid until the end of the scope in which it is declared.

Now let's change `hello2.d`:

```
import mypack.greeting;
void main() {
   mypack.greeting.sayHello();
}
```

Here, we're calling `sayHello` with its **Fully Qualified Name** (**FQN**). This is always possible, but it's only a requirement when two imported modules contain conflicting symbols. The FQN can be used to specify the symbol that is desired. One way to minimize the chance of conflict is to use `static imports`.

```
static import mypack.greeting;
```

Static imports *force* the use of the FQN on symbols. Calling `sayHello` without the FQN will fail to compile unless there is another symbol with the same name in scope. Another approach is to use `named imports`.

```
import greet = mypack.greeting;
```

Essentially, this works the same as the static import, except that now symbols in the imported module are accessed through an identifier of your choosing. In this example, calls to `sayHello` must now be made as `greet.sayHello`.

Public imports and FQNs

When a module that contains public imports is imported, symbols in the publicly imported module gain an alternate FQN. When `mypack.greeting` publicly imports `std.stdio`, then `mypack.greeting.writeln` becomes an alias for `std.stdio.writeln`. Both can be used in modules that import `mypack.greeting`.

Finally, all import declarations except selective imports support multiple, comma-separated module names. A single selective import can follow other imports, but it must be at the end. Multiple modules in a static import are all static. Standard imports and named imports can be mixed freely.

```
import std.stdio, std.file, // OK
       std.conv;
import IO = std.stdio, std.file, // OK: Two named imports and
       Conv = std.conv;          // one standard import
import std.stdio : writeln, std.conv; // Error: selective import
                                      // in front
import std.file, std.stdio : writeln; // OK: selective import at
                                      // at the end
import std.stdio : writeln, writefln; // OK: Selective import with
                                      // multiple symbols
static import std.stdio, std.file, // OK: All three imports
              std.conv;            // are static
```

The special package module

`package.d` is D's approach to importing multiple modules from a package in one go. In it, the package maintainer can publicly import modules from the package as desired. Users may then import all of them at once using the package name. The compiler will load `package.d` as if it were any other module. Given a package `somepack`, with the modules `one`, `two`, and `three`, we can save the following as `somepack/package.d`:

```
module somepack;
public import somepack.one, somepack.two, somepack.three;
```

With this in place, all three modules can be imported at once with the following declaration:

```
import somepack;
```

Any modules that are not imported in `package.d` are not visible unless imported explicitly. `package.d` is still a D source module, so any valid D code is allowed.

Comments

D supports the same types of comment syntax found in other C-family languages. C-style block comments open with /* and close with */, with any number of lines in between. They are not allowed to nest. Single-line comments open with // and terminate with the end of the line.

```
/* Hi! I'm a C-style,
 block comment. */
// I'm a single-line comment.
/* Nested block comments… /* like this one */ are illegal */
```

D also has a block comment syntax that supports nesting. This is great for quickly commenting out multiple lines of code that might already contain block comments. This syntax opens with /+ and closes with +/. Any number of lines and any number of comments can fall in between. The first +/ encountered matches the most recent /+.

```
/+ This is the first line of the comment.
   /* This is a nested comment. */
   /+ This is another nested comment. +/
The is the last line +/
```

Finally, D allows documentation comments, or Ddoc comments. This type of comment opens with /** and closes with */, or the equivalent /++ and +/. The single-line version is ///. Ddoc is used to generate source code documentation. When placed before any declaration in module scope, the comment becomes the documentation for that declaration. The Ddoc output, which is HTML file by default, can be generated with DMD by passing -D on the command line.

```
/**
The function to which control is passed from DRuntime.

This implementation prints to stdout the command used to execute this
program. It ignores errors.

Params:
    args - the command line arguments passed from DRuntime.
*/
void main(string[] args) {
    writeln(args[0]);
}
```

You can head over to http://dlang.org/ddoc.html when you're ready to begin writing source code documentation. It covers everything you need to know to get started. Refer to the Phobos source for examples.

Variable declaration and initialization

Variables in D must be declared somewhere before they can be used. Variable declarations generally take the same form as in other C-family languages: the name of a type followed by an identifier. The following two lines declare four variables named someNumber, a, b, and c, all of which are of type int:

```
int someNumber;
int a, b, c;
```

Earlier in this chapter, we looked at how scopes affect declarations. With variable declarations, one thing that must be kept in mind is **shadowing**. This occurs when a variable in a given scope is named the same as a variable in a parent scope. Shadowing module scope variables is legal; every reference to the symbol before the local declaration refers to the module scope variable and every reference after the local declaration (within the same local scope) refers to the local variable. It is an error for a local variable to shadow a variable in any outer scope except module scope.

```
int x;
void main() {
    writeln(x); // OK: refers to module scope x
    int x; // OK: shadowing module scope variables allowed
    writeln(x); // OK: refers to local x
    int y;       // Function scope
    // Opening a new scope
    {
        int y; // Error: local y is shadowing main.y
        int z;
    }
    // Opening a new scope
    {
        // OK: This scope and the one above are independent of
        // each other.
        int z;
    }
}
```

Variables in any function or block scope can be declared `static`, causing the value of the variable to persist beyond the lifetime of the scope. Such variables are only accessible within the scope in which they are declared. Applying `static` to a variable in module scope has no meaning.

Static variables and variables in module scope can be explicitly initialized to any value that can be known at compile time. This includes literals and constant values (along with any expression that can be evaluated at compile time, as you'll learn in *Chapter 4, Running Code at Compile Time*). Variables in function and block scopes can additionally be initialized to runtime values. Variables that are not explicitly initialized are default-initialized to a type-specific value. In explicit initialization, the type name can be replaced with `auto` to trigger type inference. Consider the following example:

```
auto theAnswer = 42;
int noMeaning, confused = void;
```

Here, `theAnswer` is explicitly initialized to the integer literal `42` and the compiler infers it to be of type `int`. The variable `noMeaning` is initialized to the default value for the `int` type, which is `0`. Poor `confused` is not initialized at all. The keyword `void` instructs the compiler to turn off default initialization for this variable. However, it's still going to refer to whatever happens to be living at its address when the program starts up. Forgetting to initialize variables is a common source of bugs in many C programs. With default initialization, D makes it easy to either avoid such bugs completely, or track them down when they do appear.

One last thing to keep in mind about variable declarations is that all module scope variables are thread-local by default. This is very, very different from how other C-family languages do things. This means that, if you are using multiple threads, every thread gets its own copy of the variable. One thing that will certainly surprise C and C++ programmers is that even static variables in a function or block scope are thread-local. Typically in C, functions intended to be used in multiple threads have to avoid static variables like the plague. This is not the case in D. We'll come back to static declarations when we go through functions later in this chapter.

Basic types

Most of D's basic data types will be familiar to C-family programmers. In this section, we're first going to look at what the basic data types are. Then we'll discuss a couple of features that are related not only to the basic types, but to all types.

The types

First up, D includes the special type void to mean *no type*. There is no such thing as a variable of type void. As in C, void is used to indicate that a function does not return a value. void pointers can be declared to represent pointers to any type.

Instances of the bool type are guaranteed to be eight bits in size and can hold one of two possible values: true and false. In any expression that expects a Boolean value, any zero value is converted to false and non-zero is converted to true. Conversely, in any expression that expects a numeric type, false and true are converted to 0 and 1. Variables of type bool are initialized to false by default.

D supports signed and unsigned versions of integral types in 8-, 16-, 32-, and 64-bit flavors. The default initialization value of each is 0. The following table lists the size in bits along with the minimum and maximum values for each integral type. Note that the unsigned types are named by prefixing a u to the name of their signed counterparts.

Name	Size	Minimum Value	Maximum Value
byte	8	-128	127
ubyte	8	0	255
short	16	-32,768	32,767
ushort	16	0	65,535
int	32	-2,147,483,648	2,147,483,647
uint	32	0	4,294,967,295
long	64	-9,223,372,036,854,775,808	9,223,372,036,854,775,807
ulong	64	0	18,446,744,073,709,551,615

D supports three floating-point types. In addition to the traditional 32-bit float and 64-bit double, there is a third type called real. The latter is known to be of the *largest* floating point size representable in hardware. On x86, that is either 80-bits or the size of a double, whichever is larger. In reality, all floating point operations in D *may* be performed in the largest hardware size even when the operands are declared as float or double. Floating point computations and representations in D follow the IEEE Standard for Floating-Point Arithmetic (IEEE 754). The pages http://dlang.org/float.html and http://dlang.org/d-floating-point.html are recommended reading.

Floating-point types are default-initialized to a type-specific value representing **NaN** (**Not a Number**). When a floating-point variable is assigned a value too high or too low for it to represent, it is set to a value representing infinity or negative infinity respectively.

There are three types in D which are intended to represent UTF code units. The default initialization value for each type is an invalid Unicode value. The following table lists each character type, its size in bits, its Unicode encoding, and its initialization value in hexadecimal notation.

Name	Size	Encoding	Init Value
char	8	UTF8	0xFF
wchar	16	UTF16	0xFFFF
dchar	32	UTF32	0x0000FFFF

Literals

D supports several different formats for basic type literals. We'll look at each in turn.

Integer literals

Integer literals can take three forms: decimal, hexadecimal, and binary. Hexadecimal numbers are denoted by the `0x` or `0X` prefixes and binary numbers by `0b` or `0B`. Any leading `0`s after the prefix can be omitted. For example, `0x00FF` and `0xFF` are identical, as are `0b0011` and `0b11`. Any other integer literal, as long as it does not begin with `0`, is interpreted as decimal. Each format also allows for any number of underscores in any position except the first.

```
int d1 = 1000000;
int d2 = 1_000_000;
int h1 = 0x000000FF;    // Hexadecimal for 255
int h2 = 0X00_00_00_FF; // Ditto
int h3 = 0xFF;          // Ditto
int b1 = 0b01010101;    // Binary for 85
int b2 = 0B0101_0101;   // Ditto
int b3 = 0b101_0101;    // Ditto
```

Octal literals are supported in Phobos via the `std.conv.octal` function.

```
import std.conv : octal;
int oct = octal!377;
```

The ! in `octal!377` is the syntax for template instantiation, which we'll examine in *Chapter 5, Generic Programming Made Easy*.

By default, all integer literals are inferred as `int` unless they require more than 32 bits, in which case they are inferred as `long`. Literals too big for `long` refuse to compile without help. That comes in the form of the `uL` and `UL` suffixes, which both force a literal to be interpreted as `ulong`. There are also the suffixes `u` and `U` to force `uint`, and `L` to force `long`. All of these suffixes work with decimal, hexadecimal, and binary literals, as well as the octal template (`octal!377uL`). In the following example, the `typeid` expression is used to obtain a textual version of each literal's type, which `writeln` then prints to `stdout`. Can you guess what the output of each is going to be? One of these lines will cause a *signed integer overflow* error.

```
writeln(typeid(2_147_483_647));
writeln(typeid(2_147_483_648));
writeln(typeid(2_147_483_648U));
writeln(typeid(9_223_372_036_854_775_807));
writeln(typeid(9_223_372_036_854_775_808));
writeln(typeid(9_223_372_036_854_775_808UL));
writeln(typeid(10));
writeln(typeid(10U));
writeln(typeid(10L));
writeln(typeid(10UL));
```

Floating-point literals

Floating-point literals can be represented in both decimal and hexadecimal forms. They are interpreted as `double` by default. Appending `f` or `F` will force a `float` and appending `L` will force a `real`. Note that `3.0`, `3.0f`, and `3f` are all floating point literals, but `3` and `3L` are integrals.

```
writeln(typeid(3.0));
writeln(typeid(3.0f));
writeln(typeid(3.0F));
writeln(typeid(3.0L));
writeln(typeid(3f));
```

Exponential notation is also supported as is the rarely-used hexadecimal format for floating point. The latter takes some getting used to if you aren't familiar with it. A description of both can be found on my D blog at `http://dblog.aldacron.net/floating-point-literals-in-d/`.

Character literals

The type of a character literal depends on how many bytes are required to represent a single code unit. The byte size of each code unit depends on the encoding represented by the type. The difference can be seen here:

```
char c1 = 'a';   // OK: one code unit
char c2 = 'é';   // Error: two code units
wchar wc = 'é';  // OK: one code unit
```

In UTF-8, which is what the `char` type represents, one code unit is eight bits in size. The literal `'a'` fits nicely in eight bits, so we can store it in a variable of type `char`. The literal `'é'` requires two UTF-8 code units, so it cannot be represented by a single `char`. Since it's only one code unit in UTF-16, the type of the literal is `wchar`.

Conversions

D has some rules that make it easy to know when one type can be converted to another through implicit conversion, and when a cast needed to force explicit conversion. The first rule we'll see concerns integral types: *narrowing conversions are never implicit*. Exhibit A:

```
int a = 100;
ubyte b = a;
```

Because `int` is a 32-bit value and `ubyte` is an 8-bit value, it doesn't matter that `100` will fit into a `ubyte`; it's a narrowing conversion and D just doesn't allow those implicitly. It can be coerced with a cast:

```
ubyte b = cast(ubyte)a;
```

In this case, the value `100` will be assigned to b successfully. However, if it were a value that does not fit in eight bits, such as `257`, the cast would cause all but the eight least significant bits to be dropped, resulting in b having a completely different value. Note that going from an unsigned type to the signed type of the same size is not considered a narrowing conversion. The compiler will always implicitly convert in this case, and vice versa. Just be aware of the consequences. For example:

```
ubyte u = 255;
byte b = u; // b is -1
```

Next we can say that *floating point types are never implicitly converted to integral types, but integral types are always implicitly converted to floating point.*

```
float f1 = 3.0f;
int x1 = f1;    // Error
int x2 = 2;
float f2 = x2; // OK: f2 is 2.0
```

You can cast f1 to int and the assignment to x will compile, but in doing so you'll lose the fractional part of the float.

When a literal is assigned to a variable, the compiler uses a technique called **value range propagation** to determine whether or not to allow compilation without a cast. Essentially, if the literal can be represented by the type it's being assigned to, then the assignment (or initialization) will compile. Otherwise, the compiler produces an implicit conversion error, which can be eliminated by a cast. Some examples of this are as follows:

```
ubyte ub = 256;     // Error
byte b1 = 128;      // Error
byte b2 = 127;      // OK
float f = 33;       // OK
int i = 3.0f;       // Error
```

The last scenario to consider is when multiple types are used in binary expressions, which are expressions that have two operands. Take the addition expression as an example. What type is a?

```
byte b = 10;
short s = 1024;
auto a = b + s;
```

Answering this question requires knowing the rules for arithmetic conversions. If either operand is real, double, or float, then the other operand is converted to that type. If the operands are both integral types, integer promotion is applied to each of them. Types smaller than int (bool, byte, ubyte, short, ushort, char, wchar) are converted to int; dchar is converted to uint; however, int, uint, long, and ulong are left untouched. Once integer promotion is complete, the following steps are taken in order:

- If both operands are the same type, no more conversions are necessary
- If both are signed or both are unsigned, the smaller type is converted to the larger
- If the unsigned type is smaller than the signed type, it's converted to the signed type
- The signed type is converted to the unsigned type

Applying these rules to the snippet above, neither b nor s are floating-point types, so integer promotion takes place. Both types are smaller than int, so both are promoted to int. Next, we find that, since both types are now int, no further conversions are necessary and the operation can take place. So a is of type int. Change all three variables to ubyte and the same rules apply, a common source of confusion for new D users who don't understand why they get a compiler error in that case.

Alias declarations

An **alias declaration** allows an existing type (and other symbols, as we'll see later) to be referred to by a different name. This *does not* create a new type. Consider the following:

```
alias MyInt = int;
MyInt mi = 2.0;
```

The second line will fail to compile, producing an error message telling you that `double` cannot be implicitly converted to `int`. There's no mention of `MyInt` at all, because to the compiler, it isn't a type. It's simply a synonym for `int`.

Two aliases that are declared by default are `size_t` and `ptrdiff_t`. The former is defined to be an unsigned integral type large enough to represent an offset into all addressable memory. The latter is defined to be a signed basic type the same size as `size_t`. In practice, that means the respective types are `uint`/`int` in 32-bit and `ulong`/`long` in 64-bit.

Properties

You can think of properties as values that can be queried to divine information about types or type instances. Some properties are common to all types, others are type-specific. Some are context-dependent, meaning they can return different values depending on whether the query is made on a type, a variable, or a literal. Others are context-neutral, meaning they always return the same value for any given type and instances of that type. The following snippet demonstrates accessing a property:

```
writeln(int.sizeof);
writeln(3.sizeof);
int a;
writeln(a.sizeof);
```

Properties are accessed using dot notation on a type, a literal, or a variable, with the name of the property following the dot. The `.sizeof` property is one of those properties common to all types. It's also one that is context-neutral. Run the snippet and you'll find that the same value is printed for `.sizeof` on the type `int`, the integer literal 3, and the variable `a`.

There are five common properties that are available on every type. The two we most often care about are `.init` and `.sizeof`. The former tells you the default initialization value of a given type; the latter tells you the size, in bytes, of a given type as `size_t`. You can read about all the basic type properties, including those not shown anywhere in this section, at `http://dlang.org/property.html`.

Most built-in types have a few type-specific properties. The integral types all have properties called `.min` and `.max` that return the minimum and maximum values representable by variables of that type. Floating-point types have a number of properties, most of which are only of interest to people doing fairly involved floating-point work. Of general interest may be `.nan` and `.inf`, which return the values of NaN and infinity. `.max` returns the maximum value representable and its negation is the minimum.

```
writeln(float.max);      // Maximum float value
writeln(-float.max);     // Minimum float value
```

We're not going to go into all floating-point properties here. We will, however, take a look at an example of a program that reproduces the integral types table from earlier in this section.

```
auto formatStr = "%10-s %10-s %20-s %20-s";
writefln( formatStr, "Name", ".sizeof", ".min", ".max");
writefln(formatStr, "byte", byte.sizeof, byte.min, byte.max);
writefln(formatStr, "ubyte", ubyte.sizeof, ubyte.min, ubyte.max);
writefln(formatStr, "short", short.sizeof, short.min, short.max);
writefln(formatStr, "ushort", ushort.sizeof, ushort.min,
ushort.max);
writefln(formatStr, "int", int.sizeof, int.min, int.max);
writefln(formatStr, "uint", uint.sizeof, uint.min, uint.max);
writefln(formatStr, "long", long.sizeof, long.min, long.max);
writefln(formatStr, "ulong", ulong.sizeof, ulong.min, ulong.max);
```

`writefln` was introduced in the previous chapter. It uses the same format specifiers that C uses, most of which have the same meaning. You'll find that `%s` is quite different, though. In C, it indicates that an argument is a string. In D, it means the default formatting for the given type should be used. For example:

```
writefln("Float.max is %s and int.max is %s", float.max, int.max);
```

Here, the compiler will substitute the value of `float.max` for the first `%s` and use the default `float` formatting. Similarly, `int.max` replaces the second `%s` with the default formatting for `int`. If you make a mistake and have more specifiers than arguments, you'll have no trouble compiling but will get a `FormatException` at runtime. If you have more arguments than specifiers, the extra arguments will be ignored.

We aren't using plain old %s in our program. We've added 10 and - between % and s. Format specifiers begin with % and end with a character. Several things can go in between. The 10 indicates that we want an argument to be printed in a field at least ten characters wide. The - means we want to left-justify the text within the field. %-10s and %10-s are the same. In other words, the string Name has four characters. Left justified in a field of ten characters, it will be followed by six spaces. The actual output looks like this:

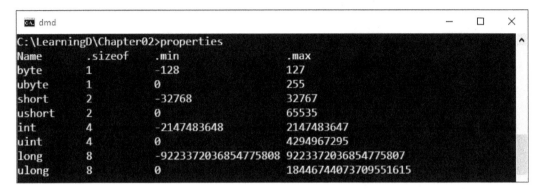

You can read more about format strings and format specifiers at http://dlang. org/phobos/std_format.html.

Basic operators

This section is a whirlwind tour of the basic operators D supports. For the most part, things are the same as they are in C. There are a few minor differences that will be highlighted as we come to them. More operators will appear later in this chapter and throughout the book. You can read more about D's operators at http://dlang.org/ expression.html.

Arithmetic operators

All of the common **arithmetic operators** are available: +, -, *, / and %, representing addition, subtraction, multiplication, division, and modulus respectively. Additionally, D has an **exponentiation operator**, ^^, which raises the left operand to an exponent (power) represented by the right operand. For example, 2^2 can be expressed as 2 ^^ 2.

D also supports the standard increment and decrement operators. In the prefix form (`++x` and `--x`), the result of the expression is the new value. In the postfix form (`x++` and `x--`), the result is the original value of the operand. To be more explicit, under the hood D is doing something like this for the prefix version:

```
x = x + 1;
return x;
```

And this for the postfix version:

```
auto temp = x;
x = x + 1;
return temp;
```

In the postfix form, if the resulting value is never used, then the compiler can optimize `temp` away and it will effectively be the same as the prefix version. For example:

```
int x = 2;
x++;    // Identical to ++x - no temporary
```

Like C++, D allows the increment and decrement operators to be overloaded by custom types. Unlike C++, D guarantees that the temporary variable in a postfix expression can *always* be optimized away when it isn't needed, even if the operand is a user-defined type. Even so, it's considered best practice to use the prefix form unless the behavior of the postfix expression is desired.

Bitwise operators

I assume you already know that there are eight bits in a byte, that bits can be 1 or 0, and that **bitwise operators** can be used to selectively turn bits on or off, reverse their state, or move them around. D supports the binary bitwise operators &, |, and ^, representing binary AND, OR, and XOR, and the unary operator ~, representing the one's complement. The left and right shift operators, << and >>, are also supported.

Additionally, D has the unsigned right shift operator, >>>. Anyone with a Java background will be familiar with this. When the left operand is an unsigned type, >> and >>> behave identically. When operating on a signed type, the right shift operator, >>, preserves the sign bit. This means that right shifting a positive value will yield a positive value and right shifting a negative value produces a negative value. The unsigned right shift operator treats the sign bit as any other bit and does not preserve it. Essentially, it's the same as casting the signed type to an unsigned type and performing a right shift.

```
int a = -3;
writeln(a >> 4);              // -1
```

```
writeln(a >>> 4);              // 268_435_455
writeln(cast(uint)a >> 4);     // 268_435_455
```

You've already learned about the **assignment operator**, =. Although the same operator is used for both assignment and initialization, the language does make a distinction when overloading operators on user-defined types. Additionally, all of the binary arithmetic operators and the bitwise operators have compact forms, referred to as **opAssign** operators, that store the result of the expression in the left operand. These are +=, -=, *=, /=, %=, ^^=, &=, |=, ^=, <<=, >>= and >>>=.

Relational and logical operators

Relational operators determine the relationship between two operands in terms of equality and ordering (greater than and less than). Relational expressions evaluate to true or false. D supports the same relational operators found in other C-family languages: ==, !=, <, >, <=, >=, representing equal, not equal, less than, greater than, less than or equal, and greater than or equal. Due to the potential for rounding errors and the existence of special values such as NaN and infinity, floating-point comparisons can be tricky. The Phobos module std.math provides functions such as isIdentical, isInfinity, isNaN, and approxEquals to help.

The binary is operator is similar to the equality operator ==. More technically, x is y is referred to as the **identity expression**. For value types, this is usually the same as x == y, though this isn't always true for floating point values and struct instances. For example:

```
float f;              // Initialized to float.nan
writeln(f == f);      // false
writeln(f is f);      // true
```

Instances of a struct type that has overridden the equality operator will usually cause == and is to produce different results. Otherwise, the default behavior of struct equality is the same as is, which is to make a bit-by-bit comparison (structs are introduced in *Chapter 3, Programming Objects the D Way*, and operator overloading in *Chapter 5, Generic Programming Made Easy*). The difference between == and is becomes most apparent when working with reference types, as we'll observe later.

Logical operators produce true or false. For anyone with C-family experience, there is nothing special or surprising about them in D: x && y evaluates to true if both operands are true; x || y evaluates to true if either operand is true; !x evaluates to true if the operand is false.

The cast operator

The **cast operator** converts a variable from one type to another. It looks like this:

```
auto y = cast(T)x;
```

Here, T represents the type to which x is cast. If the cast is not legal, the compiler will emit an error. The traditional C-style cast, which is (T) without the cast keyword, is not supported. Additionally, D does not support multiple cast operators for different types of casts as C++ does. Though, as we'll see in the next chapter, D's cast has a special feature when x is a class instance and T is a class or interface.

Derived data types

In this section, we're going to observe D's take on pointers, arrays, strings, and associative arrays. Much of what we'll cover here is very different from other C-family languages.

Pointers

As in other languages that support them, pointers in D are special variables intended to hold memory addresses. Take a moment to compile and run the following:

```
int* p;
writeln("p's value is ", p);
writeln("p's type is ", typeid(p));
writeln("p's size is ", p.sizeof);
```

First, look at the declaration. It should look very familiar to many C-family programmers. All pointer declarations are default initialized to null, so here the first call to writeln prints "null" as the value. The type of p printed in the second writeln is int*. The last line will print 4 in 32-bit and 8 in 64-bit.

So far so good. Now look at the following line and guess what type b is:

```
int* a, b;
```

No, b is not an int, it is an int*. The equivalent C or C++ code would look like this:

```
int *x, *y;
```

In D, x would be interpreted as int* and y as int**, causing a compiler error. Every symbol in a declaration *must have* the same type. No matter how many identifiers are in a pointer declaration, only one * is needed and it applies to each of them. As such, it's considered best practice to put the * next to the type, as in the first declaration, rather than next to the identifiers. Otherwise, pointers in D function much as they do elsewhere. The unary & operator can be used to take the address of any variable and the * operator can be used to dereference a pointer to fetch the value it's pointing at. Pointer types can be inferred like any other type. Changing the value to which a pointer points will be reflected when the pointer is next dereferenced.

```
auto num = 1;
auto numPtr = &num;
writefln("The value at address %s is %s", numPtr, *numPtr);
num = 2;
writefln("The value at address %s is %s", numPtr, *numPtr);
```

Here, the address of num is assigned to numPtr. Since num is inferred to be int, the type of numPtr is inferred as int*. Both calls to writeln first print the value of numPtr, which is the address of num, then dereference numPtr to print the value of num. Memory addresses are printed as hexadecimal numbers by default. The following is the output:

The value at address 18FE34 is 1

The value at address 18FE34 is 2

void pointers are used to represent pointers to any type, but it's rare to use them in D except when interfacing with C APIs. Dereferencing a void pointer directly is an error; it must first be cast to the appropriate pointer type. Pointers to other types can be implicitly converted to void*, though the reverse is not allowed.

```
auto num = 1;            // int
void* voidPtr = &num;   // OK: int* converts to void*
writeln(*voidPtr);      // Error: void has no value
writeln(*cast(int*)voidPtr); // OK: dereferencing int*.
```

All of the pointers we've seen so far point to values on the stack. Pointers can also point to blocks of heap memory. We can allocate heap memory using the new expression (you'll learn how to allocate multiple values with new when we take a look at arrays).

```
int* intPtr = new int;   // Allocate memory for a single int
*intPtr = 10;
```

The heap and the stack work as they do in C, except that D has a garbage collector involved. Memory allocated with `new` is managed by the GC. Additionally, using certain language features can implicitly cause GC memory to be allocated. We'll discuss those cases when we come across them.

It's also possible to bypass the garbage collector completely and use alternative allocators such as C's `malloc`.

```
import core.stdc.stdlib : malloc, free;
int* intsPtr = cast(int*)malloc(int.sizeof * 10); // Ten ints
free(intsPtr);
auto dontDoThis = malloc(int.sizeof);
auto thisIsOK = cast(int*)malloc(int.sizeof);
```

The variable `dontDoThis` is inferred to be `void*`, which usually isn't what you want. Always pay attention when using type inference. Another point of note is that allocating memory in this manner loses the benefit of default initialization. Any memory allocated through `malloc` should be treated just as it would be in C. It's also worth noting here that D supports pointer arithmetic, which you could use to iterate `intsPtr`. You can also use the array index operator, `[]`, to access elements of `intsPtr`. Both approaches are frowned upon in D, however. It's much safer to convert `intsPtr` to an array.

Arrays

Arrays in D are a popular feature, slices in particular. They aren't your grandpa's arrays, though. D does things a bit differently than elsewhere in the C family. We're going to spend a few pages digging into them so that you can avoid common beginner mistakes.

Array basics

The first thing to understand about arrays in D is that they are fat pointers; each array carries around both a length and a pointer to the memory block where its elements are stored. Conceptually, you can think of an array as a `struct` that looks like this:

```
struct(T) {
  size_t length;
  T* ptr;
}
```

`T` is the type of the array elements. On every array, both `.length` and `.ptr` are accessible as properties.

Static arrays are allocated on the stack. They have a fixed length that does not change.

```
int[3] stat1;
writeln(stat1);
```

Compile this snippet and the `writeln` will print `[0, 0, 0]`. Three `int` values were allocated on the stack and have all been initialized to `int.init`. A **dynamic array** can grow and shrink as required. The syntax of a dynamic array declaration looks like this:

```
int[] dynArray1;
```

Unlike `stat1`, this array is empty. No space is allocated for any elements, only enough stack space to hold the metadata. The default initializer for a dynamic array is the empty array, `[]`. Its `.length` will be `0` and its `.ptr` will be `null`. We can allocate space for the array elements using `new`.

```
dynArray1 = new int[3];
int[] dynArray2 = new int[10];
```

> Some D users think the syntax `auto arr = new int[3]` is too similar to the static array declaration `auto arr = int[3]`. D now supports an alternative syntax, `new int[](3)`. This new syntax is recommended, but old habits die hard. There is a large body of D code that uses the older syntax.

The first array will now have three `int` values, the second will have ten, and all of the values will be default initialized to `int.init`. Actually, the runtime will probably have allocated more room than necessary. You can see this with the `.capacity` property.

```
writeln("#1:", dynArray1.capacity);
writeln("#2:", dynArray2.capacity);
```

`.capacity` returns the maximum length the array can grow to before reallocation is needed. The two `writeln` calls above print `3` and `15` for me. This first number tells us that `new int[3]` allocated exactly enough space for three `int` values. If we append a new value to `dynArray1`, a reallocation will take place. The second number tells us that `new int[10]` allocated enough space for fifteen `int` values. Since we only used ten, there's still space for five more elements to be appended before a reallocation is needed. The allocation algorithm is an implementation detail, so you can't rely on fifteen elements always being allocated when you request ten. What you *can* rely on is that enough space will be allocated for the number of elements you requested.

This default behavior is fine in many situations, but when you know you're going to be appending numerous items to an array, you can use the `reserve` function to be more efficient.

```
int[] dynArray3;
dynArray3.reserve(20);
writefln("%s, %s", dynArray3.length, dynArray3.capacity);
```

We've asked the runtime to reserve enough space for twenty `int` values, but none of that space is being used. This is an important difference between `new` and `reserve`. The former will allocate the space and return an array containing the number of elements you requested, that is, the new memory is not empty. The latter only allocates the space if the current capacity is smaller than the size requested, but the newly allocated space is empty. You can see this when `writefln` prints `0, 31` to the screen. There are no elements in the array, but a total of 31 can be appended before a reallocation is needed.

This brings us to the **append operator**. Using this, you can append individual elements to an array. `dynArray3` is empty, so let's give it some values.

```
dynArray3 ~= 2;
dynArray3 ~= 10;
writeln(dynArray3);
```

This will print `[2, 10]`. Now let's combine `dynArray3` with `dynArray1` to create a new array. To do this, we can use the **concatenation operator**, `~`.

```
auto dynArray4 = dynArray3 ~ dynArray1;
writeln(dynArray4);
```

Remember that `dynArray1` contains three `int` values that were initialized to `0`, so the `writeln` in this snippet will print `[2, 10, 0, 0, 0]`. Since both operands of the concatenation operator are of type `int[]`, the type inferred for `dynArray4` is `int[]`. We can also add elements to a dynamic array by manipulating `.length` directly.

```
dynArray1.length += 10;
```

If there is enough capacity to hold all ten values, no reallocation takes place. Otherwise, more space is allocated. If the current memory block cannot be extended, then a new block is allocated and the existing elements are copied to it. Finally, ten new elements are default initialized in the newly allocated space. Conversely, you can shrink the array by decreasing the length. Be aware that, when you do so, you're causing the capacity to be reset to `0`. This has a special significance that will be explained soon in this chapter.

To get at a specific value in any array, use the index operator, `[]`. Arrays use zero-based indexes. The special operator `$` is a synonym for `array.length`; it's only defined inside the brackets and always applies to the array being indexed.

```
writeln(dynArray4[0]);   // Print the first element
writeln(dynArray4[2]);   // Print the third element
writeln(dynArray4[$-1]); // Print the last element
```

The index operator works on both static and dynamic arrays. By default, D will do bounds checking at runtime to make sure that you don't read or write past either end of the array, a common source of exploits and other bugs in C and C++ software. Doing so will result in a runtime error reporting a range violation. You can turn bounds checking off by passing `-boundscheck=off` to the compiler.

Rectangular arrays

A **rectangular array** (sometimes called a **jagged array**) is an array of arrays. As we'll soon see, new D programmers often find them confusing. The thing to keep in mind is that they are no different from normal arrays. Declaring them has the same form of `elementType[numberOfElements]` that is used with any array. It's just that, in a rectangular array, the type of the array elements happens to be another array. Consider the following declaration of a normal array:

```
int[3] arr;
```

The `arr` array is a static array of three `int` elements, visually clarified by putting parentheses around the type:

```
(int)[3] arr;
```

Now look at the following declaration of a rectangular array:

```
int[3][2] ra1;
```

The `ra1` array is a static array of two `int[3]` elements. Again, putting parentheses around the type makes it clear.

```
(int[3])[2] ra1;
```

Fetching the element at any index in `arr`, such as `arr[0]`, returns an `int`. In the same manner, `ra1[0]` returns an `int[3]`. We can, in turn, get at its first element with `[0]`, which when implemented as a single statement looks like: `ra1[0][0]`. I want to stress that none of this is special syntax; we have two index operators in the declaration solely because the type of `arr` is itself an array type. Since `ra1[0]` returns an array, then an the additional `[0]` indexes into the returned array.

Now, about that confusion I mentioned. Many programmers are familiar with C's **multidimensional arrays**. There's a major difference in how they are declared in C and how rectangular arrays are declared in D. To help illustrate this, consider the following grid:

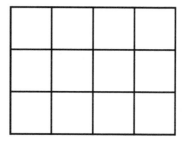

One way to describe this is as a grid of three rows and four columns. In C, this could be expressed in code like so:

```
int cgrid[3][4];
cgrid[1][0] = 10; // Set the first element of the second row
```

In D, we have to look at it a bit differently. In order to access the array elements the same way as in C, where [1] [0] is the second row and first column, we have to envision each row as an array of four elements. Given that the [4] is part of the array type, the order of the indexes in the declaration will be the reverse of those in C.

```
int[4][3] dgrid;
dgrid[1][0] = 10;
```

To be clear, the declaration is not creating a column-major array; it's still row-major exactly like the C array, so that [1] [0] is the second row and first column in both. The only difference is that the [4] is part of the array type. Keep that in mind and you should have no trouble keeping things straight.

Here's another example of a rectangular array:

```
int[][3] ra2 = [
    [0, 1],
    [2, 3, 4, 5],
    [6, 7, 8]
]
writeln(ra2[0].length);
writeln(ra2[1].length);
writeln(ra2[2].length);
```

This is a static array of three `int []`s, where each element array has a different length. In a C multidimensional array, all of the elements are stored in a contiguous block of memory. In D, this is true when all parts of a rectangular array are static, such as `int [3] [3]`. Any dynamic component in a rectangular array can point to its own separate block of memory, in which case you can't rely on it being contiguous. It's possible to create a dynamic array of dynamic arrays: `int [] []`. It's also possible to have more than two components, such as `int [] [] [3]`.

Slices

When thinking about slices, it helps to consider that dynamic arrays *are* slices and slices *are* dynamic arrays.

```
auto tenArray = [5,10,15,20,25,30,35,40,45,50];
auto sliced = tenArray[0 .. 5];
```

Here, `tenArray` is an array of `int`s. It's initialized with an array literal, a feature we'll examine shortly. I've taken a slice from `tenArray` and assigned it to a variable. The slice operator looks like this: `[m .. n]`, where the first element of the slice is `source[m]` and the last is `source[n-1]`. So the first value of `sliced` is `tenArray[0]` and the last is `tenArray[4]`. Pass it to `writeln` and you'll see `[5, 10, 15, 20]`. Print the length of `sliced` and you'll see 5, but the capacity may surprise you.

```
writeln(sliced.capacity);
```

This will print 0. When a slice begins life, no new memory is allocated. Instead, it is backed by the source array. Continuing from the preceding snippet:

```
tenArray[0] = 10;
writeln(sliced);
writeln(tenArray);
```

Running this will show that `tenArray[0]` and `sliced[0]` are both set to 10. The same thing works the other way; any changes made to `sliced` will be reflected in `tenArray`. To reinforce this point, add the following lines to the example:

```
writeln(sliced.ptr);
writeln(tenArray.ptr);
```

Both pointers are pointing to the same memory block. Now, what do you think would happen if we were to append a new item to `sliced`, either by increasing the `.length` or through the `~=` operator? The answer lies in that `.capacity` of 0.

The zero capacity indicates that appending to this slice in place may overwrite the existing elements in memory, that is, those belonging to the original array. In order to avoid any potential overwrite, attempting to append will cause the relationship between the two arrays to be severed. A new memory block will be allocated, which is large enough to hold the existing elements plus the appended one, and all of the elements copied over. Then the `.ptr` property of the slice will be set to the address of the new memory and its `.capacity` to a non-zero value.

```
sliced ~= 55;
writefln("Pointers: %s %s", tenArray.ptr, sliced.ptr);
writefln("Caps: %s %s", tenArray.capacity, sliced.capacity);
```

Running this code will print two different memory addresses. `sliced` is no longer backed by the memory of `tenArray` and now has a capacity of 7. We can say that `sliced` has become its own array. Sometimes, this isn't the desired behavior. I mentioned earlier that decreasing the `.length` of an array will reset its capacity to 0. To demonstrate, here's a little slicing trick that has the same effect as decreasing the array length:

```
auto shrink = [10, 20, 30, 40, 50];
shrink = shrink[0 .. $-1];
writeln(dontShrink);
```

Four elements are sliced from `shrink` and then the slice is assigned back to `shrink`. This is the same as decreasing `shrink.length` by one and also results in a zero capacity. Either way, the last element in the original array, the number 50, still exists at the same location in memory. The reason `.capacity` gives us a 0 here is that, if we were to append to `shrink`, we would overwrite the 50. If another slice is still pointing to the same memory block, it would be affected by any overwrites. To avoid any unintended consequences, D will play it safe and reallocate if we append.

Sometimes it doesn't matter if anything is overwritten. In that case, it's wasteful to reallocate each time the slice shrinks. That's where `assumeSafeAppend` comes in.

```
assumeSafeAppend(shrink);
```

Calling this after decreasing the length will maintain the original capacity, allowing all appends to use the existing memory block. Decreasing the length again will also reset the capacity to 0, requiring another call to `assumeSafeAppend` if we want to continue reusing the same memory block.

It's possible to remove an element from the middle of an array by taking a slice from in front of it and another from behind it, then concatenating them together. As concatenation allocates a new array, this isn't the most efficient way to go about it. A much better alternative is a function from `std.algorithm` called `remove`. Let's say we want to remove the `30` from `shrink` above. It's at the index `2`, so:

```
import std.algorithm : remove;
shrink = shrink.remove(2);
```

Now `shrink` contains the elements `[10, 20, 40, 50]`. We'll look at the details of `remove` in *Chapter 7, Composing Functional Pipelines with Algorithms and Ranges*.

Sometimes, you want to slice an entire array. There's a shortcut for that. Instead of slicing with `[0..$]`, you can use empty brackets, or no brackets at all.

```
auto aSlice = anArray[];
auto anotherSlice = anArray;
```

It's possible for static and dynamic arrays to be implicitly converted both ways. When going from dynamic to static, the lengths must match exactly. When going from static to dynamic, the compiler achieves the conversion by taking a slice of the static array:

```
int[] dyn = [1,2,3];
int[3] stat1 = dyn;      // OK: lengths match
int[4] stat2 = dyn;      // Error: mismatched array lengths
int[] sliced1 = stat1;   // OK: same as stat1[]
```

The memory for `dyn` is allocated on the heap, but `stat1` lives on the stack. When we initialize `stat1`, the elements of `dyn` are copied over and we now have two distinct arrays. In the last line, `sliced1` is just like any other slice we've seen so far, no matter that it's a slice of a static array. Its `.ptr` property will be identical to `stat1.ptr` and it will have a capacity of `0`, so we can append to or expand it without worrying about any impact on `stat1`. However, if `stat1` goes out of scope while `sliced1` still points to its memory, bad things can happen. If you can't guarantee that `stat1` is going to stick around, you can use the `.dup` property to copy it.

```
int[] sliced1 = stat1.dup;
```

This allocates memory for a dynamic array and copies into it all of the elements from `stat1`. A similar property, `.idup`, creates an immutable copy of an array. The details of immutable arrays will be discussed later in the chapter.

D arrays aren't the only things you can slice. Imagine that you've been given an array of integers, but as an `int*` and an associated length variable rather than an `int[]`. If you want to stay with your C roots, you can go ahead and use pointer arithmetic to your heart's content. If, on the other hand, you'd prefer the convenience of a D array, the language has got you covered: just slice the pointer. Assuming a C-style `int*` array called `parray`, the length of which is stored in a variable named `len`:

```
int[] array = parray[0 .. len];
```

How convenient is that? Be careful, though. As when slicing an array, the slice here is backed by the original pointer. In fact, `array.ptr` is exactly the same address as `parray`. This comes with the same potential consequences of slicing a static array. If `parray` is freed behind your back, or otherwise becomes an invalid memory location, `array` isn't going to be valid anymore, so the slice of `parray` should be `.duped`.

```
auto array = parray[0 .. len].dup;
```

Array literals

Take a look at the following array declarations, all initialized with array literals:

```
auto arr1 = [1.0f,2.0f,3.0f];    // float[]
auto arr2 = [1.0f,2.0,3.0];      // double[]
auto arr3 = [1.0,2.0f,3.0f];     // double[]
```

This snippet demonstrates that array literals are inferred as dynamic arrays by default. It also shows how the base type of an array is inferred. We see that `arr1` contains three `float`s, so it is of type `float[]` as one would reasonably expect. In the other arrays, we first see a `float` followed by two `double`s, then a `double` followed by two `float`s, yet both arrays are inferred as `double[]`. The compiler looks at the type of each element and determines their common type. This type becomes the type of the array and all elements are implicitly converted. For example, given an array comprised of `short`s and `char`s, the common type is `int`; in an array that contains one or more `long`s and a mix of smaller integer types, the common type is `long`.

We can use array literals with the append and concatenation operators.

```
int[] buildMe;
buildMe ~= [1, 2, 3, 4] ~ 5;
```

Static arrays can also be initialized with array literals, as long as the lengths match.

```
int[3] arr4 = [1,2,3];       // OK
int[3] arr5 = [1,2,3,4];     // Error: mismatched array lengths
```

Arrays and void

We've seen that `void` can be used to turn off default initialization for a variable. This is true for static arrays as well. Normally, every element of a static array will be initialized at the point of declaration. If the array is in global scope, this isn't such a big deal, but if it's in a function that is frequently called, the time taken to initialize all of the array elements can be a performance drain if the array is large.

```
float[1024] lotsOfFloats = void;
```

This will allocate 1,024 `float` values on the stack, but they will not be initialized to nan. Normally, you shouldn't turn off default initialization unless profiling shows it helps.

Uninitialized dynamic arrays

Allocating a dynamic array with new, such as new `float[10]`, will always initialize the elements with their `.init` value. Default initialization can be avoided in this case by allocating through `std.array.uninitializedArray` instead of calling new directly:

```
auto arr = uninitializedArray!(float[])(10)
```

It's also possible to declare arrays of type `void[]`. Like the universal pointer, this is the universal array. A couple of use cases can be found in the Phobos module `std.file`. The `read` function there returns a `void[]` array representing the bytes read from a file. The `write` function accepts a `void[]` buffer of bytes to write. You can cast from `void[]` to any array type and all array types are implicitly convertible to `void[]`.

Array operations

To close our array discussion, we're going to look at how arrays can serve as operands for many of the operators we discussed earlier. First up, let's take a look at a couple of special cases of the assignment operator.

We've seen `.dup` always allocates a new array, which is wasteful when the goal is to copy elements from one array into an existing one. In an assignment expression, if both arrays are the same type, or the right operand is implicitly convertible to the left, we can add empty brackets to the left operand.

```
int[] a1 = new int[10];
int[] a2 = [0,1,2,3,4,5,6,7,8,9];
a1[] = a2;
```

We know that the first line allocates ten integers and initializes them all to 0. We know that the array literal assigned to a2 allocates memory for ten integers and initializes them to the values in the bracket. We know that a1 = a2 would cause both arrays to share the same memory. By adding the empty index operator to the left operand, we're telling the compiler to do the equivalent of going through a2 and assigning each element to the corresponding position in a1. In other words, a1[0] = a2[0], a1[1] = a2[1], and so on. Although the end result looks the same as a1 = a2.dup, there is a major difference. Calling .dup will cause a1.ptr to point to the memory allocated by .dup; with the bracketed assignment, a1.ptr will be unchanged. The first two calls to writeln in this snippet will print the same address and the last one will print something different.

```
int[] a1 = new int[10];
writeln(a1.ptr);
int[] a2 = [0,1,2,3,4,5,6,7,8,9];
a1[] = a2;
writeln(a1.ptr);
a1 = a2.dup;
writeln(a1.ptr);
```

Two big caveats here. First, even when the target of the assignment is a dynamic array, the lengths of both arrays *must exactly match*. The second caveat is that the memory of the two arrays cannot overlap. Consider the following:

```
int[] a4 = [1,2,3,4,5];
int[] a5 = a4;
a5[] = a4;
```

This will give you a runtime error complaining about overlapping memory. This is an obvious case, as we know that the assignment of a4 to a5 will result in both arrays pointing to the same location. Where it isn't so obvious is with slices from pointers, or allocating your own array memory outside the GC via malloc. Vigilance is a virtue.

The empty index operator also allows us to assign a single value to every index in an array. Consider the following:

```
int[10] sa1 = 10;
sa1[] = 100;
```

Here, every element of `sa1` is initialized to `10`. In the next line, all ten elements are assigned the value `100`. This also shows that the empty index operator works with static arrays equally as well as dynamic arrays. We can apply several other operators to arrays. For example:

```
int[] a = [2,3,4];
a[] ^^= 2;
writeln(a);
int[] b = [5,6,7];
int[3] c = a[] + b[];
writeln(c);
```

If you try something like `writeln(a[] + b[])` you'll get a compiler error telling you that such operations on arrays require destination memory to write the result. There's no such thing as an implicit temporary for this sort of thing. I encourage you to experiment with the basic operators from earlier in this chapter to see what works with arrays and what doesn't. For example, the shift operators do not accept arrays as operands.

Finally, let's talk about array equality. This is our first opportunity to see the difference between `==` and `is` with reference types. Examine the following snippet:

```
auto ea1 = [1,2,3];
auto ea2 = [1,2,3];
writeln(ea1 == a2);
writeln(ea1 is a2);
```

Here we have two dynamic arrays with identical elements. The first `writeln` contains an equality expression. This will do an element-by-element comparison to see if each is the same value and evaluate to `true` if so. The `is` operator in the second `writeln` tests if the two arrays have the same identity. It doesn't care about the elements. So what's our snippet going to print?

Given that both `a1` and `a2` have the same number of elements and each element has the same value, it's rather obvious that the first `writeln` will print `true`. The `is` operator in the second `writeln` is going to look at the pointer and length of each array. If they are pointing to the same place and the length is the same, the result is `true`. In this case, `a1` and `a2` are pointing to different memory blocks, so we have a result of `false`.

The gist of it is that `==` on an array is related to its elements, while `is` on an array is related to its metadata. Both can be used to compare an array to `null`: a `== null` will return true if `a.length` is `0`; `a is null` will return true if `a.length` is `0` and `a.ptr` is `null`.

Strings

There are three string types in D: `string`, `wstring`, and `dstring`. They aren't actual types, but rather are each an alias to an immutable array of `char`, `wchar`, and `dchar` respectively. The D documentation says that strings are a special case of arrays. We can sum it up by saying that the compiler has some awareness of the string types, but they are not built-in types and they are, at heart, simply arrays. They are also treated specially by many functions in the standard library.

String essentials

Because strings are arrays, any properties available on arrays are also available on strings, but the `.length` property doesn't tell you how many letters are in a string; it tells you the number of Unicode code units. Remember from our discussion on basic types that each character type in D represents a single Unicode code unit. One or more code units can form a code point. In UTF-8, where each code unit is only eight bits, it's common for code points to be composed of multiple code units. A code point that requires two code units in UTF-8 could be represented as one code unit in UTF-16. The following example introduces D's string literals to demonstrate the code unit/code point dichotomy:

```
string s = "soufflé";
wstring ws = "soufflé"w;
dstring ds = "soufflé"d;
```

String literals in D are indicated by opening and closing double quotes (`""`). By default, they are understood by the compiler to be of type `string`. Appending a `w` to the end makes a `wstring` and a `d` similarly forces a `dstring`. The word `soufflé` has seven letters, but if you query `s.length`, you'll find it returns `8`. Both `ws.length` and `ds.length` return `7` as expected. This discrepancy is because the letter é requires two code units in UTF-8. In both UTF-16 and UTF-32, a single code unit is large enough to hold it. In fact, a single code unit in UTF-32 is always equivalent to a single code point, as 32 bits is large enough to hold any Unicode character.

Unicode is an important component in modern software development, yet is often misunderstood. For details, a great place to start is the Unicode FAQ at http://unicode.org/faq/. There are also a number of informative introductory articles that can be found through a quick web search.

Double-quoted string literals in D are always parsed for the standard escape sequences such as the end-of-line character (`'\n'`), the tab character (`'\t'`), and the null-terminator (`'\0'`). A single string literal declared over multiple lines will cause any newlines to be embedded in the string.

```
auto s1 = " Hi
I
  am a multi-line
    string";
writeln(s1);
```

Multiple strings declared in succession with no terminating semicolon between them are concatenated into a single string at compile time.

```
auto s2 = "I am" " a string which is"
          " composed of multiple strings"
          " on multiple lines.";
```

Many of the operations you'll commonly perform on strings are scattered throughout Phobos. Most of what you want is found in the `std.string` module. Other modules include `std.ascii`, `std.uni`, `std.utf`, `std.format`, `std.path`, `std.regex`, `std.encoding`, and `std.windows.charset`. Because strings are dynamic arrays, you can also use them with the functions in `std.array`. Since dynamic arrays are also ranges, many functions in `std.algorithm` also accept strings.

Another useful module for strings is `std.conv`. There you'll find a number of functions for converting from one type to another. Two particularly useful functions are `to` and `parse`. The former takes almost any type and converts it to almost any other. For example, given an `int` that you want to convert to a `string`, you can do the following:

```
import std.conv : to;
int x = 10;
auto s = to!string(x);
```

We've already seen the template instantiation operator, `!`, when we looked at `std.conv.octal`. Here, we're telling the template to take the runtime parameter x and turn it into the type indicated by the compile time parameter following the `!` operator. We'll see more about the difference between runtime and compile-time parameters in *Chapter 5, Generic Programming Made Easy*.

Conversely, sometimes you have a string from which you want to extract another type. You can do this with to, but it will throw an exception if there are inconvertible characters in the string. An alternative that doesn't throw an exception is parse. When it encounters inconvertible characters, it will stop parsing and return whatever it has parsed so far:

```
import std.conv : to, parse;
int s1 = "10";
int x1 = to!int(s1);        // OK
int s2 = "10and20";
int x2 = parse!int(s2);     // OK: x2 = 10
int x3 = to!int(s2);        // ConvException
```

If you have one or more values that you want to insert into specific places in a string, you can use std.format.format. The std.format module includes several functions, such as format, that assist in creating formatted strings.

```
auto height = 193;
auto weight = 95;
auto fs = format("Bob is %s cm and weighs %s kg", height, weight);
```

The syntax and specifiers are the same used with writef. The format function always allocates a new string from the GC heap, but another version, sformat, allows you to pass a reusable buffer as a parameter and returns a slice to the buffer.

The empty string, "", has a length of zero. Its .ptr property, however, is not null. For compatibility with C, all string literals in D are null-terminated, so even the empty string points to a piece of memory containing a '\0'. Going with what we know about arrays, this means "" == null is true and "" is null is false.

Alternative string literals

In addition to the double-quoted string literals we've gone through, D supports the following string literals:

WYSIWYG strings

Any character in a **WYSIWYG (What You See is What You Get)** string is part of the string, including escape sequences. There are two WYSIWYG syntaxes, r"wysiwyg" and `wysiwyg` (these are backticks, not single quotes). Because the former uses double quotes and does not allow escape sequences, it's impossible to include double quotes in the string itself. The backtick syntax allows you to do that, but then you can't have backticks in the string.

```
writeln(r"I'm a WYSIWYG string'```'\t\n");
writeln(`me, too!\n\r"'''"`);
```

Delimited strings

Delimited strings allow you to choose how to denote the beginning and end of a string, but there are some special rules. These literals begin with `q"` and end with `"`. Any delimiter you choose must immediately follow the opening quote and immediately precede the ending quote. There are a few nesting delimiters that are recognized by default: `[]`,`()`,`<>` and `{}`. Because these nest, you can use the same characters inside the string. Any nested delimiters must be balanced.

```
writeln(q"(A Delimited String (with nested parens))");
writeln(q"[An [Unbalanced nested delimiter]");
writeln(q"<Another unbalanced> nested delimiter>");
writeln(q"{And }{again!}");
```

In the first line, the nested parentheses are balanced and so become part of the string. The second line has an opening delimiter, but no closing delimiter to balance it. The opposite is true in the third line, while the last line has an unbalanced pair.

You can also use a custom identifier as the delimiter with the following guidelines:

- The opening and closing identifier must be the same
- A newline must immediately follow the opening identifier
- A newline must immediately precede the closing identifier
- The closing identifier must start at the beginning of the line

The first newline is not part of the string, but all subsequent newlines are, including the one preceding the closing identifier:

```
auto s = q"STR
I'm a string with a custom delimiter!
STR";
```

Strings delimited by identifiers are sometimes referred to as **heredoc strings**. Delimited strings are useful when long blocks of text need to be included in the source. They behave just like WYSIWYG strings, with the addition that they allow the use of both backticks and double quotes in the string.

Token strings

Token strings are string literals that must contain valid D tokens. These are great to use when generating code at compile time. Text editors that can perform syntax highlighting on D can highlight the code inside the string. Token strings open with q{ and close with }. Any newlines inside the literal are part of the string and the nesting of braces is allowed.

```
auto code = q{
int x = 10;
int y = 1;
};
```

Associative arrays

Associative arrays allow you to map keys of any type to values of any type.

```
int[string] aa1;   // int values, string keys
string[int] aa2;   // string values, int keys
```

The default initialization value for an associative array, if you print it, looks like the empty array, []. They may look the same, but they are two different beasts. Associative arrays have no .ptr or .capacity, though they do have a .length that is 0 by default. You can't call reserve, modify .length, or use the concatenation operator on an associative array. What you *can* do is add values like this:

```
aa1["Ten"] = 10;
aa2[10] = "Ten";
```

If the key already exists in the array, its existing value will be overwritten. If it doesn't exist, it will be added. Although aa2[10] looks like a regular array index operation, it is not. With an array, the indexes are sequential. If the index 10 does not exist, you've earned a range violation. With an associative array, you've added a new key and value pair. You can also initialize an associative array with literals, like this:

```
auto aa3 = ["x":22.0, "y":3.0f, "z":5.0f, "w":1.0];
```

Literals take the form of a bracketed sequence of comma-separated KeyType : ValueType pairs. In this particular declaration, the type of aa3 is inferred as double[string]. The type of double is inferred in the same way it would be with standard arrays; it's the common type of all of the values.

To remove an item from an associative array, use the `remove` function. This is not the same as `std.algorithm.remove` for arrays; no imports are required. If the key does not exist, it does nothing and returns `false`, otherwise it removes the key and its associated value and returns `true`.

```
aa3.remove("w");
```

There are two options for reading values from associative arrays. The most obvious is to read a key index directly.

```
auto x = aa1["x"];    // OK: key exists
auto w = aa1["w"];    // We removed it -- range violation
```

If you want to avoid the range violation for a nonexistent key, you can use the `in` operator instead. This takes a key as the left operand and an associative array as the right operand. If the key exists, it returns a pointer to the value. Otherwise, it returns `null`.

```
auto px = "x" in aa3;    // type double*, valid address
auto pw = "w" in aa3;    // type double*, null
```

Once a pointer is received from the `in` operator, it needs to be dereferenced to get at the value. We haven't looked at the `if` statements yet, but I assume you know what they are. So I'm going to show you a common D idiom. It's possible to combine the `in` operator with an `if` statement to perform an action on a value if a key is present.

```
if(auto px = "x" in aa3)
    writeln(*px);
```

You can fetch all of the keys and values in two ways. The efficient way is to call `.byKey` and `.byValue`. Both of these return ranges without allocating any heap memory or making any copies. We will explore ranges in *Chapter 6, Understanding Ranges*, at which point you'll understand how they can be efficient. Sometimes, you really do need to make a copy. For those situations, there are the `.keys` and `.values` properties. These each allocate a dynamic array and copy the keys and values respectively.

Control flow statements

D includes the traditional loop and conditional statements found in other C-family languages. It also supports the infamous `goto` statement. It has a couple of other useful statements, such as a built-in `foreach` statement and a rather unique `scope` statement. In this section, we're going to look at examples of each of the first two. Because of their relation with exceptions, `scope` statements are included in detail in the next chapter.

Traditional loops

In terms of looping constructs, we have `for`, `do`, and `do-while`. The syntax and behavior should be familiar. Here is an example of each iterating over an array:

```
auto items = [10,20,30,40,50];
for(int i=0; i<items.length; ++i)
  writeln(items[i]);

int i = 0;
while(i < items.length)
  writeln(items[i++]);

i = 0;
do {
  writeln(items[i++]);
} while(i < items.length);
```

No surprises there. The braces are optional with `for` and `while` when they only contain one statement. When a loop with an empty body is desired, the following syntax is not allowed in D:

```
int sum;
for(int i=0; i<10; sum += i++)
    ;
```

Replace the semicolon with { } and it will compile.

You can also find the traditional `break` and `continue` statements in D. The latter stops the current loop iteration and goes back to the top and the former exits the current loop completely. To break out of nested loops, D supports labeled breaks:

```
auto array = [10,20,30,40,50];
EXIT_LOOPS: for(int i=0; i<array.length; ++i) {
    for(int j=array.length - 1; j>=0; --j) {
        auto val = array[i] + array[j];
        if(val == 100) break EXIT_LOOPS;
        writeln(val);
    }
}
```

A labeled break will break out of the loop associated with the given label. In this snippet, the outer loop is the closest one to the label, so that's the loop we're breaking out of.

The foreach loop

The `foreach` loop is a special loop construct that does some things behind the scenes so you don't have to. First, let's see what it looks like, and then I'll tell you how it works. Reusing the same `items` array from above, we can do this:

```
foreach(elem; items)
    writeln(elem);
```

Essentially, `foreach` maintains the index for us and infers the type of `elem`, streamlining the syntax. You can specify a type for the element, as in `foreach(uint elem; items)`. You can also do this:

```
foreach(elem; 0..10)
    writeln(elem);
```

The `0..10` is a sequence of numbers that is only valid in specific contexts, such as in the slice operator and the `foreach` loop. This loop will print from `0` to `9` because, just as with the slice operator, the end number is exclusive. Since we're iterating an array, the loop can also tell us the current index. Simply add another variable and a comma.

```
foreach(index,elem; items)
    items[index] = elem+10;
```

By default, the index is of type `size_t`, but you can declare it to be `int` or `uint`. If the only reason you want the index is to modify the array elements, there's another way to do it. Use `ref`.

```
foreach(ref elem; items)
    elem += 10;
```

While it's fine to modify the individual elements of the iteration target in the `foreach` loop via a reference or the index operator, you should never modify its structure. For example, you cannot append or remove elements to or from an array, or otherwise modify its length in any way and expect no problems to arise. This holds true for any sort of range or container you are iterating. The compiler may let you get away with it, but you're entering undefined territory at runtime and can be certain something's going to break.

As hinted earlier, `foreach` doesn't operate only on arrays. It can iterate over any type that implements either the `opApply` function or, if that isn't present, the input range interface. We'll see the former in the next chapter and the latter in *Chapter 6, Understanding Ranges*. There is another statement called `foreach_reverse` that works like `foreach`, except that it iterates backwards, starting with the last element and ending with the first. It works with arrays and any type that implements either the `opApplyReverse` function or the bidirectional range interface.

There is some special behavior when iterating over arrays of characters and associative arrays. Character arrays, be they of the string family or of a mutable variety, can be decoded on the fly. Consider the following example:

```
foreach(c; "soufflé") {
   writeln(c);
}
```

Every character up through the letter `'l'` will print as expected, but the letter `'é'` is never printed. What actually does get printed depends on the platform. Never forget that characters in D are Unicode code units. By default, `c` is of type `immutable(char)` because `soufflé` is a `string` literal, or `immutable(char)[]`. In this case, since we know that the `é` requires two code units, we can fix this either by appending a `w` to `soufflé` to make it a `wstring` literal, or by declaring `c` as a `wchar`. By taking the latter approach, every character of the string will automatically be decoded from UTF-8 to UTF-16. When working with variables instead of literals and a suffix can't be appended, it's better to declare `c` as `dchar`. This way, no matter how many bytes are required to represent a letter, `c` will be big enough to hold them all. Just keep in mind that there is a cost associated with decoding each character.

It's also possible to use `foreach` on associative arrays. In this case, if you declare only one identifier, you are iterating the values. Declare two identifiers and the first one becomes the key. Types can be inferred as follows:

```
auto aa = ["One":1, "Two":2, "Three":3];
foreach(key,val; aa)
   writefln("%s = %s", key, val);
```

Alternatively, you can iterate on one of the following: `byValue()`, `byKey()`, `.keys`, or `.values`. You'll recall from the discussion of associative arrays that the first two return ranges and the remaining two each allocate a new array and copy over the keys or values. The first two are more efficient, but when using them you're iterating the associative array directly. In this case, attempting to modify the associative array during iteration by adding or removing elements will almost certainly cause something to break. When iterating on `.keys` or `.values`, it's a separate, copied array that is being iterated, so the associative array can be freely modified during iteration.

Traditional conditionals

First up, we have the traditional **if statement**. It looks and behaves like `if` statements in other C-family languages.

```
int x = 100;
if(x >= 200)
   writeln("200 or higher!");
```

```
else if( x >= 100)
  writeln("100 or higher!");
else
  writeln("Less than 100!");
```

Next up is the **conditional expression**, also referred to as the **ternary operator**. If its condition is `true`, it returns the second operand, otherwise it returns the third.

```
string isFour = (2 + 2 == 4) ? "It's a 4!" : "It's not a 4!";
```

The D documentation specifies that the expression in the condition of `if` statements and conditional expressions must produce a type that can be converted to `bool`. This isn't the same as a normal implicit conversion. For example, the expression `someBool = somePointer` will fail, because pointers are not implicitly convertible to `bool`. However, `if(somePointer)` is valid, as the conversion in this case is achieved via a cast inserted by the compiler. The same holds for the conditions in loops.

Finally, we have the traditional `switch` statement. In D, you must have a default case. Leaving it out will fail to compile.

```
int x = 10;
switch(x) {
  case 2:
    writeln("It's 2!");
    break;
  case 4:
    writeln("It's 4!");
    break;
  case 10:
    writeln("It's 10!");
    break;
  default:
    writeln("It's something else!");
    break;
}
```

Sometimes you want to cover case statements with one block. The C way is to list each case statement explicitly.

```
int i = 2;
switch(i) {
  case 1:
  case 2:
  case 3:
    writeln("OK");
    break;
  default: break;
}
```

You can do this in D too, and it works as expected. However, adding the highlighted line in the following code is a problem.

```
switch(i) {
   case 1:
   case 2:
      writeln("Warning!");
   case 3:
      writeln("OK");
      break;
   default: break;
}
```

This will give you an *implicit fall-through* warning if warning messages are enabled (with -wi) and an error if warnings are treated as errors (-w). It is intended to be a deprecated feature at some point. If you really want to fall through to the third case, then you can do so explicitly with goto case.

```
case 2:
   writeln("No Warning!");
   goto case;
```

It's also possible to jump to any specific case. For example:

```
switch(i) {
   case 1:
      goto case 3;
   case 2:
      writeln("No Warning!");
      goto case;
   case 3:
      writeln("OK");
      break;
   default: break;
}
```

D also supports the **case range statement** when the case values are sequential.

```
switch(i) {
   case 1: .. case 3:
      writeln("OK");
      break;
   default: break;
}
```

Leave out the .. and you're only covering two cases. Additionally, `switch` statements in D accept strings.

```
string s = "Yadda Yadda";
switch(s) {
  case "Yadda": writeln("One Yadda"); break;
  case "Yadda Yadda": writeln("Two Yaddas"); break;
  default: break;
}
```

You can also use `return` in place of `break` to exit the current function, and use `continue` when the `switch` is inside a loop. There is also a special form of `switch`, called a `final switch`, which can be useful in specific circumstances. We'll take a look at that in the next chapter, since it's closely related to enumerations.

The goto statement

Whether or not you think `goto` is evil, it is supported in D. It's the familiar C-style `goto` you're used to, not the old style that lets you jump around anywhere in your code base.

```
int x;
INC: writeln(x++);
if( x < 10) goto INC;
```

A do-it-yourself loop is one of the worst examples of `goto` there is, despite its ubiquity. However, it's short and easy to understand. One of the use cases of `goto` that most people agree is legitimate, that of cleaning up resources in a function, is quite useful in C, but is made mostly obsolete in D by the scope statement. It's still useful for explicit fall-through in `switch` statements.

The D `goto` has one important difference from the one in C: it is an error to skip variable initialization.

```
goto SKIP_I;    // Skipping initialization of i -- error!
int i = 2;
SKIP_I:
writeln(i);
```

Type qualifiers – const and immutable

Both `const` and `immutable` are type qualifiers. This means that, when applied to any type, they actually create a new type. For example, the following equivalent declarations all create a type that is called `const(int)`.

```
const int x = 10;
const(int) y = 11;
const z = 12;
```

In the declaration of z, the compiler will infer the type. For a basic type such as `int`, it makes no difference which syntax is used. However, we'll see shortly that things can be a bit confusing with derived data types, so you may want to get into the habit of using the syntax in the second line when you need to explicitly specify the type. In the rest of this section, we're going to explore the contracts of both `const` and `immutable`, then take a look at how they apply to the types we've seen so far.

The contracts

When you declare a variable as `immutable`, you are stating unequivocally that it is never, ever going to change throughout the lifetime of the program. This is a very strong contract and the compiler is going to run on the assumption that you really mean what you say. This allows the potential for optimizations that otherwise would not have been possible.

Anything declared as `const` is making a guarantee that no data will be modified through that particular reference. This is less strict than the contract of `immutable`, because it's still possible for the data to be modified through another, non-`const` reference.

Another property of `const` and `immutable` is that they are both transitive. This means that, if you apply them to a thing, then anything else that is reachable through that thing is also `const` or `immutable`. You'll get a basic sense of this in this chapter, but you'll achieve full clarity in the next chapter when you learn how to qualify user-defined types.

With the basic types

Applying `const` and `immutable` to one of the basic types is straightforward. Despite the difference in the contracts, there is effectively no difference between them in this case as the basic types are all value types. When one is assigned to another, the right operand is copied to the left operand. There's no way to change the original value through the new one.

```
immutable x = 10;
const y = 11;
const int z;
z = 12;    // Error
```

All three variables are completely protected from mutation beyond the point of declaration. x is forever 10, y is forever 11, and z is doomed to remain 0, the value of int.init.

With pointers

When applying const or immutable to a pointer declaration, you first need to decide if it should apply only to the data, or to the pointer as well.

```
const(int)* q;        // Mutable pointer to const data
const(int*) r;        // const pointer to const data
const int* s;         // const pointer to const data
```

Without parentheses, it's easy to forget which kind of pointer you have. Also, note that none of these guys are initialized; two of them are forever null. In the first declaration, q is a mutable pointer. It need not point at the same location forever. It can be assigned a new address at any time, but the data stored at that address can never be mutated. r and s are const pointers, yielding an error if you try to point them somewhere else.

```
int x = 10;
q = &x;      // OK: mutable pointer
r = &x;      // Error: const pointer
*q = 11;     // Error: const data
```

Where the contract of const comes into play is that it's possible mutate const data through a different pointer where const is not involved, as shown in this example:

```
const(int)* cp;
int* p;
int x = 10;
cp = &x;        // OK
p = &x;         // OK
```

There are two ways to modify x behind cp's back. First, you can assign a value to x directly. Second, you can do it through the pointer p. const pointers are often used as function parameters, where the function is promising it won't modify your data through the pointer during the function's lifetime.

The syntax for `immutable` is the same. The difference is in the contract. If you have a pointer to immutable data, then the data must be `immutable` through all other pointers to that data. The original data must also be `immutable`. Consider the following:

```
immutable(int)* ip;
int x = 10;
ip = &x;          // Error: x is not immutable
immutable int y = 11;
ip = &y;          // OK
```

You cannot assign `ip` a pointer to x because then there are no guarantees that x will never be mutated elsewhere in the program. It works for y because y is immutable data and cannot be modified directly. That said, you could always cast immutable away. Consider the following two lines:

```
immutable int y = 10;
immutable(int*) py = &y;
```

We know that it's an error to assign a new address to `py` because the pointer, not just the data, is declared as `immutable` (the `*` is inside the parentheses). Attempting to assign the address of a mutable `int` to `py` will result in a compiler error, but take a look at this:

```
writeln(py);
int** ppy = cast(int**)&py;
int j = 9;
*ppy = &j;
writeln(py);
```

This prints two different addresses, showing a successful violation of `immutable`'s contract. Doing something like this could lead to corrupt data, a segfault, an access violation, or who knows what else. In fact, here's a demonstration of "who knows what else":

```
immutable int x = 10;
int* px = cast(int*)&x;
*px = 9;
writeln(x);
```

This snippet takes the same approach used to modify `py` above. Compiling and running this, though, actually prints 10. The compiler, assuming that an `immutable int` is never going to be modified, has changed `writeln(x)` to `writeln(10)`. This is one of the optimizations enabled by `immutable`. Taken together, these two examples demonstrate why casting away `immutable` is never a good idea. It is undefined behavior and anything can happen.

The same can be said for `const`. It's not a violation of the `const` contract to modify source data through another reference, but it certainly is a violation to cast `const` away and modify it. There's more to the `const` story, but it's more clearly demonstrated in the context of user-defined types in the next chapter.

With arrays

The general idea with arrays is the same as with pointers. For example:

```
const(int)[] t;      // Mutable array, const data
const(int[]) u;      // const array, const data
const int[] v;       // const array, const data
```

Here, none of the metadata associated with u or v can be modified through u or v. Not the pointer, the length, the capacity, nothing. As with pointers, it's still possible for another, mutable slice to reference the same data. What about t?

```
t[0] = 1;        // Error: const data
t ~= [3,2,1];    // OK: mutable array
t.length = 30;   // OK: mutable array
```

The first line fails as one would expect; you can't modify `const` data. The last two lines show what it means to have a mutable array. Tacking a slice onto the end of it does not violate the contract, since none of the original elements are mutated and they are all still reachable from their original indexes in the array, no matter that they may have been copied elsewhere during a reallocation. The only modification was to the array metadata. Ditto for the assignment to `length`. This all also holds true for `immutable`. I trust you can work out how its contract would apply if you swap it in for `const` in this example.

You can also apply `const` and `immutable` to associative arrays and strings. Recall that strings are declared as arrays with `immutable` data. If you want to further make the array metadata `immutable` or `const`, you can do it as with any other data type, such as `immutable(string)`, which is effectively `immutable(immutable(char)[])`. This is exactly the same as `immutable(char[])`.

Conversions

Types that are passed around by value are implicitly convertible between `immutable`, `const`, and unqualified; `immutable` and unqualified are both implicitly convertible to `const`, but not the other way around.

```
immutable int x = 10;
int y = x;                  // OK: value types
immutable(int)* ipx = &x;
const(int)* cpx = ipx;      // OK: immutable to const
const(int)* cpy = &y;       // OK: unqualified to const
int* px = ipx;              // Error
```

You can think of `const` as a bridge between the three. This is particularly helpful with function parameters if the mutability of the source variable is irrelevant.

Functions

The following two statements are true about D function declarations:

- Functions can be declared in module scope or as members of an aggregate type
- There's no need to separate the declaration of a function from its implementation, though it is still possible to do so

We've seen two functions already in the form of `main` and `sayHello`, both of which had a `void` return type. Here's one that takes three `unsigned bytes` representing red, green, blue, and alpha color components and returns a packed 32-bit RGBA value as a `uint`.

```
uint packRGBA(ubyte r, ubyte g, ubyte b, ubyte a = 255) {
    return (r << 24) + (g << 16) + (b << 8) + a;
}
```

As you can see, D isn't shaking things up in the world of function declaration syntax. We have a return type, `uint`, the function name, `packRGBA`, and a parenthesized parameter list. The last parameter has a default value of `255`, so the function can be called with only three arguments instead of four. Both the following are valid:

```
auto white = packRGBA(255, 255, 255);
auto transWhite = packRGBA(255, 255, 255, 127);
```

Default arguments in D work as they do in C++. Parameters with default arguments can only be followed in the parameter list by other parameters with default arguments. When calling a function with multiple default arguments, any arguments provided by the caller are applied in order.

```
int illegal(int a = 1, int b);     // Error
int legal(int a = 1, int b = 10); // OK
legal();        // OK a = 1, b = 10
legal(2);       // OK a = 2, b = 10
legal(2,11);    // OK: a = 2, b = 11
```

Like most other declarations, functions can be declared in any scope. The same scoping rules apply.

```
void manyFuncs() {
   int innerNumber1() {
      writeln("Number1");
      return 1;
   }
   {
      void innerNumber2() {
         writeln("Number2");
      }
      innerNumber2();
   }
   for(int i=0; i<10; ++i) {
      void innerNumber3() {
         writeln(i);
      }
      innerNumber3();
   }
   innerNumber1();
}
```

Yes, you can declare functions in `for` loops. When calling a function with no arguments, the parentheses can be omitted.

```
manyFuncs();
manyFuncs;
```

What's more, if a module-scope function has only one parameter, then Universal Function Call Syntax can be used and the parentheses can still be dropped.

```
auto inc(int x) { return ++x; }
```

Both of the following are valid:

```
auto n1 = 2.inc;
auto n2 = n1.inc();
```

Again, the parentheses are optional in both cases. What's the difference? Nothing that is enforced by the compiler. It's useful for implementing properties. In fact, when you access the `.capacity` of an array, you're really calling a module-scope function that takes an array as the first parameter. It isn't a built-in property as `.length` or `.ptr` are.

One place where the parentheses are often dropped is function chaining.

```
auto n3 = 2.inc.inc.inc.inc.inc;
```

This is a common idiom when working with ranges and algorithms, as you'll learn in *Chapter 7, Composing Functional Pipelines with Algorithms and Ranges*, although you're usually chaining several functions together rather than multiple calls to one. Later in the book, we'll also take a look at D's support for **variadic functions**.

Overloaded functions

Any function in D can be overloaded by declaring another function with the same return type, same name, and different parameters. A simple example is as follows:

```
void print(int i) { writeln(i); }
void print(string s) { writeln(s); }
```

When the compiler encounters a call to one of these functions, such as print(10), it goes through a defined process to determine the best match. It looks at each parameter in the parameter lists to determine how well the types of the arguments match the types of the parameters by assigning match levels to each function. The function with the highest match level wins. In this case, that would be the `int` version of print because the type of the literal 10 makes an exact match with the type of the function's single parameter. For more on how overload matches are determined, refer to `http://dlang.org/function.html#function-overloading`.

ref and out

In D, it's impossible to declare a variable as a reference. However, it *is* possible to declare function parameters and return types as references. We do so with `ref`.

```
void swap(ref int x, ref int y) {
    auto tmp = x;
    x = y;
    y = tmp;
```

```
  }
  void main() {
    int x = 10;
    int y = 20;
    swap(x, y);
    writeln(x, ", ", y);
  }
```

One important thing to know about `ref` is that it is a **storage class**, not a type qualifier, so it does not become part of the type. It's illegal to use parentheses, like `ref(int)`.

It's also important to understand the effect of `ref` on arrays. Consider the following:

```
  void append(int[] arr, int val) {
    arr ~= val;
  }
```

And to test it:

```
  auto a1 = [10,20,30];
  a1.append(40);
  writeln(a1);
```

You'll see that the appended value was not printed. This sometimes confuses new D programmers who may be under the impression that arrays are passed around by reference. It's an easy assumption to make, especially since modifying the existing elements as we did in `update` is reflected in the original array. But recall our discussion about slices. The array itself is conceptually a length and a pointer. While a slice can share memory with its source array, its length and pointer are completely independent. As such, a slice is passed *by value* to a function. Inside a function, any modification to the length or pointer of a slice parameter is modifying the metadata of the parameter, not that of the source array. To enable modification of the source array's metadata, the parameter must be declared `ref`. Change `append` to look like this:

```
  void append(ref int[] arr, int val) {
    arr ~= val;
  }
```

With this version, `writeln` prints the appended value. There's a side-effect of adding `ref` here, though. Recall that static arrays are implicitly convertible to dynamic arrays. With `ref`, the function will no longer accept slices of static arrays.

```
  int[3] a2 = [10, 20, 30];
  append(a2, 40);      // Error!
```

This call to append causes a compiler error. Remember, the length of a static array is fixed; a2 will contain exactly three elements for the entirety of its existence. The compiler isn't going to allow you to pass a slice of a static array into a function where it is possible to modify the length of the source array through the slice.

When the parameter itself is a static array, the entirety of the array, including its elements, is copied into the function.

```
void setArrayIndex1(int[3] copy) {
   copy[1] = 2; // Changes second element only of copy.
}
```

The second element of the source array is unchanged by this function; only the second element of copy is modified. To modify the source array, once again use ref.

```
void setArrayIndex1(ref int[3] copy) {
   copy[1] = 2; // Changes second element of source array.
}
```

You can also have references to const or immutable data.

```
void silly(ref const(int) a, ref const(int) y) {}
```

This function is named silly because it really is silly to have a reference to const(int). It's effectively the same as int. This really only has meaning when used with user-defined types, as we'll see in the next chapter.

When the purpose of applying ref to a function parameter is solely to pass a value back to the call site, out can replace ref. An out parameter's only purpose in life is to hold an output value from a function. A key difference is that an out parameter is initialized to the .init value of its type when the function is entered. Using it in place of ref clearly documents that the value of any argument passed in that parameter slot is ignored.

You can also return values by ref, but it doesn't work the way a C++ programmer might expect. Consider this:

```
void main() {
    int y;
    ref int getRef() {
        return y;
    }
    auto i = getRef();
    i = 10;
    writeln(y);
}
```

Compile and execute the preceding code and you'll find it prints 0, not 10. The reason is best illustrated by attempting to compile this line:

```
ref int ri;
```

This results in the following compiler error (assuming a source file named foo.d):

Error: variable foo.main.ri only parameters or foreach declarations can be ref

To be clear, a ref return value is actually returned from the function by reference, but if it's stored in a variable, that variable cannot be declared ref. Unlike const and immutable, ref is not a type qualifier; it's a storage class only. So in this example, if assigning 10 to i has no effect on y, then what good is a ref return value? Replace the two highlighted lines with this one.

```
getRef() = 10;
```

Now the writeln at the end will show you that y has actually been set to 10. You can also declare a function to return auto ref. In that case, the compiler will use the function's return statement(s) to infer if the return value can be ref or not. For example, a local variable would be returned by value, but a local static variable by reference.

inout parameters

Sometimes, the mutability of a function return type needs to match the mutability of one of the parameters. For example:

```
const(int)[] writeAndReturn(const(int)[] arr) {
    write(arr);
    return arr;
}
```

To support the same function for both immutable and unqualified arrays, it's necessary to write one overload for each. This is such a common requirement that there's a keyword to handle it automatically: inout

```
inout(int)[] writeAndReturn(inout(int)[] arr) {
    writeln(arr);
    return arr;
}
```

Now, no matter which type of array is passed to the function, the return type will match it. Internally, the function will treat it as `const`.

```
immutable(int)[] ia = [10,20,30];
int[] a = [1,2,3];
writeln(typeid(writeAndReturn(ia)));
writeln(typeid(writeAndReturn(a)));
```

lazy parameters

When a parameter is declared `lazy`, then any expression passed in that position is not evaluated immediately when the function is entered, but when the parameter is used. The difference can be seen in the following complete program:

```
import std.stdio;
void normalParam(int x) {
  writeln("Entered normalParam");
  writeln(x);
}
void lazyParam(lazy int x) {
  writeln("Entered lazyParam.");
  writeln(x);
}
int getInt() {
  writeln("Entered getInt");
  return 10;
}
void main() {
  normalParam(getInt());
  lazyParam(getInt());
}
```

Here's the output:

A great example of its usage is with string parameters intended to be used for logging. If a function is passed the output of `std.format.format`, or a string concatenation, you'll save some work if the string is never used.

Function attributes

There are a number of attributes that can be applied to a function declaration as a contract statement. A discussion of each is better suited to different parts of the book, but this is a good place to discuss the syntax. The attributes `nothrow` and `@nogc` will serve to demonstrate. The former prevents the throwing of exceptions in a function; the latter similarly prohibits garbage collection.

One thing that will certainly leap out right off the bat is that one of these has an `@` in front and the other doesn't. This is largely an artifact of history. D supports user-defined attributes (which are explored in *Chapter 4, Running Code at Compile Time*), a feature that makes use of the `@` symbol in attribute names. Attributes defined by the language since the introduction of UDAs take the same form. The `nothrow` attribute predates this.

Function attributes can be applied at the beginning or end of a function declaration. You can apply one or all of them, in any order.

```
void func1() pure nothrow @nogc;
pure nothrow @nogc void func2();
```

You can also apply them to several functions at once using the attribute syntax we saw back at the beginning of the chapter:

```
// Valid until the closing brace
pure nothrow {
  void func1() {};
  void func2() {}
}
// Valid until the end of the current scope
pure nothrow:
  void func3() {};
  void func4() {};
```

Return statements and memory

When using the `return` statement in a function, be very careful about what it is that you're returning. Anything that lives on the stack will no longer be available once the function exits. If a pointer or reference to such data is returned, you're looking at undefined behavior. Anything returned by value, including the basic types, is fine. Slices are no problem as long as they are not backed by a local static array or any other memory allocated on the stack. Just make sure you've got the function declaration straight and that you remember that static arrays live on the stack.

```
int[3] returnAStaticArray1() {
```

```
        int[3] statArray;
        return statArray;
    }
    int[] returnAStaticArray2() {
        int[3] statArray;
        return statArray; // Error: escaping reference to local
    }
```

The first function here is on solid ground. Because the return type is a static array, the return statement will cause the entire array, including its contents, to be copied to the call site. If statArray had been declared with a different length, like int[4], this would fail to compile. The return type and the actual type returned must match exactly.

The second function fails to compile because the memory for statArray exists on the function stack. The return statement causes the static array to be sliced. Because the slice would be pointing to stack memory, its .ptr would become invalid as soon as the function stack is overwritten. You can fix this with the .dup property.

```
    int[] returnAStaticArray2() {
        int[3] statArray;
        return statArray.dup; // OK
    }
```

This will allocate a copy of statArray on the heap, making it safe to access outside the function. The same sort of caution is needed in any function that returns a pointer or reference to any value on the local stack.

```
    int* returnAnIntPointer1() {
        int x = 10;
        return &x; // Error escaping reference to local
    }
```

The solution, again, is to allocate space on the heap. This time there's no .dup property.

```
    return new int(x);
```

The compiler is smart enough to catch many instances of this for you, but it can't catch them all. It pays to be vigilant.

Function pointers and delegates

Function pointers can be declared as variables. They look like this.

```
void function(int) funcPtr;
```

Function pointers are default initialized to `null`. In this example, only the type of the parameter is listed, but you can give it a name if you want. Like any other variable, function pointers can be explicitly initialized and you can assign values to them. In C, the address of a pointer is taken by simply using the name of the function. This is one aspect of C that D did away with; taking the address of a function requires an `&` just as it does with a variable. The function can be called through the pointer using the normal syntax.

```
void myFunc(int x) { writeln(x); }
void main() {
  void function(int) funcPtr = &myFunc;
  funcPtr(22);  // call MyFunc
}
```

You can pass a function pointer around like any other variable. The function pointed to can only access non-static variables declared in its own scope or in module scope. If you need multiple function pointers with the same signature, use `alias`.

```
alias MyFuncPtr = void function(int);
```

Let's rewrite the `myFunc` example given in the preceding code so that it's an inner function:

```
void main() {
  void myFunc(int x ) { writeln(x); }
  void function(int) funcPtr = &myFunc;
  funcPtr(22);  // call MyFunc
}
```

Try to compile this and you'll get an implicit conversion error. This is because taking the address of an inner function does not give you a function pointer, but a **delegate**. An inner function is declared in a function or block scope. Sometimes, inner functions may need access to other static local variables or variables declared in a parent scope. Consider the following:

```
void proxy(void delegate() dg) {
  dg();
}
```

```
void main() {
  int x = 100;
  void myDel() {
    writeln(x);
  }
  proxy(&myDel);
}
```

Here, a delegate is passed as a function parameter. Note that the delegate declaration looks like a function pointer declaration, except that it uses `delegate` in place of `function`. When the address of `myDel` is passed to `proxy`, it completely leaves the scope of `main`. Since `x` is declared in `main`'s scope, it is not accessible outside that function. But our delegate is called in `proxy` and it must be able to access `x`. Furthermore, what would happen if the address of a delegate is stored in a variable to be called later on, well after the scope in which it was declared has exited? The stack memory where it was declared would no longer exist. When a delegate needs to reference such a variable, the compiler allocates some memory, saves in it the state of the local stack, and gives the delegate a pointer to it (this is called a **closure**).

Place the `static` keyword in front of the `myDel` declaration and things are different. A static inner function, like a static variable, exists outside the local stack. It's still only visible in the local scope, but it is stored elsewhere. Taking the address of a static inner function results in a regular function pointer. It only has access to global variables and any static variables declared before itself in the local scope.

You can also create function pointers and delegates from literals.

```
auto fp1 = function int(int  i) { return i * 2; };
auto d1 = delegate void { writeln(fp1(10)); };
auto fp2 = function (int i) => i + 1; ;
auto d2 = delegate () => "Hello";
```

`fp1` is a normal function literal. It is a function that returns `int` and accepts a single integer parameter `i`. `d1` is a normal delegate literal. It returns `void` and has no parameters (optional empty parentheses could follow the return type). The bottom two are a shorthand form called **lambdas**. For both, the return type is inferred (`int` for `fp2`, `string` for `d2`). `fp2` takes an `int` parameter, `d2` takes none. In this case, the empty parentheses are required.

There are even shorter lambda forms, as shown in the following snippet:

```
void performTest(int a, int b, bool function(int, int) test) {
  writeln("The result is ", test(a, b));
}
performTest(1, 2, (a, b) { return a == b; });
performTest(1, 2, (a, b) => a < b );
```

The first call to `performTest` uses a lambda syntax that looks like a full function literal minus the `function` keyword and return type. The second call uses the shortest form. In both cases, empty parentheses indicate no parameters, but are not optional. Both of these syntaxes can be used anywhere a function pointer or delegate is expected.

MovieMan – first steps

A lot of features have been covered in this chapter, but only a small handful are needed for the `MovieMan` module we're about to implement. We'll put more of them to use as we add to the project in later chapters. Throughout the book, the full path of any example source module is referred to as `$LEARNINGD/ChapterNum/filename.d`. This is impractical for the `MovieMan` code listings, as the project will be implemented across multiple chapters. When referring to `MovieMan` source modules, the form `$MOVIEMAN/filepath/filename.d` will be used, where `$MOVIEMAN` is the root directory of either the DUB project we created in the first chapter or of any other location you choose to initialize the `MovieMan` project with DUB.

The io module

Create an empty file in your text editor and save it as `$MOVIEMAN/source/movieman/io.d`. This module will consist of a few module-scope functions that read text from standard input and print text to standard output. We're going to implement the entire module in this chapter so that we don't need to revisit it later on. We'll start with the module declaration and an import of `std.stdio` as the first two lines.

```
module movieman.io;
import std.stdio;
```

There are two primary forms of input that `MovieMan` requires. `strings` are used to input movie titles and `uints` are for case numbers, page numbers, and menu commands. To read `strings`, we'll implement `readString`, the primary workhorse of the `io` module.

```
string readString() {
   import std.string : chomp;
   return readln().chomp;
}
```

readString calls two functions that we haven't seen. std.stdio.readln is what does the work of reading a line of text from stdin. It returns a string containing the text along with the platform-specific line terminator. Retaining the line terminator would cause extra work later on to avoid breaking the format of the program's output, so we turn to std.string.chomp to handle it here instead. This function can be given any delimiter, which it will look for at the end of a string. It the delimiter is found, it returns the string without the delimiter; otherwise, it returns the original string. When no delimiter is specified, it looks for several non-text characters. Refer to http://dlang.org/phobos/std_string.html#.chomp for details.

The next function will be readUint. It takes a string returned from readString and parses it for a uint value via std.conv.to. Recall from the discussion of strings that to throws an exception if the string cannot be converted. Any number that the user types in will represent either a case number, a page number, or a menu command, none of which can ever be 0. To handle the exception, we can make use of a feature that we won't discuss until the next chapter, though it's one that many readers will be familiar with: the try...catch block. If to throws an exception, we can catch it and simply return 0.

```
uint readUint() {
   import std.conv : to;
   try {
      return readString().to!uint;
   }
   catch(Exception e) {
      return 0;
   }
}
```

readString and readUint are the building blocks of the rest of the module. The first higher-level function we'll implement is called readTitle. It asks the user to enter a movie title, then calls readString to get the input, which it immediately returns.

```
string readTitle() {
   writeln("\nEnter a movie title:");
   return readString();
}
```

There's no check to see if we have an empty string here. This will be handled at a higher level in the program. Next is a function we'll call readNumber. It asks the user to enter a case or page number, then calls readUint to read the input. The function takes one argument, a string whose value should either be "case" or "page", which it inserts into the output.

```
uint readNumber(string label) {
```

```
    writefln("\nEnter a %s number:", label);
    return readUint();
}
```

Next, we have a pair of overloaded functions that will be used when a user needs to choose one or more actions, both named `readChoice`. The functions display one or more options, asking the reader to choose one or to press Enter for the default option. These functions will only be called in specific circumstances, such as when the user has made a selection from the main menu and needs to decide on how to proceed. The default option can be defined as aborting the current action. No action that moves the program forward or makes a change in the program state should be the default. The name of the default option is specified in the second parameter, the default value of which is `"abort"`.

```
    bool readChoice(string msg1, string msg2 = "abort") {
        writefln("\nEnter 1 to %s.", msg1);
        writefln("Press Enter to %s.", msg2);
        return readUint() == 1;
    }
    uint readChoice(string[] msgs, string msg2 = "abort") {
        writeln();
        foreach(i, msg; msgs)
            writefln("Enter %s to %s.", i+1, msg);
        writefln("Press Enter to %s.", msg2);
        return readUint();
    }
```

When the user types any input, she must press *Enter* in order for `readln` to pick it up. If Enter is pressed without any input, the line returned from `readString` will only contain a line terminator. This will cause an exception to be thrown inside `readUint`, which will catch it and return 0. The downside is that there is no way to tell if the user simply pressed Enter or typed in a bunch of gibberish. We could parse the input string to see if it only contains a line terminator, or use the operating system API to check if the Enter key was pressed, but there's really no reason to do so. Since the default option in any call to `readChoice` is to abandon whatever action is in progress, it doesn't matter what the input is, if it wasn't one of the possible options. On invalid input, the program can go back to a previous screen and the user can start again if a mistake was made.

We could conceivably do without the first version of readChoice, as the second one can handle a single action just fine. But this is a good opportunity to demonstrate one aspect of thinking in D. The second version takes an array as the first parameter. Using only one option with this function would require one of the following approaches:

```
readChoice(["Option"]);        // Approach 1
string[1] option = ["Option"];  // Approach 2
readChoice(option);
```

The first approach allocates a dynamic array on the GC heap every time it is executed. A D programmer should always be aware of which language features are allocating GC memory. For a simple little project like MovieMan, this isn't likely to ever be an issue, but readChoice could still be called numerous times in a normal run of the program. It isn't going to hurt to avoid gratuitous allocations from the GC heap. The second approach avoids the repeated allocation, but (for me, at least) it's just plain annoying to use a single-element array for what really should be a single variable.

The final function in the io module prints a header, followed by a list of numbered options. In the next chapter, we'll use this function to print menus.

```
void printList(string header, string[] list) {
  writeln("\n", header);
  foreach(i, line; list)
    writefln("\t%s. %s", i+1, line);
  writeln();
}
```

On the surface, there doesn't appear to be much difference in the output of readChoice and printList, but they are used in different contexts. In the next chapter, we'll implement a class called Menu that manages its own array of options and uses printList simply for display. The format of the output is different between the two functions as a visual cue to distinguish between primary menus and submenus

The app module

The file $MOVIEMAN/source/app.d was generated by DUB when the project was initialized. Open this file and replace its contents with the following code:

```d
import std.stdio;
import movieman.io;
void main() {
  auto title = readTitle();
  writeln("The title is: ", title);

  auto number = readNumber("page");
  writeln("The number is: ", number);

  auto bchoice = readChoice("continue", "abort");
  writeln("You chose to: ", bchoice ? "continue" : "abort");

  auto choices = ["Eat Pizza", "Sleep",
  "Watch 'Game of Thrones'", "Play Skyrim"];
  auto uichoice = readChoice(choices, "do nothing");
  if(uichoice == 0)
    writeln("You chose to do nothing.");
  else
    writeln("You chose to ", choices[uichoice-1]);

  printList("What do you feel like doing?", choices);
  uichoice = readUint();
  writeln("You chose option #", uichoice);
}
```

Now you can cd to $MOVIEMAN, type dub, and follow the instructions. In the next chapter, we'll work further on the UI.

Summary

In this chapter, you've learned the basic building blocks of the D Programming Language. We've examined the basic types and operators, complex types, control flow statements, the type qualifiers `const` and `immutable`, and functions. We've also taken the first steps toward implementing `MovieMan`, our sample project.

In the next chapter, we'll continue our journey through the basic features and take a look at the different user-defined types that D supports. Most of the chapter will be focused on object-oriented programming in D and you'll learn how to apply some OOP features to `MovieMan`.

3
Programming Objects the D Way

In this chapter, we're going to build upon the foundation established in the previous chapter by looking at D's user-defined types, its support for object-oriented programming, and some peripherally related features. By the end of the chapter, we'll be finished with the basics of D and ready for more advanced topics. Here's our checklist:

- User-defined types: enumerations, unions, structs, and classes
- Working with objects: protection attributes, constructors, and destructors
- Contract programming: contracts and invariants
- Error handling: exceptions and asserts
- MovieMan: adding menus via user-defined types

User-defined types

This section shows how to define custom types using `enum`, `union`, `struct`, and `class`. The latter two will be the focus for most of the remainder of the chapter.

Enumerations

The **anonymous enumeration** in D declares a set of immutable values. A major difference from C is that it's possible to specify the underlying type. When no fields are explicitly assigned a value, the underlying type of an `enum` defaults to `int`. Note that user-defined type declarations in D do not require a semicolon at the end:

```
enum {top, bottom, left, right}           // type is int
enum : ubyte {red, green, blue, alpha}    // type is ubyte
```

The members of each will be initialized with sequential values starting at 0. In the second declaration, the underlying type is explicitly set to `ubyte` by appending a colon and the type name to the `enum` keyword. enum values aren't restricted to integrals, or even just the basic types. Any type that D supports, be it one of the derived data types or even a user-defined type, can back an enum. Where possible, the compiler will infer the type:

```
enum {one = "One", two = "Two"}   // type is immutable(char)[]
```

An anonymous enum with only one member is eligible for some special treatment:

```
enum {author = "Mike Parker"}
enum author = "Mike Parker";
enum string author = "Mike Parker";
```

As shown in the second line, the braces can be dropped. The third line explicitly specifies a type, but in this form there's no colon. An `enum` declared without braces is called a **manifest constant**.

An anonymous enum does not create a new type, but a **named enumeration** does:

```
enum Side {top, bottom, left, right}
enum Color : ubyte {red, green, blue, alpha}
```

The name is used as a namespace and the members are accessed via the dot operator. Printing the `typeid` of one of these produces a fully-qualified name that includes the enum name (`Side` or `Color`, in this case). All user-defined types get this treatment.

Named enums have properties. `.init` equates to the value of the first member of the enum; its `.sizeof` is that of the underlying type. The type-specific properties `.min` and `.max` return the lowest and highest member values respectively.

One special feature designed to work specifically with enums is the `final switch` statement. For example, to switch on a value of the `Side` type:

```
auto s = Side.bottom;
final switch(s) {
    case Side.top: writeln("On top"); break;
    case Side.bottom: writeln("On the bottom"); break;
    case Side.left: writeln("On the left"); break;
    case Side.right: writeln("On the right"); break;
}
```

A big benefit is that the compiler will give you an error if you forget to add a case for one of the `enum` members. It also adds a default case that asserts if a non-member value somehow slips through, making it an error to add a default case. If two or more members have the same value, only one need appear in a final switch.

Unions

For the most part, unions in D work as they do in C:

```
union One {
    int a = 10;
    double b;
}
```

The members of a union share the same memory, which is large enough to hold the biggest type. In this declaration, the biggest type is double, so an instance of One takes up 8 bytes. D diverges from C in terms of initialization. Every variable in D is by default initialized and a union instance is no exception. By default, the first member is initialized to its .init value if not explicitly initialized, as in the previous example. It is an error to initialize other members.

To explicitly initialize an instance of a union, you can use the name:value syntax with braces. Given the nature of unions, it's an error to initialize more than one field:

```
One o2 = { b:22.0 };
```

 Unions are great for compatibility with C, but there is an alternative in the standard library that offers better type safety. The module std.variant exposes the Variant type. See http://dlang.org/phobos/std_variant.html for details.

Structs and classes

D's implementations of the struct and class types are a major source of misunderstanding for C-family programmers new to D. Here are declarations of each:

```
struct MyStruct {
    int a, b;
    int calculate() { return a + b; }
}
class MyClass {
    int a, b;
    int calculate() { return a + b; }
}
```

The declarations have the same syntax. The biggest difference is hidden here:

```
MyStruct ms;
MyClass mc;
```

In D, a `struct` is a value type. It's enough to declare an instance for it to be created on the stack and ready to go. At this point, a call to `ms.calculate` will successfully compile. The same cannot be said for `mc`. A `class` is a reference type. It isn't enough to declare an instance, as that only produces an uninitialized reference, or handle. It is a common error for new D programmers coming from C++ to try using uninitialized class references. Before `mc.calculate` can be called, an instance must be allocated:

```
mc = new MyClass;
auto mc2 = new MyClass;
```

This has implications for how instances are passed to and returned from functions. Since a `struct` is a value type, instances are copied. `ms.sizeof` is 8 bytes, the size of two `int`s, which means passing `ms` to a function will cause 8 bytes to be copied:

```
void modMS(MyStruct ms1, ref MyStruct ms2, MyStruct* ms3) {
  ms1.a = 1;  // Modifies local copy
  ms2.a = 2;  // Modifies original
  ms3.a = 3;  // Ditto.
}
```

Since the first argument is passed by value, any modifications to `ms1` only affect the function's copy, but modifications to `ms2` and `ms3` will be reflected in the original variable. It's different with `mc`:

```
void modMC(MyClass mc) {
  mc.a = 1;  // Modifies original.
}
```

As `MyClass` is a reference type, there's no need to declare a pointer or `ref` parameter to modify the original variable. `mc.sizeof` is 4 on 32-bit architectures and 8 on 64-bit. This is the size of the reference, not the size of the instance itself.

Struct pointers

A `struct` pointer can be obtained by taking the address of an instance or allocating an instance on the heap. C and C++ programmers take note: in D, there's no `->` for any type of pointer. There is only the dot operator.

When a `class` or `struct` instance is instantiated, it gets its own copy of any member variables. If a member variable is declared as `static`, only one thread-local copy of it exists. Each member is by default initialized to its `.init` value unless an initialization value is specified. Member functions are normal functions that accept a hidden `this` argument as the first parameter (accessible inside the function scope), representing the instance. Taking the address of a member function produces a delegate. Static member functions have no `this` parameter and taking the address of one yields a function pointer:

```
struct MembersOnly {
    static int x;
    int y;
    int z = 10; // Initialized to 10 for all instances
    static void printX() {
        writeln(x);
    }
    void printYZ() {
        writefln("%s, %s", this.y, z); // this.y is the same as y
    }
}
```

Non-static members may only be accessed using an instance name as a namespace:

```
MembersOnly mo;
writeln(mo.z);
mo.printYZ();
```

Static members must be accessed using the type name as a namespace:

```
MembersOnly.x += 1;
MembersOnly.printX();
```

The with Statement

Any time a namespace is required, it can be temporarily bypassed via the `with` statement. It works with all of the types described here, as well as with static imports:

```
MembersOnly mo;
with(mo) {
    printYZ(); // Same as mo.printYZ().
}
```

Working with objects

If you have experience with object-oriented programming, you'll find much of D's OOP support familiar. As such, I need to reiterate my warning from before: D is not C++, Java, or C#. Familiarity can help you pick some things up more quickly, but it can also lead you to take other things for granted. This section introduces D's OOP features.

Encapsulation with protection attributes

There are four levels of protection in D: `public`, `package`, `private`, and `protected`. The first three apply to classes, structs, and modules, but `protected` only has meaning with classes. We'll examine it later when we talk about inheritance.

Public

Anything declared `public` in a module, whether it's in module scope or as part of a `class` or `struct` declaration, is visible anywhere it's imported. With the exception of import declarations, all declarations in a module, `class` or `struct` are implicitly `public`. Save the following as `$LEARNINGD/chapter03/protection1.d`:

```
module protection1;
import std.stdio;  // private, only visible in this module
class MyClass {
  void sayHello() { writeln("Hello"); }
}
struct MyStruct {
  void sayHello() { writeln("Hello"); }
}
```

Now create a new file in the same directory, let's call it `importer1.d`, and add this:

```
void main() {
  import protection1;
  auto mc = new MyClass;
  mc.sayHello();
  MyStruct ms;
  ms.sayHello();
}
```

Compile both files. Every symbol declared in `protection1.d` is visible in `importer.d`, so there are no errors on compilation.

Private

Go back to `protection1.d` and add this right after the module declaration:

```
private:
```

As this uses the colon syntax rather than braces, every symbol following this line — until another protection attribute is encountered — is now private to the `protection` module. The import of `std.stdio` was already private, so this has no effect on it. Compile both modules again. Now two compiler errors are produced reporting that `MyClass` and `MyStruct` are private. That's just what one would expect. Now save the following as `protection2.d` in the same directory:

```
module protection2;
import std.stdio;
class MyClass {
    private void sayHello() { writeln("Hello"); }
}
struct MyStruct {
    void sayHello() {
        MyClass mc = new MyClass;
        mc.sayHello();   // calls private member function of MyClass
    }
}
```

Then save this as `importer2.d`, compile, and run:

```
void main() {
    import protection;
    MyStruct ms;
    ms.sayHello();
}
```

This will be a big surprise to most folks. In D, anything declared `private` is *private to the module*. In other words, `MyClass.sayHello` is accessible everywhere inside the `protection` module. There's no such thing as *private to the type* in D. Unlike C++, D does not have the concept of a `friend` function, as the same behavior arises via the `private` and `package` attributes.

Package

Any symbol-declared `package` is accessible only to modules in the same package or in any of its subpackages. To demonstrate, create two packages, `encap` and `encap.internal`, and populate them with a few modules. Filenames are commented:

```
// $LEARNINGD/chapter03/encap/support.d
module encap.support;
package void supportFunction() {
  import std.stdio: writeln;
  writeln("Providing support!");
}
// $LEARNINGD/chapter03/encap/base.d
module encap.base;
void primaryFunction() {
import encap.support;
  supportFunction();
}
// $LEARNINGD/chapter03/encap/internal/help.d
module encap.internal.help;
void helperFunction() {
  import encap.support;
  supportFunction();
  import std.stdio: writeln;
  writeln("Helping out!");
}
```

There are three modules: `encap.base`, `encap.support`, and `encap.internal.help`. Each module declares one function, two of which are `public` and one of which is `package`. Now create `$LEARNINGD/chapter03/packtest.d`, like so:

```
void main() {
  import encap.base;
  primaryFunction();
}
```

Finally, compile it all with the following command:

dmd packtest.d encap/base.d encap/support.d encap/internal/help.d

Ideally, the only function in the `encap` package that should be accessible to the outside world is `primaryFunction`. However, `encap.internal.help.helperFunction` is `public`. The default package protection does not extend accessibility to super packages, so `helperFunction` *has* to be `public` in order for it to be accessible inside `encap`. This comes with the consequence that it's also accessible outside the package. Actually, something can be done about that. Go back to `encap.internal.help` and change the declaration of `helperFunction` to look like this:

```
package(encap) void helperFunction() {…}
```

Specifying a package name with the `package` attribute makes the symbol accessible in that package and all of its subpackages. With this, `helperFunction` is still accessible in `encap.base` and is no longer accessible outside the `encap` package hierarchy.

Voldemort types

The preceding paragraphs use the terms **accessible** and **accessibility** quite a bit. We saw that, when the declarations of `MyStruct` and `MyClass` are private, instances cannot be instantiated in another module; the symbols are inaccessible. There's more to the story. Save the following as `$LEARNINGD/chapter03/priv.d`:

```
module priv;
private struct Priv {
   int x, y;
}
Priv makeAPriv(int x, int y) {
   return Priv(x, y);
}
```

You might assume that `public` members in a `private struct` declaration are meaningless. Test that assumption with `$LEARNINGD/chapter03/privtest.d`:

```
import std.stdio;
import priv;
void main() {
   auto priv = makeAPriv(10, 20);
   writeln(priv.x);
}
```

Pass both files to the compiler; not only will it compile them, but running the resulting executable will print `10`, the correct value of `priv.x`. The symbol may not be accessible, but the type itself is. Change the highlighted line to the following:

```
Priv priv = makeAPriv(10, 20);
```

This yields a compiler error similar to the one we saw earlier with `MyStruct` and `MyClass`. This is another benefit of type inference; a type can be completely hidden while only exposing its interface.

We can take this a couple of steps further. The type is still exposed in the function declaration, but, by replacing `Priv` with `auto`, the compiler will infer the return type. Also, since types can be declared inside a function, the declaration of `Priv` can be moved out of module scope and into the function's scope. In this case, we *have to* use `auto` to infer the return type, since the type does not exist outside the function scope and cannot be part of the declaration:

```
auto makeAPriv(int x, int y) {
    struct Priv {
        int x, y;
    }
    return Priv(x, y);
}
```

With these changes to the `priv` module, the original `privtest.d` will still compile. The `Priv` symbol is not accessible anywhere outside `makeAPriv`. We can refer to `Priv` as a type that shall not be named, or a **Voldemort type**.

Constructors and destructors

Constructors and destructors can be implemented for classes, structs, and even modules. However, there are differences with each that need to be accounted for.

Class constructors and destructors

We've not explicitly declared any constructors in any class declarations so far, but we've still been able to construct new instances. That's because the compiler automatically adds a default constructor if no constructors are implemented. A default constructor is one that takes no arguments:

```
class OneCon {
    private int x;
    this(int x) { this.x = x; }
}
```

`OneCon` has an explicitly implemented constructor, so `new OneCon()` will not compile. To create a new instance of `OneCon`, a constructor argument must be provided:

```
auto oc = new OneCon(10);
```

Before the constructor is run, x will be initialized by default. Since no default initialization value was specified in the declaration, it will be initialized to `int.init`. After that, the constructor is executed and the parameter x is assigned to the member x. Note `this.x` is used to specify the member variable, which is legally shadowed by the parameter of the same name. The `this` reference is accessible in every non-static function of both classes and structs. To avoid the need to use `this` so often in member functions, I prefer to prefix private member variable names with an underscore.

To enable default construction when another constructor is defined, a default constructor must also be provided. That would look like this:

```
class TwoCon {
  private int _x;
  this() { this(10); }
  this(int x) { _x = x; }
}
```

The default constructor here sets x to `10` by calling the single-argument constructor. Note that, unlike Java, D places no restrictions on where such a call can take place inside a constructor, meaning it need not be the first line. To invoke a default constructor, parentheses are optional:

```
auto tc1 = new TwoCon();
auto tc2 = new TwoCon;
```

Perhaps the biggest issue for C++ programmers in D is the class destructor:

```
class Decon {
  this() { writeln("Constructed!"); }
  this() { writeln("Destroyed!"); }
  void print() { writeln("Printing."); }
}
void printDecon() {
  auto d = new Decon;
  d.print();
}
void main() {
  printDecon();
  writeln("Leaving main.");
}
static ~this() {
  writeln("Module destructor.");
}
```

Running this shows that the message in the class destructor is printed *after* the one in the static module destructor (more on that soon). Remember, the new expression allocates memory from the GC heap. That means the garbage collector is managing the memory behind the Decon instance. The GC will call the destructor when the memory is released, but not before. The language does not specify when the memory is released. In fact, the language says there is *absolutely no guarantee that a class destructor will ever be executed*. Let me repeat: you cannot depend on a class destructor ever being run. It's better to think of a class destructor in D as a closer relative of the Java finalizer than the C++ destructor. Attempting to use them for C++ style RAII is going to be painful.

In practice, the GC implementation that is used as I write runs in two scenarios: when new memory is allocated, and during the shutdown phase of DRuntime. In the previous example, the GC is never run once the Decon instance is allocated until the app terminates. The current implementation of DRuntime happens to run static destructors before terminating the GC, but that may not always be true. Nor is there any guarantee that the GC will call any destructors during termination.

Replacing the single call to printDecon with a loop that calls it ten times prints ten destructor messages on termination. The GC will only release memory, and therefore call destructors, as needed, and it never needs to during runtime in this case. Call it a thousand times in a loop and the GC will need to do some work; some of the destructors are called inside printDecon, with others called at termination.

One more potential problem spot is that class destructors in D are *nondeterministic*, meaning that their order of execution is unpredictable. The GC can call destructors in any order. A direct consequence of this is that manipulating GC-managed memory inside a class destructor will inevitably cause an abrupt termination of the program:

```
class Innocent {
    void bye() { writeln("Bye!"); }
}
class Boom {
    Innocent _inno;
    this() { _inno = new Innocent(); }
    ~this() { _inno.bye(); }
}
```

It's quite easy to believe that because _inno is a member of Boom, it will always be valid when the destructor is run. That's just not the case. From the garbage collector's perspective, the only notable fact about _inno being a member of Boom is that, if any given Boom instance is no longer accessible (that is, it's eligible for collection), then _inno is also no longer accessible. As long as no other references to that instance of Innocent exist, it can be collected at any time. It is quite possible for the instance behind _inno to be destroyed before the destructor is run on the Boom instance. In that case, you'll see a segfault when _inno.bye() is eventually called in the destructor. Never access GC-managed memory inside a class destructor.

Struct constructors and destructors

A `struct` instance can be explicitly initialized using struct literals or C-style initializers:

```
auto ms1 = MyStruct(10, 11);// struct literal
MyStruct ms2 = {10, 11};    // C-style, not preferred
MyStruct ms3 = {b:11, a:10};// Named initializers
```

In the first two lines, the members are initialized in the order they were declared, so 10 goes to a and 11 goes to b. If there are fewer initializers than members, the remaining members will be default-initialized using the `.init` value for the relevant type. If there are more initializers than members, a compiler error results.

Struct literals are convenient for simple types (though they can become an annoyance if the type declaration changes), but they only allow for direct initialization of member variables. If more complex initialization is required, struct constructors should be used. A `struct` does not have a default constructor. It doesn't have one generated for it, nor can one be explicitly implemented. Default construction for a struct is the same as setting it to its `.init` value. Look at the following declaration:

```
struct StructCon {
    int x, y;
    this(int val) { x = y = val; }
}
```

This type has two publicly accessible members and a constructor that sets each member to the same value. Here are different ways to declare a `StructCon` instance:

```
StructCon s1;              // .init: x = 0, y = 0
auto s2 = StructCon();     // .init literal: x = 0, y = 0
auto s3 = StructCon(12);   // constructor: x = y = 12
```

In the first declaration, s1 is default initialized. In the second, s2 is explicitly initialized with the default `.init` value, making it equal to s1. In the declaration of s3; both x and y are assigned the value 12. When a struct constructor is defined, struct literals can no longer be used to initialize any instances of that type.

Default initialization can be turned off completely:

```
struct StructCon {
    int x, y;
    this(int val) { x = y = val; }
    @disable this();
}
```

The highlighted line tells the compiler that instances of StructCon cannot be implicitly default initialized; they must be explicitly initialized with the .init value or through the constructor. Be aware that this has far-reaching consequences. Consider the following example:

```
struct Container {
    StructCon sc;
}

Container container; // Error: default construction disabled
```

In order for container to be default constructed, its member sc must be as well, but default construction is disabled for StructCon. To fix it, initialize sc explicitly:

```
StructCon sc = StructCon.init;
```

A struct in D can have a special constructor called the postblit constructor. On the surface, it looks much like a C++ copy constructor, but it isn't. When a struct instance is copied in D, a bitwise copy, or blit, is performed. If the type has a postblit constructor, it is invoked after the copy is complete. They can be used to fix up anything that needs fixing up after the copy. The following example is a good use case:

```
struct PostBlit {
    int[] foo;
}
void printPtr(PostBlit cpb) {
    writeln("Inside: ", cpb.foo.ptr);
}
void main() {
    auto pb = PostBlit([10,20,30]);
    writeln("Outside: ", pb.foo.ptr);
    printPtr(pb);
}
```

When pb is passed into printPtr, a copy is made, meaning the array member foo is copied as well. Recall that, when arrays are passed around, only the metadata, and not the elements, gets copied. As such, the two writeln calls in this example print the same address. Pass pb into a function that operates on the array and it will be subject to the same array issues discussed in the previous chapter. To prevent the original elements from being accessed, a deep copy of the array is needed. Using the postblit constructor:

```
this(this) { foo = foo.dup; }
```

Add this to the `PostBlit` declaration and two different addresses will be printed. Remember, the `struct` bits have already been copied by the time the `postblit` constructor is run, so duping the slice creates a deep copy of the original array. By assigning the new slice to `foo`, `cbp` inside `printPtr` is fixed up with a completely separate array from the original.

Let's try one more thing. Replace the `postblit` constructor with the following line:

```
@disable this(this);
```

Recompiling produces an error. Disabling the `postblit` constructor completely prevents any instance of `PostBlit` from being copied.

Disable anything

Not only constructors, but any function can be annotated with `@disable`, be they free functions or members of a `class` or `struct`. You can even apply it to destructors, though good luck with compiling your program if you do. `@disable` is most often used to prevent default construction and copying of `struct` types.

Now that you've seen so much that likely appears foreign to you, it may be a relief to know that `struct` destructors behave more like they do in C++:

```
struct Destruct {
  ~this() { writeln("Destructed!"); }
}
void doSomething() {
  writeln("Initializing a Destruct");
  Destruct d;
  writeln("Leaving the function");
}
void main() {
  doSomething();
  writeln("Leaving main");
}
```

Compiling and running this example should demonstrate that the `destructor` is run on the `Destruct` instance as soon as `doSomething` exits. In this case, a `struct` destructor is both reliable (it will always be called) and deterministic—if you declare multiple `struct` instances in any scope, they will be destroyed in the reverse order of declaration when the scope is exited.

Static constructors and destructors

Consider the following example:

```
module classvar;
class A {}
A anInstance = new A;
```

Adding an empty `main` function to this module and compiling produces this error:

classvar.d(3): Error: variable classvar.anInstance is mutable. Only const or immutable class thread local variables are allowed, not classvar.A

As `anInstance` is mutable and thread-local, we can't initialize it with a runtime value (which is exactly what we get from the `new` expression). Were it declared `immutable`, `const`, `shared` or `__gshared` (more on these later), it would compile, but it can be made to compile without them if the assignment of `new A` is moved to a static constructor:

```
A anInstance;
static this() {
  anInstance = new A;
}
```

When the program is executed, DRuntime will call the static constructor before `main` is entered. Let's do a little experiment. Create two modules: `stat1.d` and `stat2.d`. Here's the implementation of `stat1`:

```
module stat1;
static this() { writeln("stat1 constructor"); }
```

`stat2.d` should look the same (with the name changed, of course). Now create a module, let's call it `statmain.d`, consisting solely of an empty `main` function. Compile it like so:

dmd statmain.d stat1.d stat2.d

When you run the executable, you should see that `stat1 constructor` is printed first, followed by `stat2 constructor`. Now let's change the compilation order:

dmd statmain.d stat2.d stat1.d

Running this will show you that the order of the output has also been reversed.

Although neither `stat1` nor `stat2` was imported anywhere, their constructors are still run. In this case, the order of execution is not specified and is implementation-dependent. Now add the following line to the top of `stat1.d`:

```
import stat2;
```

Compile again, using both of the above command lines. This time, you'll see that the stat2 constructor is executed first in both cases. This is because the language guarantees that the static constructors of any *imported* modules will be executed before the static constructor, if any, of the *importing* module. Since stat1 imports stat2, then the latter's constructor is always executed before that of stat1.

Static destructors are always executed in the reverse of the order in which the static constructors were called. Let's add destructors to both stat1 and stat2:

```
static ~this() { writeln("stat1 destructor"); }
```

When stat1 imports stat2, the destructor for stat1 is always run first. Remove the import and the destructor execution order is always the opposite of the constructor execution order, whatever that may be.

Static constructors and destructors can also be declared in class or struct scope:

```
class Stat {
  private static Stat anInstance;
  static this() {
    writeln("Stat constructor");
    anInstance = new Stat;
  }
  static ~this() { writeln("Stat destructor") }
}
```

Add this to stat1 and you'll find the previous order of execution depends on the order of declaration: multiple static constructors in a module are executed in lexical order, with destructors executed in the reverse order. The reason to use a static class or struct constructor is the same as that for using module constructors: to initialize variables that can't be initialized at compile time. Since private variables are visible in the entire module, a module constructor can do the job as well:

```
static this() { Stat.anInstance = new Stat; }
```

Static constructors and destructors are always executed once per thread. We'll skip the details for now but, to guarantee that a static constructor or destructor is executed only once for the lifetime of the program, use the shared storage class:

```
shared static this() { }
```

All static constructors marked shared are executed before those that aren't.

Inheritance and polymorphism

In D, inheritance is only available for `class` types. It looks much like Java's: multiple inheritance is prohibited and there is no such thing as public or private inheritance. All classes inherit from a DRuntime class called `Object`. Take this empty class declaration:

```
class Simpleton {}
```

One of the member functions in `Object` is the `toString` function. You can invoke it manually when you need it, but any time a class instance is passed to one of the `write` or `format` functions, `toString` will be invoked inside it. Try the following:

```
module inherit;
import std.stdio;
class Simpleton {}
void main() {
   writeln(new Simpleton);
}
```

This will print `inherit.Simpleton`. The `Object.toString` implementation always prints the fully qualified name of the class. By default, class member functions in D are *virtual*, meaning that they can be overridden by subclasses. Let's make a class that overrides the `toString` method to print a message:

```
class Babbler {
   override string toString() {
      return "De do do do. De da da da.";
   }
}
```

Instantiate a `Babbler` instead of a `Simpleton` in the example and it prints the message from `Babbler.toString`. The `override` keyword must be applied to any member function that overrides a super class function. To call the super class implementation, prefix `super` to the function name:

```
override string toString() {
   import std.format : format;
   return format("%s: %s", super.toString(),
   "De do do do. De da da da.");
}
```

Structs and the Object functions

Although a struct cannot be extended and does not descend from Object, it is still possible to implement some of the Object functions for the runtime and library to make use of. For example, if you add a toString function to a struct declaration, it will work with writeln, the same as it does for classes. override isn't used here, since there's no inheritance.

Let's add a new function to generate a message and have toString call that instead:

```
protected string genMessage() {
  return " De do do do. De da da da.";
}
override string toString() {
  import std.format : format;
  return format("%s says: %s", super.toString(), genMessage());
}
```

Notice how genMessage is protected. This makes the function accessible only to subclasses of Babbler. Let's extend Babbler and override genMessage:

```
class Elocutioner : Babbler {
  protected override string genMessage() {
    return super.genMessage() ~
      " That's all I want to say to you.";
  }
}
```

Now you can take an Elocutioner and use it anywhere a Babbler is expected, such as an argument to a function that takes a Babbler parameter, or in an array of Babbler. OOP programmers will know this as **polymorphism**:

```
void babble(Babbler babbler) {
  writeln(babbler);
}
void main() {
  babble(new Elocutioner);
}
```

Only public and protected functions can be overridden. Although private and package functions are still accessible to subclasses declared in the same module and package respectively, they are implicitly final. A member function explicitly declared final, no matter its protection level, cannot be overridden by subclasses, though it can still be overloaded. Adding final to a class declaration prevents the class from being extended.

One point that often bites new D programmers is that overriding a function hides all overloads of the overridden function in the super class. An example:

```
class Base {
  void print(int i) {
    writeln(i);
  }
  void print(double d) {
    writeln(d);
  }
}
class Sub : Base {
  override void print(int i) {
    super.print(i * 10);
  }
}
void main() {
  auto s = new Sub;
  s.print(2.0);
}
```

This produces a compiler error saying that `Sub.print` is not callable using `double`. To fix it, add an alias inside `Sub`:

```
class Sub : Base {
  alias print = super.print;
  override void print(int i) {
    super.print(i * 10);
  }
}
```

Note that the name of the super class, in this case `Base`, can be substituted for `super`.

Calling functions outside the class namespace

Imagine a `class` or `struct` with a member function named `writeln`. Inside any other functions in the class scope (or that of its subclasses) a call to `writeln` will always call the member function, and not the function in `std.stdio`. To break out of the class namespace, prepend a dot to the function call: `.writeln`.

D also supports abstract classes, as in the following two declarations:

```
abstract class Abstract1{}
class Abstract2 {
  abstract void abstractFunc();
}
```

Abstract1 is explicitly declared abstract, whereas Abstract2 is implicitly so, since it has at least one abstract member function. Neither class can be instantiated directly. Further, any class that extends Abstract2 must either provide an implementation for abstractFunc or itself be declared abstract:

```
class Subclass : Abstract2 {
  override void abstractFunc() { writeln("Hello"); }
}
```

It's always possible to upcast an instance of a subclass to a super class. For example:

```
auto eloc = new Elocutioner;
Babbler babb = eloc;
```

However, it's not always possible to go in the other direction, or downcast. Given an instance of Babbler, explicitly casting it to an Elocutioner will succeed only if the original instance was an Elocutioner. If it was created directly as a Babbler, or perhaps another subclass called Orator, the cast will fail. In that case, the result is null:

```
if (cast(Elocutioner)babb) {
  writeln("It's an elocutioner!");
}
```

Interfaces

So far, we've been talking about implementation inheritance. D also supports interface inheritance. Again, this only works for classes. As in Java, an interface in D is declared with the interface keyword and can contain member functions that have no implementation. Any class that implements an interface must implement each function or declare them abstract. In this case, the override keyword is not needed. Interfaces cannot be instantiated directly:

```
interface Greeter {
  void greet();
}
class EnglishGreeter : Greeter {
  void greet() { writeln(this); }
  override string toString() { return "Hello"; }
}
```

An instance of `EnglishGreeter` can be passed anywhere a `Greeter` is wanted. Be careful, though:

```
void giveGreeting(Greeter greeter) {
  greeter.greet();
  writeln(greeter);    // Error!
}
```

Remember that, when given a `class` instance, `writeln` calls its `toString` function. While `EnglishGreeter` does have a `toString` overriding the one that it inherited from `Object`, inside `giveGreeting` the instance is being viewed as a `Greeter`, not an `EnglishGreeter`. In D, interfaces *do not* inherit from `Object`, so there is no `toString` function for the `writlen` to call.

An `interface` can have `static` member variables and functions (the functions must have an implementation). These behave exactly as they do in a `class` or a `struct`. They can be accessed using the `interface` name as a namespace and the functions cannot be overridden. An `interface` can also have implementations of per-instance member functions, but these must be marked with `final` and cannot be overridden:

```
interface Boomer {
    final string goBoom() { return "Boom!"; }
}
class BoomerImp : Boomer {
    override string toString() { return goBoom(); }
}
```

A single class can implement multiple interfaces. Additionally, extending any class that implements any interface causes the subclass to inherit the interfaces, for example subclasses of `EnglishGreeter` are also `Greeter`s.

Fake inheritance

One interesting feature of D is called **alias this**. Although it works with classes, the biggest benefit is to be seen with `struct` types, since they can't use inheritance:

```
struct PrintOps {
  void print(double arg) { writeln(arg); }
}
struct MathOps {
  PrintOps printer;
  alias printer this;
  double add(double a, double b) { return a + b; }
}
```

Notice the syntax of the highlighted line. It differs from the standard `alias` syntax. This indicates that, when a function is called on `MathOps` that is not part of the `MathOps` declaration, the compiler should try to call it on the `printer` member instead:

```
MathOps ops;
auto val = ops.add(1.0, 2.0); // Calls Mathops.add
ops.print(val);               // Calls Printer.print
```

Here, the call to `ops.print` in the highlighted line is the same as calling `ops.printer.print`. Obviously this isn't exactly the same thing as inheritance, but it's a simple way to reuse code. It's also handy when working with template functions. As I write, the language only allows one `alias this` per `struct` or `class` declaration, but multiple `alias this` may be supported in the future.

Nested classes

It's possible to nest one class declaration inside another:

```
class Outer {
  private int _x;
  this(int x) { _x = x; }
  Inner createInner() { return new Inner; }
  override string toString() { return "Outer"; }
  class Inner {
    override string toString() {
      writeln(_x);
      return this.outer.toString ~ ".Inner";
    }
  }
}
```

The first highlighted line shows that an instance of an inner class can be allocated from inside an outer class. The bottom two highlighted lines demonstrate that `Inner` has access to the members of `Outer`. As `Inner` has no member named _x, it can access the _x member of `Outer` directly. However, both classes have a `toString` method, so we have to use `this.outer.toString` to call outer's implementation. This is like using `super` to call a super class function from a subclass.

Since the declaration of `Inner` is public, the `createInner` function isn't needed to get a new `Inner` instance; it can be allocated directly. An instance of `Outer` is needed to do so:

```
auto outer = new Outer(1);
auto inner1 = outer.new Inner;   // OK
auto inner2 = new Outer.Inner;   // Error -- need Outer 'this'
auto inner2 = new outer.Inner;   // Error -- same as above
```

By prefixing the name of the outer class instance variable to `new`, that instance is associated with the inner class instance.

When a nested class is declared as `static`, an instance of the outer class is no longer needed. However, a static nested class no longer has an associated outer class instance, which means that there is no `.outer` property. Change the declaration of `Inner` to be `static` and it can no longer access the `_x` and `toString` members of `Outer`. In other words, a static inner class is just a normal class with an additional namespace:

```
class Outer2 {
   static class StaticInner {}
}
```

To get an instance of `StaticInner`:

```
auto inner = new Outer2.StaticInner;
```

Structs can also be nested, but in this case the type name of the outer struct simply becomes an additional namespace for the inner one, for example `Outer.Inner oi;`. The inner struct is just like any other struct, with no `.outer` property.

Objects with const and immutable

In the context of class and struct instances, it's easier to understand the relationship `const` and `immutable` have with data. Here's a simple example:

```
struct ModMe {
    int x;
}
void main() {
    immutable ModMe mm;
    immutable(ModMe) * pmm;
    mm.x = 1;    // Error
    pmm.x = 2;   // Error
}
```

The declaration of `mm` creates an instance of type `immutable(ModMe)`. Not only can no assignments be made to `mm`, `mm.x` cannot be modified. `pmm` is a pointer to immutable data, so the pointer can be reassigned, but `pmm.x` cannot be modified. Now look at this:

```
struct ModMeHolder {
    ModMe mm;
}
```

```
void main() {
    immutable ModMeHolder mmh;
    mmh.mm.x = 1;
}
```

As `immutable` is transitive, applying it to `mmh` causes `mm` to also be immutable. If, in turn, it had any `class` or `struct` instance members, they would also become immutable. As they say, it's turtles all the way down. The same is true for `const`, but recall that its contract is not as strict as that of `immutable`:

```
ModMe mm;
const(ModMe)* pmm = &mm;
mm.x = 10;
writeln(pmm.x);
```

Attempting to modify `pmm.x` would be an error, since `pmm` is a pointer to `const` data, but it's perfectly legal to modify the original data behind `pmm`'s back.

Changing the previous `ModMeHolder` example to use `const` instead of `immutable` will not change the outcome. This sometimes causes consternation for C++ programmers experimenting with D. Imagine you want to implement a class that increments an internal counter every time a function is called. Pass an instance of that class to a function that attempts to call its incrementing member function through a `const` reference and a compiler error will result. In C++, programmers can get around this by declaring the counter as `mutable`. Not so in D.

D `const` is strictly *physical const*. This can be seen as a guarantee that not a single bit of an instance can ever be modified through a `const` reference, internally or externally. The alternative is `logical const`. With this definition, a reference appears `const` to the outside world, but the instance is able to modify its internal structure. While this may seem quite useful to the programmer, it completely breaks any guarantee of transitivity. If the compiler cannot guarantee transitivity, then any assumptions it makes about the state of an instance are invalid. This could have wide-ranging consequences. For example, it could be a source of race conditions in a multi-threaded program. The short of it is, in order to guarantee transitivity, logical const does not exist in D as I write. Who can say, though, what the future holds.

`const` and `immutable` can be applied to `class` and `struct` declarations, but any instances of such types must still be declared as `const` or `immutable`.

const as a storage class

We've only seen `const` used as a type qualifier thus far, but when applied to a function it is a storage class. As in C++, this is used to allow member functions to be called from a `const` or `immutable` reference:

```
class CallMe {
    void foo() {}
    void bar() const {}
}
void main() {
    const CallMe cm = new CallMe;
    cm.foo();   // Error - mutable function on const reference
    cm.bar();   // OK
}
```

`const` can be applied to the front of the function declaration as well as at the end. This has implications for how `const` return values are declared:

```
const AStruct returnSomething() {}
```

It's easy to assume this is returning a constant struct instance, but that is not the case. This is a function with a `const` storage class. For clarity, it's good practice to apply `const` at the end of a function declaration when needed and to declare `const` return values using the type qualifier syntax, `const(AStruct)`.

Error handling

D includes support for exception-based error handling. Another option is a popular feature called the **scope** statement.

Scope guards

In a C function that manipulates a locally allocated buffer, it's not unusual to see a series of `if...else` blocks where, after the failure of some operation, either the buffer is freed directly or via a `goto` statement. In D, we need neither idiom:

```
void manipulateData() {
    import core.stdc.stdlib : malloc, free;
    auto buf = cast(ubyte*)malloc(1024);
    scope(exit) if(buf) free(buf);
    // Now do some work with buf
}
```

Here, memory is allocated outside the GC with `malloc` and should be released when the function exits. The highlighted `scope(exit)` allows that. Scope statements are executed at the end of any scope in which they are declared, be it a function body, a loop body, or any block scope. `exit` says the statement should *always* be executed when the scope exits. There are two other possible identifiers to use here: `success` means to execute only when the scope exits normally; `failure` executes only after an uncaught exception. Braces were not used here since this is a one-liner but, as with any other block statement, they can be. Multiple scope guard blocks can be declared in any scope. They are executed in the reverse order of declaration.

Exception handling

DRuntime declares three globally accessible classes that form the bedrock of the exception mechanism: `Throwable`, `Error`, and `Exception`. The latter two are both subclasses of the first. Instances of the `Error` class are intended to represent unrecoverable errors, while the `Exception` class represents errors are potentially recoverable. I'll refer to both as *exceptions* throughout the book except when I need to talk specifically about the types.

Exceptions can be *thrown* and *caught*. Only instances of classes in the `Throwable` hierarchy can be thrown, including subclasses of `Error` and `Exception`. To throw an exception, use the `throw` statement:

```
throw new Exception("Very bad things have happened here.")
```

The text given to the constructor is accessible via the `.msg` property. The `toString` function of an exception includes the message, along with the fully qualified class name of the instance and a backtrace showing where the exception occurred. Normally, the backtrace only shows memory addresses but if the source is compiled with the `-g` option, a more human-readable backtrace is generated.

To catch an exception, use the standard `try` followed by one or more `catch` blocks, a `finally` block, or both. Each has its own scope and optional braces:

```
void main() {
    import std.exception : ErrnoException;
    try {
        auto file = File("log.txt", "w");
        file.writeln("Hello, file!");
    }
    catch(ErrnoException ee) {
        // Do something specific to the ErrnoException
        writeln(ee);
    }
```

```
        catch(Exception e) {
            // Do something specific to the Exception
            writeln(e);
        }
        finally
            writeln("Good bye!");
    }
```

Since `file` is declared in the `try` block, it is not visible in either the `catch` or `finally` blocks. The `catch` blocks are only run when the corresponding exception is thrown inside the `try`, while the `finally` is always run when the `try` block exits. Scope statements are syntactic sugar for `try...catch` blocks (and `scope(exit)` adds a `finally`). With multiple `catch` blocks, any subclasses having super classes in the chain should be declared first. Since `ErrnoException` is a subclass of `Exception`, it has to come first; if `Exception` were first, `ErrnoException` would never be caught.

> When you find yourself wanting to catch specific exceptions, the Phobos documentation lists the exceptions a function may throw (they aren't listed in function declarations as in Java; there are no checked exceptions in D). It does so via the `Throws:` field in Ddoc comments. When releasing your own APIs to the public, you should do the same for your documentation. For our previous example, you can look at the documentation for `std.stdio.File` at `http://dlang.org/phobos/std_stdio.html#.File` to see which functions throw which exceptions.

Exceptions that are not caught will filter up the call stack and ultimately cause the program to exit, with the result of its `toString` implementation printed to the console. Generally, you should only catch `Exception` or its subclasses. When `Exception` is thrown, things that normally run as a scope are exited, such as struct destructors and scope statements, are still guaranteed to run; there is no such guarantee when `Error` is thrown, meaning the program could possibly be in an invalid state by the time the `catch` block runs. As a general rule, never catch `Throwable` (you can't know whether it's an `Error` or `Exception` until after it's caught) and only catch `Error` if you really know what you are doing. When you do, rethrow it as soon as you're finished with it. A program should never attempt to recover when `Error` is thrown.

When a function is annotated with `nothrow`, the compiler requires that any function it calls also be marked `nothrow`. `Exceptions` cannot be thrown from inside such a function, but `Errors` are still allowed. Try to compile this:

```
void saveText(string text) nothrow {
    auto file = File("text.txt", "w");
    file.writeln(text);
}
```

You should see four errors. Three of them tell you that the constructor and destructor of the `File` type, as well as its `writeln` method, are not marked `nothrow`. The last one says that `saveText` is marked `nothrow` even though it may throw. In order to live up to the promise of `nothrow`, the function body should be wrapped up in a `try...catch` block:

```
try {
    auto file = File("text.txt", "w");
    file.writeln(text);
}
catch(Exception e) { /* Log the message */ }
```

`Exception` and `Error` can be subclassed to create custom exceptions. When doing so, at least one of the super class constructors must be called from the subclass. `Exception` has constructors with the following signatures:

```
this(string msg, string file = __FILE__, size_t line = __LINE__,
    Throwable next = null)
this(string msg, Throwable next, string file = __FILE__,
    size_t line = __LINE__)
```

The `next` parameter is used to set up a chain of exceptions, but is primarily used internally. Most notable here are the `__FILE__` and `__LINE__` identifiers. C and C++ programmers will reflexively think of preprocessor macros that have the same name. If you happen to be one of them, please push that thought from your mind right now. The purpose of these identifiers is the same as the C macros, but they are implemented as special constants that the compiler substitutes directly where encountered. Moreover, using the macros as default values in C++ would cause the line number and filename of the *function declaration* to be inserted. In D, it's the line number and filename of the *call site*. When extending `Exception` (`Error` constructors don't have the same signatures), be sure to add the same parameters to your own constructor(s) and pass the values on to the super class constructor. The feature is useful elsewhere, particularly for custom logging functions intended to log the file name and line number of the caller.

Contract programming and unit tests

D has built-in support for contract programming and unit testing. D's contract programming implementation consists of two loosely related features: **invariants** and **function** contracts. None of these features would be as useful as they are without the assert expression.

Before we dig into the details, I'd like to point out that all of these features, except unit tests, are enabled by default. Passing `-release` to the compiler will disable asserts, function contracts, and invariants. Typically, you'll want to leave that flag out during development and use it when you are ready to start testing the release version.

Assert contracts

The `assert` expression evaluates a Boolean expression and throws an `AssertError` when the result is `false`. The basic syntax takes two forms:

```
assert(10 == 10);
assert(1 > 0, "You've done the impossible!");
```

Both of these examples will always evaluate to true since the Boolean expressions use constants. If the second one did somehow fail, the text message following the expression would be printed as part of the `AssertError` message.

When the assert condition can be evaluated to `0` at compile time, the expression is always compiled in, even when `-release` is enabled. This is useful in code you expect to be unreachable, such as in the `default` case of a `switch` statement that covers a limited number of cases. All of the following forms trigger the special behavior:

```
assert(0);
assert(false);
assert(10 - 10);
assert(1 < 0);
```

The D reference documentation explicitly says that `assert` is the most basic contract. As such, it allows the compiler the freedom to assume that the condition is always true and to use that information to optimize any subsequent code, even when asserts are disabled. The rationale is that the assert expression establishes a contract and, since contracts must be satisfied, an assert failure means the program has not satisfied the contract and is in an invalid state. In practical terms, this means that the language allows the compiler to behave as if assert expressions are being used as intended: to catch logic errors. They should never be used to validate user input or test anything that is subject to failure at runtime; that's what exceptions are for.

Function contracts

Function contracts allow a program's state to be verified before and after a function is executed. A contract consists of three parts: in, body, and out. Of the three, only body is required, as it's the actual implementation of the function. For example:

```
void explicitBody() body { writeln("Explicit body."); }
void implicitBody() { writeln("Implicit body"); }
```

Every function has a body, but the keyword is not necessary unless either in or out, or both, is also used. The declarations can appear in any order:

```
enum minBuffer = 256;
size_t getData(ubyte[] buffer)
in {
  assert(buffer.length >= minBuffer);
}
out(result) {
  assert(result > 0);
}
body {
  size_t i;
  while(i < minBuffer)
    buffer[i++] = nextByte();
  return i;
}
```

This example shows a function, getData, that has both in and out contracts. Before the body of the function is run, the in contract will be executed. Here, the length of buffer is tested to ensure that it is large enough to hold all of the data. If the in contract passes, the body is run. When the function exits normally, the out contract is executed. The syntax out(result) makes the return value accessible inside the out contract as a variable named result (it's worth noting that function parameters can be used in an out contract). This implementation just makes sure the return value is greater than 0.

Invariants

Invariants are added to a struct or class declaration in order to verify that something about the state of an instance, which must be true, is actually true. For example:

```
class Player {
  enum MaxLevel = 50;
  private int _level;
```

```
    int level() { return _level; }
    void levelUp() {
      ++_level;
      if(_level > MaxLevel)
        _level = MaxLevel;
    }
    invariant {
      assert(_level >= 0 && _level <= MaxLevel);
    }
}
```

In this example, `_level` cannot be modified directly outside the module; it's a read-only property. It can only be modified through `levelUp`. By adding an `invariant` that verifies `_level` is within the expected range, we guarantee that any accidental modification will be caught. For example, what if we modify the `levelUp` function and accidentally remove the `> maxLevel` check, or if we do some work elsewhere in the module and modify `_level` directly? The invariant is a safeguard.

Invariants are run immediately after a constructor, unless the instance was implicitly constructed with `.init`, and just before a destructor. They are run in conjunction with function contracts, before and after non-private, non-static functions, in this order:

- In contract
- Invariant
- Function body
- Invariant
- Out contract

Something that's easy to overlook is that invariants are not run when a member variable is accessed directly, or through a pointer or reference returned from a member function. If the variable affects the invariant in any way, it should be declared `private` and access should only be allowed through getter and setter functions, always returning by value or `const` reference.

Non-private and non-static member functions cannot be called from inside an invariant. Attempting to do so will enter an infinite loop, as the invariant is run twice on each function invocation. Additionally, the invariant can be manually checked at any time by passing a `class` instance, or the address of a `struct` instance, to an `assert`:

```
auto player = new Player;
assert(player);
assert(&structInstance);
```

Unit tests

Unit tests are another tool to verify the integrity of a code base. They are implemented in `unittest` blocks. Any number of `unittest` blocks can be added at module scope and in `class`, `struct`, and `union` declarations. It is idiomatic to place a `unittest` block immediately after the function it is testing. Anything valid in a function body can go into them, as they are functions themselves. Here's a simple example:

```
int addInts(int a, int b) { return a + b; }
unittest {
    assert(addInts(10, 1) == 11);
    assert(addInts(int.max, 1) == int.min);
}
```

To enable `unittest`s in an executable, pass the `-unittest` flag to the compiler. This will cause DRuntime to run each unit test when the program is executed after static constructors and before `main`. All unit tests in a given module are run in lexical order, though the order in which modules are selected for execution is unspecified. However, it is often more convenient to compile and test a single module, rather than an entire program. To facilitate this, DMD provides a switch that will automatically generate a `main` function if one does not already exist. This creates an executable from a single module that can be used to specifically run the `unittest`s in that module.

Save the previous snippet in a file called `utest.d`. Then execute the following command:

dmd -unittest --main -g utest.d

Run the resulting binary and you shouldn't see any output. Note `-g` on the command line. When running `unittest`s, it's always helpful to generate debug info to get the full stack trace. Let's look at that now. Change the 11 to 12 so that the first `assert` fails. You should get an `AssertError` with a stack trace pointing to the failure. `--main` tells the compiler to generate a `main` function for the module. This is useful to test modules in isolation.

The `unittest` blocks can be decorated with function attributes, such as `nothrow`. This really comes in handy when testing template functions, for which the compiler is able to infer attributes. They can also be documented with Ddoc comments. This will cause the code inside the block to become an example in the documentation for the preceding function or type declaration. To prevent this behavior, the `unittest` can be declared `private`. There is also a feature available at compile time to determine whether `unittest`s are currently enabled, but we'll save that for the next chapter.

MovieMan – adding menus

It's time now to take some of the features covered in this chapter and apply them to
MovieMan. The code listings here will, unfortunately, be incomplete in the interests of
keeping the page count down. However, the complete implementation can be found
in the Chapter03/MovieMan directory of the downloadable source code.

The MovieMan menus are implemented as a small set of classes: Menu, MainMenu,
and DisplayMenu. We could debate composition versus inheritance, or the
use of classes to implement such simple menus, but my priority is to provide
a demonstration of D features.

The Menu base class

To get started, save a file called $MOVIEMAN/source/movieman/menu/menu.d. At the
very top, add the following lines:

```
module movieman.menu.menu;
import std.stdio;
import movieman.io;
```

Next, we'll make an empty class declaration that we'll fill in a little at a time:

```
class Menu {
}
```

The Menu class will have three private members:

```
private:
    string _header;
    string[] _items;
    bool _shouldExit;
```

_header is the title of the menu and _items is the text specifying the available
actions, each of which will be displayed in a numbered list for the user to input a
selection. _shouldExit is a flag that will be set when a subclass is ready to exit the
menu loop. Now we've got a few protected functions, starting with the constructor:

```
protected:
    this(string header, string[] items) {
        _header = header;
        _items = items;
    }
```

A `protected` constructor is normally used to allow subclasses access while preventing instances of the class from being instantiated outside the class scope. That's the exact behavior we want for `Menu`, but it isn't necessary to make the constructor `protected` in this case as the very next function is `abstract`; I simply prefer to make all constructors in an abstract class `protected`:

```
abstract void handleSelection(uint selection);
```

Subclasses will override `handleSelection` in order to respond to the user's selection of a menu item. The next function, `exitMenu`, is called when a subclass is ready to give up control and terminate the loop that prints the menu and reads the user's selection:

```
void exitMenu() { _shouldExit = true; }
```

The next two functions ensure that a title or number entered by the user is valid and print an "abort" message if not. The former only checks whether `title is null` for now and the latter if the number is `0`. The label parameter is used in the error message:

```
bool validateTitle(string title) {…}
bool validateNumber(uint number, string label) {…}
```

The last function in `Menu` is the one that drives things:

```
public:
  final void run() {
    do {
      printList(_header, _items);
      auto selection = readUint();
        if(!selection || selection > _items.length)
          writefln("Sorry, that's an invalid selection. Please try
          again.");
        else
          handleSelection(selection);

    } while(!_shouldExit);
  }
}
```

The `public:` keyword before the function declaration "turns off" the `protected:` added previously. The `final` in the declaration prevents subclasses from overriding `run`. The implementation is a loop that begins with a call to `movieman.io.printList` to display the header and the numbered menu items. It then asks the user to enter a number, which it sends to the subclass to handle if it is in the range of valid options (which is `1` to `items.length`, inclusive), then the loop goes back up to the top and the menu is displayed again, unless `exitMenu` is called.

The MainMenu class

Save a new file as `$MOVIEMAN/source/movieman/menu/main.d`. Add the following lines to the top:

```
module movieman.menu.main;
import movieman.menu.menu;
final class MainMenu : Menu {
}
```

Note that the class is declared `final`. Given that there's no need to ever subclass `MainMenu`, we can use this not just as a preventative measure, but also as an optimization hint. For example, the compiler can be sure that none of the member functions will ever be overridden and can safely inline calls to them. Now, inside `MainMenu`:

```
private:
enum Options : uint {
  addMovie = 1u,
  displayMovie,
  exit,
}
Menu _displayMenu;
```

The `Options` enumeration will be used to determine the action to take in `handleSelection`. The user can choose to add a new movie, display one or more movies, or exit the program. The `_displayMenu` member is an instance of `DisplayMenu`, declared as an instance of the `Menu` base class. It is created in one of two private functions, `onDisplayMovie`, when the user chooses to display a movie:

```
void onDisplayMovie() {
  import movieman.menu.display : DisplayMenu;
  if(_displayMenu is null)
    _displayMenu = new DisplayMenu;
    _displayMenu.run();
}
```

A local selective import is used since `DisplayMenu` is not used anywhere else in the module. `_displayMenu` is allocated only if it's `null`, then its `run` function is called. The second private function adds a movie to the database:

```
void onAddMovie() {
    import movieman.io;
    import std.stdio : writeln;
    auto title = readTitle();
    if(!validateTitle(title))
        return;
    auto caseNumber = readNumber("case");
    if(!validateNumber(caseNumber, "case"))
        return;
    auto pageNumber = readNumber("page");
    if(!validateNumber(pageNumber, "page"))
        return;
    if(readChoice("add this movie to the database"))
        writeln("Adding movie!");
    else
        writeln("\nDiscarding new movie.");
}
```

This function asks the user to enter a title, case number, and page number. If any one of these is invalid, the function returns without making any changes. Finally, it gives the user a chance to verify the information is correct via `readChoice`. If the user approves, a message is printed saying the movie has been added. Later in the book, this will be changed to add a movie to the database. Next:

```
protected:
    override void handleSelection(uint selection) {
        final switch(cast(Options)selection) with(Options) {
            case addMovie:
                onAddMovie();
                break;
            case displayMovie:
                onDisplayMovie();
                break;
            case exit:
                exitMenu();
                break;
        }
    }
```

This function uses a `final switch` to cover every member of the `Options` enumeration. `with(Options)` is used as a convenience to avoid adding the namespace in every `case`. Notice that there's no private function to handle the `exit` option. Instead, the `exitMenu` function implemented in the base class is called. Finally, the `public` constructor:

```
public:
  this() {
    auto options = [
      "Add Movie",
      "Display Movie(s)",
      "Exit"
    ];
    super("Select one of the following actions.", options);
  }
}
```

When a class has no default constructor, either implicit or explicit, then any subclasses must call one of the constructors that have been implemented. The `MainMenu` class must call `Menu`'s sole constructor. Before doing so, an array of menu items is allocated as `options` with an array literal. Using the literal directly in the constructor call would have been somewhat less readable. Finally, the `Menu` constructor is called via `super`.

The DisplayMenu class

This `DisplayMenu` class will eventually print movie data to the screen and provide the option to edit movies in the database. The implementation is similar to the `MainMenu` class, though the only function currently implemented is `handleSelection`, which does the work of reading input and printing responses (there's no movie data yet to display or edit). Before looking at the implementation in the downloadable source, consider how you might implement `DisplayMenu`, using `MainMenu` as a guide.

Summary

In this chapter, we've taken an introductory look at D's support for user-defined types and object-oriented programming. We've looked at how these features differ from other C family languages. We've also learned about scope guards, exception handling, contract programming, and unit tests. Finally, we've added some menu classes to `MovieMan`.

In the next chapter, we look at features that allow you to do neat stuff at compile time.

4
Running Code at Compile Time

The title of this chapter refers to **Compile Time Function Execution (CTFE)**. This is primarily what makes D's generative programming capability as powerful as it is. Given that a function meets certain constraints, the compiler can execute it in order to produce values at compile time. These can then be used to generate new code. The very basics of CTFE can be explained with a couple of paragraphs, but there are a number of related features that can be used to increase its benefits. These features can also be used independently to conditionally control which parts of the program are compiled, or to generate code without ever running a function. We're going to spend the entire chapter examining these features in preparation for the next chapter on templates; D's compile-time features coupled with templates make for amazing possibilities.

- Pragmas: Compile-time messages, libraries, and function inlining hints
- Conditional compilation: `version`, `debug`, and `static if` conditions
- Compile-time strings: The `import` expression and string mixins
- Compile-time function execution
- Odds and ends: `static assert`, alignment, compile-time reflection, and user-defined attributes

Pragmas

A **pragma** statement is a directive for the compiler to perform a specific task at compile time. In C and C++, it's a preprocessor directive, but in D it's an actual statement. At the time of writing, there are five predefined pragmas. We'll go through three of them here; the other two are for more advanced usage. The language also allows for vendor-specific pragmas. When a compiler encounters one that it doesn't recognize, such as one from a different compiler vendor, it is required to emit an error. Vendor-specific pragmas can be used by versioning them, something you'll learn how to do in the next section. For more on pragmas, refer to http://dlang.org/pragma.html.

The lib pragma

The `lib` pragma is a way to instruct the compiler in code as to which libraries should be linked at compile time. Here's an example.

```
pragma(lib, "OpenGL32.lib");
```

This will cause the compiler to insert a directive into the object file that the linker can then use to link a library into the executable, `OpenGL32.lib` in this case. While it's a useful feature, there are some potential issues to be aware of.

First, the library names are always going to be platform-specific. The preceding example is specific to Windows. Later in this chapter, I'll show you how to version sections of your code to target specific platforms, but bear in mind that you'll generally need at least two lib pragmas for a multi-platform project: one for Windows and one for POSIX.

Second, just as when passing the name of a library on the command line, any libraries passed through the `lib` pragma will be searched for on the global search path, including any paths specified on the command line. While there is no way to specify a search path via a `pragma`, it's possible to specify a complete path to a library, like so:

```
pragma(lib, `C:\dlang\libs\MyLib.lib`);
```

Notice the format of the string. When compiling using DMD on Windows with the OPTLINK linker (the default 32-bit configuration), it's necessary to specify paths using backslashes, as OPTLINK doesn't understand forward slashes. To avoid the need to escape the backslashes ('\\'), I've used a WYSIWYG string. When using the MS linker, forward slashes suffice.

Third, you might one day have the idea of adding a `lib` pragma in one of the source modules of a library you distribute, hoping to make it more convenient for users by having it link to itself. In my experience, this tends to cause more trouble than it's worth. The potential for conflict with the user's preferred build system is high. I've actually seen a couple of libraries distributed with full paths specified in `lib` pragmas, something that's almost guaranteed to cause a build failure out of the box. It's generally a better idea to let the user, or the user's preferred build tool, decide how to link with your library and any of its dependencies so that conflicts can be avoided. An exception will be if the library depends on a system library that should be generally available on most systems. Adding a `lib` pragma in one of your modules for that library should be safe if it's properly versioned.

Finally, when linking multiple libraries via `lib` pragmas, the order in which they are declared matters when linking with the GNU linker. The compiler will queue them up in lexical order and pass them all to the linker, but the GNU linker requires that dependencies be ordered after dependents. For example, if a hypothetical `libA3` depends on `libA2`, and `libA2` depends on `libA1`, then they need to be passed along in the following order: `libA3`, `libA2`, and `libA1`. To ensure DMD does the right thing, the `lib` pragmas must be ordered the same way.

```
pragma(lib, "A3");
pragma(lib, "A2");
pragma(lib, "A1");
```

This also holds true when passing libraries on the command line. When using `lib` pragmas, it's quite easy to get a working program on Windows that fails to link on Linux or Mac. The lesson here is to always familiarize yourself with the system tools you're working with before using any features that depend on the toolchain.

The `lib` pragma is most useful when compiling your own executables. The format for specifying global library search paths varies across compilers and systems (we'll take a look at some examples later in the book), so including the full path to a library in the source is one option that may be preferable to specifying it in the build system, except when using libraries that are managed by DUB.

The msg pragma

When generating code at compile time, it's sometimes necessary to output error or debug messages. `writeln` and friends are not executable at compile time, so they aren't going to help. Enter the `msg` pragma.

```
pragma(msg, "Hi! I'm a compile-time message.");
```

When the compiler encounters this `pragma`, it will immediately print the message to the console. This usually isn't the desired behavior; it's often more useful to have it printed out only in specific circumstances. Very soon, we'll take a look at other compile time features that make that possible.

The inline pragma

The compiler does not attempt to inline function calls unless `-inline` is passed on the command line. The `inline` pragma can be used to affect its behavior.

```
pragma(inline, false) void dontInlineMe() {...}
pragma(inline, true):
   void pleaseInlineMe() {...}
   int meToo() {...}
pragma(inline): // go back to the default behavior
```

Here, `dontInlineMe` will never be inlined, even when the compiler thinks it's a good idea to do so. If the compiler is unable to inline either of the next two functions, it will generate an error. Finally, `pragma(inline)` restores the default behavior, so any functions declared from that point on in the module will be inlined or not, at the compiler's discretion. To be very clear, none of these have any effect if `-inline` is not passed on the command line.

Conditional compilation

The C preprocessor makes it possible to conditionally compile certain blocks of code using `#define` and related directives. Once again, D achieves similar results using built-in compile-time statements, such as `version`, `debug`, and `static if`.

The version condition

A `version` condition is used to instruct the compiler to generate code for anything in the `version` block only if the specific condition is defined. Here's an example:

```
version(Windows)
   pragma(msg, "We are compiling on Windows.");
else version(OSX)
   pragma(msg, "We are compiling on a Mac OS X system.");
else version(Posix)
   pragma(msg, "We are compiling on a Posix system.");
```

This example uses the predefined versions `Windows`, `OSX`, and `Posix`. Swap the order of the `Posix` and `OSX` versions and the `Posix` block, not the `OSX` block, will run on Mac OS X. Remove the `else` statements and then both the `Posix` and `OSX` blocks will compile on Mac. `Posix` is defined on all POSIX systems, which includes Linux, Mac OS X, and the various BSDs. In addition to Windows and OSX, other system-specific versions include `linux`, `FreeBSD`, `OpenBSD`, `NetBSD`, `DragonFlyBSD`, `BSD` (for other flavors of BSD), `Solaris`, and more. You can find a list of predefined versions at `http://dlang.org/version.html#predefined-versions`.

 The fact that the `linux` version isn't capitalized is sort of an accident of history. `linux` is a predefined preprocessor symbol with the GCC compiler. Back in the D1 days, the same symbol was included in D under the assumption that Linux programmers would find it familiar. Over the years, some users have asked that it be deprecated and replaced with the capitalized form, but that hasn't happened as a great deal of D code already uses it. As such, it remains an anomaly among the predefined versions. It's also an occasional source of bugs. One such bug actually made it into Phobos, where some Linux-specific networking code was versioned with `Linux` instead of `linux`!

`version` *does not* create a new scope; anything declared inside a `version` block belongs to the enclosing scope. For example:

```
module timestuff;
// These imports are at global scope.
version(Windows) import core.sys.windows.windows;
else import core.sys.posix.time;

void doSomeTimeStuff() {
  // These variables are in function scope
  version(Windows) {
    SYSTEMTIME sysTime;
    // Do something with sysTime
  } else {
    timeval tv;
    // Do something with tv
  }
  int hour = sysTime.wHour;   // Compiles only on Windows!
}
```

New D programmers are often surprised that they are unable to use version with Boolean expressions, for example version (Windows || linux). Such a feature has been requested, but was rejected on the grounds that it leads to error-prone code. One way to handle this is to use a version specification. These can be declared in module scope, never in a local scope, and allow you to specify new versions in code.

```
version(Windows)
    version = WindowsOrLinux;
else version(linux)
    version = WindowsOrLinux;
```

Now version (WindowsOrLinux) can be used with one major caveat: version specifications only exist within the module in which they are declared. To use WindowsOrLinux in multiple modules, the preceding code must be included at the top of every module that needs it; it can't be implemented once and imported everywhere. Note that using a version before it is set is an error.

```
version(DoIt) pragma(msg, "DoIt!");
version = DoIt;     // Error
```

In addition to predefined operating system versions, there are versions for the currently recognized D compilers, CPU architectures, endianness, feature availability, and more. Additionally, version (unittest) is enabled only when -unittest has been passed to the compiler, version (assert) is satisfied only when asserts are enabled, and version (none) can be used to disable a block of code.

D allows custom versions to be specified on the command line with the -version compiler switch. For example:

dmd -version=SayHello foo.d

With this command line, the following snippet will print Hello, World!.

```
version(SayHello) writeln("Hello, World!");
else writeln("I have nothing to say.");
```

It's also possible to specify an integer version, which the compiler interprets as a version level. Any code in such a block will only be compiled when the number is greater than or equal to the number specified.

```
version(10) pragma(msg, "Ten is enabled!");
```

This form must use integer literals and can be specified either on the command line or with a version specification in code. To see the preceding message:

```
dmd -version=10 foo.d
```

Anything in a `version` block must be syntactically valid D. This can have unexpected consequences. It's possible when using different compilers, or even different versions of the same compiler, that code in a version block will not be syntactically valid, causing a compiler error. For this reason, some prefer to use `version(none)` to disable unused code rather than commenting it out; it helps ensure the code will not go stale.

The debug condition

Where `version` is intended to be used to facilitate porting across different platforms and configuring different program features, `debug` is intended to enable the inclusion of code used for debugging. It's only available when `-debug` is passed on the command line. Here's a simple example. Note that it uses no identifiers and no numeric debug level.

```
debug writeln("Debugging enabled.");
else writeln("Debugging disabled.");
```

Compile this with `-debug` and the first line will print; compile without that flag and the second line will print. If you need them, you can also use identifiers and numeric levels.

```
debug(Graphics)
   writeln("Graphics debugging enabled.");
debug(10)
   writeln("Debug level 10 enabled.");
```

Identifiers and levels can be specified in code using a debug specification, for example `debug=10`, where they do not create a new scope, or on the command line, for example `-debug=Graphics`. A debug specification is only valid for the module in which it is declared, but using the command-line flag enables it for the entire program. The meaning of a debug identifier or level is entirely up to you; that is, specifying `–debug=Graphics` does not enable any automatic debugging for a `graphics` package or module; any code you'd like enabled only in that case must be wrapped in `debug(Graphics)` blocks. `-debug` is shorthand for `-debug=1` and, in source code, `debug` means `debug(1)`.

The static if condition

The `static if` condition is a compile time version of the `if` statement. It can be used in any scope, including module scope, and can contain multiple `else static if` branches and a single, optional `else` at the end. When the condition of any branch is met, any code inside its block will be included in the final binary. No branch in a `static if` chain creates a new scope, so any variables declared inside will belong to the enclosing scope. As with other statements, if the block contains a single expression or statement, the braces can be omitted.

There are many uses for `static if`, but one that I've found particularly helpful is to create Boolean conditions for version combinations. Let's redo the `version(WindowsOrLinux)` example from earlier. Since conditions in a `static if` are evaluated at compile time, they need to be compile-time expressions. For that, we'll enlist the help of a couple of manifest constants.

```
version(Windows) {
  enum sysWindows = true;
  enum sysLinux = false;
}
else version(linux) {
  enum sysWindows = false;
  enum sysLinux = true;
}
else {
  enum sysWindows = false;
  enum sysLinux = false;
}
```

The preceding snippet is implemented once at module scope and that module is then imported anywhere these constants are needed. A `static if` statement with a logical OR condition is used to test if the platform is Windows or Linux.

```
void main() {
  static if(sysWindows || sysLinux)
    writeln("Windows or Linux!");
  else
    writeln("Neither Windows nor Linux!");
}
```

Any compile-time expression can be used as a `static if` condition. Don't forget that most of the built-in type properties are compile-time values. For example, the following configures a `struct` based on the host platform's architecture.

```
struct SomethingSilly {
  static if(size_t.sizeof == 8)        // 64-bit
    double value;
  else static if(size_t.sizeof == 4)   // 32-bit
    float value;
  else                                 // Future proof
    pragma(msg, "Unsupported architecture.");
}
```

Compile-time strings

Literals, `const` and `immutable` variables in module scope (that aren't initialized in a static constructor), static `const` and `immutable` variables in function scope, and manifest constants and `enum` members, can all be known at compile time. In this section, the focus is specifically on compile-time strings. We're first going to see one more way to initialize them, then we'll see how any compile-time string can be used to generate code.

The import expression

The `import` expression is quite different from the `import` declaration that pulls module symbols into the current scope. This expression is used to specify any file name for the compiler to read into memory at compile time. The file will be read as text and treated as a string literal, making it possible to assign it to any variable that can be initialized at compile time.

```
import std.stdio;
immutable fileData1 = import("myfile1.txt");
enum fileData2 = import("myfile2.txt");
void main() {
  writeln(fileData1);
  writeln(fileData2);
}
```

Save this as `$LEARNINGD/Chapter04/impexp.d`. Now create a couple of text files. First up is `$LEARNINGD/Chapter04/myfile1.txt` with the following content:

```
Hello from the executable directory!
```

And then `$LEARNINGD/Chapter04/files/txt/myfile2.txt` with the following content:

```
Hello from files/txt/myfile2.txt!
```

Try to compile this with the following command line:

dmd impexp.d

You should see a couple of errors saying that you need the `-Jpath` switch. As a security precaution, the compiler requires you to specify one or more paths where it is allowed to search for files named in `import` expressions. The compiler is also free to disallow any path components from the filename. The path can be absolute or relative to the directory in which the compiler is invoked. For this example, this command line works:

dmd -J. -Jfiles/txt impexp.d

We've passed two paths with `-J`. The `.` character represents the compiler's working directory, allowing it to find `myfile1.txt`. Next we pass `files/txt` so that `myfile2.txt` can be found. Running the executable now prints the text from each file.

Although the result of an `import` expression is a `string`, it can be cast to an array of any type. Care should be taken when doing so to avoid problems with endianness or alignment. A typical use case is to load a binary file as a `ubyte` array. I've used this in a little ASCII game project to make sure a default font is always available. For example:

```
enum defFont = cast(ubyte[])import("deffont.png");
```

With that, `defFont` can be passed to a function that knows how to load PNG images from memory. This is a simple case, but imported files often need to be massaged into a different format. In some cases, it may be possible to manipulate the data at compile time using CTFE.

String mixins

The string mixin exists for one purpose and one purpose only: to generate source code from strings. This is a powerful feature that opens the door for all sorts of compile-time configuration without any external tools or a preprocessor. While they really shine when used in conjunction with CTFE and templates, neither feature is needed to demonstrate their functionality. Add the following content to `$LEARNINGD/Chapter04/version.txt`:

```
struct AppVersion {
  int major;
```

```
    int minor;
    int patch;
}
enum appVersion = AppVersion(1, 0, 1);
enum appVersionString = "1.0.1";
```

In the same directory, create a file named `mixin.d` and add the following content:

```
import std.stdio;
mixin(import("version.txt"));
void main() {
    writeln(appVersion);
    writeln(appVersionString);
}
```

Compiling with `-J.` and running will show that `version.txt` was compiled into the binary. The `import` expression pulled the file in as a string, then `mixin` took that string and inserted it into the source code at the point of declaration. After that, the compiler compiled it along with the rest of the module. String mixins often come in handy. They were used to aid in the transition from D1 to D2; they have been used in creating **DSLs (Domain-Specific Languages)**, in compile-time reflection, and more. In every case, they are doing nothing more than what you see here, which is generating source code from strings.

Compile-time function execution

Phobos ships with one of the fastest regular expression engines available. This is possible in part because of its ability to make use of CTFE and other compile-time features to compile regular expressions and generate native machine code for matching (Dmitry Olshansky's DConf 2014 talk gives insight into the regular expression engine; refer to http://dconf.org/2014/talks/olshansky.html). Keep in mind that the performance benefit doesn't come for free; the cost is paid for as an increase in compile time and the potential for code bloat. Still, CTFE can often prove to be a big enough win in terms of performance and/or maintenance costs to outweigh the drawbacks.

Any D function can be executed at compile time as long as it doesn't depend on runtime data. As an example, let's revisit the `packRGBA` function from earlier in the book.

```
uint packRGBA(ubyte r, ubyte g, ubyte b, ubyte a = 255) {
    return (r << 24) + (g << 16) + (b << 8) + a;
}
```

This function is a candidate for compile-time execution because all of the data can be known at compile time. The default value of a is a compile-time value, as are the literals used in the function body. This leaves the other parameters, r, g, and b. Whether or not they are compile-time values depends on the context. Consider the following invocations:

```
int red = 255, blue, green;
auto col = packRGBA(red, blue, green);
col = packRGBA(255, 0, 0);
```

There is no possibility whatsoever for the first call to occur at compile time; the arguments are all runtime values. The second invocation uses integer literals, so it meets the requirement that the function use only compile-time values. However, the return value is assigned to a runtime variable. In this case, the compiler doesn't need to execute the function at compile time, so it doesn't. More generally, if a function must be run at compile time, it will be; if it doesn't have to be executed at compile time, it won't be. The following examples all force the function to be called at compile time:

```
enum red = packRGBA(255, 0, 0);          // manifest constant
immutable green = packRGBA(0, 255, 0);   // module-scope immutable
const blue = packRGBA(0, 0, 255);        // module-scope constant
int white = packRGBA(255, 255, 255);     // module-scope mutable
enum Color : uint {                      // enum members
   red = packRGBA(255, 0, 0),
   green = packRGBA(0, 255, 0),
   blue = packRGBA(0, 0, 255),
}
struct FooColor {
   // Set default init value for user-defined type fields
   uint r = packRGBA(255, 0, 0);
   // Initialize static user-defined type members
   static uint green = packRGBA(0, 255, 0);
}
void someFunc() {
   // Initialize local static variables
   static auto red = packRGBA(255, 0, 0);
}
```

In each case, integer literals are used as parameters and the result is assigned in a variable or constant declaration. The compiler will pick up on all of that and execute the function at compile time without any further coercion. If CTFE is not possible in any given context, the compiler will emit an error. When the compiler does execute a function, it is acting as a D interpreter. Consider:

```
string makeID(string s, string suffix = null) {
  auto ret = "ID_" ~ s;
  ret ~= suffix;
  return ret;
}
enum ID : string {
  One = makeID("One"),
  OneEx = makeID("One", "Ex"),
}
pragma(msg, ID.One);
pragma(msg, ID.OneEx);
```

When the compiler encounters the calls to makeID in the declaration of the ID members, it determines that the function can be executed at compile time and goes into interpreter mode to do so. From inside the function, this essentially looks like any other runtime execution, and it basically is. The difference is only in the context in which it is executed. Let's modify makeID a little.

```
string prefix = "ID_";
string makeID(string s, string suffix = null) {
    auto ret = prefix ~ s;
    ret ~= suffix;
    return ret;
}
```

Now the function makes use of a mutable, module-scope variable. Although the variable is initialized with a compile time value, prefix itself is a runtime variable; it cannot be known in a compile-time context. Execute makeID at runtime and all is well, but execute it at compile-time and an error is produced saying that the static variable prefix *cannot* be read at compile time. Change makeID one more time.

```
enum usePlatformPrefix = true;
string makeID(string s, string suffix = null) {
    static if(usePlatformPrefix) {
        version(Windows) enum prefix = "WIN_ID_";
        else enum prefix = "NIX_ID_";
    }
    else enum prefix = "ID_";
```

```
        auto ret = prefix ~ s;
        ret ~= suffix;
        return ret;
    }
```

This version still uses an external variable, but this time it's a manifest constant that can be known at compile time. It's also got some new compile-time constructs inside. Here's where some people get confused. The static if and version blocks are evaluated *before the function is executed* by the interpreter, *not during CTFE*. Again, inside makeID there is no difference whether the function is executed at compile time or at runtime; the same code is run either way. Another way to look at it is that a function body is not a compile-time construct such as a static if block or a manifest constant. In a compile-time context, the function is run and its result is used in a compile-time construct; in a runtime context, the function is run and its result is used in runtime construct. To the function itself, there is absolutely no difference.

Sometimes, we really do want the implementation of a function to behave somewhat differently in compile-time and runtime contexts. To facilitate this, the language provides a special variable, __ctfe, which is true when the function is being executed by the built-in interpreter at compile time and false during normal runtime execution. A common mistake new D users make is to try and use __ctfe with static if, but it's a runtime variable. Here's an example of __ctfe being used to produce context-dependent output.

```
    string genDebugMsg(string msg) {
        if(__ctfe)
            return "CTFE_" ~ msg;
        else
            return "DBG_" ~ msg;
    }
    pragma(msg, genDebugMsg("Running at compile-time."));
    void main() {
        writeln(genDebugMsg("Running at runtime."));
    }
```

Some may cringe at the idea of introducing a runtime branch just to distinguish between the two contexts, but there's no need to worry. Because __ctfe is always false at runtime, the branch will never make it into the binary even when optimizations are not enabled.

Odds and ends

In this section, we're going to look at several compile-time features that don't fit snugly in the preceding sections.

static assert

`static assert` is a compile-time assertion that is always enabled. It can't be turned off with `-release` like a normal `assert` can. It is not affected by runtime conditionals. When its condition is evaluated to false, an error is generated and compilation halted. The following `static assert` always errors out because its condition is `0`.

```
void main() {
    if(0) static assert(0);
}
```

Like a normal `assert`, it's possible to give a `static assert` a message to be printed on failure. The following example is a good use of that feature:

```
version(Windows)
    enum saveDirectory = "Application Name";
else version(Posix)
    enum saveDirectory = ".applicationName";
else
    static assert(0, "saveDirectory not implemented.");
```

The line number at which the `assert` was encountered is always included in the output, but adding a custom message makes it easy to tell at a glance what caused the problem.

The examples above use `0` as the assert condition, but any Boolean expression that can be evaluated at compile time is eligible to fill that role. Consider the case where you want to restrict compilation to 64-bit. One approach would be to use a `version` condition like so.

```
version(D_LP64) {
  // implement code
} else static assert(0, "32-bit not supported.");
```

`D_LP64` is predefined when compiling with the `-m64` command-line switch. It means that pointers are 64-bits. The following is a single-line alternative:

```
static assert((void*).sizeof == 8, "32-bit not supported.");
```

The is expression

The previous chapter introduced the `is` operator, which performs an identity test on two variables. D also has a compile-time `is` expression, which can be used in a few different ways. First, let's look at the most basic form.

```
enum alwaysTrue = is(int);
```

This checks that the argument is a well-formed type. If so, it returns `true`. Directly pass a value or an expression, and the result is `false`. However, both can be used with `typeof`.

```
enum alwaysTrueToo = is(typeof(1+1));
```

The `==` operator can be used to test for a specific type.

```
enum isFloat = is(typeof(1+1) == float);
```

As written, this is going to set `isFloat` to `false` since the type of `1+1` is `int`. An alternative is to test if one type is convertible to another.

```
enum canBeFloat = is(typeof(1+1) : float);
```

This evaluates to `true` because `int` is implicitly convertible to `float`. Let's see a more complex example:

```
struct AType {
  int x;
  int addXTo(double d) {
    return x + cast(int)d;
  }
}
void main() {
  static if(is(typeof(AType.addXTo(30.0)))) {
    import std.stdio : writeln;
    AType t;
    writeln(t.addXTo(30.0));
  }
}
```

[

Accessing members at compile time

Don't let `AType.addXTo` confuse you. It may look like we're calling a static member function with no `static` in sight, but this isn't what's happening. This is the syntax used to access any member of a `struct` or `class` that can be known at compile time; it's happening at compile time.

]

The `is(typeof())` operator doesn't check if code will compile; it only determines if the code produces a well-formed type. This is something that's often misunderstood, especially when considering that it's possible to put complex code in an `is` expression.

```
static if(is(typeof({
        AType t;
        t.addXTo(30.0);
    }))) {  ...  }
```

Notice the opening and closing braces inside the parentheses. With this syntax, any syntactically valid D code can be used with `is(typeof())`, though it need not be semantically valid. This is an important distinction.

In addition to checking for types, the `is` expression can be used to check against certain language constructs. For example, this `static if` block determines if `AType` is a `struct` or a `class`.

```
static if(is(AType == struct)) {
    writeln("It's a struct!");
} else static if(is(AType == class)) {
    writeln("It's a class!");
}
```

With the preceding declaration of `AType`, the first `writeln` is compiled into the executable. Change the declaration of `AType` so that it's a class, and the second line is compiled in. Other specifiers can be used, such as `function`, `delegate`, `const`, `immutable`, and so on. For more on `is`, refer to `http://dlang.org/expression.html#IsExpression`.

It may be difficult to see exactly how `is` can be useful, given that in each of the above examples the type is already known. Where it really comes in handy, and where it's most often used, is when working with generic types. In the next chapter, where we cover templates, we'll start putting the `is` expression to use.

Alignment

Many C and C++ programmers will be familiar with data alignment and data structure padding given the emphasis placed on cache-friendly code these days. For those who aren't familiar with the topics, a good introduction for a broader understanding can be found at `http://en.wikipedia.org/wiki/Data_structure_alignment`. Here, we're going to focus on what it looks like in D. Consider the following example:

```
struct Packed {
    double x;
    float y;
```

```
        byte z;
        byte w;
    }
    void main() {
        import std.stdio : writeln;
        writeln(Packed.x.offsetof);
        writeln(Packed.y.offsetof);
        writeln(Packed.z.offsetof);
        writeln(Packed.w.offsetof);
    }
```

The `Packed` data structure has its members ordered from largest to smallest. The result is that the compiler is able to align each member on byte boundaries that are tightly packed. This can be verified by querying the `.offsetof` property available on all `struct` and `class` member variables. The preceding example results in the following output:

```
0
8
12
13
```

The first member of a `struct` will always have an offset of `0`. Since x is a `double` and `double.sizeof` is `8`, then the address of the variable y is going to be the address of x plus eight bytes. The following snippet shows this clearly.

```
    Packed p;
    writeln(cast(void*)&p.y - cast(void*)&p.x);
```

Note that the casts to `void*` are needed here, as `float*` and `double*` are incompatible types. This will print `8` to the console, matching the value of `Packed.y.offsetof`.

Continuing on this line, since y is a four-byte value, the offset of z is four bytes past y, or `12`. Since z is a one-byte value, the offset of w is one byte past z, or `13`. But this is not really the full story. Change the type of w from `byte` to `int` and the output becomes the following:

```
0
8
12
16
```

Even though z is only a one-byte value, w now begins four bytes past it rather than one. A more dramatic demonstration of this behavior can be seen in the following example, where the NotPacked data structure has a different set of types.

```
struct NotPacked {
    int x;
    long y;
    byte z;
    double w;
}
void main() {
    import std.stdio : writeln;
    writeln(NotPacked.x.offsetof);
    writeln(NotPacked.y.offsetof);
    writeln(NotPacked.z.offsetof);
    writeln(NotPacked.w.offsetof);
}
```

For this, the output is the following:

```
0
8
16
24
```

Ultimately, the offset of a member depends not only on the size of the preceding type, but on the default alignment of the member's type. In this example, x is still four bytes in size but, more importantly, the default alignment of long is 8. We can see this by querying its .alignof property (available on all types).

```
writeln(long.alignof);
```

This will print 8. What it means is that the memory address of any long variable must be a multiple of 8. When the compiler generates the code for any instance of NotPacked, the address four bytes past x is not going to be divisible by 8, so it puts y another four bytes further on to satisfy that requirement. byte.alignof gives us 1, so it can always immediately follow whatever is in front of it. Therefore, the offset of z is 16, which is at the very end of y. Finally, double.alignof is 8, so it's impossible for the offset of w in NotPacked to be 17. Instead, the compiler moves it to the next address that is a multiple of 8, so its offset becomes 24.

The result of all of this is that there are four unused bytes between x and y, with a further seven unused bytes between z and w. These unused bytes are called **padding** and, though they inflate the size of the data structure, they make it much more efficient for the CPU to access members in memory. NotPacked.sizeof is 32, but reorder things so that the long and double are at the top, followed by the int, then the byte last, and the size becomes 24 (there will still be three padding bytes following the byte at the end). Then it can be called a packed data structure, meaning there is no padding in the interior.

There are times when it may be desirable to pack a data structure without reordering the members. One common example is when reading and writing chunks from or to a file that follows a predefined format. Rather than reading or writing each member one at a time, it can be more efficient to transfer the entire structure in one go. Imagine a file format that specifies a header consisting of a byte value, followed by a four-byte value and ending with another byte, for a total of six bytes. As a struct, it looks like:

```
struct FileHeader {
    byte version;
    int magic;
    byte id;
}
```

Try to read or write an instance of FileHeader directly and there's a problem. You can see it clearly in the following image:

There are three padding bytes between fmtVersion and magic, with another three padding bytes past id, yielding a total of twelve bytes instead of six. Writing the entire structure directly means that the file header no longer follows the predefined format, as all the padding bytes will be written, too. Conversely, reading a properly formatted file will cause the first three bytes of magic to go into the three padding bytes after fmtVersion and id to go into the second byte of magic, resulting in all three fields having incorrect values.

Given that a `struct` is a type, it has an `.alignof` property like any other built-in type. However, the property has no predefined value; it takes on the alignment value of its largest member type. In `FileHeader`, the largest member type is `int`, with an alignment of 4, so `FileHeader` also has an alignment of 4. The alignment of a `struct` type does not just affect how instances of that type are aligned in relation to other variables, but also how memory is allocated for the instance itself. This is why `FileHeader.sizeof` is 12: its alignment is 4, so members must be allocated on four-byte boundaries.

As the earlier image demonstrates, the number of four-byte blocks that need to be allocated in this case is three. `fmtVersion` takes up only one of the bytes it was allocated. The next member is an `int`, which requires four bytes and, therefore, another block of memory; its alignment of 4 dictates that it can't use the three free bytes of the first block. Finally, because `magic` fills its entire block, a third block is allocated for `id`, which again only needs one byte, leaving three unused. If a `short` is added between `fmtVersion` and magic, the size of `FileHeader` does not change. Since `short` has an alignment requirement of two bytes and also a size of two bytes, it fits snugly in the last two bytes of the first memory block. Similarly, another `short` could be tacked on to the end and the size would remain twelve bytes.

In C or C++, the padding bytes could be eliminated by packing the data structure via a compiler-specific #pragma preprocessor directive. In D, we get something that's defined by the language instead: `align`. It can apply to one declaration or, using a colon or braces, multiple declarations. Let's make all of the `FileHeader` members byte-aligned.

```
struct FileHeader {
align(1):
  byte fmtVersion;
  int magic;
  byte id;
}
```

Now all of the members directly follow each other in memory, with no padding between.

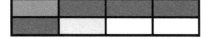

However, notice that there are still two empty bytes at the end. This is because `FileHeader.sizeof` is still 4, so memory for its members is still allocated on four-byte boundaries. To completely eliminate the padding bytes, it's necessary to add an align attribute to the `FileHeader` type as well.

```
align(1) struct FileHeader {
align(1):
    byte fmtVersion;
    int magic;
    byte id;
}
```

`FileHeader.sizeof` now gives us 6 instead of 8 or 12, meaning we have eliminated the padding bytes completely. We can now safely read and write entire arrays of `FileHeader` instances in one go without fear of data becoming corrupt because of padding. Note, however, that `FileHeader.alignof` is still 4; we have not changed how instances of the type are aligned, only how memory is allocated for its members. As with any other variable, the alignment of `struct` instances is changed by including an `align` attribute in the variable declaration.

There's a big, giant caveat to go with `align`. Data structures with erratic alignment are going to be more expensive to manipulate. Accessing a member at an odd boundary in memory can cause more work for the CPU. This is great for improving the speed of I/O, but the alignment of any data structures that are to be manipulated frequently throughout the life of a program should only be changed with great care, if at all. It's better to manually pack things by changing the order of declaration. Finally, `align` is not exclusively for use with data structures; it can be prefixed to any variable declaration in any scope. It's rare to do so, however, and using it with data structures is more common.

Classes and .alignof

Remember that querying properties on a `class` type or instance is returning values for a class reference, not an entire data structure. `.alignof` for a `class` is always 4 in 32-bit and 8 in 64-bit, no matter the alignment of the members.

Compile-time reflection

Several existing languages, particularly those that run on a virtual machine, have support for runtime reflection. If you aren't familiar with the concept, see `http://en.wikipedia.org/wiki/Reflection_(computer_programming)` for an introduction. D has some support for runtime reflection now and there are plans afoot to expand upon it. More interesting for many D users is its support for compile-time reflection. This enables a number of possibilities for both generative and generic programming that wouldn't otherwise be possible.

A language feature that exists exclusively for compile-time reflection is the `__traits` expression. It takes at least two arguments. The first is a keyword indicating the type of trait to query, followed by one or more types or expressions. Some examples:

```
enum a = __traits(isUnsigned, uint);
enum b = __traits(isUnsigned, 10 + 11);
enum c = __traits(isUnsigned, 10u + 11u);
enum d = __traits(isUnsigned, uint, 10u + 11u, 10.0 - 9.0);
```

In the declaration of a, the second argument to `__traits` is a type. Since `uint` is unsigned, a is initialized to `true`. The initialization of b uses an expression. The literals `10` and `11` are both of type `int`, so the result of the expression is also an `int`. That means b is set to `false`. c is initialized to `true`, as the result of the expression is `uint`, thanks to the u suffix on the literals. Finally, in the declaration of d, multiple arguments are passed after `isUnsigned`. In this case, all of the arguments must pass the test in order for the entire expression to return `true`. Since the last argument, `10.0 - 9.0`, results in a `double`, d is set to `false`.

There are a number of Boolean traits, but there are others that return something completely different. Take, for example, the `getMember` trait. This can be used to indirectly set or get a member variable in a `struct` or `class`.

```
struct Point {
  int x, y;
}
void main() {
  auto p = Point(10, 20);
  writeln(__traits(getMember, p, "x"));
  __traits(getMember, p, "y") = 33;
  writeln(p.y);
}
```

Remember, `__traits` is evaluated at compile time, so the two highlighted lines ultimately cause code to be generated that is the same as is generated when `writeln(p.x)` and `p.y = 33` are used. Some traits return a set of values; for example, `allMembers` returns a set of `strings` containing the names of each member of a `struct`, `class`, or `enum`.

```
pragma(msg, __traits(allMembers, Point));
```

Compiling this with the `Point` type prints:

`tuple("x", "y")`

There is a Phobos module, `std.traits`, providing alternative implementations of several built-in traits. Generally, it's encouraged to use these over the built-ins. We'll take a look at `std.traits` in the next chapter (and one convenience function before the end of this chapter). For more on built-in traits, refer to `http://dlang.org/traits.html`.

User-defined attributes

User-defined attributes, or **UDAs**, allow you to associate metadata with your variables and functions. The attributes can be examined at compile time to generate different code paths. There are different ways to implement a UDA. The simplest is to use a literal, such as the integer literal in this example.

```
@(1) int myVal;
```

To determine at compile time what attributes `myVal` has, use the `getAttributes` trait.

```
pragma(msg, __traits(getAttributes, myVal));
```

This will print the following:

`tuple(1)`

Integer literals aren't really the best option for implementing UDAs. There's absolutely no scoping for a literal and two libraries may interpret `1` quite differently. It's more appropriate to declare UDAs that have a name with some special meaning. Here's one possible approach:

```
enum NoPrint;
struct Foo {
    int x;
    @NoPrint int y;
}
```

A function (preferably a template) could be implemented that only prints data that isn't annotated with @NoPrint. Literals and manifest constants can become UDAs because they are known at compile time. Aggregate types work as well.

```
struct NoPrint {}
struct NoSave {}
enum Decoration {
  none,
  italics,
  bold,
}
struct Decorated {
  Decoration decoration;
}
struct Data {
  @Decorated(Decoration.Bold) string name;
  @Decorated(Decoration.Italics) string occupation;
  @NoSave @NoPrint int temporary;
}
```

All the attributes of a single member of a data structure can be examined with __traits.

```
pragma(msg, __traits(getAttributes, Data.temporary));
```

Compile time reflection can be used to grab the attributes of every member.

```
foreach(member; __traits(allMembers, Data)) {
  enum name = "Data." ~ member;
  writef("Attributes of %s: ", name);

  foreach(attr; __traits(getAttributes, mixin(name))) {
    static if(is(typeof(attr) == Decorated)) {
      Decoration dec = __traits(getMember, attr, "decoration");
      writef("Decoration.%s", dec);
    } else {
      writef(" %s", attr.stringof);
    }
  }
  writeln();
}
```

First up, a `foreach` loop is being run on the members of `Data`. It's worth noting that, because the return value from `__traits` is a compile-time value, the loop is actually being unrolled at compile time. The same is true for the inner loop. In order to get the attributes of any specific member of `Data`, the qualified form of the name must be used, such as `Data.occupation`. The names returned by `allMembers` are not qualified, so the qualified names have to be constructed manually: `"Data." ~ member`.

When it's time to fetch the attributes, the qualified member name must be passed to `__traits` as an identifier, and not as a string. It needs the name of the member as it is written in code, e.g. `Data.occupation` and not `"Data.occupation"`. A string mixin is used to generate an identifier from the string value of `name`. As the attributes are iterated, a test is performed on each with `is(typeof(attr) == Decorated)`.

Attributes can be types or values. This has consequences when a `struct` is used to define the attribute. `@NoSave` is a type attribute, whereas `@NoSave()` is a value attribute. The former can be tested with `is(attr == NoSave)`. The latter will fail that test, since a value can't be compared with a type. Therefore, the test in that case must be `is(typeof(attr) == NoSave)`. Notice that `Decorated` is used as a value attribute, initialized in each case with a member of the `Decoration` enumeration. The loop uses `static if` to determine if the current property is an instance of `Decorated` and, if so, uses the `getMember` trait to fetch the value of its `decoration` member.

If the attribute is not a `Decorated` instance, then the `.stringof` property is used to get the name of the attribute as a string. A type can't be printed at runtime (though it can be at compile time with a `msg` pragma), so each type must be converted to a string via `.stringof`. This is the opposite of the problem solved by string mixins, where strings are converted to symbols.

When writing a function that looks for multiple attributes, the type/value dichotomy can make for some convoluted code. Thankfully, `std.traits` provides a template function to hide all of the complexity.

```
import std.traits : hasUDA;
static if(hasUDA!(Data.temporary, NoSave))
    writeln("Data.temporary can't be saved!");
```

This will return true no matter if `Data.temporary` was annotated with `@NoSave` or `@NoSave()`. As of DMD 2.069, `std.traits` also includes the functions `getUDAs` and `getSymbolsByUDA`.

Summary

In this chapter, we have examined several different, independent compile-time features. You've learned how to use the `pragma` statement to print compile-time messages and link with libraries in code. You've taken a look at how to implement conditional compilation with `version`, `debug`, and `static if`. You've gone through the basic usage of the `import` expression and string mixins, and learned how to force functions to be evaluated at compile time. Finally, we've examined `static assert`, the `is` expression, data alignment, compile-time reflection, and user-defined attributes.

The purpose of this chapter is to set the stage for the next chapter, which introduces templates. Using templates with the compile-time features covered here opens the door to a whole new world.

5
Generic Programming Made Easy

One of the benefits of generic programming is that it enables the implementation of type-independent code. A single function can be written once to support multiple types, rather than once for each supported type. Several languages allow for generic programming to one degree or another. Some implementations are easy to use, but not very powerful; others are powerful, but difficult to learn. Throughout my time in the D community, I have seen numerous remarks in the newsgroups, reddit threads, and elsewhere, praising the simplicity and power of D templates. Combined with the compile-time features covered in the previous chapter, even novice programmers can quickly learn to do things that might seem daunting in other languages.

I have to work from the assumption that many readers will not be as familiar with generic programming as others. With that in mind, we're going to start with a look at the very basics of using templates in D and progressively work our way through to more advanced usage. We aren't going to cover everything there is to know about templates, but we'll cover enough that you'll be able to use them to great effect in your own code. The flow of the chapter looks like this:

- Template declarations: templates as code blocks, struct, class, enum, and function templates
- Template parameters: value, alias, and this parameters
- Beyond the basics: template specializations, template constraints, template mixins, and variadic templates
- Operator overloads: several overloadable operators
- MovieMan: the database

Template basics

As a barebones definition, we might say that a template is a block of code that doesn't exist until it is used. A template can be declared in a source module, but if it is never instantiated, it doesn't get compiled into the final binary. Further, there are different ways to declare a template and several ways to control how it is compiled into the binary. In this section, we're going to explore the former.

Templates as code blocks

A template declaration looks somewhat like a function declaration. It opens with the `template` keyword, followed by an identifier, a parameter list, and then a pair of braces for the body. The body may contain any valid D declaration except module declarations, as the following example demonstrates:

```
template MyTemplate(T) {
  T val;
  void printVal() {
    import std.stdio : writeln;
    writeln("The type is ", typeid(T));
    writeln("The value is ", val);
  }
}
```

The first line declares a `template` named `MyTemplate` that takes one parameter, `T`. This isn't the same as a function parameter. There are different kinds of template parameters, but in this case `T` is intended to refer to a type. It can be any type: `int`, `float`, a user-defined type, and so on. Most templates are parameterized.

After the template parameter list, multiple declarations can appear inside a pair of braces. This example declares a variable of type `T` named `val` and a function called `printVal` that uses `val`. If compiled at this point, neither `val` nor `printVal` would be present in the binary. For that to happen, the template must be instantiated at least once.

When a template is instantiated, any declarations inside it are compiled, with the given template arguments replacing its parameters. The following snippet instantiates two instances of `MyTemplate` using two different types and two different approaches:

```
MyTemplate!(int).val = 20;
MyTemplate!int.printVal();
alias mtf = MyTemplate!float;
mtf.printVal();
```

Taken together, the two snippets yield the following output:

```
The type is int
The value is 20
The type is float
The value is nan
```

The first line of `main` instantiates `MyTemplate` with `int`. This is accomplished by putting the template instantiation operator, `!`, after the template name, followed by the type argument list. In the same line, `val` is set to `20`. `MyTemplate!(int)` acts as a namespace for each declaration in the body. Both members are accessed with the dot operator.

The second line demonstrates two points. First, the parentheses around the type parameter have been dropped. When a template declaration takes only one parameter, the parentheses are usually optional in the instantiation, though sometimes they are required; for example, the brackets in an array type such as `int []` make the parentheses mandatory. Second, when `printVal` is called, it shows that the type of `T` is `int` and its value is `20`. This verifies that it refers to the same instance of the template that was instantiated in the first line, where `val` is set to `20`. If this were part of a larger program, then any usage of `MyTemplate!int`, in any module, is referring to the same instance of `val` and the same implementation of `printVal`.

The third line sets up for a different approach to instantiation by creating an `alias`. This both instantiates the template and makes `mtf` a synonym for `MyTemplate!float`. The very next line calls `printVal` through the alias. This prints the type as `float` and the value as `nan`, since `val` was never set for the `float` version of `MyTemplate`.

Template instantiation happens in the same scope as the declaration, not that of the instantiation. Consider this module, `declscope`, with its `addTwo` function:

```
module declscope;
int addTwo(int x) {
  return x + 2;
}
template NumTemplate() {
  enum constant = addTwo(10);
}
```

It should be obvious that `addTwo(10)` is calling the function declared here, but what happens when `NumTemplate` is instantiated in the following `intscope` module, which has its own `addTwo`?:

```
module intscope;
int addTwo(int x) {
  // We lied, we're adding 20
  return x + 20;
}
void main() {
  import declscope, std.stdio;
  writeln(NumTemplate!().constant);
}
```

It's easy to believe that the body of the template is being pasted somewhere around the instantiation, but that isn't the case. Compiling this and running it results in 12, not 20, meaning `declscope.addTwo` is being called inside the template. Remember, a template is only instantiated once for each set of arguments and the same instantiation can be repeated in multiple modules throughout a program. If each instantiation were scoped locally, the template would no longer work as expected.

It's also worth noting that the template in the previous example takes no parameters. When it's instantiated, the instantiation operator and parentheses are required and the parentheses have to be empty. It may appear to be pointless to have a typeless template; after all, supporting multiple types with a single block of code is a major benefit of generic programming. We'll see later that typeless templates can be put to good use.

If one instance of `val` per instantiation is not sufficient, the template body can be rewritten so that `val` and `printVal` are wrapped inside a `struct` or `class`:

```
template MyTemplate(T) {
  struct ValWrapper {
    T val;
    void printVal() {
      import std.stdio : writeln;
      writeln("The type is ", typeid(T));
      writeln("The value is ", val);
    }
  }
}
void main() {
  MyTemplate!int.ValWrapper vw1;
  MyTemplate!int.ValWrapper vw2;
  vw1.val = 20;
```

```
    vw2.val = 30;
    vw1.printVal();
    vw2.printVal();
}
```

Although it looks like `MyTemplate` is instantiated twice here, that's not what's happening. The template is still instantiated only once. Instead, two instances of `MyTemplate!int.ValWrapper` are declared. The instantiation effectively creates a new `ValWrapper` declaration as if the following had been explicitly declared:

```
struct ValWrapper {
    int val;
    void printVal() {...}
}
```

If the template is instantiated with a different type, it creates a new declaration of `ValWrapper`. If it's never instantiated, then `ValWrapper` never exists as a type. Although multiple declarations can go inside a template body, it's quite common to declare a single `struct`, `class`, function, or even a manifest constant. In that case, we can do away with the tediousness of the dot operator and take some shortcuts.

Struct and class templates

In 1975, Fleetwood Mac released an album titled *Fleetwood Mac*. Six years later, it was in reference to that album that the 10-year-old me first made the connection between the words *eponymous* and *self-titled* while listening to the radio. In D, self-titled templates are a thing. Let's rewrite `MyTemplate` once more, this time making it eponymous:

```
template ValWrapper(T) {
    struct ValWrapper {
        T val;
        void printVal() {
            writeln("The type is ", typeid(T));
            writeln("The value is ", val);
        }
    }
}
```

Now that the `template` and `struct` declarations have the same name, the dot operator can be dropped from instantiations and instances of `ValWrapper` declared directly:

```
ValWrapper!int vw;
```

That's much nicer syntax, isn't it? The language also allows for a shortcut in the `template` declaration. By simply adding the parameter list to the `struct` declaration, the `template` block is eliminated completely. The declaration then becomes:

```
struct ValWrapper(T) {
  T val;
  void printVal() {
    writeln("The type is ", typeid(T));
    writeln("The value is ", val);
  }
}
```

This is a **struct template**. The instantiation syntax is the same as it was for the first version of the eponymous template. If it is expected to be used often, alias declarations can be added at module scope to help make the instantiation syntax even cleaner:

```
alias ValWrapperI = ValWrapper!int;
alias ValWrapperF = ValWrapper!float;
```

A **class template** is similar:

```
class ValClass(T) {
private:
  T _val;
public:
  this(T val) {
    _val = val;
  }
  T val() @property {
    return _val;
  }
}
```

It can be instantiated like this:

```
auto vc = new ValClass!int(10);
```

When multiple type parameters are involved, the parentheses in the instantiation are no longer optional and two pairs are needed when invoking the constructor. The following partial implementation of a wrapper for associative arrays demonstrates:

```
class HashMap(K,V) {
  V[K] _map;
  string _name;
  this(string name) {
```

```
    _name = name;
  }
}
```

When instantiating one of these, it's going to look a bit more cluttered:

```
auto map = new HashMap!(string, int)("NameMap");
```

Always remember that the first pair of parentheses contains the template arguments and the second the constructor arguments.

It's also possible to inherit from a template `class` or `interface`:

```
interface Transformation(T) {
  T transform(T t);
}
class Double(T) : Transformation!T {
  T transform(T t) {
    return t * 2;
  }
}
```

When an instance of `Double` is instantiated, it in turn instantiates the `Transformation` interface with the same type. Then, a `Double!int` can be passed anywhere a `Transformation!int` is expected:

```
struct Value(T) {
  T val;
  Transformation!T transformation;
  T transform() {
    val = transformation.transform(val);
    return val;
  }
}
void main() {
  import std.stdio : writeln;
  auto = Value!int(10, new Double!int);
  writeln(intVal.transform());
}
```

When `Value` is instantiated with `int`, its member `transformation` is expected to be of type `Transformation!int`, which is exactly what it is initialized with when `new Double!int` is used in the struct literal. Note that, since `Value` is a template, the literal form must also be a template instantiation. Though not covered here, it's also possible to declare union templates.

Enum templates

An **enum template** is a templated manifest constant. Let's look at the long form first:

```
template isLongOrInt(T) {
    enum isLongOrInt = is(T == long) || is(T == int);
}
```

Dig around the source for Phobos and you'll find several declarations like this, all written before the shortened syntax was introduced for enum templates. Now we can do this:

```
enum isLongOrInt(T) = is(T == long) || is(T == int);
```

Instantiating an enum template causes the value of the manifest constant in the template body to be substituted at the point it is used at:

```
writeln(isLongOrInt!long);
writeln(isLongOrInt!float);
```

In this snippet, the first instantiation will be replaced at compile time by `true` and the second by `false`. It's conceptually the equivalent of the following:

```
enum isLongOrInt_Long = true;
enum isLongOrInt_Float = false;
writeln(isLongOrInt_Long);
writeln(isLongOrInt_Float);
```

These really come in handy when working with repetitive `static if` conditions or, as we'll see later in this chapter, template constraints. When a compile-time condition needs frequent use, consider turning it into an enum template.

Function templates

We've already made use of a few function templates in the book, such as `std.conv.to` and, believe it or not, `std.stdio.writeln`. Before we look into why the former requires the template instantiation operator and the latter doesn't, let's first take a look at what a function template declaration looks like. First, the long form:

```
template sum(T) {
    T sum(T lhs, T rhs) {
        return lhs + rhs;
    }
}
```

And now, the more common short form:

```
T sum(T)(T lhs, T rhs) {
    return lhs + rhs;
}
```

There are two pairs of parentheses in the declaration. As is obvious in the long form, the first pair holds the template parameters and the second is for the function parameters. Instantiating and calling a function template can be done in two ways, as seen here:

```
auto doubles = sum!double(2.0, 3.0);
auto floats = sum(2.0f, 3.0f);
writeln(typeid(floats));
```

The first line instantiates the template in the same way we've seen for every case we've examined so far, by specifying the types in the argument list. Again, the parentheses are optional on a single argument, but are required if there are more. The second line is more interesting in this example. Notice that there is neither an instantiation operator nor a template argument anywhere to be found (the same is true for `writeln`). This is because the compiler is able to infer T from the function arguments, so there's no need to specify them. This is called **Implicit Function Template Instantiation (IFTI)**. IFTI is quite convenient, but isn't always possible. Consider this example that wraps `std.conv.to` in order to convert a `struct` member variable into a different type:

```
struct Value {
    private int _val;
    T getAs(T)() {
        import std.conv : to;
        return to!T(val);
    }
}
```

First, note that the member function `getAs` is a template, but `Value` itself is not. Member function templates are instantiated like any other function template, except that they must be called through the dot operator on the type instance like a normal member function:

```
auto value = Value(100);
auto valstr = value.getAs!string();
```

Take out the !string bit and there is no way for the compiler to know that value.val should be converted to a string and not a double, a bool, or anything else. In that case, IFTI will fail with a compiler error. Modify getAs to take an argument to use as a default value, then the situation changes:

```
T getAs(T)(T defVal) {
    import std.conv : to;
    try {
        return to!T(val);
    } catch(Exception e) {
        return defVal;
    }
}
```

Now the compiler has enough information to implicitly deduce the type of T from the type of defVal in the function call, for example value.getAs("DefaultVal").

Reducing dependencies

In the getAs example, std.conv : to is a local import. As it is inside a template, std.conv will never be imported if the template is never instantiated. Keeping imports local when writing templated code is a great way to reduce dependencies and good practice even in non-templated code.

Special features

There are a couple of special features of function templates that are not available to normal functions. First, consider the following:

```
int addTwo()(int x) {
    return x + 2;
}
int addTwoInt(int x) nothrow {
    return addTwo(x);
}
```

Recall that a function marked nothrow can only call other functions marked nothrow. There is no guarantee that the compiler will always have the source available for a normal function, but the source for a template must always be available. Due to this, the compiler can safely use the source of any function template to infer certain function attributes (@safe, pure, nothrow, and @nogc). In this case, when addTwoInt calls addTwo, the compiler verifies that addTwo can't throw anything and allows compilation. If addTwo were to directly throw an Exception or call a function that isn't nothrow, then it would no longer be inferred as nothrow itself.

Another feature of function templates is **auto ref parameters**. Consider this:

```
void printLargeStruct (const(LargeStruct) p) {…}
void printLargeStruct(ref const(LargeStruct) p) {…}
```

If the first version of `printLargeStruct` were the only one, it would accept both l-values and r-values. The l-values would be copied, something that's inefficient for a large struct. By also declaring a `ref` version of the function, we ensure that l-values will be passed by reference. However, maintaining two versions of the same function is error-prone. With a function template that takes `auto ref` parameters, one implementation can handle both:

```
void printLargeStruct()(auto ref const(LargeStruct) p) {…}
```

Note that both `addTwo` and `printLargetStruct` have empty template parameter lists. Function templates with empty parameter lists are sometimes used in place of normal functions solely to get the benefits of `auto ref`.

One last thing to say about function templates: they cannot be virtual. All member functions in a `class` declaration are virtual by default and can be overridden by subclasses, but templated member functions cannot be.

More template parameters

While types are perhaps the most common form of template parameter, there are others. We're going to examine three of them, beginning with value parameters.

Value parameters

The following example is a partial implementation of a wrapper for D's array type:

```
struct Array(T, size_t size = 0) {
  static if(size > 0)
    T[size] elements;
  else
    T[] elements;
  enum isDynamic = Size == 0;
}
```

`Array` is a struct template that has two parameters, a type parameter `T` and a value parameter `size`. We know that `T` is a type parameter because it's a single identifier. Whether it's called `T`, or `Type`, or `Foo`, or whatever, a solitary identifier in a template parameter list represents a type. `size` is identifiable as a value parameter because it is composed of a specific type followed by an identifier, just as if it were in the parameter list of a function. A value parameter binds to any expression that can be evaluated at compile time, such as literals and function calls. Notice that `size` is assigned a default value. This means an argument corresponding to `size` is optional during instantiation, meaning `Array` can be instantiated with one argument for `T`.

Template parameters are always compile-time entities. The implementation of `Array` makes use of that fact to decide whether it should be a static or a dynamic array. This is accomplished at compile time with a `static if`. If `size` is greater than `0`, the member variable `elements` is declared as a static array with length `size`; otherwise, `elements` is a dynamic array. The manifest constant `isDynamic` is initialized as a Boolean with `size == 0`, causing any read of its value to be replaced by the compiler with `true` or `false` directly.

Here are two possible instantiations of `Array`:

```
Array!int arr1;
assert(arr1.isDynamic);
Array!(float, 10) arr2;
assert(!arr2.isDynamic);
```

As the asserts verify, the first instantiation yields an instance of `Array` wrapping a dynamic array. Since `size` is an optional argument, it's still possible to drop the parentheses when only the first argument is specified in the instantiation. The second instantiation results in an instance containing a static array of type `float` and length `10`. Though the example uses a literal to specify `size`, any compile-time expression that results in a `size_t` can be used. For example, given this function:

```
double getADouble() { return 100.0; }
```

We can use CTFE to instantiate the template like so:

```
Array!(float, cast(size_t)getADouble()) arr3;
```

Alias parameters

While types and values as template parameters open the door to a variety of possibilities, D goes further and allows the use of symbols as template parameters. This is possible through the use of **alias parameters**.

The following function template takes any symbol and prints its string representation to standard output:

```
void printSymbol(alias Name)() {
    writeln(Name.stringof);
}
```

Here the template is instantiated with several different symbols:

```
int x;
printSymbol!x();                  // Variable name
printSymbol!printSymbol();        // Function template name
printSymbol!(std.conv.to)();      // FQN of function template
printSymbol!(std.stdio)();        // Module name
```

Note that the parentheses around the solitary template arguments are required for the last two instantiations due to the dots in the symbol names. The output looks like this:

x

printSymbol(alias Name)()

to(T)

module stdio

In addition to symbols, alias parameters can also bind to any expression that can be evaluated at compile time, including literals:

```
enum number = 10;
printSymbol!number();
printSymbol!(1+3)();
printSymbol!"Hello"();
printSymbol!(addTwo(3))();
```

Together with the following function:

```
int addTwo(int x) { return x + 2; }
```

This yields the following output:

10

4

"Hello"

5

As I write, D does not support any of the keyword types as template alias parameters, so instantiations such as `printSymbol!int` and `printSymbol!class` will not compile.

This parameters

Recall that every class instance has a reference to itself called `this`. The following `class` declaration includes a function that prints the type of `this`:

```
class Base {
  void printType() { writeln(typeid(this)); }
}
class Derived : Base {}
```

Now let's see what it prints in two specific circumstances:

```
Derived deri = new Derived;
Base base = new Derived;
deri.printType();
base.printType();
```

Running this will show that, in both cases, the printed type is `Derived`, which is the actual type of both instances. Most of the time, this is exactly the desired behavior, but now and again it might be useful to know the static (or declared) type of an instance, rather than the actual type. The static type of `base` is `Base`, as that is the type used in the declaration. A `this` parameter can be used to get the static type. These are special in that they can only be used with member functions. Change the declaration of `Base` to this:

```
class Base {
  void printType(this T)() { writeln(typeid(T)); }
}
```

Calling this version of `printType` will print `Derived` for `deri` and `Base` for `base`. This is most useful in template mixins, which we'll see later in the chapter.

Template `this` parameters can also be used in `struct` declarations, though their usefulness is more limited given that structs in D are not polymorphic. However, a possible use case is demonstrated in the following declaration:

```
struct TypeMe {
  void printType(this T)() const {
    writeln(T.stringof);
  }
}
```

As `printType` is declared as `const`, it can be called on any instance of `TypeMe`, whether it was declared as `const`, `immutable`, or unqualified. The template `this` parameter can be used to determine which:

```
const(TypeMe) ct;
immutable(TypeMe) it;
TypeMe t;
ct.printType();
it.printType();
t.printType();
```

Beyond the basics

A lot can be accomplished using the template features we've examined so far. In this section, we're going to see how to make our templates more powerful, through features that are easy to learn and use. We'll start with template specializations.

Template specializations

All instantiations of a template get the same implementation of the template body. Parameters may be substituted in different places, but the overall implementation doesn't change. However, there are times when it's useful for a template to behave differently when instantiated with different types. Simple cases, where one or two lines are different for one or two types, are easy to configure at compile time with `static if`, but sometimes the code is hard to read. In more complex cases, such as when different types require completely different implementations, `static if` is not practical.

Template specializations allow us to implement multiple versions of the same template for different types. Earlier, we implemented a function template called `sum` that takes two arguments and adds them together. Let's assume for the sake of this example that, when dealing with floating point types, we'd like to round to the nearest whole number. Such a simple case can be implemented with `static if` and `std.traits.isFloatingPoint`:

```
T sum(T)(T lhs, T rhs) {
  import std.traits : isFloatingPoint;
  T ret = lhs + rhs;
  static if (isFloatingPoint!T) {
    import std.math : round;
    ret = round(ret);
  }
  return ret;
}
```

Easily done, but look at the tradeoff; the simple one-line function body is now seven lines long. Also, there's a new dependency on std.traits just to determine whether we're dealing with a floating point type. We can do better. A template can be made to specialize on a type by declaring the type identifier as normal, followed by a colon and the name of the specialized type. The following version of sum specializes on all floating point types:

```
T sum(T : real)(T lhs, T rhs) {
    import std.math : round;
    return round(lhs + rhs);
}
```

Since all floating point types are implicitly convertible to real, this will catch them all. Unfortunately, this won't quite do the trick by itself:

```
T sum(T)(T lhs, T rhs) {
    return cast(T)(lhs + rhs);
}
T sum(T : real)(T lhs, T rhs) {
    import std.math : round;
    return round(lhs + rhs);
}
void main() {
    import std.stdio : writeln;
    writeln(sum(10, 20));
}
```

Save this as $LEARNINGD/Chapter05/sum.d. Attempting to compile should produce the following compiler errors:

```
sum.d(9): Error: cannot implicitly convert expression
(round(cast(real)(lhs + rhs))) of type real to int

sum.d(12): Error: template instance sum.sum!int error instantiating
```

The second error indicates that the template failed to instantiate. The first error, which comes from inside the template body, shows the reason instantiation failed. Recall that integrals are implicitly convertible to floating point types, but the reverse is not true. In the example, sum is instantiated with int, since that's the type of both 10 and 20. This matches the specialization because int is implicitly convertible to real. The error happens because the instantiation of sum expects to return int, but it's actually trying to return real, which is the return type of round. Since real is not implicitly convertible to int, the compiler errors out and the template fails to instantiate. To fix this, add a new specialization to catch only integrals.

Since all integrals are implicitly convertible to `ulong`, and since it's a better match for integrals than `real`, it can be used to get the job done. With two specializations to catch floating point and integral types, the original will pick up anything remaining, such as arrays, pointers or user-defined types. To disallow those, simply delete the original template and keep the two specializations:

```
import std.stdio;
T sum(T : ulong)(T lhs, T rhs) {
  writeln("Integral specialization.");
  return cast(T)(lhs + rhs);
}
T sum(T : real)(T lhs, T rhs) {
  writeln("Floating-point specialization.");
  import std.math : round;
  return round(lhs + rhs);
}
void main() {
  writeln(sum(10, 20));
  writeln(sum(10.11, 3.22));
}
```

Specialization on pointers and arrays

When `sum` is instantiated, it isn't necessary to explicitly specify a type; the type is implicitly deduced from the function arguments. Unfortunately, when a type is implicitly deduced, it's possible that no specialization will match. In practice, this isn't a problem for most types. While it works just fine for the `sum` template with integrals and floating point types, you would be in for a surprise if you tried to specialize on a pointer or array.

Let's leave `sum` behind and implement a new function template called `printVal`. This will take a single argument of any type and print it to standard output. The base form of the template looks like this:

```
void printVal(T)(T t) {
  writeln(t);
}
```

Try to instantiate this with any type and it will work flawlessly. The only potential issue is what to do about pointers. By default, `writeln` prints the address of a pointer. If that's the desired behavior, then nothing further need be done. What if, instead, we want to print the value the pointer is pointing to? In that case, we need a specialization. Specializing on a specific type of pointer is no different than doing so for any type:

```
void printVal(T : int*)(T t) {
  writeln(*t);
}
```

But who wants to write a version of `printVal` for every conceivable pointer type? To specialize on any pointer, no matter the base type, the following syntax is used:

```
void printVal(T : U*, U)(T t) {
   writeln(*t);
}
```

The second template parameter, `U`, is what allows this function to specialize on any pointer. Whatever type `U` is, then `T` is specialized on a pointer to that type. Explicit instantiation can look like either of the following lines:

```
printVal!(int*, int)(&x);
printVal!(int*)(&x);
```

When there are multiple template parameters, it's not necessary to pass an argument for all of them if the remainder can be deduced. In the second declaration, the compiler can deduce that, if `T` is `int*`, then `U` must be `int`. This can be verified by adding `writeln(U.stringof)` to `printVal`. IFTI also works:

```
printVal(&x);
```

The same form can be used to specialize on arrays:

```
void printVal(T: U[], U)(T t) {
   foreach(e; t)
      writeln(e);
}
void main() {
   printVal([10, 20, 30]);
}
```

Note that, as I write, the documentation says that IFTI will not work with templates that use type specialization. That came as a surprise to several users involved in a forum discussion, since it's been working in the compiler for quite a while. Given the history of D development, it is more likely that the documentation will be changed to match the behavior than the other way around, but the possibility does exist that the behavior could change at some point. Anyway, for now it works and code in the wild is using it.

Template constraints

Template specialization is useful, but it can be hard sometimes be difficult to get right and doesn't fit every use case. Template constraints offer a more comprehensive alternative. The following two implementations of sum achieve the same result as the two specializations from earlier:

```
import std.traits;
T sum(T)(T lhs, T rhs) if(isFloatingPoint!T) {
  import std.math : round;
  return round(lhs + rhs);
}
T sum(T)(T lhs, T rhs) if(isIntegral!T) {
  writeln("Integral");
  return cast(T)(lhs + rhs);
}
```

These can be instantiated using implicit type deduction:

```
writeln(sum(10,20));
writeln(sum(22.11,22.22));
```

A template constraint is an if statement where the condition is any expression that can be evaluated at compile time. When the compiler finds a potential match for a set of template arguments, then the condition must evaluate to true in order for the match to succeed. Otherwise, the match fails and the compiler will try to find another.

The conditions in this example are isFloatingPoint and isIntegral, both of which are templates found in std.traits. Using this approach, there's no ambiguity; an int can only match the template with the isIntegral condition. These are essentially shortcuts for what would be, if implemented manually, a string of is expressions. For example, a test for floating point would look like: if(is(T == float) || is(T == double) || is(T == real)). Imagine doing the same for all the integral types.

The constraints could be rewritten to if(is(T : real)) and if(is(T : ulong)), to test whether T is implicitly convertible to real or ulong. On the surface, this looks similar to template specialization. However, there's a big difference in the result. When a type matches more than one specialization, the one that is more specialized wins and becomes the match. Conversely, when constraints are matched on more than one template, a compiler error is produced instead; constraint matching is more precise.

Template constraints aren't just an alternative to specialization. They are also a means of limiting a template to specific instantiations. Consider the case where it's desirable to define a function interface intended to be used among a number of different `class` and `struct` types. If it were only restricted to classes, then each `class` could extend and implement an actual `interface`, but that's not possible with structs in D. Constraints can be used to make sure that any `class` or `struct` instance provides a specific interface.

As a simple example, imagine a function called `printOut` that is defined to take no parameters, to return `void`, and to print a `class` or `struct` instance to standard output. In any given template, we want to know that it's actually possible to call `printOut` on an instance, either as a member function or via UFCS. Since this is something that is likely to be repeated in multiple templates, it will be useful to implement an enum template that checks whether `printOut` exists on any given type. A good name for it would be `hasPrintOut`. It might look like this:

```
enum hasPrintOut(T) = is(typeof(T.printOut));
```

We saw the `is(typeof())` idiom in the previous chapter. Here, we're only checking whether the given type has a member function named `printOut`, but not whether the return type matches that of the expected interface. For a simple example like this, that doesn't matter. Now, with `hasPrintOut` in hand, a constraint can be implemented on any template that wants to call `printOut` on any type. For example:

```
void print(T)(T t) if(hasPrintOut!T) {
   t.printOut();
}
```

Template constraints can be as simple or as complex as they need to be. A proper implementation of `hasPrintOut` would verify that the return type and function parameter list match the interface. Such complex constraints, or those used often, should generally be wrapped up in a separate template such as `hasPrintOut` or `isFloatingPoint` to keep the declaration clean and readable.

Template mixins

Earlier, we saw that template instantiations have the scope of the declaration, not the instantiation. Template mixins turn that upside down. A template mixin is a special kind of template that can essentially be copied and pasted into a different scope. On the surface, they appear to be identical to the string mixins we saw in *Chapter 4, Running Code at Compile Time*. Digging a little deeper shows they aren't quite the same:

```
mixin template Mixalot() {
   int count = 10;
   int increase(int x) {
      return x + count;
```

```
        }
    }
```

First up, note that the declaration is a regular template declaration with the `mixin` keyword in front. It can have any number of valid declarations in the body, excluding module declarations. Although this particular mixin has no parameters, they can be parameterized like other templates. To instantiate a mixin, we again use the `mixin` keyword. When the mixin has no parameters, the instantiation operator and parentheses can be elided, as in the following example:

```
int count = 100;
mixin Mixalot;
writeln(increase(20));
writeln(count);
```

Here, the declarations inside `Mixalot` are inserted directly into the current context. `increase` can be called without the need to prefix it with a `Mixalot` namespace. However, compile and run this and you'll find that the first `writeln` prints `30`, not `120`, and the second prints `100` instead of `10`. As mixins have their own scope, `increase` sees the `count` declared inside `Mixalot`, not the one declared in `main`. Inside `main`, the local `count` declaration overrides the one in `Mixalot`. Let's see what happens if we change `Mixalot` to be a string mixin:

```
enum Mixalot = q{
int count = 10;
int increase(int x) {
  return x + count;
}
};
void main() {
  import std.stdio : writeln;
  int count = 100;
  mixin(Mixalot);
  writeln(increase(20));
  writeln(count);
}
```

This yields an error to the effect that `main.count` is already defined. String mixins don't have their own scope.

When a template mixin is parameterized, it must be instantiated with the instantiation operator. The following example does so, while demonstrating a common use case of template mixins: implementing a common interface among different `struct` declarations:

```
mixin template ValueImpl(T) {
  private T _value;
```

```
    T value() {
      return _value;
    }
    void value(T val) {
      static bool isSet;
      if(!isSet) {
        _value = val;
        isSet = true;
      }
    }
  }
  struct Value {
    mixin ValueImpl!int;
  }
  struct ExtendedValue {
    mixin ValueImpl!int;
    float extendedValue;
  }
  void printValue(T)(T t) if(is(typeof(T.value))) {
    import std.stdio : writeln;
    writeln(t.value);
  }
  void main() {
    Value val;
    val.value = 20;
    printValue(val);
    ExtendedValue exval;
    exval.value = 100;
    printValue(exval);
  }
```

Variadic templates

A **variadic template** is one that accepts any number of template parameters as types, expressions, or symbols, from none to many. The following is an example:

```
  void printArgs(T...)() if(T.length != 0) {
    foreach(sym; T)
      writeln(sym.stringof);
  }
```

`T...` is a compile-time list of arguments generated from any instantiation of the template. `T` is the alias used to refer to the list inside the template body. Some prefer to use `Args...` instead, but any legal identifier is allowed. There are no function parameters here, as this particular function doesn't need them. The template argument list can be manipulated much like an array; it can be indexed and sliced, and the `.length` can be read (though not written to). Again, this all happens at compile time. The template constraint in this example ensures that the template cannot be instantiated with an empty template argument list, meaning `printArgs!()` will fail to compile.

The body of `printArgs` consists of a `foreach` loop that iterates every item in the argument list. A special property of `foreach` is that it can iterate a compile-time argument list like this *at compile time*. This means that the loop is unrolled; code is generated for the loop body for each item in the list. In this case, the only thing generated per iteration is a single call to `writeln`. Here's some code to clarify this:

```
printArgs!(int, "Pizza!", std.stdio, writeln);
```

When the compiler encounters this line, the template is instantiated with a compile-time argument list that consists of a type, a compile-time value, and two symbols (a module name and a function name). The result of the loop in the function body will be to generate the equivalent of the following (the output of each is shown in comments):

```
writeln(int.stringof);          // int
writeln("Pizza".stringof);      // "Pizza"
writeln((std.stdio).stringof);  // module stdio
writeln(writeln.stringof);      // writeln()
```

This is what is executed at runtime. If the `writeln` calls were replaced with a `msg` pragma, then the template would have no runtime component at all.

`T...` is only visible inside the template. However, it's possible to get a handle to an argument list outside an eponymous `alias` template:

```
template ArgList(T...) {
   alias ArgList = T;
}
```

Alternatively, the short form:

```
alias ArgList(T...) = T;
```

With this, it's possible to generate a compile-time list of types, expressions, or symbols that can be used in different ways, some of which we'll see shortly. For now:

```
printArgs!(ArgList!(int, string, double));
```

This results in the same output as if `int`, `string`, and `double` had been passed directly to `printArgs`. Any function that accepts `T...` can accept the result of an alias template. It's not necessary to implement your own generic alias template, however, as the `std.meta` module in Phobos provides one in the form of `AliasSeq`. The `Seq` part means *sequence*.

That's the basic functionality of variadic templates. There's more to cover in order to fully understand their power, but before we dive into more usage we first have to take an unfortunate, but necessary, detour to discuss terminology.

Terminology

If you visit `http://dlang.org/template.html#TemplateTupleParameter`, you'll find that the documentation refers to `T...` as a **template tuple parameter**. Dig around some more and you may find other references in the documentation, tutorials, forums, and blog posts to the terms **type tuple** and **expression tuple** (or value tuple). `AliasSeq!(int, string, double)` produces a type tuple, as all of the arguments are types; `AliasSeq!(42, "Pizza!", 3.14)` results in an expression tuple, where all of the members are expressions (values). `T...` can also be a list of symbols, but it's rare to refer to a *symbol tuple*. When the members are mixed, as in `printArgs!(int, "Pizza!", std.stdio)`, there is no special name.

There is an obvious discrepancy in the name `AliasSeq` and the term *tuple*. There is some history here that is still playing out as I write. Shortly after I wrote the first draft of this chapter, there was a debate in the forums regarding the naming of `std.typetuple.TypeTuple`. The debate resulted in the name change of both the module and the template, to `std.meta.AliasSeq`. The discussion arose in the first place because there has always been some confusion around the use of *tuple* in D.

Some readers may be familiar with tuples from other languages, where they are often used as a runtime list that can hold multiple values of differing types. Phobos provides such a construct in the form of `std.typecons.Tuple`, instances of which can be created with the convenience function `std.typecons.tuple` (note the lowercase `t`):

```
auto tup1 = tuple!(int, string, double)(42, "Pizza", 3.14);
auto tup2 = tuple!("name", "x", "y")("Position", 3.0f, 2.0f);
```

The first version creates a `Tuple` with three members. The types of the members are specified as template arguments and the optional initial values as function arguments. Each member can be accessed with the index operator, so `tup1[0]` is `42`. In the second form, the template arguments give names to each member and the types are deduced from the function arguments. This produces a `Tuple` instance on which `tup2[1]` and `tup2.x` both return `3.0f`.

`Tuple` is implemented as a `struct` and is useful for returning multiple values from a function, or in any place where multiple values of different types need to be packaged together. Talking about tuples in D, though, has always been a bit problematic. Does it mean `std.typecons.Tuple` or `T...`? Another issue has been that `TypeTuple` could create not only type tuples, but expression tuples, symbol tuples, and any possible compile-time tuple. The name certainly wasn't conducive to easy understanding.

Now that we have `std.meta.AliasSeq` to create compile-time tuples and `std.typecons.Tuple` to create runtime tuples, that doesn't mean all is well quite yet. People still refer to `T...` as a tuple, and sometimes as a compile-time argument list, a sequence, and now even an AliasSeq. In *Chapter 4, Running Code at Compile Time*, I explicitly avoided the use of tuple when talking about `__traits`, even though the documentation for some of the traits declares the return value to be a tuple. For example `allMembers` returns a tuple of string literals. Then there's the use of *Template Tuple Parameters* in the template documentation, and the `.tupleof` property of structs (which we'll look at soon).

So we have a situation where a movement has begun to make tuples less confusing, but has only just gotten started. As I write, no one has yet agreed on how exactly to refer to `T...` in a discussion, but I must choose a term to use in this book. It is certainly now discouraged to use tuple in this context, but any other term I select may be made obsolete if the community eventually settles on a different term. Given that the documentation still uses tuple in many places and that the `.tupleof` struct property still exists, I will use tuple for the remainder of this discussion to refer to `T...` or any compile-time argument list, such as that returned by the `allMembers` trait. I have the benefit of formatting, so `tuple` and `Tuple` will refer to the symbols in `std.typecons`, while tuple will refer to the compile-time version. Keep yourself up to date by reading the latest documentation and following the forum threads to know how to map the term tuple used here to the term being used at the time you read the book. Now, back to the usage of variadic templates and tuple parameters.

More on usage

Instances of a type tuple (no expressions or symbols allowed in this case) can be declared using an alias template as the type, or an `alias` to the template:

```
import std.meta : AliasSeq;
AliasSeq!(int, string, double) isdTuple1;
alias ISD = AliasSeq!(int, string, double);
ISD isdTuple2;
```

Instances are runtime constructs, which are given special field names for the members. As implemented, `printArgs` will not print the field names of a tuple instance. Instead, it will print `sym`, the name of the alias in the `foreach`, for each member. No problem. Let's make a new function called `printTuple`:

```
void printTuple(T...)() if(T.length != 0) {
  foreach(i, _; T)
    writeln(T[i].stringof);
}
```

The point of this loop is to avoid using the alias, so _ is used as a visible indication that it won't be used. Instead, the current index is used to access tuple items directly. This will properly print the field names. `printTuple!isdTuple1` produces this:

__isdTuple1_field_0

__isdTuple1_field_1

__isdTuple1_field_2

This explicitly shows the difference between a tuple instance and the compile-time entity; `printTuple!ISD` will print the type names. Moreover, the instance will have been initialized with the `.init` values of each type in the tuple. This can be verified with the following runtime loop:

```
foreach(item; isdTuple1)
  writeln(item);
```

It prints:

0

nan

The default initializer for a `string` is the empty string, so nothing is printed in the second line. Values can be assigned to the instance just like any other variable:

```
isdTuple1[0] = 42;
isdTuple1[1] = "Pizza!";
isdTuple1[2] = 3.14;
```

Tuple instances can also be expanded, or unpacked, anywhere a comma-separated list of values is expected. Consider this function:

```
void printThreeValues(int a, string b, double c) {
    writefln("%s, %s, %s", a, b, c);
}
```

Given that `isdTuple1` and `isdTuple2` each have three members that match the types of the function arguments (in the same order), either can be passed to the function like so:

```
printThreeValues(isdTuple1);
```

Structs have the property `.tupleof`, which can be used to convert all of a struct's members to a tuple. It can then also then be unpacked:

```
struct UnpackMe {
    int meaningOfLife;
    string meaningOfFood;
    double lifeOf;
}
```

Instead of passing each member individually to `printThreeValues`:

```
auto um = UnpackMe(42, "Pizza!", 3.14);
printThreeValues(um.tupleof);
```

Unpacking also works for compile-time tuples:

```
void printThreeTemplateParams(T, string U, alias V)() {
    writefln("%s, %s, %s", T.stringof, U, V.stringof);
}
```

The following tuple matches the parameter list:

```
printThreeTemplateParams!(AliasSeq!(int, "Hello", std.stdio));
```

Instances can also be declared as function parameters:

```
void printTuple2(T...)(T args) {
  foreach(i, _; T)
    pragma(msg, T[i].stringof);
  foreach(item; args)
    writeln(item);
}
```

This can be called like a normal function and the members of `T...` will be deduced:

```
printTuple2(42, "Pizza!", 3.14);
```

As you can see, there are a number of different ways to use tuples. The instances described in this section seem quite similar to the `std.typecons.Tuple` type mentioned earlier, but they have very different implementations. At this point, I hope you understand why there is a movement afoot to change the tuple terminology.

Operator overloading

The time has come to return to user-defined types and see how to implement operator overloads. It's important to note before we get started that D does not support operator overloads as free functions; they must be part of a `class` or `struct` declaration. We'll be turning away from templates for part of this discussion; some operator overloads are required to be templates, but others can either be templates or normal member functions. We'll look at the latter group first. For the official documentation on operator overloading, pay a visit to `http://dlang.org/ operatoroverloading.html`.

Non-templated operator overloads

There are a handful of operator overloads that are not required to be templates. These cover the comparison operators, the function call operator, and the assignment operator, as well as the index, index-assign, and dollar operators. We'll visit them each in that order.

Comparison overloads – opEquals and opCmp

The equality operators `==` and `!=` are overloaded with `opEquals`. The comparison operators `>`, `<`, `>=` and `<=` are all overloaded with `opCmp`. There are some important considerations to keep in mind when implementing these overloads, but before we dig into that, let's look at the syntax and usage of each.

opEquals

The signature of `opEquals` is going to differ, depending on whether it's being implemented for a class or a `struct`. For classes, it's an override of a default implementation in `Object`. It should look like this:

```
class EqualClass {
  override bool opEquals(Object o) {...}
}
```

In a class, the very first thing any `opEquals` implementation ought to do is to test whether the argument can be cast to the enclosing type, in this case `EqualClass`:

```
if(auto ec = cast(EqualClass)o) {
  // Return true if both refer to the same instance.
  if(ec is this) return true;
  // Now test any members here.
}
return false;
```

There are multiple possible signatures for `opEquals` on a `struct`. Some possibilities:

```
struct EqualStruct {
  bool opEquals(const(EqualStruct) es) {...}
  bool opEquals(ref const(EqualStruct) es) {...}
  bool opEquals(const(EqualStruct) es) const {...};
}
```

Note that, if the type is intended to be used in an associative array, one of the first two versions must be used. All of these could be replaced with a template form that takes no template parameters and uses `auto ref` on the function parameter:

```
struct EqualStruct {
  bool opEquals()(auto ref const(EqualStruct) es) const {...}
}
```

Given two instances a and b, when either a `==` b or a `!=` b is encountered, the following sequence is initiated:

- If the expression is a `!=` b, it is rewritten as `!(a == b)`.

- If both operands are class instances, the expression is rewritten as `.object.opEquals(a, b)`, which has the following implementation:

```
bool opEquals(Object a, Object b) {
    if (a is b) return true;
    if (a is null || b is null) return false;
```

```
        if (typeid(a) == typeid(b)) return a.opEquals(b);
        return a.opEquals(b) && b.opEquals(a);
    }
```

- For non-class instances, `a.opEquals(b)` and `b.opEquals(a)` are both attempted. If both resolve to the same `opEquals` implementation, then `a.opEquals(b)` is selected; if one is a better match than the other, it is selected; if one compiles and the other doesn't, it is selected.

- No match has been found and an error is emitted.

opCmp

`opCmp` should be declared like this for a class:

```
class CmpClass {
    override int opCmp(Object o) {...}
}
```

This again, is overriding a default implementation in `Object`. As with `opEquals`, a struct can have a number of possible overloads, such as:

```
struct CmpStruct {
    int opCmp(const(CmpStruct) es) {...}
    int opCmp(ref const(CmpStruct) es) {...}
    int opCmp(ref const(CmpStruct) cs) const {...}
}
```

Alternatively, the condensed template form:

```
struct CmpStruct {
    int opCmp()(auto ref const(CmpStruct) es) const {...}
}
```

`opCmp` should return a negative value if the ordering of `this` is lower than that of the argument, a positive number if it is higher, and `0` if they are equal. Given objects `a` and `b`, when an expression containing one of the comparison operators is encountered, each is rewritten twice as shown in the following table:

Expression	Rewrite 1	Rewrite 2
a < b	a.opCmp(b) < 0	b.opCmp(a) > 0
a <= b	a.opCmp(b) <= 0	b.opCmp(a) >= 0
a > b	a.opCmp(b) > 0	b.opCmp(a) < 0
a >= b	a.opCmp(b) >= 0	b.opCmp(a) <= 0

Both rewrites are tried and:

- If only one compiles, it is selected
- If both resolve to the same function, the first rewrite is selected
- If they resolve to different functions, the best match is selected
- An error is emitted

Considerations

When an object does not have an opEquals, a default implementation is used for any equality comparisons. For structs, this implementation does a member-wise comparison on each instance; for classes, it's a simple identity comparison, for example a is b. Attempting an ordering comparison on any struct instance for which opCmp is not defined results in a compiler error; it's a runtime error for classes.

Often, the behavior of the default opEquals is exactly what is required for a struct type. Consider a 2D point object, or an RGB color object. Both are types where it makes sense for equality to mean member-wise comparison. More importantly, neither type has any standard concept of ordering. For classes, an identity comparison is rarely the desired behavior, so opEquals should usually be implemented for any class that requires comparison.

When ordering is necessary, it's important to ensure that opCmp and opEquals are consistent. For example if a.opCmp(b) returns 0, then a.opEquals(b) should return true. If not, this can introduce subtle bugs that can be difficult to track down. Best practice dictates that, when implementing one, you should implement the other.

Function call overloads

opCall allows a user-defined type to be callable like a function. It can be declared to have any return type, and any number and combination of parameters. It can also be static. Here's an example:

```d
struct PrintAction {
  void opCall(string arg1, int arg2) {
    import std.stdio : writefln;
    writefln(`Taking action on "%s" and %s`, arg1, arg2);
  }
}
void main() {
  PrintAction print;
  print("A Number", 42);
}
```

Imagine a function template that accepts, and calls in certain circumstances, anything that is callable: a function pointer, a delegate, or a struct or class with `opCall`. Such a template opens up many options in how you design your program; you aren't restricted to only using delegates, or only using classes that extend an interface. Note that implementing `opCall` on a struct disables all struct literals for that type.

Assignment overloads

The assignment operator is overloadable with `opAssign`. Generally, it can take any sort of parameter, with one restriction. On classes, the identity assignment is prohibited. In other words, given a class `C`, it is illegal to declare an `opAssign` that accepts another `C` or any type that is implicitly convertible to `C`. This is because classes have reference semantics, meaning that the reference on the left-hand side would rebind to the reference on the right-hand side. In other words, in `myC = yourC`, the original instance referred to by `myC` would have its `opAssign` run, but `myC` would no longer refer to it; `myC` and `yourC` now refer to the same instance. Structs, being value types, have no such restriction:

```
class C {
  private int _x;
  void opAssign(int x) { _x = x; }  // OK
  // Error: Identity assignment overload is illegal
  // void opAssign(C c) { _x = c._x; }
}
struct S {
  private int _x;
  void opAssign(int x) { _x = x; }  // OK
  void opAssign(S s) { _x = s._x; }  // OK
}
void main() {
  S s1, s2;
  s1 = 10;
  s2 = s1;
  writeln(s2);
  auto c = new C;
  c = 10;
  writeln(c._x);
}
```

In this example, the `opAssign` declarations all return `void`, but it's often a good idea to return `this` in structs to enable assignment chaining: `a = b = c`.

Index overloads

When a user-defined type needs to behave like an array, there are a handful of overloads that can be implemented. We'll look at two of them here: opIndex and opIndexAssign.

opIndex

There are different ways to use opIndex, two of which we'll cover here. First, we'll consider the form that takes one or more integral parameters, preferably of type size_t. When there is only one parameter, it corresponds to the index of a one-dimensional array, while two parameters are the indexes of a two-dimensional array, and so on. As we saw in *Chapter 2*, *Building a Foundation with D Fundamentals*, D does not have built-in support for multi-dimensional arrays, but opIndex allows adding multi-dimensional access to user-defined types. The syntax is [m,n] rather than [m][n].The function can return whatever type is appropriate, preferably by reference to allow direct modification:

```
struct Matrix3 {
  double[3][3] values;
  ref double opIndex(size_t i, size_t j) {
    return values[i][j];
  }
}
```

The second use case of opIndex is to add support for the empty slice operator. Given a type T that needs to support slicing, the empty slice operator can be overloaded by implementing opIndex with no arguments. The following example does just that:

```
struct Numbers(T) {
  T[] _values;
  T[] opIndex() {
    return _values[];
  }
}
```

This following snippet slices a Numbers instance in order to iterate over it:

```
auto nums = Numbers!int([10, 20, 30, 40]);
foreach(n; nums[]) {
  writeln(n);
}
```

Of course, there's more to slicing than just the empty slice. For that, we have the opSlice function. When we cover it later in the chapter, we'll also see a third use case for opIndex.

opIndexAssign

When a user-defined type needs to accept assignment to an index, it can implement opIndexAssign. This allows assignments of the form t[i] = x. Like opIndex, multiple indexes are supported, but the first parameter is the assigned value. Revisiting the Matrix example, here's an implementation that takes two indexes:

```
double opIndexAssign(double val, size_t i, size_t j) {
  return _values[i][j] = val;
}
```

With this, it's now possible to assign a value to a matrix such as m[0, 1] = 10.0. We're going to revisit both opIndex and opIndexAssign later in the chapter when we discuss opSlice.

opDollar

This is not an index overload, but it's closely related. Recall that inside the array and slice operators, $ is a shortcut for the .length property of the current array. User-defined types can override this with opDollar:

```
struct Numbers(T) {
  T[] _values;
  T[] opIndex() {
    return _values[];
  }
  size_t opDollar() { return _values.length; }
}
```

Templated operator overloads

With the power of templates, it's possible to configure a single function at compile time to overload multiple operators, or to take different code paths for different operators. We're going to cover unary operators, binary operators, the cast operator, the op-assign operators, and the slice operator.

Unary overloads

In any expression with a unary operator applied to an object a, the expression is rewritten as a.opUnary!"op"(), where op is one of -, +, ~, *, ++, and --. This takes no function parameters and can return any value (even void, but that diminishes its usefulness). It requires one template value parameter, a string representing the overloaded operator.

A common approach to implement this is to use template constraints on the value. This example does just that to implement everything but the pointer dereference operator, *:

```
struct Number(T) {
  T value;
  T opUnary(string op)() if(op != "*") {
    mixin("return " ~ op ~ "value;");
  }
}
```

Notice the string `mixin` in the function body. This is used in order to generate the actual code for the correct expression. Without that, it would be necessary to use a `static if` chain to compare `op` against each supported operator and manually implement the expression for each. To verify it works as expected:

```
auto num = Number!int(10);
writeln(-num);
writeln(++num);
writeln(--num);
writeln(+num);
writeln(~num);
```

As `opUnary` is a template, all of the template options are at your disposal. Don't like having a single implementation for all of those operators? No problem. Go ahead and implement multiple versions of `opUnary` with different constraints. Or maybe forgo constraints altogether and use `static if` inside the body, or use specialization instead: `opUnary(string op : "*")()`. There's no one right way to do it. Note that the compiler uses `opUnary` for both prefix and postfix increment and decrement operators. It's not possible, nor is there a need, to distinguish between them inside `opUnary`.

Binary overloads

Given two objects in an expression `a op b`, where `op` is one of +, -, *, /, %, ^^, &, |, ^, <<, >>, >>>, ~, or in, the expression is rewritten as both `a.opBinary!"op"(b)` and `b.opBinaryRight!"op"(a)`, and the best match selected. If both equally match, there is an error. They can return any value and the function parameter can be any type. As they are templates, everything that held true in the discussion of `opUnary` applies here as well. Consider this partial implementation of a 3D vector:

```
struct Vector3 {
  float x, y, z;
  Vector3 opBinary(string op)(auto ref const(Vector3) rhs)
  if(op == "+" || op == "-")
```

```
  {
    mixin(`return Vector3(
      x` ~ op ~ `rhs.x,
      y` ~ op ~ `rhs.y,
      z` ~ op ~ `rhs.z);`
    );
  }
  Vector3 opBinary(string op : "/")(float scalar) {
    return this * (1.0f/scalar);
  }
  Vector3 opBinary(string op : "*")(float scalar) {
    return Vector3(x*scalar, y*scalar, z*scalar);
  }
  Vector3 opBinaryRight(string op : "*")(float scalar) {
    return this * scalar;
  }
}
```

The first `opBinary` handles both addition and subtraction with `Vector3`. For this case, it doesn't make sense to implement `opBinaryRight`. That would actually cause both rewrites to match equally and lead to a compiler error. The body is implemented using a WYSIWYG `string` in a simple string mixin. The second and third implementations handle division and multiplication by scalars. A single implementation could have handled both operators using a `static if` block, but that is more verbose. Finally, `opBinaryRight` is implemented only for the scalar multiplication. It's reasonable to accept `2.0f * vec` to be the same as `vec * 2.0f`. The same does not hold for division. The following verifies that all works as expected:

```
auto vec1 = Vector3(1.0f, 20f, 3.0f);
auto vec2 = Vector3(4.0f, 2.0f, 5.0f);
writeln(vec1 + vec2);
writeln(vec1 - vec2);
writeln(vec2 * 2.0f);
writeln(2.0f * vec2);
writeln(vec1 / 2.0f);
```

Cast overloads

Given a cast of any user-defined type `a` to any type `T`, the compiler rewrites the expression to `a.opCast!(T)`. Additionally, given any circumstance where a user-defined type can be evaluated to `bool`, such as `if(a)` or `if(!a)`, the compiler will attempt to cast the type to `bool` with `a.opCast!(bool)` and `!a.opCast!(bool)`. Implementations of `opCast` should take no function parameters and return a value of a type that matches that of the template parameter. The following is a simple `Number` type that supports casting to `bool` and any numeric type:

```
struct Number(T) {
  import std.traits : isNumeric;
  T value;
  bool opCast(C)() if(is(C == bool)) const {
    return value != 0;
  }
  C opCast(C)() if(isNumeric!C) const {
    return cast(C)value;
  }
}
```

The following snippet shows `opCast` in action:

```
auto num1 = Number!int(10);
Number!int num2;
writeln(cast(bool)num1);
writeln(cast(bool)num2);
writeln(cast(byte)num1);
```

Operator assignment overloads

Given two objects in an expression `a op= b`, where op is one of +, -, *, /, %, ^^, &, |, ^, <<, >>, >>>, ~, or in, the expression is rewritten as `a.opOpAssign!"op"(b)`. As an example, let's add support for +=, -=, *=, and /= to the previous `Vector3`:

```
struct Vector3 {
  float x, y, z;
  ref Vector3 opOpAssign(string op)(auto ref Vector3 rhs)
  if(op == "+" || op == "-")
  {
    mixin("x" ~ op ~ "= rhs.x;
    y" ~ op ~ "= rhs.y;
    z" ~ op ~ "= rhs.z;");
    return this;
  }
}
```

opAssign versus opOpAssign

That these two operator overloads have such similar names makes it easy to mix them up. More than once I have unintentionally implemented `opAssign` when I really wanted `opOpAssign`. I even did it while implementing the `Vector3` example. When your `opOpAssign` isn't working properly, the first thing to check is that you didn't type `opAssign` by mistake.

Slice operator overloads

Overloading the slice operator in D requires two steps: add an `opSlice` implementation, and a special version of `opIndex`. Before describing how the functions should be implemented, it will help to show how they are used. The following lines show both a one-dimensional slice and a two-dimensional slice:

```
auto slice1 = oneD[1 .. 3];
auto slice2 = twoD[0 .. 2, 2 .. 5];
```

The compiler will rewrite them to look like this:

```
oneD.opIndex(opSlice!0(1, 3));
twoD.opIndex(opSlice!0(0, 2), opSlice!1(2, 5));
```

`opSlice` must be a template. The single-template parameter is a value representing the dimension that is currently being sliced. The two function parameters represent the boundaries of the slice. They can return anything the implementation requires in order to perform the slice.

`opIndex` is a normal function as before and should be declared to accept one parameter per supported dimension. What's different now is that the type of the parameter no longer needs to be an integral; it can be any type required to produce a slice. Additionally, the return value should be whatever type is produced from slicing this type.

Let's look at a one-dimensional array wrapper as a simple example:

```
struct MyArray(T) {
  struct SliceInfo {
    size_t start, end;
  }
  private T[] _vals;
  T opIndex(size_t i) {
    return _vals[i];
  }
```

```
    T[] opIndex(SliceInfo info) {
      return _vals[info.start .. info.end];
    }
    SliceInfo opSlice(size_t dim)(size_t start, size_t end) {
      return SliceInfo(start, end);
    }
}
```

The internally declared `SliceInfo` is the key to making the slice work. `opSlice`
simply returns an instance initialized with the beginning and end indexes it's given.
The slice overload of `opIndex` then takes that data and produces a slice:

```
auto ma = MyArray!int([10, 20, 30, 40, 50]);
writeln(ma[1 .. 3]);
```

This prints [20, 30] as expected. Support for multidimensional arrays works
the same way, just with extra dimensions. Here's a custom two-dimensional array
to demonstrate:

```
struct My2DArray(T) {
  struct SliceInfo {
    size_t start, end;
  }
  private T[][] _vals;
  this(T[] dim1, T[] dim2) {
    _vals ~= dim1;
    _vals ~= dim2;
  }
  T opIndex(size_t i, size_t j) {
    return _vals[i][j];
  }
  auto opIndex(SliceInfo info1, SliceInfo info2) {
    return My2DArray(
      _vals[0][info1.start .. info1.end],
      _vals[1][info2.start .. info2.end]
    );
  }
  SliceInfo opSlice(size_t dim)(size_t start, size_t end) {
    return SliceInfo(start, end);
  }
}
```

Notice that the template parameter in `opSlice` is never used at all; it's just not needed in this simple case. Also notice that `opIndex` is defined to return a `My2DArray` instance containing the sliced array data. That is likely the best return type to use in this specific case (after all, slicing `T[]` returns `T[]`), but there is enough flexibility to tailor the behavior for specific circumstances. We could just as easily implement it like this:

```
auto opIndex(SliceInfo info1, SliceInfo info2) {
    return _vals[0][info1.start .. info1.end] ~
    _vals[1][info2.start .. info2.end];
}
```

This concatenates the two slices into a single slice, which it then returns. It could also return a range (which we will get to in the next chapter), or any other type that we need a slice to represent.

Other overloads

The aforementioned overloads are called every time a specific symbol in the source code is encountered, such as `*` or `cast` or `()`. This subsection covers overloads that are called in more narrow circumstances.

opDispatch

Given a variable `t` of type `T` and a call to a member function `t.func`, the compiler will report an error if `T` does not implement `func`. The templated `opDispatch` acts as a catch-all when an attempt is made to access any member that doesn't exist on a type. The name of the member is passed as a template value parameter in a process called **forwarding**:

```
struct NoMembers {
    void opDispatch(string s)() {
        import std.stdio : writeln;
        writeln("Attempted to access member ", s);
    }
}
void main() {
    NoMembers nm;
    nm.doSomething();
    nm.someProperty;
}
```

This gives the following output:

```
Attempted to access member doSomething
Attempted to access member someProperty
```

With a good mix of D's compile-time features, some creative things can be done with this. Take a look at the HodgePodge type:

```
struct HodgePodge {
  void printTwoInts(int a, int b) {
    writefln("I like the ints %s and %s!", a , b);
  }
  int addThreeInts(int x, int y, int z) {
    return x + y + z;
  }
}
```

The following snippet has an opDispatch implementation that can take any number of arguments and return any type. It uses compile-time reflection to determine whether the member function in the template argument exists in HodgePodge, ensures the number of function arguments match, and calls the function if they do:

```
struct Dispatcher {
  private HodgePodge _podge;
  auto opDispatch(string s, Args...)(Args args) {
    static if(__traits(hasMember, HodgePodge, s)) {
      import std.traits : ParameterTypeTuple;
      alias params =
      ParameterTypeTuple!(mixin("HodgePodge." ~ s));
      static if(params.length == args.length)
        mixin("return _podge." ~ s ~ "(args);");
    }
  }
}
```

auto allows for any type to be returned. The first template parameter s is bound to the missing member name. If the function call includes arguments, they will be passed after s. In this case, a tuple parameter is declared to catch all of them. In the body, static if and __traits are used to determine whether HodgePodge has a member named s. If so, ParameterTypeTuple from std.traits is used to get a tuple containing the types of all of the function parameters. A string mixin generates HodgePodge.memberName for the template instantiation. It's not the types we're interested in, but the number of them, so it checks whether the number of function arguments matches the number given to opDispatch. If so, a string mixin generates both the function call and return.

Note that this implementation doesn't support member variables or variadic member functions. Trying to access any of these through this implementation of opDispatch leads to an error message saying that Dispatcher doesn't have that missing member. Fixing that is left as an exercise for the reader.

opApply

In order to directly iterate a user-defined type in a foreach loop, it must either implement the opApply function or a range interface (something we'll see in the next chapter). opApply must be declared to return int and to take a delegate as its only parameter. The delegate should also return int, but can have multiple parameters of any type. The delegate is provided to the function from the runtime. The implementation of opApply should do whatever internal iteration it needs, call the delegate at each step of iteration, and if the delegate returns non-zero, immediately return that value. If the internal iteration runs its course, the function should return 0:

```d
struct IterateMe {
  enum len = 10;
  int[len] values;
  void initialize() {
    foreach(i; 0..len) {
      values[i] = i;
    }
  }
  int opApply(int delegate(ref int) dg) {
    int result;
    foreach(ref v; values) {
      result = dg(v);
      if(result)
        break;
    }
    return result;
  }
}
void main() {
  IterateMe im;
  im.initialize();
  foreach(i; im)
    writeln(i);
}
```

Here's an example using multiple parameters with the delegate:

```
struct AA {
  int[string] aa;
  void initialize() {
    aa = ["One": 1, "Two":2, "Three": 3];
  }
  int opApply(int delegate(string, ref int) dg) {
    int result;
    foreach(key, val; aa) {
      result = dg(key, ref val);
      if(result)
        break;
    }
    return result;
  }
}
void main() {
  import std.stdio : writefln;
  AA aa;
  aa.initialize();
  foreach(k, v; aa)
    writefln("%s: %s", k, v);
}
```

To iterate the type with `foreach_reverse`, implement `opApplyReverse` in the same manner, but iterate over the internal array in the opposite direction.

toHash

`toHash` isn't an operator overload, but it's a function that any user-defined type can implement and it's tightly connected with `opEquals`. It's called on any type that is used as an associative array key, takes no parameters, and must return `size_t`. The signature for classes is:

```
override size_t toHash() @trusted nothrow;
```

And for structs or unions:

```
size_t toHash() const @safe pure nothrow;
```

The only requirement is that `toHash` and `opEquals` be consistent. Given objects `a` and `b`, if calling `opEquals` on them returns `true`, then their `toHash` functions must return the same value. If this requirement is not met, the object will not behave properly as an associative array key. All objects, even structs and unions, have a default `toHash` that is used when a custom version is not implemented; however, when overloading `opEquals`, it's best to also implement a custom `toHash` to ensure that they remain consistent.

MovieMan – the database

`MovieMan` does not use any database software, but it still needs to store the movie data the user enters. Ideally, the data would be stored on disk, preferably in a platform-specific, per-user, application data directory, but the goal behind `MovieMan` is to demonstrate D language features, not to develop a fully featured program. To keep things simple, the book implementation will keep the movie data in memory. A good exercise for the reader after finishing the book could be to implement the saving and loading of the movie data to and from disk.

This section lays out the database API. It won't be fully implemented at this point; we'll complete the implementation later with features from the next two chapters. Using the skeleton API we develop here, we'll also flesh out the menu classes we implemented back in *Chapter 3, Programming Objects the D Way*.

db.d

`$MOVIEMAN/source/movieman/db.d` is the home of the `Movie` type and the database, a simple array wrapped by a custom type. The following two lines go at the top of the file:

```
module movieman.db;
import std.stdio;
```

Next is the declaration of the `Movie` type. It's a simple **POD (Plain Old Data)** type with no member functions. Later, we'll add an `opCmp` implementation to use for sorting:

```
struct Movie {
  string title;
  uint caseNumber;
  uint pageNumber;
}
```

Before we see the DB API, let's add the following to the bottom of the file:

```
private:
  DBTable!Movie _movies;

  struct DBTable(T) {
    T[] _items;
  }
```

DBTable is a template, though in the book it's only ever going to be instantiated with one type. As an exercise, you might expand the program to manage audio CDs or books, in which case the templated type will come in handy. For now, we're going to add only one member function to DBTable: an overload of the append operator that we'll use to add new movies to the database. Later we'll add logic to this function to indicate the array should be sorted:

```
  void opOpAssign(string op : "~")(auto ref T t) {
    _items ~= t;
  }
```

The last function we'll implement fully in this module is addMovie. Go back up and add the following below the declaration of Movie but above the private:, as it needs to be a public function:

```
  void addMovie(Movie movie) {
    _movies ~= movie;
    writefln("\nMovie '%s' added to the database.", movie.title);
  }
```

The deleteMovies function will eventually remove one or more movies from the database, but for the moment all it does is pretend:

```
  void deleteMovies(Movie[] movies) {
    writeln();
    foreach(ref movie; movies)
      writefln("Movie '%s' deleted from the database.",
      movie.title);
  }
```

movieExists will be used to determine whether a movie has already been added to the database. It does a simple comparison of the titles, as it's possible for multiple movies to exist on the same page in the same case. It's also possible for more than one movie to have the same title, but that will be accounted for in the menu handler. For now, this function always returns false:

```
  bool movieExists(string title) {
    return false;
  }
```

Finally, there are four versions of getMovies: one to get all movies, one to fetch movies by title, one to fetch by case, and one to fetch by case and page number. For now, each simply returns the entire movie array:

```
auto getMovies() {
    return _movies._items;
}
auto getMovies(string title) {
    return _movies._items;
}
auto getMovies(uint caseNumber) {
    return _movies._items;
}
auto getMovies(uint caseNumber, uint pageNumber = 0) {
    return _movies._items;
}
```

Back to the menus

The menu classes can be updated to use the new database API, but before doing so we're going to need a utility function to print a movie to the screen. Idiomatic D encourages the use of generic functions that can be used with multiple types. From that perspective, something like this might be useful:

```
void printObject(T)(T obj) {
    import std.uni : asCapitalized;
    foreach(mem; __traits(allMembers, T)) {
        writefln("%s: %s", mem.asCapitalized, __traits(getMember, obj,
        mem));
    }
}
```

This uses compile time reflection to get a tuple of all of an object's member names and values, printing each pair on its own line to standard output. Note that it uses the function std.uni.asCaptialized to capitalize the member name without allocating any memory. That's an aesthetic touch, but doesn't really look that good with the Movie type, given that caseNumber is transformed into Casenumber. We can't change the name to case, since that's a keyword, but something such as folder could work. Change pageNumber to page and you're good to go. Or, you could forgo genericity in this case and simply do this:

```
import movieman.db;
void printMovie(Movie movie) {
    writeln("Title: ", movie.title);
    writeln("Case: ", movie.caseNumber);
```

```
        writeln("Page: ", movie.pageNumber);
    }
```

With this in place, we can go back to $MOVIEMAN/source/movieman/menu/main.d
and add the highlighted lines to the onAddMovie member function of MainMenu:

```
    void onAddMovie() {
        import movieman.db : Movie, addMovie;
        import movieman.io;
        import std.stdio : writeln;

        auto title = readTitle();
        if(!validateTitle(title))
            return;

        auto caseNumber = readNumber("case");
        if(!validateNumber(caseNumber, "case"))
            return;

        auto pageNumber = readNumber("page");
        if(!validateNumber(pageNumber, "page"))
            return;

        auto movie = Movie(title, caseNumber, pageNumber);
        printMovie(movie);

        if(readChoice("add this movie to the database"))
            addMovie(movie);
        else
            writeln("\nDiscarding new movie.");
    }
```

All of the highlighted lines are new, but the call to addMovie replaces the call to
writeln that was used as a placeholder. Next, open display.d from the same
folder. Add the following highlighted line to the top of the page:

```
    import movieman.io,
           movieman.db,
           movieman.menu.menu;
```

Then go down to the handleSelection member function. We're only going to make
one modification so that you can display any movie data you enter. We'll finalize the
implementation when we come back to it later in the book. Replace the code in the
all case of the switch with the highlighted lines:

```
    override void handleSelection(uint selection) {
        final switch(cast(Options)selection) with(Options) {
            case byTitle:
```

```
        auto title = readTitle();
        writeln("Displaying ", title);
        break;
    case allOnPage:
        auto caseNumber = readNumber("case");
        auto pageNumber = readNumber("page");
        writefln("Displaying all on page %s of case %s", pageNumber,
        caseNumber);
        break;
    case allInCase:
        auto caseNumber = readNumber("case");
        writeln("Displaying all in case ", caseNumber);
        break;
    case all:
        auto movies = getMovies();
        foreach(movie; movies) {
          printMovie(movie);
          if(!readChoice("show the next movie"))
            break;
        }
        break;
    case exit:
        exitMenu();
        break;
    }
}
```

Now, when you run the program, you can add movie data, then select **2. Display Movie(s)** from the main menu, and finally choose **4. Display All Movies** from the display menu to see the data you've entered. In *Chapter 7, Composing Functional Pipelines with Algorithms and Ranges*, we'll finish off this version of MovieMan.

Summary

This has been a heavy chapter. We've covered the basics of templates in D, such as how to declare them, and have seen the different types of templates and template parameters available. We then got a little more advanced with template specializations, template constraints, template mixins, and variadic templates with tuples. After that we saw how to implement operator overloading for user-defined types and closed out with some additions to `MovieMan`.

In the next chapter, we're going to begin the final stretch of the language feature discussion. We'll dig into ranges—what they are, how to create them, and the basics of using them—in preparation for putting them to good use with functional pipelines in the subsequent chapter.

6
Understanding Ranges

Since they were first introduced, ranges have become a pervasive part of D. It's possible to write D code and never need to create any custom ranges or algorithms yourself, but it helps tremendously to understand what they are, where they are used in Phobos, and how to get from a range to an array or another data structure. If you intend to use Phobos, you're going to run into them eventually. Unfortunately, some new D users have a difficult time understanding and using ranges.

The aim of this chapter and the next is to present ranges and functional style in D from the ground up, so the you can see they aren't some arcane secret understood only by a chosen few. Then, you can start writing idiomatic D early on in your journey. In this chapter, we lay the foundation with the basics of constructing and using ranges in two sections:

- Ranges defined
- Ranges in use

Ranges defined

In this section, we're going to explore what ranges are and examine concrete definitions of the different types of ranges recognized by Phobos. First, we'll dig into an example of the sort of problem ranges are intended to solve and, in the process, develop our own solution. This will help form an understanding of ranges from the ground up.

The problem

As part of an ongoing project, you've been asked to create a utility function, `filterArray`, that takes an array of any type and produces a new array containing all of the elements from the source array that satisfy a Boolean condition. The algorithm should be nondestructive, meaning it should not modify the source array at all. For example, given an array of integers as the input, `filterArray` could be used to produce a new array containing all of the even numbers from the source array.

It should be immediately obvious that a function template can handle the requirement to support any type. With a bit of thought and experimentation, a solution can soon be found to enable support for different Boolean expressions, perhaps a string `mixin`, a delegate, or both. After browsing the Phobos documentation for a bit, you come across a template, `std.functional.unaryFun`, that looks like it will help with the implementation. Its declaration is as follows:

```
template unaryFun(alias fun, string parmName = "a");
```

The `alias fun` parameter can be a string representing an expression, or any callable type that accepts one argument. If it is the former, the name of the variable inside the expression should be the value of `parmName`, which is `"a"` by default. The following snippet demonstrates this:

```
int num = 10;
assert(unaryFun!("(a & 1) == 0")(num));
assert(unaryFun!("x > 0", "x")(num));
```

If `fun` is a callable type, then `unaryFun` is documented to alias itself to `fun` and the `parmName` parameter is ignored. The following snippet calls `unaryFun` first with a `struct` that implements `opCall`, then calls it again with a delegate literal:

```
struct IsEven {
  bool opCall(int x) {
    return (x & 1) == 0;
  }
}
IsEven isEven;
assert(unaryFun!isEven(num));
assert(unaryFun!(x => x > 0)(num));
```

With this, you have everything you need to implement the utility function to spec:

```
import std.functional;
T[] filterArray(alias predicate, T)(T[] source)
  if (is(typeof(unaryFun!predicate(source[0]))))
{
```

```
    T[] sink;
    foreach(t; source) {
      if(unaryFun!predicate(t))
        sink ~= t;
    }
    return sink;
  }
  unittest {
    auto ints = [1, 2, 3, 4, 5, 6, 7];
    auto even = ints.filterArray!(x => (x & 1) == 0)();
    assert(even == [2, 4, 6]);
  }
```

The `unittest` verifies that the function works as expected. As a standalone implementation, it gets the job done and is quite likely good enough. But what if, later on down the road, someone decides to create more functions that perform specific operations on arrays in the same manner? The natural outcome of that is to use the output of one operation as the input for another, creating a chain of function calls to transform the original data.

The most obvious problem is that any such function that cannot perform its operation in place must allocate at least once every time it's called. This means that chain operations on a single array will end up allocating memory multiple times. This is not the sort of habit you want to get into in any language, especially in performance-critical code, but in D you have to take the GC into account. Any given allocation could trigger a garbage collection cycle, so it's a good idea to program to the GC; don't be afraid of allocating, but do so only when necessary and keep it out of your inner loops.

In `filterArray`, the naïve appending can be improved upon, but the allocation can't be eliminated unless a second parameter is added to act as the sink. This allows the allocation strategy to be decided at the call site rather than by the function, but it leads to another problem. If all of the operations in a chain require a sink and the sink for one operation becomes the source for the next, then multiple arrays must be declared to act as sinks. This can quickly become unwieldy.

Another potential issue is that `filterArray` is **eager**, meaning that every time the function is called, the filtering takes place immediately. If all of the functions in a chain are eager, it becomes quite difficult to get around the need for allocations or multiple sinks. The alternative, **lazy** functions, do not perform their work at the time they are called, but rather at some future point. Not only does this make it possible to put off the work until the result is actually needed (if at all), it also opens the door to reducing the amount of copying or allocating needed by operations in the chain. Everything could happen in one step at the end.

Finally, why should each operation be limited to arrays? Often, we want to execute an algorithm on the elements of a list, a set, or some other container, so why not support any collection of elements? By making each operation generic enough to work with any type of container, it's possible to build a library of reusable algorithms without the need to implement each algorithm for each type of container.

The solution

Now we're going to implement a more generic version of `filterArray`, called `filter`, that can work with any container type. It needs to avoid allocation and should also be lazy. To facilitate this, the function should work with a well-defined interface that abstracts the container away from the algorithm. By doing so, it's possible to implement multiple algorithms that understand the same interface. It also takes the decision on whether or not to allocate memory completely out of the algorithms. The interface of the abstraction need not be an actual interface type. Template constraints can be used to verify that a given type meets the requirements.

You might have heard of **duck typing**. It originates from the old saying, *If it looks like a duck, swims like a duck, and quacks like a duck, then it's probably a duck.* The concept is that if a given object instance has the interface of a given type, then it's probably an instance of that type. D's template constraints and compile-time capabilities easily allow for duck typing. We've already seen some of this in *Chapter 5, Generic Programming Made Easy*. We're going to see more here, as it's a key component of range-based programming in D.

The interface

In looking for inspiration to define the new interface, it's tempting to turn to other languages such as Java and C++. On the one hand, we want to iterate the container elements, which brings to mind the iterator implementations in other languages. However, we also want to do a bit more than that, as demonstrated by the following chain of function calls:

```
container.getType.algorithm1.algorithm2.algorithm3.toContainer();
```

Conceptually, the instance returned by `getType` will be consumed by `algorithm1`, meaning that, inside the function, it will be iterated to the point where it can produce no more elements. But then, `algorithm1` should return an instance of the same type, which can iterate over the same container, and which will in turn be consumed by `algorithm2`. The process repeats for `algorithm3`. This implies that instances of the new type should be able to be instantiated independent of the container they represent.

Moreover, given that D supports slicing, the role of getType could easily be played by opSlice. Iteration need not always begin with the first element of a container and end with the last; any range of elements should be supported. In fact, there's really no reason for an actual container instance to exist at all in some cases. Imagine a random number generator. We should be able to plug one into the preceding function chain just by eliminating the container and replacing getType with the generator instance. As long as it conforms to the interface we define, it doesn't matter that there is no concrete container instance backing it.

The short version of it is, we don't want to think solely in terms of iteration, as it's only a part of the problem we're trying to solve. We want a type that not only supports iteration, of either an actual container or a conceptual one, but one that also can be instantiated independently of any container, knows both its beginning and ending boundaries, and, in order to allow for lazy algorithms, can be used to generate new instances that know how to iterate over the same elements.

Considering these requirements, Iterator isn't a good fit as a name for the new type. Rather than naming it for what it does or how it's used, it seems more appropriate to name it for what it represents. There's more than one possible name that fits, but we'll go with Range (as in, a range of elements). That's it for the requirements and the type name. Now, let's move on to the API.

For any algorithm that needs to sequentially iterate a range of elements from beginning to end, three basic primitives are required:

- There must be a way to determine whether or not any elements are available
- There must be a means to access the next element in the sequence
- There must be a way to advance the sequence so that another element can be made ready

Based on these requirements, there are several ways to approach naming the three primitives, but we'll just take a shortcut and use the same names used in D. The first primitive will be called empty and can be implemented either as a member function that returns bool or as a bool member variable. The second primitive will be called front, which again could be a member function or variable and which returns T, the element type of the range. The third primitive can only be a member function and will be called popFront, as conceptually it is removing the current front element from the sequence to ready the next element.

A range for arrays

Wrapping an array in the Range interface is quite easy. It looks like this:

```
auto range(T)(T[] array) {
  struct ArrayRange(T) {
    private T[] _array;
    bool empty() {
      return _array.length == 0;
    }
    ref T front() {
      return _array[0];
    }
    void popFront() {
      _array = _array[1 .. $];
    }
  }
  return ArrayRange!T(array);
}
```

By implementing the iterator as a `struct`, there's no need to allocate GC memory for a new instance. The only member is a slice of the source array, which again avoids allocation. Look at the implementation of `popFront`. Rather than requiring a separate variable to track the current array index, it slices the first element out of `_array` so that the next element is always at index `0`, consequently shortening the length of the slice by one so that, after every item has been consumed, `_array.length` will be `0`. This makes the implementation of both `empty` and `front` dead simple.

`ArrayRange` can be a `Voldemort` type because there is no need to declare its type in any algorithm it's passed to. As long as the algorithms are implemented as templates, the compiler can infer everything that needs to be known for them to work. Moreover, thanks to UFCS, it's possible to call this function as if it were an array property. Given an array called `myArray`, the following is valid:

```
auto range = myArray.range;
```

Next, we need a template to go in the other direction. This needs to allocate a new array, walk the iterator, and store the result of each call to `front` in the new array. Its implementation is as follows:

```
T[] array(T, R)(R range) {
  T[] ret;
  while(!range.empty) {
    ret ~= range.front;
    range.popFront();
  }
  return ret;
}
```

This can be called after any operation that produces any `Range` in order to get an array. If the range comes at the end of one or more lazy operations, this will cause all of them to execute simply by the call to `popFront` (we'll see how shortly). In that case, no allocations happen except as needed in this function when elements are appended to `ret`. Again, the appending strategy used here is naïve, so there's room for improvement in order to reduce the potential number of allocations. Now it's time to implement an algorithm to make use of our new range interface.

The implementation of filter

The `filter` function isn't going to do any filtering at all. If that sounds counterintuitive, recall that we want the function to be lazy; all of the work should be delayed until it is actually needed. The way to accomplish that is to wrap the input range in a custom range that has an internal implementation of the filtering algorithm. We'll call this wrapper `FilteredRange`. It will be a `Voldemort` type, which is local to the `filter` function. Before seeing the entire implementation, it will help to examine it in pieces as there's a bit more to see here than with `ArrayRange`.

`FilteredRange` has only one member:

```
private R _source;
```

R is the type of the range that is passed to `filter`. The `empty` and `front` functions simply delegate to the source range, so we'll look at `popFront` next:

```
void popFront() {
    _source.popFront();
    skipNext();
}
```

This will always pop the front element from the source range before running the filtering logic, which is implemented in the private helper function `skipNext`:

```
private void skipNext() {
    while(!_source.empty && !unaryFun!predicate(_source.front))
        _source.popFront();
}
```

This function tests the result of `_source.front` against the predicate. If it doesn't match, the loop moves on to the next element, repeating the process until either a match is found or the source range is empty. So, imagine you have an array `arr` of the values `[1,2,3,4]`. Given what we've implemented so far, what would be the result of the following chain?:

```
arr.range.filter!(x => (x & 1) == 0).front;
```

As mentioned previously, `front` delegates to `_source.front`. In this case, the source range is an instance of `ArrayRange`; its front returns `_source[0]`. Since `popFront` was never called at any point, the first value in the array was never tested against the predicate. Therefore, the return value is 1, a value which doesn't match the predicate. The first value returned by `front` should be 2, since it's the first even number in the array.

In order to make this behave as expected, `FilteredRange` needs to ensure the wrapped range is in a state such that either the first call to `front` will properly return a filtered value, or `empty` will return `true`, meaning there are no values in the source range that match the predicate. This is best done in the constructor:

```
this(R source) {
    _source = source;
    skipNext();
}
```

Calling `skipNext` in the constructor ensures that the first element of the source range is tested against the predicate before `front` is ever called; however, it does mean that our filter implementation isn't completely lazy. In an extreme case, when `_source` contains no values that match the predicate; it's actually going to be completely eager. The source elements will be consumed as soon as the range is instantiated. Not all algorithms will lend themselves to 100 percent laziness. No matter. What we have here is lazy enough. Wrapped up inside the `filter` function, the whole thing looks like this:

```
import std.functional;
auto filter(alias predicate, R)(R source)
  if(is(typeof(unaryFun!predicate))) {
    struct FilteredRange {
       private R _source;
       this(R source) {
          _source = source;
          skipNext();
       }
       bool empty() { return _source.empty; }
       auto ref front() { return _source.front; }
       void popFront() {
          _source.popFront();
          skipNext();
       }
       private void skipNext() {
          while(!_source.empty &&
             !unaryFun!predicate(_source.front))
             _source.popFront();
```

```
        }
    }
    return FilteredRange(source);
}
```

It might be tempting to take the filtering logic out of the `skipNext` method and add it to `front`, which is another way to guarantee that it's performed on every element. Then no work would need to be done in the constructor and `popFront` would simply become a wrapper for `_source.popFront`. The problem with that approach is that `front` can potentially be called multiple times without calling `popFront` in between, meaning the predicate will be tested on each call. That's unnecessary work. As a general rule, any work that needs to be done inside a range to prepare a front element should happen as a result of calling `popFront`, leaving `front` to simply focus on returning the current element.

The test

With the implementation complete, it's time to put it through its paces. Here are a few test cases in a `unittest` block:

```
unittest {
    auto arr = [10, 13, 300, 42, 121, 20, 33, 45, 50, 109, 18];
    auto result = arr.range
                        .filter!(x => x < 100 )
                        .filter!(x => (x & 1) == 0)
                        .array!int();
    assert(result == [10,42,20,50,18]);

    arr = [1,2,3,4,5,6];
    result = arr.range.filter!(x => (x & 1) == 0).array!int;
    assert(result == [2, 4, 6]);

    arr = [1, 3, 5, 7];
    auto r = arr.range.filter!(x => (x & 1) == 0);
    assert(r.empty);

    arr = [2,4,6,8];
    result = arr.range.filter!(x => (x & 1) == 0).array!int;
    assert(result == arr);
}
```

Assuming all of this has been saved in a file called `filter.d`, the following will compile it for unit testing:

```
dmd -unittest -main filter
```

That should result in an executable called `filter` that, when executed, should print nothing to the screen, indicating a successful test run. Notice the test that calls `empty` directly on the returned range. Sometimes, we might not need to convert a range to a container at the end of the chain. For example, to print the results, it's quite reasonable to iterate a range directly. Why allocate when it isn't necessary?

The real ranges

The purpose of the preceding exercise was to get a feel of the motivation behind D ranges. We didn't develop a concrete type called `Range`, just an interface. D does the same, with a small set of interfaces defining ranges for different purposes. The interface we developed exactly corresponds to the basic kind of D range, called an **input range**, one of two foundational range interfaces in D (the upshot of that is that both `ArrayRange` and `FilteredRange` are valid input ranges, though, as we'll eventually see, there's no reason to use either outside of this chapter). There are also certain optional properties that ranges might have that, when present, some algorithms might take advantage of. We'll take a brief look at the range interfaces now, then see more details regarding their usage in the next section.

Input ranges

This foundational range is defined to be anything from which data can be sequentially read via the three primitives `empty`, `front`, and `popFront`. The first two should be treated as properties, meaning they can be variables or functions. This is important to keep in mind when implementing any generic range-based algorithm yourself; calls to these two primitives should be made without parentheses. The three higher-order range interfaces, we'll see shortly, build upon the input range interface.

To reinforce a point made earlier, one general rule to live by when crafting input ranges is that consecutive calls to `front` should return the same value until `popFront` is called; `popFront` prepares an element to be returned and `front` returns it. Breaking this rule can lead to unexpected consequences when working with range-based algorithms, or even `foreach`.

Input ranges are somewhat special in that they are recognized by the compiler. Recall the coverage of `opApply` in the previous chapter; it's what enables iteration of a custom type with a `foreach` loop. An alternative is to provide an implementation of the input range primitives. When the compiler encounters a `foreach` loop, it first checks to see if the iterated instance is of a type that implements `opApply`. If not, it then checks for the input range interface and, if found, rewrites the loop. For example, given a range `someRange`:

```
foreach(e; someRange) { ... }
```

This is rewritten to something like this:

```
for(auto __r = range; !__r.empty; __r.popFront()) {
    auto e = __r.front;
    ...
}
```

This has implications. To demonstrate, let's use the `ArrayRange` from earlier:

```
auto ar = [1, 2, 3, 4, 5].range;
foreach(n; ar) {
    writeln(n);
}
if(!ar.empty) writeln(ar.front);
```

The last line prints 1. If you're surprised, look again at the `for` loop that the compiler generates. `ArrayRange` is a struct, so when it's assigned to `__r`, a copy is generated. The slices inside, `ar` and `__r`, point to the same memory, but their `.ptr` and `.length` properties are distinct. As the length of the `__r` slice decreases, the length of the `ar` slice remains the same. This behavior was covered in the discussion of slices back in *Chapter 2, Building a Foundation with D Fundamentals*, and again when we talked about `postblit` constructors in *Chapter 3, Programming Objects the D Way*, but it's easy to forget.

When implementing generic algorithms that loop over a source range, it's not a good idea to rely on this behavior. If the range is a class instead of struct, it *will be* consumed by the loop, as classes are references types. Furthermore, there are no guarantees about the internal implementation of a range. There could be struct-based ranges that are actually consumed in a `foreach` loop. Generic functions should always assume this is the case.

To test if a given range type R is an input range:

```
import std.range : isInputRange;
static assert(isInputRange!R);
```

There are no special requirements on the return value of the `front` primitive. Elements can be returned by value or by reference, they can be qualified or unqualified, they can be inferred via `auto`, and so on. Any qualifiers, storage classes, or attributes that can be applied to functions and their return values can be used with any range function, though it might not always make sense to do so.

Forward ranges

The most basic of the higher-order ranges is the forward range. This is defined as an input range that allows its current point of iteration to be saved via a primitive appropriately named `save`. Effectively, the implementation should return a copy of the current state of the range. For ranges that are `struct` types, it could be as simple as:

```
auto save() { return this; }
```

For ranges that are `class` types, it requires allocating a new instance:

```
auto save() { return new MyForwardRange(this); }
```

Forward ranges are useful for implementing algorithms that require lookahead. For example, consider the case of searching a range for a pair of adjacent elements that pass an equality test:

```
auto saved = r.save;
if(!saved.empty) {
  for(saved.popFront(); !saved.empty;
                r.popFront(), saved.popFront()) {
    if(r.front == saved.front)
      return r;
  }
}
return saved;
```

Because this uses a `for` loop and not a `foreach` loop, the ranges are iterated directly and are going to be consumed. Before the loop begins, a copy of the current state of the range is made by calling `r.save`. Then, iteration begins over both the copy and the original. The original range is positioned as the first element, and the call to `saved.popFront` in the beginning of the loop statement positions the saved range as the second element. As the ranges are iterated in unison, the comparison is always made on adjacent elements. If a match is found, `r` is returned, meaning that the returned range is positioned at the first element of a matching pair. If no match is found, `saved` is returned—since it's one element ahead of `r`, it will have been consumed completely and its `empty` property will be `true`.

The preceding example is derived from a more generic implementation in Phobos, `std.range.findAdjacent`. It can use any binary (two-argument) Boolean condition to test adjacent elements and is constrained to only accept forward ranges.

It's important to understand that calling `save` usually does not mean a deep copy, but it sometimes can. If we were to add a `save` function to the `ArrayRange` from earlier, we could simply return `this`; the array elements would not be copied. A class-based range, on the other hand, will usually perform a deep copy because it's a reference type. When implementing generic functions, you should never make the assumption that the range does not require a deep copy. For example, let's assume a range `r`:

```
auto saved = r;        // INCORRECT!!
auto saved = r.save;   // Correct.
```

If `r` is a class, the first line is almost certainly going to result in incorrect behavior.

To test if a given range `R` is a forward range:

```
import std.range : isForwardRange;
static assert(isForwardRange!R);
```

Bidirectional ranges

A **bidirectional range** is a forward range that includes the primitives `back` and `popBack`, allowing a range to be sequentially iterated in reverse. The former should be a property, the latter a function. Given a bidirectional range `r`, the following forms of iteration are possible:

```
foreach_reverse(e; r) writeln(e);
for(; !r.empty; r.popBack)
    writeln(r.back);
}
```

Like its cousin `foreach`, the `foreach_reverse` loop will be rewritten into a `for` loop that might not consume the original range; the `for` loop shown here does consume it.

To test whether a given range type `R` is a bidirectional range:

```
import std.range : isBidirectionalRange;
static assert(isBidirectionalRange!R);
```

Random-access ranges

A **random-access range** is a bidirectional range that supports indexing and is required to provide a length primitive if it isn't infinite (two topics we'll discuss shortly). For custom range types, this is achieved via the `opIndex` operator overload. It is assumed that `r[n]` returns a reference to the (n+1)th element of the range, just as when indexing an array.

To test whether a given range R is a random-access range:

```
import std.range : isRandomAccessRange;
static assert(isRandomAccessRange!R);
```

Dynamic arrays can be treated as random-access ranges by importing `std.array`. This pulls functions into scope that accept dynamic arrays as parameters and allows them to pass all the `isRandomAccessRange` checks. This makes our `ArrayRange` from earlier obsolete. Often, when you need a random-access range, it's sufficient just to use an array instead of creating a new range type. However, char and wchar arrays (string and wstring) are not considered random-access ranges, so they will not work with any algorithm that requires one.

Getting a random-access range from char[] and wchar[]

Recall that a single Unicode character can be composed of multiple elements in a char or wchar array, which is an aspect of strings that would seriously complicate any algorithm implementation that needs to directly index the array. To get around this, the thing to do in the general case is to convert `char[]` and `wchar[]` into `dchar[]`. This can be done with `std.utf.toUTF32`, which encodes UTF-8 and UTF-16 strings into UTF-32 strings. Alternatively, if you know you're only working with ASCII characters, you can use `std.string.representation` to get `ubyte[]` or `ushort[]` (on dstring, it returns `uint[]`). This will also avoid auto-decoding in algorithms that work with input ranges, as calling popFront on any string will decode the next front element into UTF-32.

Output ranges

The output range is the second foundational range type. It's defined as anything that can be sequentially written to via the primitive put. Generally, it should be implemented to accept a single parameter, but the parameter could be a single element, an array of elements, a pointer to elements, or another data structure containing elements. When working with output ranges, never call the range's implementation of put directly; instead, use the Phobos utility function `std.range.put`. It will call the range's implementation internally, but it allows for a wider range of argument types. Given a range r and element e, it would look like this:

```
import std.range : put;
put(r, e);
```

The benefit here is that, if e is anything other than a single element, such as an array or another range, the global put does what is necessary to pull elements from it and put them into r one at a time. With this, you can define and implement a simple output range that might look something like this:

```
MyOutputRange(T) {
  private T[] _elements;
  void put(T elem) {
    _elements ~= elem;
  }
}
```

Now you need not worry about calling put in a loop, or overloading it to accept collections of T. For example:

```
MyOutputRange!int range;
auto nums = [11, 22, 33, 44, 55];
import std.range : put;
put(range, nums);
```

 Note that using UFCS here will cause compilation to fail, as the compiler will attempt to call MyOutputRange.put directly, rather than the utility function. However, it's fine to use UFCS when the first parameter is a dynamic array.

To test whether a given range R is an output range:

```
import std.range : isOutputRange;
static assert(isOutputRange!(R, E));
```

Here, E is the type of element accepted by R.put.

Optional range primitives

In addition to the five primary range types, some algorithms in Phobos are designed to look for optional primitives that can be used as an optimization or, in some cases, a requirement. There are predicate templates in std.range that allow the same options to be used outside of Phobos.

hasLength

Ranges that expose a `length` property can reduce the amount of work needed to determine the number of elements they contain. A great example is the `std.range.walkLength` function, which will calculate and return the length of any range, whether it has a length primitive or not. Given a range that satisfies the `std.range.hasLength` predicate, the operation becomes a call to the `length` property; otherwise, the range must be iterated until it is consumed, incrementing a variable every time `popFront` is called. Generally, `length` is expected to be a `O(1)` operation. If any given implementation cannot meet that expectation, it should be clearly documented as such. For non-infinite random-access ranges, `length` is a requirement. For all others, it's optional.

isInfinite

An input range with an `empty` property which is implemented as a compile-time value set to `false`, is considered an infinite range. For example:

```
struct IR {
    private uint _number;
    enum empty = false;
    auto front() { return _number; }
    void popFront() { ++_number; }
}
```

Here, `empty` is a manifest constant, but it could alternatively be implemented as follows:

```
static immutable empty = false;
```

The predicate template `std.range.isInfinite` can be used to identify infinite ranges. Any range that is always going to return `false` from `empty` should be implemented to pass `isInfinite`. Wrapper ranges (such as the `FilterRange` we implemented earlier) in some functions might check `isInfinite` and customize an algorithm's behavior when it's `true`. Simply returning `false` from an `empty` function will break this, potentially leading to infinite loops or other undesired behavior.

Other options

There are a handful of other optional primitives and behaviors, as follows:

* `hasSlicing`: This returns `true` for any forward range that supports slicing. There are a set of requirements specified by the documentation for finite versus infinite ranges and whether `opDollar` is implemented.

- hasMobileElements: This is true for any input range whose elements can be moved around in memory (as opposed to copied) via the primitives moveFront, moveBack, and moveAt.

- hasSwappableElements: This returns true if a range supports swapping elements through its interface. The requirements differ depending on the range type.

- hasAssignableElements: This returns true if elements are assignable through range primitives such as front, back, or opIndex.

At http://dlang.org/phobos/std_range_primitives.html, you can find specific documentation for all of these tests, including any special requirements that must be implemented by a range type to satisfy them.

Ranges in use

The key concept to understand ranges in the general case is that, unless they are infinite, they are consumable. In idiomatic usage, they aren't intended to be kept around, adding and removing elements to and from them as if they were some sort of container. A range is generally created only when needed, passed to an algorithm as input, then ultimately consumed, often at the end of a chain of algorithms. Even forward ranges and output ranges with their save and put primitives usually aren't intended to live beyond an algorithm.

That's not to say it's forbidden to keep a range around; some might even be designed for long life. For example, the random number generators in std.random are all ranges that are intended to be reused. However, idiomatic usage in D generally means lazy, fire-and-forget ranges that allow algorithms to operate on data from any source and minimize memory allocations.

For most programs, the need to deal with ranges directly should be rare; most code will be passing ranges to algorithms, then either converting the result to a container or iterating it with a foreach loop. Only when implementing custom containers and range-based algorithms is it necessary to implement a range or call a range interface directly. Still, understanding what's going on under the hood helps in understanding the algorithms in Phobos, even if you never need to implement a range or algorithm yourself. That's the focus of the remainder of this chapter.

Custom ranges

When implementing custom ranges, some thought should be given to the primitives that need to be supported and how to implement them. Since arrays support a number of primitives out of the box, it might be tempting to return a slice from a custom type, rather than a struct wrapping an array or something else. While that might be desirable in some cases, keep in mind that a slice is also an output range and has assignable elements (unless it's qualified with `const` or `immutable`, but those can be cast away). In many cases, what's really wanted is an input range that can never be modified; one that allows iteration and prevents unwanted allocations.

A custom range should be as lightweight as possible. If a container uses an array or pointer internally, the range should operate on a slice of the array, or a copy of the pointer, rather than a copy of the data. This is especially true for the `save` primitive of a forward iterator; it could be called more than once in a chain of algorithms, so an implementation that requires deep copying would be extremely suboptimal (not to mention problematic for a range that requires `ref` return values from `front`).

Now we're going to implement two actual ranges that demonstrate two different scenarios. One is intended to be a one-off range used to iterate a container, and one is suited to sticking around for as long as needed. Both can be used with any of the algorithms and range operations in Phobos.

Getting a range from a stack

Here's a barebones, simple stack implementation with the common operations `push`, `pop`, `top`, and `isEmpty` (so named to avoid confusion with the input range interface). It uses an array to store its elements, appending them in the `push` operation and decreasing the array length in the `pop` operation. The top of the stack is always `_array[$-1]`:

```
struct Stack(T) {
    private T[] _array;
    void push(T element) {
        _array ~= element;
    }
    void pop() {
        assert(!isEmpty);
        _array.length -= 1;
    }
    ref T top() {
        assert(!isEmpty);
        return _array[$-1];
    }
    bool isEmpty() { return _array.length == 0; }
}
```

Rather than adding an `opApply` to iterate a stack directly, we want to create a range to do the job for us so that we can use it with all of those algorithms we'll look at in the next chapter. Additionally, we don't want the stack to be modified through the range interface, so we should declare a new range type internally. That might look like this:

```
private struct Range {
    T[] _elements;
    bool empty() { return _elements.length == 0; }
    T front() { return _elements[$-1]; }
    void popFront() { _elements.length -= 1; }
}
```

Add this anywhere you'd like inside the stack declaration. Note the implementation of `front`. Effectively, this range will iterate the elements backwards. Since the end of the array is the top of the stack, that means it's iterating the stack from the top to the bottom. We could also add `back` and `popBack` primitives that iterate from the bottom to the top, which would require adding a `save` primitive since bidirectional ranges must also be forward ranges.

Now, all we need is a function to return a `Range` instance:

```
auto elements() { return Range(_array); }
```

Again, add this anywhere inside the `Stack` declaration. A real implementation might also add the ability to get a range instance from slicing a stack. Now, test it out:

```
Stack!int stack;
foreach(i; 0..10)
    stack.push(i);
writeln("Iterating...");
foreach(i; stack.elements)
    writeln(i);
stack.pop();
stack.pop();
writeln("Iterating...");
foreach(i; stack.elements)
    writeln(i);
```

One of the great side-effects of this sort of range implementation is that you can modify the container behind the range's back and the range doesn't care:

```
foreach(i; stack.elements) {
        stack.pop();
        writeln(i);
}
writeln(stack.top);
```

This will still print exactly what was in the stack at the time the range was created, but the `writeln` outside the loop will cause an assertion failure because the stack will be empty by then. Of course, it's still possible to implement a container that can cause its ranges not just to become stale, but to become unstable and lead to an array bounds error, an access violation, or something similar. However, D's slices used in conjunction with structs give a good deal of flexibility.

A name generator range

Imagine that we're working on a game and need to generate fictional names. For this example, let's say it's a music group simulator and the names are those of group members. We'll need a data structure to hold the list of possible names. To keep the example simple, we'll implement one that holds both first and last names:

```
struct NameList {
private:
    string[] _firstNames;
    string[] _lastNames;
    struct Generator {
        private string[] _first;
        private string[] _last;
        private string _next;
        enum empty = false;
        this(string[] first, string[] last) {
            _first = first;
            _last = last;
            popFront();
        }
        string front() {
            return _next;
        }
        void popFront() {
            import std.random : uniform;
            auto firstIdx = uniform(0, _first.length);
            auto lastIdx = uniform(0, _last.length);
            _next = _first[firstIdx] ~ " " ~ _last[lastIdx];
        }
    }
public:
    auto generator() {
        return Generator(_firstNames, _lastNames);
    }
}
```

The custom range is in the highlighted block. It's a `struct` called `Generator` that stores two slices, `_first` and `_last`, which are both initialized in its only constructor. It also has a field called `_next`, which we'll come back to in a minute. The goal of the range is to provide an endless stream of randomly generated names, which means it doesn't make sense for its `empty` property to ever return `true`. As such, it is marked as an infinite range by the manifest constant implementation of `empty` that is set to `false`.

This range has a constructor because it needs to do a little work to prepare itself before `front` is called for the first time. All of the work is done in `popFront`, which the constructor calls after the member variables are set up. Inside `popFront`, you can see that we're using the `std.random.uniform` function. By default, this function uses a global random number generator and returns a value in the range specified by the parameters—in this case `0` and the length of each array. The first parameter is inclusive and the second is exclusive. Two random numbers are generated, one for each array, and then used to combine a first name and a last name to store in the `_next` member, which is the value returned when `front` is called. Remember, consecutive calls to `front` without any calls to `popFront` should always return the same value.

> `std.random.uniform` can be configured to use any instance of one of the random number generator implementations in Phobos. It can also be configured to treat the bounds differently. For example, both could be inclusive, exclusive, or the reverse of the defaults. See the documentation at `http://dlang.org/phobos/std_random.html` for details.

The `generator` property of `NameList` returns an instance of `Generator`. Presumably, the names in a `NameList` would be loaded from a file on disk or, from a database, or perhaps even imported at compile-time. It's perfectly fine to keep a single `Generator` instance handy for the life of the program as implemented. However, if the `NameList` instance backing the range supported reloading or appending, not all changes would be reflected in the range. In that scenario, it's better to go through `generator` every time new names need to be generated.

Now, let's see how our custom range might be used:

```
auto nameList = NameList(
    ["George", "John", "Paul", "Ringo", "Bob", "Jimi",
     "Waylon", "Willie", "Johnny", "Kris", "Frank", "Dean",
     "Anne", "Nancy", "Joan", "Lita", "Janice", "Pat",
     "Dionne", "Whitney", "Donna", "Diana"],
    ["Harrison", "Jones", "Lennon", "Denver", "McCartney",
     "Simon", "Starr", "Marley", "Dylan", "Hendrix", "Jennings",
     "Nelson", "Cash", "Mathis", "Kristofferson", "Sinatra",
```

```
            "Martin", "Wilson", "Jett", "Baez", "Ford", "Joplin",
            "Benatar", "Boone", "Warwick", "Houston", "Sommers",
            "Ross"]
    );
    import std.range : take;
    auto names = nameList.generator.take(4);
    writeln("These artists want to form a new band:");
    foreach(artist; names)
        writeln(artist);
```

First up, we initialize a `NameList` instance with two array literals, one of first names and one of last names. Next, the highlighted line is where the range is used. We call `nameList.generator` and then, using UFCS, pass the returned `Generator` instance to `std.range.take`. This function creates a new lazy range containing a number of elements, four in this case, from the source range. In other words, the result is the equivalent of calling `front` and `popFront` four times on the range returned from `nameList.generator`. However, since it's lazy, the popping doesn't occur until the `foreach` loop. That loop produces four randomly generated names that are each written to standard output. One iteration yielded the following names for me:

```
    These artists want to form a new band:
    Dionne Wilson
    Johnny Starr
    Ringo Sinatra
    Dean Kristofferson
```

Other considerations

The `Generator` range is infinite, so it doesn't need `length`. There should never be a need to index it, iterate it in reverse, or assign any values to it. It has exactly the interface it needs. But it's not always so obvious where to draw the line when implementing a custom range. Consider the interface for a range from a queue data structure.

A basic queue implementation allows two operations to add and remove items — `enqueue` and `dequeue` (or `push` and `pop` if you prefer). It provides the self-describing properties `empty` and `length`. What sort of interface should a range from a queue implement?

An input range with a `length` property is perhaps the most obvious, reflecting the interface of the queue itself. Would it make sense to add a `save` property? Should it also be a bidirectional range? Should the range be random-access? There are queue implementations out there in different languages that allow indexing, either through an operator overload or a function such as `getElementAt`. Does that make sense? Maybe. More importantly, if a queue doesn't allow indexing, does it make sense for a range produced from that queue to allow it? What about slicing? Or assignable elements? For our queue type at least, there are no clear-cut answers to these questions.

A variety of factors come into play when choosing which range primitives to implement, including the internal data structure used to implement the queue, the complexity requirements of the primitives involved (indexing should be a `O(1)` operation), whether the queue was implemented to meet a specific need or is a more general-purpose data structure, and so on. A good rule of thumb is that, if a range can be made a forward range, then it should be. Other than that, which range options should be applied is wholly dependent on context.

In the next chapter, we'll add a range interface to the custom `Array` type in `MovieMan`. It's an example of drawing the line at a minimal interface that meets a specific need.

Custom algorithms

When implementing custom, range-based algorithms, it's not enough to just drop an input range interface onto the returned range type and be done with it. Some consideration needs to be given to the type of range used as input to the function and how its interface should affect the interface of the returned range. Consider the `FilteredRange` we implemented earlier, which provides the minimal input range interface. Given that it's a wrapper range, what happens when the source range is an infinite range? Let's look at it step by step.

First, an infinite range is passed in to `filter`. Next, it's wrapped up in a `FilteredRange` instance that's returned from the function. The returned range is going to be iterated at some point, either directly by the caller or somewhere in a chain of algorithms. There's one problem, though: with a source range that's infinite, the `FilteredRange` instance can never be consumed. Because its `empty` property simply wraps that of the source range, it's always going to return `false` if the source range is infinite. However, since `FilteredRange` does not implement `empty` as a compile-time constant, it will never match the `isInfiniteRange` predicate itself. This will cause any algorithm that makes that check to assume it's dealing with a finite range and, if iterating it, enter into an infinite loop. Imagine trying to track down that bug.

One option is to prohibit infinite ranges with a template constraint, but that's too restrictive. A better way around this potential problem is to check the source range against the `isInfinite` predicate inside the `FilteredRange` implementation. Then, the appropriate form of the `empty` primitive of `FilteredRange` can be configured with conditional compilation:

```
import std.range : isInfinite;
static if(isInfinite!T)
   enum empty = false;
else
   bool empty(){ return _source.empty; }
```

With this, `FilteredRange` will satisfy the `isInfinite` predicate when it wraps an infinite range, avoiding the infinite loop bug.

Another good rule of thumb is that a wrapper range should implement as many of the primitives provided by the source range *as it reasonably can*. If the range returned by a function has fewer primitives than the one that went in, it is usable with fewer algorithms. But not all ranges can accommodate every primitive.

Take `FilteredRange` as an example again. It could be configured to support the bidirectional interface, but that would have a bit of a performance impact as the constructor would have to find the last element in the source range that satisfies the predicate in addition to finding the first, so that both `front` and `back` are primed to return the correct values. Rather than using conditional compilation, `std.algorithm` provides two functions, `filter` and `filterBidirectional`, so that users must explicitly choose to use the latter version. A bidirectional range passed to filter will produce a forward range, but the latter maintains the interface.

The random-access interface, on the other hand, makes no sense on `FilteredRange`. Any value taken from the range must satisfy the predicate, but if users can randomly index the range, they could quite easily get values that don't satisfy the predicate. It could work if the range were made eager rather than lazy. In that case, it would allocate new storage and copy all the elements from the source that satisfies the predicate, but that defeats the purpose of using lazy ranges in the first place.

Summary

In this chapter, we've taken an introductory look at ranges in D and how to implement them in containers and algorithms. For more information on ranges and their primitives and traits, see the documentation at `http://dlang.org/phobos/std_range.html`. In the next chapter, we're going to continue looking at ranges by exploring more of `std.range` and `std.algorithm` in order to get comfortable with using ranges and algorithms in a functional style.

7
Composing Functional Pipelines with Algorithms and Ranges

A frequent source of difficulty for new D users with no background in functional programming is that making sense of the range-based functions from Phobos can be rather daunting, particularly when looking at a long chain of function calls with names that seem as if they come from an alien language. As an old C programmer myself, I still think of hash maps when I see `std.algorithm.map`, and the C function `itoa` pops into my head when I see `std.range.iota`. Until that "eureka" moment where it all falls into place, knowing which functions are used for what, and where to find them in Phobos, can be a challenging task. It's for this reason that some new D programmers tend to avoid ranges and algorithms altogether.

In this chapter, we're going to work on getting past that first hurdle with range-based functions in Phobos. We're going to look into how to use D ranges in a functional style and, in the process, explore the standard library modules that make it possible. We'll begin with an introduction to composable pipelines and then, through the rest of the chapter, take a look at a variety of functions from Phobos that can be combined in interesting ways. By the end of the chapter, you should be able to understand the idiomatic D snippets that people post in the community forums, know where to look in Phobos for the algorithms you need, and understand how to compose functional pipelines yourself. The chapter is shaped like so:

- Functional programming and composable pipelines: an introduction and some examples
- Navigating Phobos: `std.range`, `std.algorithm`, and `std.array`
- Wrapping up MovieMan

Functional programming and composable pipelines

A major goal of functional programming is **functional purity**. This means that functions should be implemented such that they have no side effects. A pure function does not modify any global state or mutate any data structures in place. Take the example of appending an item to a list. In C, it might look like this:

```
list_append(list, item);
```

This will add `item` to `list` in place. When `list_append` returns, the state of `list` has been mutated. This is a side effect, making it an impure function. In a functional language, it would look more like this:

```
list2 = list_append(list1, item);
```

In this form, `list1` is immutable; new items cannot be added or inserted. Instead, this function returns a new list, `list2`, containing all of the elements of `list1` followed by the new addition, `item`. Immutability coupled with purity can make it easier to reason about a program's behavior. It also leads naturally to functions which are self-contained, tightly-sealed units, with no dependency on external state. This in turn makes it natural to string multiple functions together in a pipeline, where the output of one becomes the input of the next (sometimes, even a function can become the input of another).

The idea of chaining function calls together in a program is not new or particularly special. It's been a common idiom in Java for years, where the member functions of a class are often implemented to return a reference to the class instance, making something like the following possible:

```
myClass.operation1(10).operation2(30).process();
```

We can call this sort of operation chaining a pipeline, but it isn't very composable. The `process` function (or *method*, as member functions are called in Java) most likely depends on the state modified by `operation1` and `operation2`, both of which might also be dependent on the order in which they will be compiled. This makes it impossible to swap their positions in the call chain, or replace either of them with a different implementation. It would be necessary to read the documentation to know for sure, but class methods written with chaining in mind aren't usually designed for composability.

Composable pipelines are more flexible than regular function chains in that each operation is independent of the others. This allows them to be placed at any point in a pipeline; the order of operations is dictated not by the operations themselves, but usually by the format of the desired output or other external constraints. The benefits are so great that support for them has begun to appear in non-functional languages, though usually without the strict guarantees that functional languages provide. Another difference is that functions in non-functional languages generally are not first-class citizens. In a functional language, a function can be passed as an argument to another function, or returned as the result of a function, with each instance carrying its own state (this sort of stateful function instance is often called a **closure**). Contrast this with C, in which function pointers can be passed to and returned from functions, but pointers to the same function all share the same state.

While variables in D are not immutable by default, we have observed that they can be made so. D also has the concept of functional purity, though we will only go through it briefly in *Chapter 11, Taking D to the Next Level*. Functions are not first-class citizens in D, but the language does have closures in the form of delegates. While it's possible to conceive of a composable pipeline implementation using D's delegates, ranges present a much more flexible alternative. With the variety of range interfaces available, and the ease with which they can be implemented to perform lazily, they provide a great abstraction for the inputs and outputs in composable pipelines.

There's a lot more to functional programming than composable pipelines. Refer to the article at https://en.wikipedia.org/wiki/Functional_programming for a more in-depth introduction.

A simple example

You're working on a tactical combat game where squads of robot warriors duke it out on a battlefield. You decide to implement a function that allows the AI to reorganize two squads such that the members with the most health remaining are placed in one, while those with the least are placed in the other. A naïve implementation follows:

```
class Robot {
  int health;
  this(int health) { this.health = health; }
  // Other members
}

// Assumes a squad size of 5 for simplicity
void healthBasedSwap(ref Robot[] squad1, ref Robot[] squad2) {
  import std.algorithm : sort;
```

```
    auto tmp = squad1 ~ squad2;
    tmp.sort!((a,b) => a.health > b.health)();
    squad1 = tmp[0 .. 5];
    squad2 = tmp[5 .. $];
}
```

This function first concatenates the two arrays, then sorts the elements of the resulting array in descending order with `std.algorithm.sort`. Finally, the sorted array is sliced such that the first five elements, the robots with the highest health, are assigned to `squad1` and the remainder to `squad2`. In order for this to work properly, both `squad1` and `squad2` must be declared with the `ref` storage class. Remember that any changes to the existing elements of an array function parameter are reflected in the source array, except for those made to the `length` or `ptr` properties. This function modifies the `ptr` property of each array when it assigns the slices, so without `ref` the changes would only be local. The `ref` requirement could be eliminated, but this would require copying the data, for example, `squad1[]` = `temp[0 .. 5]`.

The following `unittest` verifies that the function works as expected. Note that the test declares an inner function to help assemble the `Robot` arrays and includes a local import. This serves as a reminder that a `unittest` is just a special kind of function.

```
unittest {
  Robot[] makeRobots(int[] healthVals) {
    Robot[] bots;
    foreach(val; healthVals)
      bots ~= new Robot(val);
      return bots;
  }
  import std.algorithm : equal;
  auto squad1 = makeRobots([10, 76, 22, 67, 55]);
  auto squad2 = makeRobots([33, 94, 17, 27, 16]);
  healthBasedSwap(squad1, squad2);
  assert(squad1.equal!((a,b) => a.health == b.health)
  (makeRobots([94, 76, 67, 55, 33])));
  assert(squad2.equal!((a,b) => a.health == b.health)
  (makeRobots([27, 22, 17, 16, 10])));
}
```

This implementation gets the job done, but it's not an ideal solution. Every time it's called, the concatenation allocates new memory. This can add up if it's called frequently. Not only that, it's considered best practice in D to minimize memory allocations using lazy ranges. The idea is to avoid allocation completely where possible and, where it's not, only allocate at the point where the memory is actually needed. As it turns out, the allocation in `healthBasedSwap` can easily be done away with.

 Walter Bright gave a talk on the topic of memory allocation avoidance using lazy ranges at DConf 2015. You can watch the video, and download the slides at `http://dconf.org/2015/talks/bright.html`.

A D newcomer who is unfamiliar with ranges may attempt to avoid allocation by looping through the two arrays and swapping values as needed, perhaps using a static array to help out. This approach can be efficient and the algorithm, depending on its implementation, could likely be made generic so that it can be used elsewhere. On the other hand, a D user who understands ranges and uses them on a regular basis would likely never consider such an approach. Instead, he would reach for Phobos and the many range utilities suited to his purpose. Consider the following reimplementation of `healthBasedSwap`:

```
void healthBasedSwap(Robot[] squad1, Robot[] squad2) {
    import std.algorithm : sort;
    import std.range : chain;
    squad1.chain(squad2).sort!((a,b) => a.health > b.health)();
}
```

The most obvious property of this version is that it's shorter than the original. If it were in a module where other functions from `std.algorithm` and `std.range` are used, the imports could be moved to the top of the module and the function would become a one-liner. It's also true to say that the reduced number of statements makes it easier to reason about what the code is doing, but this is predicated on the assumption that the reader understands `std.range.chain`.

In this particular case, the name of `std.range.chain` is fairly descriptive and the pipeline is short, so it may look more like a familiar Earthly language rather than Martian. `chain` takes any number of input ranges and returns a range that presents them all as a single sequence. So, we've managed to replace the concatenation in the original implementation with something that effectively has the same end result without the allocation. Nothing is copied, nothing is moved. In fact, no action is taken at all, other than constructing and returning the output range; `chain` results in a lazy range.

`std.algortithm.sort`, on the other hand, is eager. In the function above, its return value is never used. This is because the input to `sort` is sorted in place; its output is only needed if it is to be handed off to another algorithm. Sorting in place can avoid allocation. It's also the reason the parameters in this version of `healthBasedSwap` are not declared `ref`; only the content of each array is modified, not the `length` or `ptr` properties.

To sum up, `sort` is passed given the output of `chain` and sees a single random-access range rather than two separate ones. Because `squad1` is the first parameter to `chain`, it corresponds to indexes `0-4`, while indexes `5-9` map to `squad2`. Because the delegate passed as a predicate to `sort` specifies descending order (the default is ascending), the end result is that `squad1` contains the five highest values and `squad2` the five lowest. This can be verified with the same `unittest` used with the first implementation. Now, `squad1` can carry on the fight while `squad2` withdraws for repairs.

A more complex example

You are making a word search game. You download the English Open Word List, a set of words provided freely by Ken Loge, from `http://dreamsteep.com/projects/the-english-open-word-list.html`. Your plan is to load the words into memory at startup, randomly shuffle them, then for each new round select 10 of them to hide in the puzzle space. You also decide to constrain the length of the selected words based on the size of the puzzle space (there are no words longer than 10 characters in the EOWL).

An imperative implementation of the `pickWords` function might look like this:

```
string[] pickWords(string[] words, size_t maxLen, string[] sink) {
  size_t matches;
  foreach(s; words) {
    if(s.length <= maxLen) {
      sink[matches] = s;
      if(++matches == sink.length)
        break;
    }
  }
  return sink[0 .. matches];
}
```

This implementation does not allocate memory. It takes an array to use as a sink. It returns a slice of `sink`, allowing the calling code to recognize the number of elements assigned to the array. To see why this is a good idea, consider the following code:

```
static string[10] arr;
arr[0] = "Hello";
writeln(arr);
```

This will print `Hello` followed by nine empty strings. `sink` might be the same length as the source array, or it might only be a slice of it. In the latter case, the `.length` property of the source array will always report the number of allocated elements, but not the number actually assigned to it in `pickWords`. By returning a slice of `sink`, the caller can read `.length` on the return value to get the actual number of elements assigned.

This function isn't bad, but let's rework it to use a range-based functional pipeline.

```
string[] pickWords(string[] words, size_t maxLen, string[] sink) {
    import std.algorithm : filter, copy;
    import std.range : take;
    auto remaining = words
        .filter!(s => s.length <= maxLen)
        .take(sink.length)
        .copy(sink);
    return sink[0 .. sink.length - remaining.length];
}
```

The highlighted lines have replaced the `foreach` loop, resulting in a code that looks cleaner and can be easier to follow. We can read it from top to bottom: iterate `words`; only consider strings whose length is less than or equal to `maxLen`; take up to `sink.length` of those; copy them all to `sink`. The return value assigned to `remaining` comes from the last call in the chain, `copy`. It's always of the same type as the target range, which in this case is `string[]`, and its `.length` is the number of empty slots remaining in the target range. So if `sink` is filled up, it will return 0. The number of elements copied is determined by subtracting `remaining.length` from `sink.length`, which is what happens at the end to generate the returned slice.

This function looks more like idiomatic D, but an idiomatic D programmer probably isn't going to stop there. Two things stand out about it. First, `words` and `sink` aren't just arrays, they're ranges, too. That's why they can be used with the functions from `std.algorithm` and `std.range`. Second, the words themselves are just range elements, meaning that the algorithm could apply to any elements of any range. All that would be required is a way to specify the predicate, which right now compares the length of each word. From that perspective, a more generic `pickElements` function could be envisioned, but that will be left as an exercise for the reader.

Sometimes we can't

In the downloadable source code for the book, under `Chapter07`, you'll find the modules `words1.d` and `words2.d`. These files contain the implementations of `pickWords`, along with a `main` function that loads the word list, shuffles it, then calls `pickWords` and prints the selected strings to standard output. In both files, the following lines load and shuffle the word list:

```
import std.array : split;
import std.file : readText;
import std.random : randomShuffle;
auto wordList = readText("words.txt").split();
wordList.randomShuffle();
```

There are two things that are worth noting about this snippet. First off, the two highlighted lines are just screaming to be combined, but they can't be. The reason is that `randomShuffle` has a return value of `void`, so it can't be used in any pipeline that's making an initialization or an assignment.

Second, `std.array.split` is an eager function. When given a string, it splits on whitespace by default and returns an array of strings. Another function, `std.algorithm.splitter`, will lazily split strings on whitespace, but if you replace the call to `split` above with a call to `splitter`, it will no longer compile. This is because `splitter` returns an input range. If the source range is a forward or bidirectional range, the returned range will have those properties as well. `randomShuffle`, however, requires a random-access range as input. In other words, a range returned from `splitter` cannot be used with `randomShuffle` until it is first converted to a random-access range, which is usually accomplished by calling `std.array.array`.

Ultimately, it doesn't matter in this case whether the splitting operation is lazy or eager; the end result still needs to be an array of strings, which can be obtained equally well by `split` and `splitter.array`. The point of this little diversion is that when first learning your way around range-based functions in Phobos, it's not uncommon to run into situations where you can't get some of them to work together. Always pay attention to the documented inputs and outputs for any functions you use. For example, the documentation for the single-argument version of `randomShuffle` has this as a header:

```
void randomShuffle(Range)(Range r) if (isRandomAccessRange!Range);
```

The void return value is a quick indication that it can't be used directly in a pipeline. The template constraint shows that the type Range must be a random-access range, so we know that we can pass arrays to it directly, but other types of ranges must first be converted. There has been discussion in the D forums about the proliferation of template constraints in the Phobos documentation and how it can look like gibberish to new users. The flipside is that if you understand the meaning of the predicates in those constraints, then you can understand at a glance what sort of input a function requires.

Navigating Phobos

Although there are range-based functions in many modules in Phobos, the focus of this section is on those found in std.range, std.algorithm, and std.array. The functions in these modules are often central to composable pipelines. We aren't going to cover all of them, just enough to give you a taste of what is possible and where to find the functions you might need. An in-depth treatment of these modules would span more pages than we have room for.

> Note that while many of the functions in these modules are usable in function pipelines, some of them are not, either because they have a return type of void, or they do not take a range as the first parameter. Although this chapter is focused on composable pipelines, we will still take a look at a few of these misfit functions as they can be quite useful to initialize a range before pipelining or to do something with the result of a pipeline.

std.range

The std.range package exposes two modules, std.range.interfaces and std.range.primitives, and a number of functions are located in its package.d file.

The interfaces module provides a number of object-based interfaces that can be used for special cases when runtime polymorphism is required for ranges. For example, if it were necessary to store instance of a number of different input range types in an array, then the InputRange interface could be used as the array type. We can safely ignore this module for now, as it plays no special role in composable pipelines.

The templates for testing range properties that we saw in the previous chapter, such as isInputRange and hasLength, all live in the primitives module, along with some utility functions for directly manipulating ranges. These are useful for implementing range-based algorithms, but are irrelevant to our purposes in this chapter.

The bulk of the functions in the `std.range` package that typically play a role in composable pipelines are found in the `std.range` module itself (`package.d`). The documentation at `http://dlang.org/phobos/std_range.html` says the following:

> "… *this module provides a rich set of range creation and composition templates that let you construct new ranges out of existing ranges…*"

Actually, most range-based functions create new ranges from existing ranges, including many of those in `std.algorithm`. We saw this sort of thing first-hand when we implemented our own custom `filter` function in *Chapter 6, Understanding Ranges*. The key difference is that the only purpose of these functions in `std.range` is to create a new range. They aren't used to apply any sort of transformation to the elements, or otherwise manipulate the elements, in any way. Any work carried out inside the range is done to produce values, not transform them.

At the time of writing, the documentation does not divide the `std.range` functions into different categories, but it's helpful to do so for our purposes. It's also helpful to think of them not in terms of functions, but rather in terms of the ranges they produce. We can roughly categorize them into three groups: generative ranges, selective ranges, and compositional ranges. Not all of the functions from `std.range` will be covered here, but enough to serve as a foundation for learning more from the documentation.

Generative ranges

The functions in this group do not get their elements from other ranges, but rather generate them on the fly. These are used to create ranges from scratch, often to contain a sequence of numbers. It's much more convenient to call one of these functions than to implement a new range, or fill out an array literal, when all that is needed is a quick, one-off sequence.

iota

This function is the simplest in this category. The word *iota* is the name of a letter from the Greek alphabet. It has been used in some programming languages to represent a consecutive sequence of integers. The range returned by this function is a consecutive sequence, but it need not be of integers. All of the built-in numeric types are supported, as well as any user-defined type that overloads the `++`, `<` and `==` operators. It takes up to three parameters. The following lines demonstrate this function:

```
import std.range : iota;
// Prints 0 - 9
foreach(i; iota(10)) writeln(i);
// Prints 1 - 10
```

```
foreach(i; iota(1, 11)) writeln(i);
// Prints all even numbers from 2 - 20
foreach(i; iota(2, 21, 2)) writeln(i);
```

The two-argument version takes a start value and an end value as parameters. The single-argument version is equivalent to `iota(0, arg)`, where `arg` is `10` in the example. The third parameter represents the step value, or the amount by which to increment the current element on each iteration. The step value is `1` when it isn't specified. As with the slice operator, the start value is inclusive and the end value is exclusive, hence `iota(1, 3)` yields a range that starts with `1` and ends with `2`. The type of range returned by `iota` depends on the type of the inputs. For built-in types, the return type is a random access range, but for user-defined types it is a basic input range.

recurrence

A recurrence equation recursively defines a sequence of numbers. Given an initial number to begin the sequence, subsequent numbers are each defined as a function of the preceding numbers. A well-known example of this is the Fibonacci sequence.

`std.range.recurrence` takes one or more function arguments that represent the initial state of the new range. As a template parameter, it accepts the recurrence relation in the form of a string, delegate or other callable type. The returned range is a forward range. This example generates the first 20 Fibonacci numbers.

```
import std.range : recurrence, take;
auto r1 = recurrence!("a[n-1] + a[n-2]")(0, 1).take(20);
```

When using a string as the recurrence equation, `a` represents the current state and `n` represents the current index. The following example uses a delegate to achieve the same result as `iota(2, 21, 2)`.

```
auto r2 = recurrence!((a,n) => a[n-1] + 2)(2).take(10);
```

sequence

This function is similar to `recurrence`, but the numbers are generated differently. Instead of an equation where the value of n depends on the previous values, `sequence` uses a closed form expression, where the nth value is a function of the initial value and n itself. The following example generates a sequence of the first 10 even numbers.

```
import std.range : sequence, take, dropOne;
auto r = sequence!("n*2").dropOne.take(10);
```

The call to `dropOne` (the description of which is coming up shortly) ensures the generated sequence doesn't start with `zero`. `sequence` returns a random-access range.

Selective ranges

A selective range is produced from a source range to selectively iterate the source elements. This group includes the `take` and `drop` families of ranges, `stride`, and `retro`.

take

The `take` function and a variation called `takeExactly` both accept two arguments, a range and the number of elements to take from it. They both return a new range containing the elements taken. It is the equivalent of calling `front` and `popFront` on the source range n times and storing the result of `front` each call to in the new range. The difference between the two is that `take` will happily succeed if the source range does not contain enough elements, while the same circumstance in `takeExactly` will trigger an assertion failure.

```
import std.range : iota, take, takeExactly;
// OK -- returned range has 10 elements
auto r1 = iota(10).take(12);
// Assertion failure -- takeExactly requires 12 elements
auto r2 = iota(10).takeExactly(12);
```

The type of range returned by `take` is dependent on the properties of the source range. The documentation only specifies that if the source range has a `length` property, so does the returned range, but a look at the source shows that other properties will be configured based on the type of the source range. The same holds true for `takeExactly`, with the exception that the returned range will always support `.length`, even when the source range does not.

There are two other variations of this function. `takeOne` returns a range that contains, at the most, one element. If the source range is empty, the returned range will also be empty, otherwise it contains the first element of the source. The returned range is always a random-access range with `.length`, no matter the properties of the source range. This sets it apart from `take`. `takeNone` will always return an empty range. It's possible to call `takeNone` with no source range at all, so it can be used to create an empty range from scratch. The returned range is always a random-access range with `.length`.

drop

The drop family of selective ranges are the inverse of the `take` family. `drop`, `dropExactly` and `dropOne`, given a source range, will return a range that contains all of the elements of the source except the first n elements. It's the equivalent of `popFront` on the source range n times to discard n elements. For example, the following snippet fills a range with 20 elements, then discards the first 10. It prints the numbers 11 – 20.

```
import std.range : iota, drop;
auto r = iota(1, 21).drop(10);
foreach(i; r) writeln(i);
```

There are three other variants called `dropBack`, `dropBackExactly`, and `dropBackOne` that work with the `back` and `popBack` primitives of bidirectional ranges.

stride

This function produces a range that iterates its elements according to a step value. Given a step of n, each call to `popFront` is the equivalent of calling `popFront` on the source range n times. If the source range is random-access, iteration is performed via indexing. The following prints all even numbers from 0 to 20.

```
import std.range : iota, stride;
auto r1 = iota(21).stride(2);
foreach(i; r) writeln(i);
```

Multiple calls to `stride` on the same range results in a step that is a product of the two steps all of the arguments. For example, the following prints all the numbers divisible by 32 from 0 to 256:

```
auto r2 = iota(257).stride(2).stride(16);
foreach(i; r2) writeln(i);
```

The returned range is of the same type as the source.

retro

A significant number of range-based functions iterate their arguments based on the assumption that they are only input ranges. This means they always iterate a source range from front to back. Few functions are designed to iterate bidirectional ranges from back to front. `retro` allows any range that supports the bidirectional range interface to be iterated in reverse with any range-based function. Consider the following:

```
import std.range : iota, retro;
auto r = iota(1, 21).retro();
foreach(i; r) writeln(i);
```

Remember that `iota` returns a random-access range when its arguments are built-in types. Since random-access ranges are bidirectional, we can use `retro` on the returned range to iterate it in reverse without the need for `foreach_reverse`. If the source is a random-access range, so will be the returned range. Note that two consecutive calls to `retro` on the same range cancel each other out; the returned range will be the source range.

Compositional ranges

This category of ranges takes any number of ranges and returns a range that treats them all as a single range. Calling `front` on the range returned from one of these functions will result in `front` being called on one of the composed ranges, though which range is selected and the pattern used for multiple calls to `front` is different for each function. These functions can accept ranges with different properties. The return value of each is dependent on the properties of the source ranges. When in doubt, always consult the source.

chain

This function takes multiple ranges and produces a range that iterates each in sequence, effectively treating them as a single, concatenated range. Once `front`/`popFront` have gone through the first range, they pick up with the second, and so on. The following chains three ranges, each containing ten integers, then prints them all from `0` to `29`:

```
import std.range : iota, chain;
auto r = chain(iota(10), iota(10, 20), iota(20, 30));
foreach(i; r) writeln(i);
```

The returned range is a simple input range unless the sources are all random-access ranges with `.length`, in which case the returned range will have the same properties.

roundRobin

This function takes any number of ranges and alternates between them on each successive call to `front`. Given the ranges `r1` and `r2`, the first call to `front` returns the first element of `r1`, the second returns the first element of `r2`, the third returns the second element of `r1`, and so on. The following takes the sequences `[0, 1, 2]`, `[3, 4, 5]`, and `[6, 7, 8]`, and prints 0, 3, 6, 1, 4, 7, 2, 5, 8.

```
auto rr = roundRobin(iota(3), iota(3, 6), iota(6, 9));
foreach(i; rr) writeln(i);
```

If the sources are all forward ranges, the returned range will be, too. If all of the source ranges have `.length`, so will the returned range. Otherwise, it's a simple input range.

transposed

Consider the following array of `int[]`:

```
int[][] arr = [[1, 2, 3], [4, 5, 6]];
```

We can refer to this as an array of arrays, but since `std.array` exposes the range interface for dynamic arrays, we can also refer to it as a range of ranges. `transposed` takes a range of ranges and transforms it into a new range of ranges that looks like `[[1, 4], [2, 5], [3, 6]]`. In other words, the ith range in the result contains the ith elements of each range in the source.

```
import std.range : transposed;
auto arr = [[1, 2, 3], [4, 5, 6]];
auto r = transposed(arr);
foreach(a; r) writeln(a);
```

The source range must be a forward range with assignable elements. The returned range is a forward range that supports slicing.

zip

Given multiple ranges, `zip` allows them to be iterated in lockstep. Rather than returning an individual element, each call to front on a zipped range returns a tuple containing the corresponding elements from each source range. This allows transformations to be applied to the elements of each source range in parallel. The following iterates a zipped range and prints each tuple whose first item is even:

```
import std.range : iota, zip;
import std.algorithm : filter;
auto r = zip(iota(1, 11), iota(11, 21))
   .filter!(t => (t[0] & 1) == 0);
foreach(i; r) writeln(i);
```

The output looks like the following:

```
Tuple!(int, int)(2, 12)
Tuple!(int, int)(4, 14)
Tuple!(int, int)(6, 16)
Tuple!(int, int)(8, 18)
Tuple!(int, int)(10, 20)
```

The returned range shares the common properties of all the source ranges. For example, given three ranges, if one is a forward range, one is bidirectional, and one is random-access, the returned range will be a forward range, since it is the lowest common property among them all. This holds true for optional primitives like `.length`.

`zip` supports an optional template parameter that is expected to be a value from the `StoppingPolicy` enumeration. This is used to specify how to handle ranges of different length. `StoppingPolicy.shortest` will stop iteration as soon as `empty` returns true from any of its source ranges, while `StoppingPolicy.longest` will continue until all ranges are consumed. `StoppingPolicy.requireSameLength` will cause an exception to be thrown if any range is consumed while any of the others has elements remaining. The default is `StoppingPolicy.shortest`.

lockstep

This function works like `zip`, except that it is intended to be used in `foreach` loops and not as part of a pipeline. As such, its return value is not a range, but an object with an `opApply` implementation. This allows for an index variable to be used in the loop, something not normally possible with ranges by default (`std.range.enumerate` returns a range that allows index variables in `foreach` loops).

```
import std.range : iota, lockstep;
foreach(i, x, y; lockstep(iota(1, 11), iota(11, 21)))
    writefln("%s. x = %s and j = %s", i, x, y);
```

This results in the following output:

```
0. x = 1 and j = 11
1. x = 2 and j = 12
2. x = 3 and j = 13
3. x = 4 and j = 14
4. x = 5 and j = 15
5. x = 6 and j = 16
6. x = 7 and j = 17
7. x = 8 and j = 18
8. x = 9 and j = 19
9. x = 10 and j = 20
```

`lockstep` also accepts an optional `StoppingPolicy` template argument, with `StoppingPolicy.shortest` as the default. However, `StoppingPolicy.longest` is not supported and will cause an exception to be thrown if used.

std.algorithm

It is probably accurate to call this package the workhorse of Phobos. The range-based functions found here are used to solve a variety of problems in the D world and make up the bulk of the composable pipelines you'll see in the wild. The algorithms are split among several modules called `comparison`, `iteration`, `mutation`, `searching`, `setops`, and `sorting`. Again, there's no room for us to cover all of the functions these modules expose, but by the end of this subsection you'll have a good feel for the layout of the package and a better understanding of where to find what you need. All of the functions described here, and many more, can be found in the documentation at `http://dlang.org/phobos/std_algorithm.html`.

Comparison

The comparison algorithms take two or more ranges and return a result based on a one-by-one comparison of the elements. The result could be a range, a numeric value, a `bool`, or a tuple, depending on the algorithm. Here, we take a look at four of these functions: `equal`, `cmp`, `mismatch`, and `levenshteinDistance`. It's also worth noting that there are a few functions in this module that are not range-specific. For example, `min`, `max`, and `clamp` can be used with any built-in or user-defined type that supports `opCmp` comparisons.

equal

This function iterates two ranges in lockstep and applies a predicate to the corresponding elements of each, the default being `"a == b"`. It returns `bool`, making it convenient to use as a predicate to other algorithms. It's also useful for unit testing functions that return ranges.

```
import std.range : iota, take;
import std.algorithm : equal;
assert(equal(iota(51).take(20), iota(20)));
```

cmp

Given two ranges, this function compares the corresponding element of each range using the given predicate. The default predicate is `"a < b"`. Given an element `e1` from the first range and `e2` from the second, if `predicate(e1, e2)` is `true`, then the function returns a negative value; if `predicate(e2, e1)` is `true`, the function returns a positive value. If one of the ranges is consumed, the return will be negative if the first range has fewer elements than the second, positive for the opposite case, and `0` if both ranges are the same length.

Recall that strings are iterated by Unicode code point, so comparison will happen one code point at a time after the strings have been decoded.

```
import std.algorithm : cmp;
auto s1 = "Michael";
auto s2 = "Michel";
assert(cmp(s1, s2) < 0);
```

mismatch

This function iterates two ranges, comparing corresponding elements using the given predicate. When two elements are found that fail the predicate, the function returns a tuple of the two reduced ranges. The ranges begin with the elements that failed the predicate.

```
import std.algorithm : mismatch, equal;
auto s1 = "Michael";
auto s2 = "Michel";
auto t1 = mismatch(s1, s2);
assert(equal(t1[0], "ael"));
assert(equal(t1[1], "el"));
```

If all elements match, the tuple will contain empty ranges.

```
auto arr = [1, 2, 3];
auto t2 = mismatch(arr, arr);
assert(t2[0].length == 0);
assert(t2[1].length == 0);
```

levenshteinDistance

Given two forward ranges r1 and r2, this function returns the number of edits necessary to transform r1 into r2. This is most useful with strings, but can be used with any forward range. The following example uses levenshteinDistance to suggest a command to the user when an incorrect command is entered:

```
import std.algorithm : levenshteinDistance;
auto commands = ["search", "save", "delete", "exit"];
auto input = "safe";
size_t shortest = size_t.max, shortestIndex;
foreach(i, s; commands) {
  auto distance = levenshteinDistance(input, s);
  if(distance < shortest) {
    shortest = distance;
    shortestIndex = i;
  }
}
```

```
if(shortest != size_t.max)
    writeln("\"%s\" is an unknown command. Did you mean \"%s\"?",
        input, commands[shortestIndex]);
```

Iteration

While most of the comparison algorithms may be best suited to the end of a pipeline or to be used in isolation, the iteration algorithms tend to form the bulk of a function chain. It is not uncommon to see the same algorithm more than once in the same pipeline. Here, we look at three of them: group, map, and reduce. The filter and splitter functions we saw earlier also live in this module.

group

This function iterates a range, looks at the number of times an element appears consecutively in sequence, and returns a range containing a tuple of each element and the number of times it appears in the sequence. If you're familiar with run-length encoding, then you should easily understand group.

```
import std.algorithm : group;
auto arr = [1, 1, 1, 1, 2, 3, 3, 6, 6, 4, 3, 3, 3, 3];
auto r = arr.group();
foreach(val, count; r)
    writeln("%s appears %s times", val, count);
```

This snippet produces the following output:

1 appears 4 times

2 appears 1 times

3 appears 2 times

6 appears 2 times

4 appears 1 times

3 appears 4 times

map

Given a range as a function argument and a string or callable as a template argument, map applies the given callable to each element of the range. The return value is a range containing the transformed elements. The following example outputs the even numbers from 2 to 40.

```
import std.algorithm : map;
import std.range : iota;
auto r = iota(1, 21).map!(x => x * 2);
foreach(n; r) writeln(n);
```

`map` can accept multiple template arguments as callables. Instantiating it in this manner causes it to return a tuple containing one range for each callable. The following returns a tuple whose first element is a range containing all of the elements of the source range multiplied by 2 and the second a range containing all of the elements of the source range divided by 2.

```
import std.algorithm : map;
import std.range : iota;
auto r = iota(100, 111).map!("a", "a * 2", "a / 2");
foreach(t; r ) {
  writefln("%s * 2 = %s", t[0], t[1]);
  writefln("%s / 2 = %s", t[0], t[2]);
}
```

Although `map` is most commonly used to directly transform the elements of a range, it can be used in other ways. The English Open Word List we used earlier is distributed as a set of separate text files, one for each letter of the alphabet. The name format follows the pattern A Words.txt. I used the following script to combine all of them into a single file:

```
void main() {
  import std.stdio : File;
  import std.range : iota;
  import std.algorithm : map;
  import std.file : readText;
  import std.string : chomp;
  auto file = File("words.txt", "w");
  auto text =
  iota('A', cast(char)('Z'+1))
    .map!(c => readText(c ~ " Words.txt")
  .chomp());
  foreach(s; text)
    file.writeln(s);
}
```

The lines most relevant to this chapter are highlighted. `iota` is used to generate a range of characters from `'A'` to `'Z'`. I used `'Z'` + 1 rather than `'['` (which follows Z in the ASCII chart) as the end of the range because it's more readable. However, adding an `int` and a `char` results in an `int`, which would cause the element type of the range returned by `iota` to be `int`; hence the cast.

It's important to understand that `map` performs its transformations in `front` and never caches the result. When using it to read files or perform other potentially expensive operations, care should be taken that the operations are not performed multiple times. Remember that due to the way the `foreach` loop is rewritten by the compiler, `text` in the above example is never actually consumed. It's possible to iterate it once more, reading all of the files into memory a second time.

reduce

`reduce` takes a string or a callable as a template argument, and a range and optional initial seed value as function arguments. The seed value is used to initialize an accumulator; if no seed is specified, then the first element of the range is used. Given the call `range.reduce!(fun)`, for every element `e` of `range`, the following evaluation is made: `accumulator = fun(accumulator, e)`. Once all elements have been iterated, the value of `accumulator` is returned. Unfortunately, the two-argument form of the function accepts the seed value as the first parameter, rather than the range, which precludes it from being used with UFCS call chains in which each step returns a range. The single argument form fits right in, though. The following example sums all of the numbers in the range 0-5:

```
import std.algorithm : reduce;
import std.range : iota;
assert(iota(6).reduce!("a + b") == 15);
```

Like `map`, `reduce` can accept multiple template arguments that can be applied to the range elements. In that case, it returns a tuple containing the accumulated results of each.

Mutation

Functions in this module modify a range in some way, either by adding or removing elements. There are many properties that allow a range to be modified. All output ranges are modifiable, some ranges may allow modification through `opIndexAssign`, and others may have an assignable `front` property. The functions in this module look for one or more of these properties in order to carry out their work. We'll look at three: `copy`, `fill`, and `remove`.

copy

This function takes an input range as its first parameter and an output range as its second, copying all of the elements from the former into the latter. The copy happens eagerly, so it's great to use at the end of a pipeline and avoid the need to allocate an array, for which it was used earlier in the `words2` example. The target range must have enough room to hold all of the elements of the source range, or else an assertion failure will result. The function returns the remaining, unfilled portion of the target range when the copy is complete, as demonstrated by the following example:

```
import std.algorithm : copy;
import std.range : iota;
int[20] sink;
auto r = iota(10).copy(sink[]);
iota(10, 20).copy(r);
writeln(sink);
```

Static arrays and templates

When passing a static array to a normal function, slicing happens implicitly. When passing it to a template function where the types of the parameters are not explicitly specified in the instantiation, the slice needs to be explicit.

fill

Given an input range that has assignable elements and a single value, this function fills the range with the value. The following example fills a static array of 20 elements with the value 100:

```
import std.algorithm : fill;
int[20] sink;
fill(sink[], 100);
foreach(n; sink)
    writeln(n);
```

remove

This function removes one or more elements from a bidirectional range that has assignable elements. It is the recommended way to remove items from an array. Elements are specified for removal by offset, not by value. In other words, r.remove(0, 2) removes the first and third elements of the range. The function returns the shortened range. The length of the source array is untouched, though its contents can be shuffled or stomped. In order for the original to reflect the shortened length, it must be assigned the return value of remove. The following prints [2, 4, 5]:

```
import std.algorithm : remove;
auto arr = [1, 2, 3, 4, 5];
arr = arr.remove(0, 2);
writeln(arr);
```

The function accepts a template parameter to specify the strategy to use regarding the order of the remaining elements in the range. The default, SwapStrategy. stable, maintains the order of the remaining elements. Specifying SwapStrategy. unstable allows a more performant version of the algorithm, in which the last element in the range is swapped to the newly emptied location. The following prints [5, 2, 4]:

```
import std.algorithm : remove, SwapStrategy;
auto arr = [1, 2, 3, 4, 5];
arr = arr.remove!(SwapStrategy.unstable)(0, 2);
writeln(arr);
```

Searching

`std.algorithm.searching` contains a number of functions that provide different ways to find elements or ranges inside other ranges. We are going to discuss three of them: `find`, `count`, and `any`.

find

This function searches for a single element in any input range. It takes a template argument of a string or callable to use as a predicate, the default being `"a == b"`. There are five overloads of the function, all of which take a range in which to search (the haystack), as the first function argument and a second argument that specifies what to search for (the needle). If a match is found, the haystack is returned, advanced to the point where the match is in the front position. If no match is found, the returned range is empty. The following example shows the most basic form, looking for an element in a range of elements. It prints `[7, 8, 9]`:

```
import std.algorithm : find;
import std.range : iota;
auto r = iota(10).find(7);
writeln(r);
```

Another form searches for a range of elements inside a range of elements. It can serve as a D equivalent of the C standard library function `strstr`.

```
import std.algorithm : find;
auto s = "Like Frankie said I did it my way.";
auto r = s.find("Frankie");
if(!r.empty)     // s contains "Frankie"
   writeln(r);
```

count

This function is all about counting occurrences of needles in haystacks. If the needle is a single element, the haystack must be an input range and cannot be infinite. If the needle is a forward range, the haystack must be a forward range and cannot be infinite. In both cases, a predicate specified as a template argument is applied to every element of the haystack. The default predicate is `"a == b"`, where a is an element from the haystack and b is either the needle or an element from the needle (when the needle is a range). If the predicate passes, the count is incremented. If no needle is specified, the predicate is applied to each element in isolation. In that case, the default predicate is simply `"true"`.

```
import std.algorithm : count;
// How many 2s?
auto arr1 = [1, 2, 3, 5, 2, 6, 3, 2];
```

```
assert(arr1.count(2) == 3);
// How many occurrences of "ke"?
auto s = "Mike Parker";
assert(s.count("ke") == 2);
// How many even numbers?
auto arr2 = [2, 3, 1, 4, 5, 10, 7];
assert(arr2.count!("(a & 1) == 0") == 3);
```

any

This function returns `true` if any elements of a range satisfy the given predicate and `false` if none of them do. The default predicate, simply `"a"`, results in the use of each element's implicit Boolean value. The following checks if any of the elements multiplied by 2 is greater than 50:

```
import std.algorithm : any;
import std.range : iota;
assert(iota(50).any!("(a * 2) > 50"));
```

Set operations

In mathematics, a **set** is a collection of objects which is treated as a distinct object itself. For example, the set {1, 2, 3} consists of three objects, 1, 2, and 3, but we can refer to it as a *set of size three*. A **set operation (setop)** is used to combine two sets in a particular way to produce a new set. This module provides a number of such operations, where ranges serve as the sets. We are going to look at three, based on common set operations: `setIntersection`, `setDifference`, and `setUnion`.

Each of these functions requires their source ranges to have the same element type. Each function also assumes each range is sorted by the predicate `"a < b"`. A different predicate can be specified as a template parameter.

setIntersection

This function accepts any number of source ranges and returns a lazy range containing every element that is common between all of the source ranges. The following prints [1, 2, 5, 8, 10]:

```
import std.algorithm : setIntersection;
auto a1 = [0, 1, 2, 5, 6, 8, 9, 10];
auto a2 = [1, 2, 3, 4, 5, 7, 8, 10, 11, 12];
auto a3 = [0, 1, 2, 3, 4, 5, 6, 7, 8, 9, 10, 11, 12];
writeln("Intersection: ", setIntersection(a1, a2, a3));
```

setDifference

This function takes two source ranges and returns a lazy range containing elements that only appear in one, but not in the other. The following prints [0, 6, 9]:

```
import std.algorithm : setDifference;
auto a1 = [0, 1, 2, 5, 6, 8, 9, 10];
auto a2 = [1, 2, 3, 4, 5, 7, 8, 10, 11, 12];
writeln(setDifference(a1, a2));
```

setUnion

This function takes any number of ranges and returns a lazy range containing every element of every source range, sorted according to the predicate. Elements in the returned range are not unique. This is a divergence from the mathematical notion of sets, where members are expected to be locally unique. The following prints [0, 0, 1, 1, 1, 2, 2, 3, 3, 4, 4, 4, 6, 6]:

```
import std.algorithm : setUnion;
auto a1 = [0, 1, 2, 4, 6];
auto a2 = [1, 3, 4, 6];
auto a3 = [0, 1, 2, 3, 4];
writeln(setUnion(a1, a2, a3));
```

Sorting

This module contains several functions used to manipulate the order of a range. We are only going to examine two of them: sort and partition.

sort

This is an eager function that modifies the original range. It requires a random-access range and sorts its elements according to a template predicate, the default being "a < b". The function expects the predicate to behave in a particular manner. If predicate(a, b) and predicate(b, c) are true, then predicate(a, c) should also be true. Furthermore, if the former two are false, so should be the third. In many cases, such transitivity comes naturally, but care should be taken when using floating point types. Any user-defined types should have properly behaving opCmp and opEquals overloads when using the default predicate, otherwise a custom predicate should be provided.

sort supports stable and unstable sorting, with SwapStrategy.unstable being the default. In that case, Introsort is used as the sorting algorithm. When SwapStrategy. stable is specified, the Timsort algorithm is used. The former makes no allocations, while the latter will make one or more per call.

The following loads the `words.txt` file from an earlier example, randomly shuffles the words, sorts them with the default stable sort, and prints the first ten words from the list:

```
import std.algorithm : sort;
import std.range : take;
import std.array : split;
import std.file : readText;
import std.random : randomShuffle;
auto wordList = readText("words.txt").split();
wordList.randomShuffle();
writeln(wordList.sort().take(10));
```

For this specific example, an alternative would be to use `std.algorithm.sorting.topN`, which would replace `sort().take(10)` with a single call.

An error of omission

It's not uncommon for D programmers to omit the parentheses on functions called in a pipeline. Be careful about that when using `std.algorithm.sort`. As a remnant from the D1 days, arrays still have a built in `sort` property that uses quicksort. It internally uses a function pointer to make comparisons, calls to which cannot be inlined. If the parameter to `std.algorithm.sort` is an array and the parentheses are omitted, the compiler will pick up the old array property instead of the algorithm. This could be bad news for performance.

partition

Given a predicate as a template argument and a range as a function argument, this function reorders the range such that all elements that pass the predicate come first, followed by all that fail. The default swap strategy is `SwapStrategy.unstable`.

Let's revisit the robot health example from earlier in this chapter. Remember that we wanted to take two squads and reorganize them such that the five bots with the highest health are in one squad and those with the lowest in the other. Let's change that up a bit and say that we want five bots with health no lower than 30. Here's one approach:

```
void healthBasedSwap(Robot[] squad1, Robot[] squad2) {
  import std.algorithm : partition;
  import std.range : chain;
  squad1.chain(squad2).partition!("a.health >= 30");
}
```

This won't guarantee that we'll always have the five bots with the highest health, or that the result will be sorted, but it still works as a nice variation for one of the game AIs. With this implementation, the following prints [94, 76, 33, 67, 55]:

```
auto squad1 = [10, 76, 22, 67, 55];
auto squad2 = [33, 94, 17, 27, 16];
healthBasedSwap(squad1, squad2);
foreach(robot; squad1)
  writeln(robot.health);
```

std.array

This module provides several functions that operate on arrays and associative arrays. We've already seen array and split. Now we'll look at just a few more: Appender, assocArray, and join. The docs at http://dlang.org/phobos/std_array.html describe them all.

Appender

While D's array appending operator is quite convenient, it can unfortunately be inefficient if used often. Appender is a struct that can be used to efficiently append elements to an array. An Appender can be constructed directly, or one can be created via the appender convenience function. Once created, the put member function, or the append operator, is used to append individual items or entire ranges to the backing array.

There are a small number of member functions and properties that can be used on the Appender instance, such as reserve to preallocate additional space, or capacity to determine how many elements can be appended before triggering a reallocation. Appender also exposes the backing array via the data property, so it can be accessed directly to initiate a pipeline. Another potential use is to append the result of a pipeline to an Appender, rather than allocating a new array. When an instance is used multiple times, this approach can cut down on memory allocations. The following example creates a range of 50 integers and appends all of the even numbers to an Appender instance:

```
import std.array : appender;
import std.algorithm : filter, copy;
import std.range : iota;
auto app = appender!(int[]);
iota(50).filter!("(a & 1) == 0").copy(app);
foreach(n; app.data) writeln(n);
```

The `put` member function makes `Appender` an output range, allowing it to be used as the target in the call to `copy`.

assocArray

This function allocates a new associative array and populates it from an input range of key/value tuples. The `zip` algorithm is good for this, but the following example uses the range returned from `group`:

```
import std.array : assocArray;
import std.algorithm : group;
auto arr = [1, 1, 1, 2, 2, 3, 3, 3, 3, 4];
auto aa = arr.group().assocArray();
writefln("The number 3 appears %s times.", aa[3]);
```

join

This function is like a cousin of the `array` function. It takes a range of ranges and concatenates all of their elements into a single array, with the option to specify a separator to place between each element. The optional separator can be a range or an element. Let's do something with the word list example again. This time, rather than sorting it, we'll pull 10 strings from the list and join them all into a single string where each word is partitioned by a pipe character.

```
import std.range : take;
import std.array : split, join;
import std.file : readText;
import std.random : randomShuffle;
auto wordList = readText("words.txt").split();
wordList.randomShuffle();
auto arr = wordList.take(10).join("|");
writeln(arr);
```

In the `std.algorithm.iteration` module there is a function called `joiner` which is a lazy version of `join`. The following would achieve the same result:

```
auto arr = wordList.take(10).joiner("|").array;
```

Where to look for more

We've only covered a small fraction of the range-based functions in `std.range`, `std.algorithm` and `std.array`. In addition, there are a number of range-based functions scattered throughout Phobos. As I write, new range-based versions of older functions are being added, and new APIs are expected to provide a range-centric interface. Some of these functions can be used directly in a pipeline, others cannot. Some can be used with any kind of range, others require specific features. Some return a range configured based on the source range, others always return a specific type of range. In short, look for range-based functions throughout Phobos and always pay careful attention to the function signature and the documentation to learn how to make the most of them. Don't be afraid to look directly at the source to learn how a range-based function is implemented. Not only will it help you to better understand the function, but it will also help you learn techniques to implement your own composable, range-based functions.

MovieMan – wrapping up

Now that we've covered all of the language and standard library features we're going to cover, it's time to add the finishing touches to MovieMan. There are two modules that need to be modified: `movieman.db` and `movieman.menu.display`.

The db module

Open up `$MOVIEMAN/source/movieman/db.d`. We'll start with fleshing out `DBTable`. At the top of its declaration, add the highlighted line as follows:

```
T[] _items;
bool _sortRequired;
```

In order for the movies to display in a sensible order, they'll need to be sorted. We could perform the sort every time a movie is added or every time the movies are displayed. The problem with this is that sorting is going to become an expensive operation as more and more movies are added. There are different solutions to make it more efficient, but to keep things simple, we're only going to sort when it's actually needed. This is tracked by `_sortRequired`. It should be set each time a new movie is added to the database, so the `opOpAssign` member function needs to be updated.

```
void opOpAssign(string op : "~")(auto ref T t) {
  _items ~= t;
  _sortRequired = true;
}
```

Previously, the `getMovies` overloads were all implemented simply to return the `_items` member of `DBTable`. It's time to implement the means to change that by giving `DBTable` the ability to produce a range. The range will be a simple wrapper of a slice, much like the `ArrayRange` we implemented in *Chapter 6, Understanding Ranges*. We'll use `opIndex` to get the range, allowing calling code to use the slice operator with no indexes. Before the range is returned, the function will check if sorting is required and, if so, call `std.algorithm.sort` on the `_items` array. Here's the function in its entirety:

```
auto opIndex() {
    import std.algorithm : sort;
    struct Range {
        T[] items;
        bool empty() {
            return items.length == 0;
        }
        ref T front() {
            return items[0];
        }
        void popFront() {
            items = items[1 .. $];
        }
        size_t length() {
            return items.length;
        }
    }
    if(_sortRequired) {
        _items.sort();
        _sortRequired = false;
    }
    return Range(_items);
}
```

In order for this to compile, the `Movie` type needs an `opCmp` implementation. We could, instead, use a custom predicate for the sort, but what we need is a bit more complex than would be feasible in that case. Movies should be displayed by case number, then by page number, and finally, for movies on the same page, in alphabetical order. So scroll up to the top of the file and add the following to the `Movie` declaration.

```
int opCmp(ref const(Movie) rhs) {
    import std.algorithm : cmp;
    if(this == rhs)
        return 0;
```

```
      else if(caseNumber == rhs.caseNumber && pageNumber ==
      rhs.pageNumber)
         return title.cmp(rhs.title);
      else if(caseNumber == rhs.caseNumber)
         return pageNumber - rhs.pageNumber;
      else
         return caseNumber - rhs.caseNumber;
   }
```

If all fields of both instances are equal, there's nothing to do but return 0. If the case and page numbers are the same, there's nothing to do but to sort by title (same case, same page). This can be done with std.algorithm.cmp and its result returned directly. Otherwise, if only the case numbers are the same, there's nothing left but to sort by page number. This is done with a subtraction: if this.pageNumber is higher, the return value will be positive; if it's lower, the return value is negative. If the case numbers are not equal, the page numbers don't need to be tested (the movies are in different cases), so a subtraction is performed on the case numbers to sort by case. This implementation of opCmp is compatible with the default opEquals for structs (it will never return 0 when opEquals returns false), so there's no need to implement our own.

Now let's turn back to DBTable, where we need to implement removeItems, which allows us to delete an array of movies from the database. Like sorting, this is also a potentially expensive operation. Using std.algorithm.remove with SwapStrategy.stable (the default) would require looping through the array of movies, calling remove for each one, and paying the price of copying some of the elements around, in the worst case, on each iteration. Another option would be to use SwapStrategy.unstable and set the _sortRequired flag. A third option would be to figure out how we could make use of some of the many tools available in std.algorithm.

```
   void removeItems(T[] ts) {
      import std.algorithm : find, canFind, copy, filter;
      auto dirty = _items.find!(m => ts.canFind(m));
      auto tail = dirty.filter!(m => !ts.canFind(m)).copy(dirty);
      _items = _items[0 .. $ - tail.length];
   }
```

This uses a function we haven't discussed yet, std.algorithm.searching.canFind, which, given a range as a haystack and an optional needle, returns true if the needle exists in the haystack.

If it's not immediately obvious what's happening here, don't worry. This sort of thing takes a lot of getting used to. I encourage you to work through it step-by-step. It helps to copy it out of the project into a separate source file and work with data that's easy to manipulate manually. Something like this:

```
import std.stdio;
int[] _items;
void removeItems(int[] ts) {
    import std.algorithm : find, canFind, copy, filter;
    auto dirty = _items.find!(m => ts.canFind(m));
    auto tail = dirty.filter!(m => !ts.canFind(m)).copy(dirty);
    _items = _items[0 .. $ - tail.length];
}
void main() {
    _items = [10, 20, 30, 40, 50, 60, 70, 80, 90, 100];
    removeItems([20, 50, 90, 30]);
    writeln(_items);
}
```

This allows you to work with the function in isolation, adding `writeln`s where necessary and experimenting as needed until you fully understand it.

That's it for `DBTable`. Now let's turn our attention to the `deleteMovies` function. The only thing that needs to be done here is to add the highlighted line.

```
void deleteMovies(Movie[] movies) {
    _movies.removeItems(movies);
    writeln();
    foreach(ref movie; movies)
        writefln("Movie '%s' deleted from the database.",
        movie.title);
}
```

Next are the overloaded versions of `getMovies`. First up is the overload that returns all movies. We'll change it from returning `_movies._items` to returning the new input range we added. It can provide the range by slicing.

```
auto getMovies() {
    return _movies[];
}
```

The second overload takes a movie title. Because it's possible for more than one movie with the same title to be in the database, we need to use an algorithm that allows us to build a range containing all movies with the given title. That sounds like a job for `std.algorithm.filter`.

```
auto getMovies(string title) {
    import std.algorithm : filter;
    return _movies[].filter!(m => m.title == title);
}
```

Next up is the overload that takes a case number. It also uses `filter`.

```
auto getMovies(uint caseNumber) {
    import std.algorithm : filter;
    return _movies[].filter!(m => m.caseNumber == caseNumber);
}
```

Finally, `getMovies` by case and page number:

```
auto getMovies(uint caseNumber, uint pageNumber) {
    import std.algorithm : filter;
    return _movies[].filter!(m => m.caseNumber == caseNumber &&
    m.pageNumber == pageNumber);
}
```

That's all we're going to implement for the `db` module in the book. There is one other function skeleton that we added back in *Chapter 5*, *Generic Programming Made Easy*, and that is the `movieExists` function. It's intended be called from the main menu before adding a movie to the database. It should return `true` if a movie with that title already exists, and `false` if not. Currently, it always returns `false`, which is fine since it isn't actually called from anywhere. Here's a challenge for you: implement `movieExists` using one of the algorithms we've already used here in the `db` module. Then, update `$MOVIEMAN/source/movieman/menu/main.d` to call the function and, if a movie title does already exist, ask the user if he really wants to add it to the database.

The display menu

Very little has been implemented here, so we'll be making several additions. Open up `$MOVIEMAN/source/movieman/menu/display.d`. Add the highlighted import at the top of the module.

```
import std.stdio,
    std.array;
```

We need this because we're going to use `std.array.Appender` to keep track of movies that need to be deleted. We can add an instance of it to the `DisplayMenu` declaration, immediately following the `Options` enumeration.

```
enum Options : uint {
  byTitle = 1u,
  allOnPage,
  allInCase,
  all,
  exit,
}
Appender!(Movie[]) _pendingDelete;
```

Next, we have three member functions to implement in the `private:` section of `DisplayMenu`. The first, `displayRange`, takes a range of movies returned from the `getMovies` functions, iterates it, and prints each movie to the screen.

```
void displayRange(R)(R range) {
  import std.range : walkLength;
  if(range.empty) {
    write("\nSorry, there are no movies in the database that match
    your query.");
    return;
  }

  auto len = range.walkLength();
  writefln("\nFound %s matches.", len);

  foreach(ref movie; range) {
    if(!displayMovie(movie, --len >= 1))
      break;
  }
  writeln("\nThat was the last movie in the list.");
}
```

First, note that this is implemented as a template. That's because the range is a Voldemort type, so there's no way to use its type directly in a function parameter list. Using a template lets the compiler deduce the type. The first line is an import of `walkLength`, which will be used to determine how many movies are available. Next, a check is made to see if the range is empty. If so, a message to that effect is printed and we abort. After that, the number of available movies is obtained and printed, then the range is iterated with a `foreach` loop, and `displayMovie`, which we'll implement next, is called for each element. As the second argument to the function, the local copy of the range length is decremented to determine if any movies follow the current one; `displayMovie` will use this in order to decide if the user should be given the option to display the next movie.

Note that the `movie` variable in the `foreach` is declared as `ref`. This is because the user will be able to edit movies from the display menu. Using a `ref` variable allows us to take a shortcut and edit the movie data directly through the instance, rather than adding a new function to update the database.

`displayMovie` prints the movie data, then shows a submenu that allows the user to choose additional actions: edit or delete the current movie, or show the next movie (if any are available).

```
bool displayMovie(ref Movie movie, bool showNext = false) {
    static choices = [
        "edit this movie",
        "delete this movie",
        "display the next movie"
    ];

    printMovie(movie);
    auto choiceText = showNext ? choices : choices[0 .. $-1];
    auto choice = readChoice(choiceText);

    if(choice == 1) {
        editMovie(movie);
        return displayMovie(movie, showNext);
    }
    else if(choice == 2) {
        _pendingDelete ~= movie;
        writefln("\nMovie '%s' scheduled for deletion.", movie.title);
        return showNext;
    }
    else if(choice != 3) return false;
        return true;
}
```

The `choices` array is a list of options for the submenu, which is displayed using `readChoice`. If no movies follow the current one, the third option is not shown. If option one is selected, the `editMovie` function, coming up next, is called; after that, the updated movie info is displayed. If the second option is selected, the movie is appended to `_pendingDelete`. Later, when control returns to `handleSelection`, any movies added to `_pendingDelete` will be removed from the database. Finally, if option three is selected, the function returns `false`, causing control to go back to `handleSelection`; otherwise, the return value is `true`, indicating that `displayRange` should continue iterating its range of movies.

The next private function is `editMovie`. This function simply asks the user to enter the new information, then, after asking for verification, either updates the movie instance with the new info directly or aborts.

```
void editMovie(ref Movie movie) {
    enum skipIt = "skip it";
    auto title = "";
    auto msg = "No changes committed to the database.";
    uint caseNumber, pageNumber;

    scope(exit) {
        writeln("\n", msg);
        writeln("Press 'Enter' to continue.");
        readUint();
    }

    if(readChoice("to edit the movie's title", skipIt)) {
        title = readTitle();
        if(!validateTitle(title))
            return;
    }

    if(readChoice("to edit the movie's case number", skipIt)) {
        caseNumber = readNumber("case");
        if(!validateNumber(caseNumber, "case"))
            return;
    }

    if(readChoice("to edit the movie's page number", skipIt)) {
        pageNumber = readNumber("page");
        if(!validateNumber(pageNumber, "page"))
            return;
    }

    if(title != "") movie.title = title;
        if(caseNumber > 0) movie.caseNumber = caseNumber;
            if(pageNumber > 0) movie.pageNumber = pageNumber;
                msg = "Database updated.";
}
```

A few points of note. Before asking for each item, `readChoice` is called with the option to skip entering that item. When an item is entered, it is checked for validity against one of the two validation functions in the base `Menu` class. At the end of the function, only the fields for which data has been entered are modified.

Finally, `handleSelection` needs to be updated to call the new functions. The highlighted lines show the changes.

```
override void handleSelection(uint selection) {
  final switch(cast(Options)selection) with(Options) {
    case byTitle:
      auto movies = readTitle.getMovies();
      displayRange(movies);
      break;
    case allOnPage:
      auto caseNumber = readNumber("case");
      auto pageNumber = readNumber("page");
      auto movies = getMovies(caseNumber, pageNumber);
      displayRange(movies);
      break;
    case allInCase:
      auto movies = readNumber("case").getMovies();
      displayRange(movies);
      break;
    case all:
      auto movies = getMovies();
      displayRange(movies);
      break;
    case exit:
      exitMenu();
      break;
  }

  if(_pendingDelete.data.length > 0) {
    deleteMovies(_pendingDelete.data);
    _pendingDelete.clear();
  }
}
```

The block at the end will remove any movies that are pending deletion.

Making it better

There are a number of ways to improve upon MovieMan in its current form. Perhaps the most important is adding the ability to write the database to file. The menu handling code introduced early in the book could be rewritten to use features that came later, like templates. It could perhaps even be converted to a range-based implementation to be more idiomatic. New features could be added, like a database of movie directors, actors and actresses. Support could be added to accommodate music CDs in addition to DVDs. I intend to do that with my own copy of the program, as I have hundreds of music CDs in cases as well.

MovieMan is intended to be your playground. Experiment with it, play with it, and see what you can do with it. Use it to practice your D skills. Anything goes.

Summary

In this chapter, you've learned how to use composable pipelines to craft cleaner and potentially more efficient code by replacing traditional loops. We took a quick jaunt through the heart of the range-based modules in Phobos to get a feel of some of the functions and where to find others that are useful for working with ranges. Finally, we made our final updates to the desktop version of MovieMan.

In the next chapter, we're off to explore the wide world of the D ecosystem, where we'll take a look at libraries, tools, and other resources to help you on your journey.

8
Exploring the Wide World of D

Anyone learning a new programming language benefits tremendously when the language has an active and vibrant community. Learning resources such as blog posts, articles, and books help speed up the process; software such as build tools and IDEs make it easier to get new projects off the ground; libraries and language bindings reduce the amount of new code that needs to be written. D has been around long enough now that an ever-maturing ecosystem has grown up around it, making it easier than ever to jump in and start writing D programs.

In this chapter, we're going to take a tour of that ecosystem. We'll look at online resources that can be used to keep up with D's development, and you will learn more about the language, some of the tools that aid in building and debugging, a few of the text editor and IDE plugins many D users rely on, and some of the popular third-party libraries and bindings used in D programs. We're also going to dig more deeply into DMD command line options and you will learn how to add third-party dependencies to a DUB project. By the end of this chapter, you'll have a good idea of the sort of resources that are available and where to go to find more of them. The layout of this chapter is as follows:

- Online resources: A sampling of websites for enhancing your D knowledge and keeping up with D development.

- Editors and IDEs: An overview of some of the options available to D programmers.

- Tools and utilities: Software that can aid with different aspects of development with D, including a closer look at DMD.

- Libraries: An overview of the DUB package repository, how to use it, and how to register new packages, plus a peek at two collections of bindings to popular C libraries.

Online resources

A handful of online resources, like the forums and the #D IRC channel at `freenode. net`, were introduced in *Chapter 1*, *How to Get a D in Programming*, and links to the D documentation have been sprinkled throughout the book. `http://dlang.org/` should be located prominently in your bookmark list. Not only is it the gateway to the language reference and standard library documentation, but also to the official compiler releases, the forums, and the issue tracker. Additionally, there are sections in the sidebar where other useful resources can be found, such as articles on specific D topics (templates, arrays, floating point, and so on). It's also the host of a couple of subdomains we haven't yet discussed, one of which belongs to the DWiki, our first stop in this section. The following are a handful of resources any beginning D programmer should find helpful:

DWiki

The **DWiki** at `http://wiki.dlang.org/` is a portal to a wealth of D resources. Most of the items covered in this chapter are linked somewhere from this wiki. Tools, libraries, tutorials, books, videos, and more can be found there. A section titled *Core Development* lists a number of links for those interested in following the development of D itself. Some sections of the wiki are more current than others, but these days there are changes and updates on a near-daily basis. One page that may be worth keeping an eye on is at `http://wiki.dlang.org/Jobs`, which is a list of current job openings for D programmers.

Planet D

Planet D is an aggregator of D-related blog feeds. It doesn't cover every D-related blog post in existence, only those sites that have registered with the service, but it's still a useful stream to point your feed reader toward. A number of active D community members write blog posts now and again about the projects they're working on, things they like or dislike about the language, and new tricks they've discovered. These blogs are a great way to hear about new projects or learn things about the language that can help make you a better D programmer. Planet D lives at `http://planet.dsource.org/`.

reddit and StackOverflow

Not everyone using D makes use of the official forums for help and project announcements. Two alternatives are reddit and StackOverflow.

The d_language subreddit at https://www.reddit.com/r/d_language/ isn't as active as others, but people do announce projects and post questions there now and again. Additional D-related posts can be found at https://www.reddit.com/r/programming/. Personally, I've found the former to occasionally be a source for learning of projects I might not otherwise have heard of, and the latter to be a place for spirited discussion about D.

There are a number of questions about D at StackOverflow, a visit to which may prove fruitful when you encounter your own D-related issues. A quick search may yield a solution. You can always see an up-to-date list of D-related questions at http://stackoverflow.com/questions/tagged/d.

This Week in D

Adam Ruppe maintains a blog with weekly updates on the latest goings-on in the world of D. He highlights the biggest forum discussions, the latest GitHub statistics, and often has a *Tip of the Week* or an interview with someone from the D community. For those who are too busy to keep up with all of the forum activity, this is a timesaver. You can find *This Week in D* at http://arsdnet.net/this-week-in-d/.

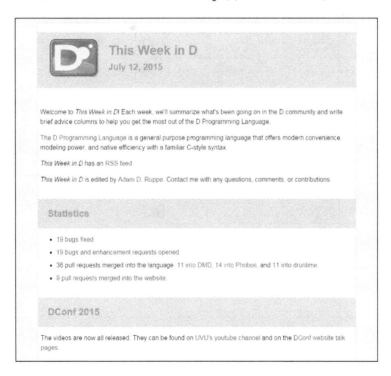

DConf

DConf is an annual D-centric conference that first launched in 2013. The conference consists of three days of presentations, mingling, and discussions about the language and how to make it better. While it's certainly nice to be able to attend the conference in person, it's sometimes live-streamed so that those who are unable to attend can still participate. More importantly, presentation slides and videos are linked directly from the DConf site at `http://dconf.org/`. They are available for any given year. To find them, click on the year of the conference in the menu bar at the top of the page and then on the **Schedule** menu item. From there, you'll find links to a summary of each presentation, where further links lead to the slides and videos.

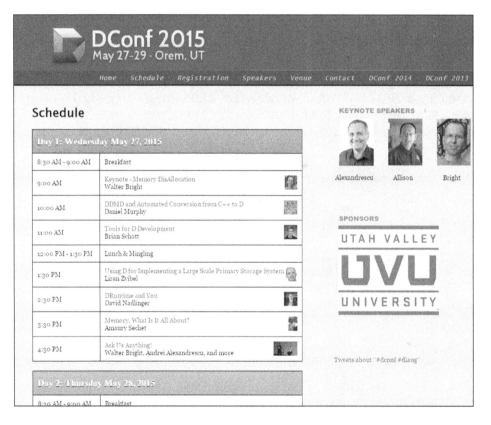

The first D conference was actually held in 2007 in Seattle, though it wasn't called DConf. Some of the slides are still available at `http://d.puremagic.com/conference2007/index.html`. The videos have since been archived on YouTube by Brad Roberts. I've created a playlist for anyone interested at `https://www.youtube.com/playlist?list=PLz50A_by6eUdcH4yL06c_XrHiIHWJNGLC`.

DSource

A long time ago, in a galaxy far, far away, there was a website that offered free project hosting for open source D projects. It was maintained by a volunteer from the D community and served on a box provided by his employer. That was then. Today, DSource is a graveyard of old D projects dating from the D1 era. In a perfect world, there would be no reason to even mention it in a modern book about D2. Unfortunately, the internet is not a perfect world.

A handful of long-lived projects that used to be hosted at DSource are still alive and well at GitHub (and most of those have a message on the project's wiki page at DSource indicating such). A persistent source of confusion for new D users, however, is that old pages referring to the old projects at DSource still pop up in search results now and again. Some of those confused new users manage to find their way to the forums or the #D channel, but there's no way to know how many turned away, thinking D is a dead or dying language, citing DSource as the evidence for it.

Though DSource sat abandoned for a very long time, another D user was ultimately able to contact the right people in order to move the entire site to his own server and take over its maintenance. It now exists in archive mode; no updates can be made to any of the projects, no posts made on the forums, no comments posted in Trac, and so on. While some in the D community would like to see it gone, there are others who see value in keeping it around as an archive of D's history.

The site is included here for two reasons. First, and most importantly, so that when DSource shows up in your search results for anything related to modern D, you can safely ignore it. The second is to let you know that there is a potential treasure trove of D history available for you to peruse. Given that most of the projects on DSource were written with D1, it can help anyone interested in observing how the language has changed and, perhaps, get some perspective on why some features are the way they are. Moreover, there is still some useful code there that could be put to good use with a bit of work to make it compatible with modern D.

Editors and IDEs

Most programmers have a preferred text editor or integrated development environment. Take a look inside the D community and you'll find a variety of preferences. This has led to a number of volunteer efforts to add support for D syntax highlighting to existing editors, or plugins for existing IDEs that provide a complete D building and debugging environment. This section highlights some of the cross-platform options used in the D community, but it is by no means an exhaustive list. More options can be found at the DWiki.

Text editors

There are a number of text editors, both commercial and free, which support D syntax highlighting either natively or through community-driven plugins.

Vim and Emacs

Many D programmers come from the Linux world, where editors like **Vim** and **Emacs** have a long tradition. Users of these editors coming to D need not fret, as support exists for both. A DWiki page at `http://wiki.dlang.org/D_in_Vim` lists a few resources for Vim users and a package for syntax highlighting can be found at `https://github.com/JesseKPhillips/d.vim`. The package is already included in Vim, but the latest updates can always be found on the GitHub page. Another interesting package for Vim users is Dutyl, a collection of D utilities, which is available at `http://www.vim.org/scripts/script.php?script_id=5003`.

Emacs users can find a major mode for D at `https://github.com/Emacs-D-Mode-Maintainers/Emacs-D-Mode`. Additionally, there is a version of **MicroEmacs** that supports D. It's maintained (and used) by D's creator, Walter Bright, at `http://www.digitalmars.com/ctg/me.html`.

Textadept

Textadept is an open source text editor with built-in support for D syntax highlighting. It also ships with built-in support for compiling with DMD. It's highly configurable via the Lua scripting language and comes in the form of multiple executables, one of which is a terminal version of the editor. You can read more about Textadept and download a copy for your platform at `http://foicica.com/textadept/`.

Sublime Text

Sublime Text is a commercial multi-platform text editor with support for a number of programming languages, including D. Syntax highlighting for D is built-in, along with support for compiling with DMD. Plugins adding auto-completion exist and the editor can be further extended with Python, adding support for other compilers or build tools like LDC or DUB. It's available at `http://www.sublimetext.com/`. If Sublime Text is your editor of choice, be sure to ask around in the #D IRC channel for information about useful plugins for D.

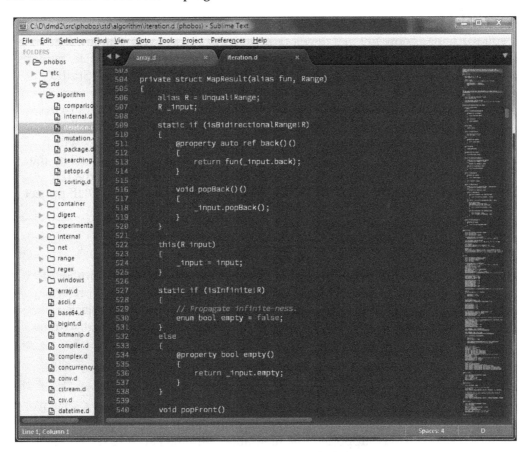

IDEs

In the past, Integrated Development Environments tended to support only one language. Today, most popular open source and commercial IDEs support multiple languages, usually through a plugin system. Sometimes the plugins ship with the IDE, sometimes they must be downloaded separately, and often they are developed by third-parties. Here, we're going to look at three plugins for three major IDEs, plus one open-source IDE that ships with support for D included.

Visual D

If you work for a company that develops any sort of software for Windows, chances are you are using a version of Microsoft Visual Studio at the office, perhaps even at home. Support for D can be added to several versions of Visual Studio through the Visual D plugin available at `https://github.com/D-Programming-Language/visuald`. It supports DMD, GDC, and LDC. It also comes with two debugging options. One is the Mago debugger, a tool developed specifically to work with D-style debug output. The other is a conversion tool, called `cv2pdb`, which translates DMD's CodeView debug output into the PDB format recognized by the modern Microsoft debugger. Both options allow debugging directly in the IDE. On a side note, DUB supports generating Visual D project files from a DUB project configuration.

Mono-D

Mono-D is a plugin for MonoDevelop/XamarinStudio. It supports a number of toolchains, including DMD, GDC, LDC, DUB, RDMD, and Make. DUB projects can be opened directly in the IDE. It also supports loading Visual D projects. You can read more about it and find download links and installation instructions at `http://wiki.dlang.org/Mono-D`.

DDT

DDT is a plugin for the open source Eclipse IDE. It has built-in support for DUB such that elements of the package configuration are listed in the Project Explorer. Debugging with GDB is supported via integration with the Eclipse CDT plugin (for C and C++ development). Eclipse users moving to D should point their browsers at `http://ddt-ide.github.io/` for more info on obtaining and using DDT.

Code::Blocks

Code::Blocks is an open source, cross-platform IDE. Though it's billed as an IDE for C, C++, and Fortran development, it also supports D. This includes support for debugging with GDB. For instructions on how to configure Code::Blocks for D development, refer to `http://wiki.dlang.org/CodeBlocks`.

Tools and utilities

Throughout the book we've been using DMD to compile examples and DUB to manage the MovieMan project. Now it's time to look at some additional tools that can be part of a productive D workflow. The first tool on the list, though, is actually DMD. We're going to take a look at some of the compiler options that can be helpful during the development of D programs.

DMD

Thus far, we haven't used many options when compiling D programs, but there are quite a few of them. As demonstrated in *Chapter 1, How to Get a D in Programming*, the list of compiler options can be displayed by invoking DMD with no command-line options. Each option is accompanied by a brief description of what it does. Here are a few of those that you may find most useful.

Optimized and debug builds

There are a few DMD options that control optimizations and debugging. The `-g` switch adds debugging information in a D-specific format. For debuggers that don't support D debug symbols, `-gc` can be used to make the compiler use C-style debug output. The `-O` switch turns on optimizations; `-inline` will activate function inlining; `-release` will turn off contracts and asserts, cause assertion failures to be classified as undefined behavior, and disable array bounds checking in functions not annotated with `@safe` (more on that in *Chapter 11, Taking D to the Next Level*). Additionally, the `-boundscheck=` switch can be used to have a little more control over array bounds checking. It takes one of three possible arguments: `on`, `safeonly`, and `off`. The first is the default in the absence of `-release`, the second the default with it.

Changing the default output

The default behavior of DMD is to name the binary output the same as the first input source or object file it is given, and to write it in the current working directory, using the appropriate platform-specific file extension. The output directory for object files and library files can be changed with the -od command-line switch. The name of the target library or executable file can be changed with the –of switch. The argument here can be a file name or a path. For example, the following line writes main.obj to the out/obj subdirectory and creates an executable named app (or app.exe on Windows) in a subdirectory named bin. The directories out, out/obj and bin will be created if they do not exist.

```
dmd –odout/obj –ofbin/app main.d
```

Compiling libraries

Creating a library requires compiling several source files into object files, then handing the object files off to a tool that packs them all into the target library. DMD allows you to condense these separate steps into a single command line with the -lib switch. With this option, any source files, object files, or library files fed to the compiler will all be combined into a single library. Let's experiment.

In $LEARNINGD/Chapter08/libs, create two modules, hello.d and goodbye.d. The former should look like this:

```
module hello;
void sayHello() {
    import std.stdio : writeln;
    writeln("Hello");
}
```

And the latter should look this:

```
module goodbye;
void sayGoodbye() {
    import std.stdio : writeln("Goodbye!");
}
```

First, let's create two separate libraries, named hello and goodbye with the following two command lines:

```
dmd -lib -odseparate hello.d
dmd -lib -odseparate goodbye.d
```

This will create two libraries (hello.lib and goodbye.lib on Windows, libhello.a and libgoodbye.a elsewhere) in a subdirectory named separate. Let's say we want to combine them into a single library. There are multiple ways to go about this. If all we have is the source code, we would do this:

```
dmd -lib -odcombined -ofgreets hello.d goodbye.d
```

Now we have greets.lib or libgreets.a in the combined subdirectory. What if we have the two libraries and no source?

```
dmd -lib -odcombined -ofgreets separate/hello.lib
separate/goodbye.lib
```

Same result. You could also pass, for example, hello.d and goodbye.lib, or hello.lib and goodbye.d, or compile the source modules into object files and pass those to the compiler instead. Each case will have the same result.

Dropping extensions

When passing files to DMD, pay attention to the file extensions. If no extension is specified, then the compiler will treat it as a source file. Forgetting to add the proper extension for a library or object file will not generate an error if a source module exists with the same path and filename.

Using libraries

Using a library with DMD can be as easy as making one, but there are some potential pain points. For the simplest cases, you can pass a library directly on the command line along with one or more source files, object files, or other libraries. As long as a main function exists somewhere in the mix, the compiler will make sure everything is passed to the linker to generate the executable. For example, given a module main.d in $LEARNINGD/Chapter08/libs, which looks like this:

```
void main() {
    import hello, goodbye;
    sayHello();
    sayGoodbye();
}
```

As we saw in *Chapter 4*, *Running Code at Compile Time*, we can add a lib pragma to the top of main.d and forgo the need to pass the library on the command line at all, but if we do decide to use the command line, there are some differences between Windows and other platforms.

On Windows, we can compile the preceding code and link with `combined/greets.lib` like so:

```
dmd main.d combined/greets.lib
```

This command line hides the linker flags from the user. Whether we're using the Digital Mars linker or the Microsoft linker, the compiler will do what needs to be done to link the binary. DMD allows flags to be passed directly to the linker with the `-L` switch. On Linux, Mac, and the BSDs, this is used to specify any libraries that should be linked with. On those platforms, the GNU linker expects libraries to be fed to it with the `-l` (lowercase L) switch. For example, given `libgreets.a` in the same directory as `main.d`, we would link with it like so:

```
dmd -L-lgreets main.d
```

The `-L` tells the compiler that what immediately follows is not for the compiler itself, but for the linker. So, now we have two different command lines for linking with libraries, one for Windows and one for other platforms. If we want to pass a common directory in which to find libraries, it gets a bit messier.

Whether we're passing libraries on the command line or using lib `pragmas`, when we are using multiple libraries from the same path, it can help keep things neat and concise if we tell the linker to look for the libraries in a specific directory. Moreover, due to the nature of the linker on Linux and other platforms, you typically don't want to be passing a full library name (such as `libhello.a`) to the linker. This is where the pain starts to set in if you are using a make file or custom build script to compile on multiple platforms, or on Windows with multiple compilers or architectures.

To specify a common directory, we have to explicitly pass the appropriate flag to the linker via `-L`, but the DM linker and the MS linker take different options. Not only that, if you throw in other platforms, you've got a third option to deal with. In short, telling the linker to search for libraries in the separate subdirectory and link with both the `hello` and `goodbye` libraries looks like the following with the different linkers:

- With the Digital Mars linker:

  ```
  dmd -L+separate\ main.d hello.lib goodbye.lib
  ```

- With the Microsoft linker:

  ```
  dmd -m64 -L/LIBPATH:separate main.d hello.lib goodbye.lib
  ```

- With the GNU linker:

  ```
  dmd -L-Lseparate -L-lgoodbye -L-lhello main.d
  ```

This is where something like DUB really comes in handy. No matter which compiler, which platform, or which linker, it abstracts away all these differences so that you never have to worry about them.

Finally, it's worth noting that DMD looks for the LIB environment variable when it's time to link. If you have any special paths where you like to store libraries, you can add that path to LIB, either on the command line, via a shell script, or in the DMD configuration file.

Warnings

Warnings in DMD are not enabled by default. There are two ways to turn them on. With the -w switch, warnings will be treated as errors and cause compilation to halt. The -wi switch will allow compilation to continue, printing each warning to stderr as they are encountered. Whichever approach you prefer, it's a good idea to compile your project with these once in a while, if not all the time, to try and squelch any warnings that may arise.

Profiling

There are a number of profiling tools out there that may be usable with D when working with the GCC or Microsoft toolchains, but DMD ships with an easy-to-use option that allows you to get an idea of where your D program is spending its time. It's a simple command-line switch, -profile, which results in a binary that generates profiling information on execution.

In the $LEARNINGD/Chapter08/profile directory, you'll find a source file, main.d:

```d
uint calc(uint x, uint y) {
    return x + y;
}
uint select() {
    import std.random : uniform;
    return uniform(1u, 1001u);
}
void main() {
    import std.stdio : writeln;

    for(size_t i=0; i<100; ++i) {
        writeln("Starting calculations...");
        uint result;
        for(size_t j=0; j<20; ++j)
            result += calc(select(), select());
        writeln("The accumulated result: ", result);
    }
}
```

Compile this file with the following command:

```
dmd -profile main.d
```

Executing the resulting binary will produce two new files, `trace.def` and `trace.log`. The former is intended to be passed to the linker, telling it the optimal order in which to link the program's functions. The latter has two sections that display information about the program's call tree and the function timings.

The first section appears to be a jumbled mess of mangled function names and numbers, but there is a method to the madness: it's a call tree. Each entry is separated by dashed lines, with the first function called in the program (the main function) listed at the very bottom of the tree. Scroll down until you see the last few sections that look like this:

```
- - - - - - - - - - - - - - - - -
          4000   _Dmain
_D4main6selectFZk    4000    2736    471
          4000   _D3std6random27__T7uniformVAyaa2_5b29TkTkZ7uniformFNfkkZk

- - - - - - - - - - - - - - - - -
            1  main
_Dmain 1          119380 464
           100   _D3std5stdio16__T7writelnTAyaZ7writelnFNfAyaZv
          4000   _D4main6selectFZk
          2000   _D4main4calcFiiZk
           100   _D3std5stdio18__T7writelnTAyaTkZ7writelnFNfAyakZv

- - - - - - - - - - - - - - - - -
main   0     0     0
            1   _Dmain
```

The entry at the bottom tells us that the `main` function (which is actually internal to `DRuntime`) calls `_Dmain` exactly one time (`_Dmain` is the name by which `DRuntime` knows our `main` function in `main.d`). Moving up to the next entry, we see `1 main` in the first line. This tells us this entry is for a function that's called one time from `main`. Next we have the name of that function (`_Dmain`), followed by all of the functions that it calls and how many times it calls each of them. Next to `_Dmain` we see three numbers, `1`, `119380` and `464`. The first is the number of times it is called, in this case by `main`, the next two are timings in *ticks*, or the number of times the timer has incremented. The first timing is the total number of ticks taken by `_Dmain`, including the tick count of the functions it calls (call tree time).

The second is the tick count of _Dmain minus that of the functions it calls (function call time). Moving up, we see an entry for one of the functions that _Dmain calls 4000 times, select, along with the functions it calls. Select has tick counts of 2736 and 471. Every function call in the program will have an entry in the same format as those shown here.

The second section, just below the bottom entry in the call tree, starts off like this:

```
======== Timer Is 3320439 Ticks/Sec, Times are in Microsecs ========
```

This is arguably the part of the file you'll usually be most interested in. It is a table listing the number of calls and timings for each function. The headers of the table are, as shown:

```
Num         Tree        Func        Per
Calls       Time        Time        Call
```

Tree Time is the total amount of time spent inside the function, including any function calls it makes. Func Time is the total amount of time spent in the function minus any function calls it makes. Per Call is Func Time / Num Calls. Following the headers is an entry for every function, most of which are listed in their demangled forms. The entry for the select function looks like this:

```
4000        823         141               0      uint main.select()
```

A total of 4000 calls, a total time of 823 microseconds, a total function time of 141 microseconds, and a per call time of 0 (meaning less than one microsecond per call).

Code coverage analysis

Code coverage analysis is useful to find dead code in a program, to make sure that all code paths intended to be taken actually are and, when used in conjunction with unit testing, to ensure all of the code is tested. Essentially, it means analyzing the run time of a program to determine what percentage of the total number of lines of code is actually touched. DMD has built-in support for code coverage analysis via the -cov switch.

Save the following code snippet as $LEARNINGD/Chapter08/cov/main.d:

```d
import std.stdio;
void dontCallMe() {
    writeln("Not covered.");
    writeln("Me neither");
}
void callMe() {
    writeln("Covered.");
```

```
    }
    void main() {
        callMe();
        callMe();
    }
```

Compile it with the following command line:

```
dmd -cov main.d
```

Execute the resulting binary and a new file, `main.lst`, will be created in the same directory. It contains the same source code found in `main.d`, but annotated with the number of times each line of code is executed. At the end of the file, it lists the total percentage of code coverage. In our case, with five total lines of code two of which are never executed, we have achieved only 60% coverage.

```
        |import std.stdio;
        |
        |void dontCallMe() {
0000000|    writeln("Not covered.");
0000000|    writeln("Me neither");
       |}
       |
       |void callMe() {
      2|    writeln("Covered.");
       |}
       |
       |void main() {
      1|    callMe();
      1|    callMe();
       |}
```

```
main.d is 60% covered
```

The `-cov` switch takes an optional argument specifying a target coverage percentage. If the target is not met, an error will be thrown at the end of execution, letting you know before you ever look at the output file if your target is met. For example, execute the following in the same directory:

```
dmd -cov=100 main.d
```

This yields a binary, whose output is this:

```
Covered.
Covered.
Error: main.d is 60% covered, less than required 100%
```

Compile and run

When compiling an executable with the `-run` switch, DMD will launch the binary as soon as it has been compiled and linked. Any files generated during the process are temporary and will be cleaned up once execution has completed. The syntax is as follows:

```
dmd <options> -run <srcfile> <args>
```

Here, `<options>` is any number of DMD options, including source files. However, one source file must follow the `-run` switch in `<srcfile>`. Any arguments passed in `<args>` will be treated as command-line arguments for the executed program.

GDC and LDC

The **GDC** and **LDC** D compilers were mentioned briefly in *Chapter 1, How to Get a D in Programming*. Here, you'll learn more about what they are and where to get them.

GDC

The GNU D Compiler is a community-driven, GPL implementation that integrates the D front end with the GNU Compiler Collection. This integration opens the door to compiling for platforms and targets not officially supported by DMD through the use of the existing GCC toolchain to generate output. It's available through the package managers of several systems, but the latest can always be found at `http://gdcproject.org/downloads`.

At the time of writing, the Linux versions of GDC are well-tested and suitable for production code. They are often used to produce the final release version of software due to GDC's ability to better optimize than DMD. The Windows versions require installation of the `w64-mingw32` compiler, but as I write this, they are considered alpha-quality and not quite ready for production.

Most, if not all, of the supported DMD command-line options have GCC-style equivalents supported by GDC (the common GCC options are also supported). Code generated by GDC can be debugged with GDB. Iain Buclaw, the primary GDC maintainer, is also the official maintainer of D support in GDB. It is expected that GDC will one day become part of the GCC distribution. The source for GDC can be found at `https://github.com/D-Programming-GDC/GDC`. There is also a GDC-specific forum at `http://forum.dlang.org/group/gdc`.

LDC

LDC is an open-source, community-driven compiler that integrates the D frontend with the LLVM core libraries. It is available for several different platforms supported by LLVM. Where it can't be obtained through a package manager, binaries of the latest version can always be downloaded at `https://github.com/ldc-developers/ldc/releases` and the source is available at `https://github.com/ldc-developers/ldc`. At the time of writing, Windows binaries require the Visual Studio runtime, though past releases have also supported `w64-mingw32`.

In addition to LLVM-related command-line options, LDC has equivalents for many of the options supported by DMD. Output on most platforms can be debugged with GDB and with Visual Studio on Windows. Like GDC, LDC is also better at optimizing D code than DMD, so it's another alternative used for release versions of software. The LDC forum at `http://forum.dlang.org/group/ldc` is a good source of help.

RDMD

When compiling with DMD or any other D compiler, every module intended to be part of the final binary must be passed on the command line, either in the form of source code for compilation or as object or library files for linking. DUB eliminates that requirement by managing everything itself. DUB will compile all of the modules in a project's `source` directory into the output binary, though a directive can be added to the project configuration to exclude one or more files.

RDMD is a build tool that works a bit differently. First off, it has no concept of a project. All it cares about are source files, no matter where they may be located. Given a single source file, RDMD will determine all of the modules it imports, all of the modules imported by those modules, and so on, and pass all imported modules on to the compiler. In other words, if a module is not imported anywhere in a program, it is not compiled into the final binary. Once compilation is complete, RDMD will launch the newly created executable. All generated files are cached in a temporary directory so that each invocation of `rdmd` will only compile new or changed source files.

RDMD recognizes a handful of command-line options. Options not recognized by RDMD will be passed on to the compiler. For a list of supported command line-options, execute `rdmd` with no arguments. An important one is `--build-only`, which saves the compiled executable and does not run it. It also accepts a switch, `--eval`, which takes a string of code as an argument to compile and execute. Try this:

```
rdmd --eval="import std.stdio; writeln(`Hello World`);"
```

Another very useful option on systems that understand **shebang lines** (#!) in text files is the `--shebang` switch. This allows RDMD to be used to execute a D `source` file as if it were a script file, for example, `./myscript.d`. Such scripts require the very first line in the file to be a `shebang` line that contains the command line for the program that should be invoked to execute the script. RDMD requires `--shebang` to be the first option in the command-line string. For example:

```
#!/usr/bin/rdmd --shebang -release -O
import std.stdio;
void main() {
    writeln("I'm a D script!");
}
```

The same can be done with DMD using the `-run` switch, but since RDMD will automatically compile all imported modules and only those that need compiling, it's the preferable choice. RDMD ships with DMD.

DustMite

You're hacking away at your keyboard one afternoon when you decide to take a quick break and check the D forums. You see an announcement for a new release of DMD, so you decide to upgrade. A short while later, you're neck-deep in D code again and it's time to compile. You pull up a command prompt, invoke DMD, and find yourself staring at an **ICE** (**Internal Compiler Error**). Congratulations! You've just discovered a compiler bug, potentially a regression introduced by the new release.

The thing to do in this situation is to head over to `https://issues.dlang.org/` and file a bug report, but in order to do that you need to be able to provide a minimal test case that someone else can compile to reproduce the problem. Your program consists of dozens of modules and thousands of lines of code; you obviously can't upload it all. You need to reduce it somehow, but this ICE is the sort of error that makes it almost impossible to whittle things down manually. This is where **DustMite** comes in.

DustMite, which ships with DMD, takes two arguments: a path to a source directory and a string that serves as a test for a specific error. The string should contain one or more shell commands that have a return code of `0` to indicate that an error persists. The `source` directory should be cleaned of all files except D source modules and DustMite should be executed in the parent directory. With this information, DustMite will enter a cycle of removing portions of the source code and recompiling, looking for the minimal set of code that matches the command string it was given.

As an example, given a source file `main.d` in a clean directory named `projects/myproject`, we can navigate to the `projects` directory and execute the following command to get a minimal test case for an internal compiler error. The reduced source tree will be output to the `projects/myproject.reduced` directory.

```
dustmite myproject 'dmd main.d 2>&1 | grep -qF "Internal error"'
```

Linux users will be instantly familiar with the test string. First, it compiles `main.d` with DMD and redirects the output of `stderr` to `stdout`. The pipe then executes `grep`, using the output of `stdout` as its input. `grep` will search for "Internal error" and return `0` if it is found. The `q` in `-qF` tells `grep` not to print anything to `stdout` and the `F` tells it that its input is a newline-separated list of strings.

DustMite and Windows

`grep` is a utility that is not installed on Windows by default. There is a similar tool, called `findstr`, but I've been unable to get it to work with `DustMite`. Windows users might choose to use a custom script (perhaps written in D) or batch file, but it's probably more convenient to install a Windows version of `grep` and either execute DustMite in an MSYS or Cygwin command shell or, when using DUB to manage a project, simply invoke DustMite through DUB.

When you are using DUB to manage your project, you can also use it to call DustMite for you. Pass it the `dustmite` command, an output directory, and a string to use as a regex against which to test the compiler output. Here's an example:

```
dub dustmite ./output --compiler-regex="Internal error"
```

You can read more about DustMite and learn other ways to use it at https://github.com/CyberShadow/DustMite/wiki. For more about using DustMite through DUB, execute the following command:

```
dub dustmite -help
```

DCD

The **D Completion Daemon** is a client-server program that provides an auto-completion service for text editors and IDEs that support D. Many of the editors and IDEs listed earlier in the chapter are either configured to use DCD out of the box or have plugins available that support it. Essentially, the DCD server runs continuously in the background. The editor uses the client to communicate with the server, sending it all the information it needs to determine auto-completion possibilities, or suggestions for function calls, which the server then sends back to the client for display to the user. You can read more about DCD and download the source of the latest release at `https://github.com/Hackerpilot/DCD`.

DVM

When installing DMD with the Windows installer or one of the Linux packages, the compiler is automatically added to the system path for convenience (it's optional with the Windows installer). However, it's sometimes necessary to install multiple versions of DMD. Perhaps you want to test the latest beta, or you want to compile an older project with an older version of DMD and still use a newer version for your new projects. There are different ways to handle this on different systems, but they require varying degrees of effort in getting set up every time you want to add a different version of the compiler to your system. This is the problem **DVM** was created to solve.

When you download a DVM binary or build one yourself, you must first tell DVM to install itself like so:

```
dvm install dvm
```

This will cause DVM to do whatever it needs to ensure that your system is ready to start handling multiple versions of DMD. From that point, getting a new version of DMD is as simple as this:

```
dvm install 2.068.2
```

This will install version `2.068.2` of DMD. Nothing is added to the path at this point. You can install more versions of DMD as needed. Then, when you're ready to use version `2.068.2`, open up a command prompt and type the following:

```
dvm use 2.067.1
```

You can find DVM at `https://github.com/jacob-carlborg/dvm`.

Downloading the DVM binary on Windows

The link to the DVM GitHub page will, if you choose not to build from source, ultimately lead you to the page where all DVM releases are listed. There, you will find a few binaries and a couple of source archives available for download. The Windows binary is named in a format similar to this: `dvm-0.4.3-win.exe`. This looks like it could be an installer, but it is not. When running the install command, be sure to use the actual name of the binary in place of `dvm`. Alternatively, save the downloaded file as `dvm.exe`.

Libraries

There was a time when D libraries were scattered all over the internet, on several different project hosting sites and private servers. Today, though there are still some rogue projects out there that have yet to jump on the bandwagon, the DUB Registry has become the hub of D library activity. In this section, we're first going to talk about the registry itself, specifically about how to use registered projects and how to register new ones.

code.dlang.org

The DUB registry lives at `http://code.dlang.org/`. Its primary purpose is to serve as the main database for DUB-enabled projects. Although the registry is not restricted to libraries, they are where our attention will be directed. A library in the DUB registry is globally available as a dependency to any DUB-enabled project. When you have a need in your project that is not covered by the standard library, this is the first place to look before rolling up your sleeves to develop your own solution.

Using libraries from the DUB registry

As a demonstration of how to use libraries from the DUB registry as project dependencies, we're going to develop a short little program called **colors**. It takes any command line-arguments you feed it and displays it to the console with random foreground and background colors and in a random style. To do this, it uses a library developed by Pedro Tacla Yamada, called **colorize**, as a dependency.

On the main page of the DUB repository, linked above, you can find a link to the registry page for the colorize library. Following that will bring up the project information page, as shown here:

The top section of the page displays information mostly taken from the library's package configuration file. The link to GitHub was provided when the project was registered. Following that is an example of how to include the library as a dependency in your project. Finally, the last part of the page is the README file from the project's GitHub repository.

Note that although the project is registered as `colorize` in the DUB registry, it is `d-colorize` on GitHub. The part that most concerns us right now is the **Installation** section.

Version numbers in DUB packages follow the **Semantic Version** (or **SemVer**) format (see `http://semver.org/`). The basic format is `MajorVersion.MinorVersion.PatchLevel`. Additional information can be tagged on to the end, for example `1.1.0+2.068` might indicate version 1.1.0 of a library, which required version 2.068 of DMD. When adding dependencies to the DUB project configuration, a version number must be specified. There is more than one way to do it, each having different meanings.

`>=1.0.5` means any version greater than or equal to version `1.0.5`, while `<1.1.0` means any version less than version `1.1.0`, and `>=1.0.5 <1.1.0` constrains the version to the anything greater than or equal to `1.0.5` and less than `1.1.0`. The latter form has a shortcut in the form of `~>1.0.5`, which is the recommended format for most projects. See the section titled *Version specifications* at `http://code.dlang.org/package-format?lang=sdl#version-specs` for more details.

For our little example project, the first thing to do is to create a `dub.sdl` file in `$LEARNINGD/Chapter08/colors`. It looks like this:

```
name colors
description "Print randomly colored text to stdout."
copyright "Copyright © 2015, Mike Parker"
authors "Mike Parker"
dependency "colorize" version="~>1.0.5"
```

Next, create a `source` subdirectory in the same location. There, create a file `app.d`. At the top of the file, we need two imports.

```
import colorize;
```

The enumerations `fg` and `bg` in the `colorize` module represent foreground and background colors, respectively. `mode` represents different text styles. There is an overload of `std.random.uniform` which takes an enumeration as a template argument and returns a random member from the `enum`. We can use that to randomly select colors and modes in the function `coloredPrint`.

```
void coloredPrint(string msg) {
    import std.random : uniform;
    auto fore = uniform!fg;
    auto back = uniform!bg;
    auto style = uniform!mode;
    cwriteln(msg.color(fore, back, style));
}
```

The function `cwriteln` is part of `colorize`. It takes the place of `writeln`. Finally, a `main` function which ties it all together.

```
void main(string[] args) {
    import std.stdio : writeln, readln;
    writeln("Enter some text to colorize:");
    auto input = readln();
    coloredPrint(input);
}
```

The output of one run looked like this for me:

```
C:\LearningD\Chapter08\colors>dub
Performing "debug" build using dmd for x86.
colorize 1.0.5: target for configuration "library" is up to date.
colors ~master: building configuration "application"...
Linking...
To force a rebuild of up-to-date targets, run again with --force.
Running .\colors.exe
Enter some text to colorize:
What's up, Doc?
What's up, Doc?
```

That's all there is to it. No matter how complex the library, if it's in the DUB registry, DUB will manage everything for you with one simple addition to the project configuration.

Registering libraries with the DUB registry

To create a library for the DUB registry, there's a major point to keep in mind for the project configuration: do not provide an `app.d` in the project's `source` directory unless you explicitly add the line `"targetType": "library"` to the project configuration. If no target type is specified, DUB will compile an executable when it encounters an `app.d` in the source directory. If there is no `app.d`, it will generate a library instead. Let's try it.

First, let's create a `dub.sdl` in the directory `$LEARNINGD/Chapter08/mylib`, which has the following content:

```
name "mylib"
description "An example DUB-enabled library."
copyright "Copyright © 2015, Mike Parker"
authors "Mike Parker"
dependency "colorize" version="~>1.0.5"
```

The target path is never required for any DUB project. This is just a habit I've gotten into with my own projects: executables go in a `bin` subdirectory and libraries in a `lib` subdirectory. Feel free to follow your own convention. By default, DUB uses the project's root directory as the output location.

Now, let's create a file in the `source` subdirectory called `mylib.d`. It has a single function:

```
module mylib;
void sayIt() {
    import std.stdio : writeln;
    writeln("I don't care what you say anymore, this is my lib.");
    writeln("Go ahead with your own lib. Leave me alone!");
}
```

Now, we can execute `dub` in the project directory, with or without the `build` command, and we'll see a shiny new library in the `lib` subdirectory. If you were really going to register the new library with the DUB registry, you would first need to create a project either at GitHub or BitBucket (which are the only two supported providers at the time of writing), push everything in the project directory to the remote repository, and then tag a new release.

 If you've never used git before, it will be useful to start picking up the basics. It has become a big part of the D ecosystem and, at the time of writing, is the only source control system that DUB knows how to work with. You can find an introductory tutorial to git at `https://git-scm.com/book/en/v2/Getting-Started-Git-Basics`.

Once the repository is set up, you would head over to `http://code.dlang.org/` and register a new account if you don't have one already. After registering and logging in, you would then go to the **My packages** link in the menu bar (`http://code.dlang.org/my_packages`). At the top of that page is a button labelled **Register new package**.

Clicking on that button leads to a page that has a choice box and two text fields.

At the time of writing, the choice box offers two options: GitHub and BitBucket. After making the appropriate selection, you would fill in the first field with your GitHub or BitBucket account name, the second with the name of the repository, and finally click on the **Register package** button. After that, the newly registered library would show up at the top of the registry's main page on its next update (and updates happen fairly frequently).

Once a package is registered, new tagged releases in the git repository will automatically be picked up by the registry. This may take some time though, as not all packages are checked for updates at one time. To help speed things along, you can log in, go to **My packages**, click on the link for the updated library, and then click on **Trigger manual update**. If that button is greyed out and you are not able to click on it, it means that the package is already scheduled for an update.

It's inevitable that the interface will be updated at some point, making these instructions obsolete, but the basic functionality should remain consistent.

Testing DUB-enabled libraries

When developing a DUB-enabled library, there are different ways to test it without registering in the DUB registry. The simplest and easiest to explain is to execute the following: `dub add-local path/to/library/project 0.0.1`. The version specified at the end can be anything you want it to be. With this done, you can now create a separate DUB project, configured as an executable, and include version 0.0.1 of your library as a dependency. This is all local to your machine.

Browsing the DUB registry

At the time of writing, in mid-October of 2015, there are nearly 600 packages in the DUB registry and it's growing every week. The majority of the packages are libraries that scratch one itch or another. To more efficiently browse the registry and find the libraries you need, there is a mechanism that package maintainers can use to categorize their projects.

At the top of the main registry page is a choice box labeled **Select category**. There are two options, **Development library** and **Stand-alone applications**. Select the former. This will display a new choice box that allows you to select a category. Some of these may open up a third choice box to select a sub-category.

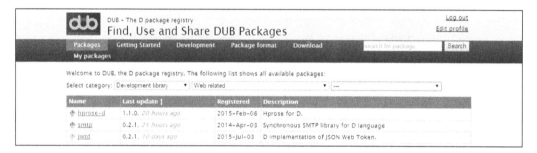

Categories can be added for your own DUB packages by logging in, clicking on **My packages** in the menu bar, and selecting the project you want to categorize. There, on the project page, you will find choice boxes allowing you to associate up to four categories with the package.

Deimos and DerelictOrg

Deimos is an organization at GitHub that serves as an umbrella for a number of static bindings to C libraries. Similarly, **DerelictOrg** (commonly referred to as Derelict) is an umbrella organization for dynamic bindings to C libraries. We're going to cover the difference between static and dynamic bindings in detail in the next chapter, but it can be summed up by saying that the former always has at least a compile-time dependency on a C library and the latter only has a run-time dependency on a C library.

Deimos is an all-encompassing collection of libraries; anyone with a static binding to a C library can have it added to Deimos, no matter the library's arena. All you need do is contact Walter Bright and request to have your library added. Some of the packages are DUB-enabled and in the DUB registry, but not all of them. The members of the Deimos group are curators.

Maintenance is handled by the community. Users can submit pull requests for the curators to apply, and request that packages be added to the DUB registry.

Derelict is a more narrowly-focused collection of bindings, primarily targeting libraries that are useful for game development and multimedia applications. The group is not as open as Deimos. New projects are rarely allowed in. While pull requests are happily accepted, the primary responsibility to maintain and develop the packages rests with the members of the organization (I created Derelict in 2004 and have been the primary maintainer ever since). Anyone is welcome to use the `DerelictUtil` package (which all Derelict packages depend on) to create their own dynamic bindings using the Derelict name, even if the packages are never added to the organization. Every package in Derelict is DUB-enabled and in the DUB registry.

There is some overlap between the two collections, where a static binding to a library exists in Deimos and a dynamic binding to the same library is in Derelict. Which you choose is quite often a matter of preference, but may sometimes be dictated by project requirements. I mention them here primarily because there are some useful bindings in Deimos that are not in the DUB registry, but also because both projects turn up in discussions in the D community on a regular basis. Deimos is located at `https://github.com/D-Programming-Deimos`, and DerelictOrg at `https://github.com/DerelictOrg`.

Summary

In this chapter, we've taken a brief tour of the D ecosystem. We've seen a few web sites that can help in your D journey, discussed DMD a little more in-depth, seen some other useful tools, and gotten a glimpse into the DUB registry and how to make use of it.

In the next chapter, we take a look in detail at a feature of D that enables it to make use of an even wider world of existing software: its ability to communicate directly with libraries that know how to speak C.

9
Connecting D with C

There are many reasons a programming language may fail to gain traction, but a surefire way to discourage adoption is to make it incompatible with C, whose ABI is the *lingua franca* of programming languages. Even if the creators of a new software project are in a position to choose any language they'd like to work with, it's unlikely that they would be willing to take the time to port or recreate the popular battle-tested C libraries they are sure to need, such as image loaders, graphics interfaces, or database drivers. The easier it is to interface with C, the better.

Binary compatibility with C was a priority with D from the beginning. This means it's possible for code written in D to directly call functions written in C (or any language that exposes a C ABI-compatible interface), and vice versa. There's no need for any intermediate layer to bridge the two languages together. This means it's easy, and often quick, to get a D and C program up and running. In this chapter, we're going to take a fairly comprehensive look at how to make D and C work together. It's impossible to cover every possible corner case that may be encountered in the pantheon of C arcana, but it's still going to be heavy on details. This chapter can serve as a reference to connect the two languages in the majority of cases. The layout looks like this:

- Preliminaries: terminology, object file formats, and linkage attributes
- Binding D to C: function prototypes and type translation
- Calling C from D: handling arrays, memory, and exceptions
- Calling D from C: how to manage DRuntime

Preliminaries

The bulk of this chapter is about C code and D code, and what you need to do in order for the two to communicate. There are a few prerequisites that need to be established before we roll up our sleeves. First, there needs to be a clear understanding of the key terminology used in this chapter, both in order to understand the content and to discuss it with others. An understanding of the different types of binary output from the different compiler toolchains is key to getting D and C binaries to link. Second, it's beneficial to know at least a little of what's going on under the hood when D and C are combined in the same program. We'll cover all of that here in this section.

Terminology

In order to avoid the potential for misunderstanding in this chapter and in conversations with other D programmers, we're going to clearly define certain terms that pop up in any discussion of connecting D with C. There are those for whom the meanings of some of these words blur together, but we're focusing strictly on how they are generally used in the D community at large.

Bindings, wrappers, and ports

The primary focus of this chapter is how to create a binding between D and C. A **binding** is a bit of code that allows one language to communicate with another. There are two other terms that sometimes get mixed up in the same context: **wrapper** and **port**. If you ever create a binding to a C library and intend to make it publicly available for others, you want to make sure you're using the correct terminology.

Different languages have different approaches to creating language bindings. Java programmers bind to foreign-language libraries through the **Java Native Interface (JNI)**. An intermediate layer, which sits between the Java code and the library, is created as a C or C++ library. The JNI is used to translate Java types and function calls to something understood by the foreign library. In this scenario, the Java code does not bind to the foreign library itself, but rather to the intermediate layer. This means there need not be a one-to-one correspondence between the types and function signatures in the library and those on the Java side. In fact, the intermediate layer can hide the library interface completely and expose an entirely new interface to the Java code, one that *wraps* the library. In that situation, the result can be called a **wrapper**.

C++ has the advantage that C++ compilers can understand C header files. No bindings need to be created to use a C library in C++. However, some C++ programmers prefer to create an object-oriented interface over a C library, using C++ features that aren't present in C. Again, this can be called a wrapper. When going the other way, from C++ to C, the terminology isn't so obvious. Much of the C++ API is hidden behind C functions. The interface has to be different simply because C does not support many C++ features. Is this a binding or a wrapper? Both terms are sometimes used in this case.

Like C++, D can communicate directly with C without the need for a JNI-like layer in the middle. However, D compilers do not know how to parse C header files. That means the function prototypes and type declarations in a C header need to be translated to D. The result is a module full of aliases, type declarations, and function prototypes that can be called a **binding**. The new D module can be imported in any D project and, once compiled and linked with the C library, will allow D code to call into the C API directly.

Several great examples of this can be found in the DRuntime source that ships with DMD. The `core.stdc` package is a collection of modules that, together, form a binding to the C library. In it you'll find function prototypes such as this one from `core.stdc.stdlib`:

```
extern(C) void exit(int status);
```

That comes with a companion set of manifest constants, which are the result of translating the C definitions for the possible values of `status`:

```
enum EXIT_SUCCESS = 0;
enum EXIT_FAILURE = 1;
enum MB_CUR_MAX   = 1;
```

When you compile any D program, the standard C library is automatically linked, so you can call `exit` and any other standard C functions any time you like. All you need is to import the correct module.

In D, there is a clear distinction between bindings and wrappers. Bindings provide no implementation of the functions in an API, only the signatures; they link directly with the equivalent symbols in a C library. A wrapper can be implemented on top of a binding to give it a more D-like interface, but the functions in a wrapper must have an implementation. As an example, you can find a binding to the 2D graphics library, SDL, at `https://github.com/DerelictOrg/DerelictSDL2`. Then at `https://github.com/d-gamedev-team/gfm/tree/master/sdl2/gfm/sdl2` is an API that uses the binding internally, but wraps the SDL interface in something more D-friendly.

That brings us to the word **port**. Typically, this term is used to indicate that a program has been translated from one language, platform, or CPU architecture to another. Looking at `core.stdc` again, some might say that the headers of the C standard library have been ported to D, but that's misleading; we cannot say that the entire library has been ported. Translating the headers is what is necessary to create a binding; translating the source is creating a port. As an example, the *colorize* package that we used in the previous chapter is a port of a Ruby library to D. Bindings have a number of constraints which ports don't have, perhaps the biggest being a dependency on the original C library.

> Once, I was scrolling through the DUB registry looking at new packages that had been added and found one that was described as a port of a C library. Clicking through and looking at the source showed it to be a binding, not a port. It may seem like a small matter to confuse terminology like that, but inaccurate terminology can lead to a surprising number of support requests and issue reports from people who don't bother to click through to the source first.

Dynamic and static – context matters

From personal experience in maintaining the Derelict bindings over several years, more confusion arises from the terms **dynamic binding** and **static binding** than from any other related terms. There are four other terms that include *dynamic* or *static* and which are often used in any discussion about compiling, linking, and using bindings: **dynamic linking**, **static linking**, **dynamic libraries**, and **static libraries**. Even if you are familiar with these terms and what they describe, you are encouraged to read through this subsection to fully understand the difference between static and dynamic bindings.

Static libraries and static linking

Static libraries are a link-time dependency. They are archives of object files that are handed off to the linker along with any other object files intended to be combined to form an executable or shared library. On Windows, they tend to have the `.lib` (Library) extension, while on other platforms (and Windows versions of GCC) they usually have the `.a` (Archive) extension. When a static library is created, no linking takes place. The compiled objects are gathered into a single library file, and there they stay until the library is ultimately handed off to a linker during the build process of an executable or shared library. This means that if the library has any other link-time or runtime dependencies, the final binary will have those dependencies as well.

The job of the linker, in addition to creating the final binary, is to make sure that any reference to a symbol in any of the object files it is given, be it a function call or a variable access, is matched up with the symbol's memory offset. With a static library, everything needed is right there for the linker to make use of. It's just the same as if every object file in the library were given to the linker individually on the command line. Linking with a static library is known as **static linking**.

Dynamic libraries and dynamic linking

Dynamic libraries (I will use shared library and dynamic library interchangeably in this book) are often a link-time dependency, but are *always* a runtime dependency. On Windows, they have the .dll (**Dynamic Link Library**) extension, while on Unix-based systems they have the .so (Shared Object) extension (Mac OS X additionally supports .dylib, or Dynamic Library files). Dynamic libraries are created by a linker, not by a library tool. This means that any link-time dependencies a shared library has are part of the library itself; any executable using the shared library need not worry about them. Runtime dependencies, by definition, still need to be available when the program is executed.

Any program that uses a dynamic library needs to know the address of any symbols it needs from the library. There are two ways to make this happen. The first, and most common, is **dynamic linking**. With this approach, the linker does the work of matching up the offsets of the library symbols with any points of access in the executable. This is similar to what it does with static linking, but in this case the library is not combined with the executable. Instead, when the executable is loaded into memory at runtime, the dynamic library is loaded by the system's dynamic linker (or runtime linker), which I'll refer to as the **system loader**. The preliminary work done by the linker allows the loader to match function calls and variable accesses with the correct memory addresses.

On Unix-based systems, dynamic linking takes place by giving the shared object file directly to the linker, along with any object files and static libraries intended to form the final executable. The linker knows how to read the library and find the memory offset of each symbol that is used by the other files it is given. On Windows, when a DLL is created, a separate library, called an **import library**, is also created. This file, somewhat confusingly, has the same .lib extension as a static library. The import library contains all of the offsets for every symbol in the DLL, so it is passed to the linker in place of the DLL itself. Some C and C++ linkers on Windows know how to fetch the memory offsets directly from a DLL, so they can be given either the import library or the DLL.

The second way to make use of a dynamic library is for the program to load it manually at runtime (often called **dynamic loading**, but we've got enough *dynamics* to deal with here already, so I'll use the term **manual loading**). Essentially, the programmer must do in code what the system loader would have done at application start up: match any use of a dynamic library's symbols in a program with the addresses of the symbols after the library is loaded into memory. This requires all functions and variables declared and used in the program to be pointers (more on that shortly). Using an API exposed by the operating system, the dynamic library is loaded into memory with a function call, then another function is used to extract the address of every required symbol, which is then assigned to an appropriate pointer.

In order for the system to load a dynamic library at runtime, it must know where the library can be found. Every operating system defines a search path for dynamic libraries. Though there are normally several locations on the search path, there are typically only one or two directories on any given system where most shared libraries live. On Windows, it's normal for any non-system libraries required by a program to ship in the same directory as the executable, with the result that multiple copies of the same library may be installed with multiple programs. On Unix-based systems, it's preferred for dependencies to be installed on the system search path through a package manager so that every program can share the same copy of the library. This is supported on OS X, but it additionally supports packing dependencies with the executable in an application bundle.

Dynamic and static bindings

Now we get to the underlying theme of this chapter. When setting out to create a D binding to a C library (or vice versa), a decision must be made on what type of binding it is going to be: a **static binding** or a **dynamic binding**. Unfortunately, *static* and *dynamic* used in this context can sometimes lead to the erroneous conclusion that the former type of binding requires static linking and the latter requires dynamic linking. Let's nip that misconception in the bud right now.

A static binding is one that always has a link-time dependency on the bound library, but that dependency can be in the form of a static library or a dynamic (or import) library. In this scenario, functions and global variables are declared on the D side, much as they would be in any C header file. The `core.stdc` package in DRuntime is a static binding to the standard C library. Let's look again at the declaration of the `exit` function:

```
extern(C) void exit(int status);
```

In order for this to compile, one of two things must happen: either the static version or the dynamic version of the C library must be passed to the linker. Either way, there is a link-time dependency. Failure to pass a library to the linker would cause it to complain about a missing symbol. If the dynamic library is linked, then there is an additional runtime dependency as well. DMD will automatically link the C standard library, though whether it does so statically or dynamically depends on the platform.

With a dynamic binding, we completely eliminate the link-time dependency, but take a guaranteed runtime dependency as a trade-off. With this approach, normal function declarations are out the window. Instead, we have to declare function pointers. In a dynamic binding to the C standard library, the declaration of the exit function on the D side would look like this:

```
extern(C) alias pexit = void function(int);
pexit exit;
```

Then, somewhere in the program, the standard C library needs to be loaded into memory, and the address of the exit symbol must be fetched and assigned to the function pointer.

Just to drive the point home, because it is so often the source of misunderstanding: static bindings can link with either static or dynamic libraries, but they must always link with something; dynamic bindings have no link-time dependencies at all, but the dynamic library must always be loaded manually at runtime.

Object file formats

One potential sore spot when working with static bindings is object file formats. Any given linker knows how to deal with a specific format, which means any object files and libraries it is given must be in that format. On Linux, Mac, and other Unix-based platforms, this isn't such a big deal. The compiler backends on all of these platforms output the same object file format, such as elf on Linux and the BSDs, or mach-o on OS X. On Windows, the picture isn't so rosy.

Among the three major D compilers on Windows, there are three linkers to contend with: the DMC linker that DMD uses by default, the MinGW linker used by GDC and one flavor of LDC, and the Microsoft linker used by DMD in 64-bit mode (and 32-bit with the -m32mscoff switch) and another flavor of LDC. Among these three linkers are two primary object formats: OMF and COFF. The DMC linker outputs object files in the ancient OMF format, whereas everything else outputs COFF. This is an issue that affects both static and import libraries.

Another potential thorn arises when dealing with static libraries generated by MinGW. Sometimes, it's possible for them to work with the Microsoft toolchain, as they use the COFF format and link with the Microsoft C Runtime. Unfortunately, there are a number of incompatibilities that can crop up in the form of linker errors. Even static libraries compiled directly with Microsoft Visual Studio can sometimes result in linker errors when given to DMD, depending on the options that were used to compile the library.

The bottom line is that, with a static binding, all static libraries, import libraries, and object files given to the linker must be in the file format the linker understands. Preferably, the libraries and object files will all have been compiled by the same toolchain. Generally, you want to follow these guidelines when compiling any C library intended to be used with a static binding in a program compiled by DMD:

- On Windows, when compiling the program with the -m32 switch (the default), all C libraries should be compiled with DMC

- On Windows, when compiling the program with -m64 or -m32mscoff, all C libraries should be compiled with the Microsoft compiler

- On other platforms, all C libraries can be compiled with either GCC or clang

If you're coming to D from a language such as Java and have never compiled a C library before, most popular C library projects for which D bindings exist provide binary distributions for different platforms and compiler toolchains. You may never need to compile any C at all. However, it's still useful to learn about some of the different build tools many C projects use. There may be times when no binary distribution is available and you have no choice but to compile it yourself.

Conversion tools

When compiling with DMD on Windows using the default architecture (-m32), COFF files can be converted to OMF using a conversion tool such as Agner Fogg's free object file converter (http://agner.org/optimize/#objconv) or the coff2omf utility that is part of the commercial Digital Mars Extended Utility Package (EUP) (http://www.digitalmars.com/eup.html). The EUP also contains a tool, coffimplib, which will create an import library in OMF format from a DLL compiled as COFF. For all three tools, the results may not be perfect.

Linkage attributes

The fundamental mechanism that affects how D and C symbols interact with one another is the **Application Binary Interface (ABI)**. This defines such things as how types are laid out in memory, what their sizes are, and so on. Most of that we don't have to worry about when creating a binding, as the compiler takes care of it for us. However, there are two aspects of the ABI to which active attention should be paid in order to ensure the binding matches up with the C library. Get this wrong and any binding you create becomes nothing more than a pile of linker errors or access violations waiting to happen. One mechanism is that of name mangling, the other is calling conventions.

Name mangling

With a language that supports function overloading, a linker needs to be able to distinguish between different overloads of a function. It also needs to be able to distinguish between any symbols of the same name in different namespaces. This is where name mangling comes into play. The compiler takes symbols declared in source code and *mangles*, or *decorates*, them with a set of characters that have predefined meanings. We can see this in D by calling the `mangleof` property on any symbol. Save the following as `$LEARNINGD/Chapter09/mangle.d`:

```
module mangle;
import std.stdio;
int x;
void printInt(int i) { writeln(i); }
void main() {
  writeln(x.mangleof);
  writeln(printInt.mangleof);
}
```

Running this results in the following output:

_D6mangle1xi

_D6mangle8printIntFiZv

A linker need not know or care what the mangled names indicate, but a tool that understands D mangling can make use of it. In both lines, `_D` indicates that this is the D name-mangling format. The `6` immediately after it says that the symbol following the number, `mangle`, has six characters. Being that `mangle` is the first symbol in the name, we know it's the name of the module. It acts as a namespace. In the first line, `mangle` is followed by `1xi`. The `1` indicates a one-character symbol name, `x` is the name, and the `i` tells us it's an `int`.

Similarly, the second line tells us that the symbol name has 8 characters and the name is printInt. F lets us know that it's a function, i that it takes an int parameter, and z, in this case, indicates that the next character represents the return type of the function. Since that happens to be v, we know the return type is void. You can read more about D's name mangling at http://dlang.org/abi.html.

Not all languages define a name-mangling format as D does. C++, for example, does not; each compiler has its own approach to name mangling, which is one of several aspects of the C++ ABI that makes it extremely difficult to bind to C++ libraries (though, as we'll see in *Chapter 11*, *Taking D to the Next Level*, there is ongoing work to make it possible in D). C, on the other hand, is the lingua franca of programming languages for a reason: it has a well-defined ABI that does not include function overloading or namespaces.

That's not to say that C compilers don't use any sort of decorations. It's still necessary to distinguish between variables that are declared locally to a compilation unit rather than globally, but this has no impact on bindings. Some compilers may decorate a C symbol in a static library with an underscore, but this is usually not an issue in practice. The short of it is that when a C header is translated into D, any symbols that need to link up on both sides cannot be declared with the default D name mangling. The C side knows nothing about D's name-mangling scheme, so nothing would ever match up unless it's disabled. We'll see how to do this soon, but first we need to talk about calling conventions.

Calling conventions

When a function is called, there are a number of steps that must be taken, both at the beginning of the call and at the end. During compilation, the compiler generates the appropriate instructions to carry out those steps. This includes instructions to preserve the contents of the CPU registers if needed, pushing function parameters on the stack or copying them into registers before the call, looking in the correct location for a return value once a function call has ended, and other low-level details that we programmers never have to manage ourselves unless we are programming in assembly. In order for the correct instructions to be generated, the requirements must be detailed somewhere of how to carry out any given function call, including whether it expects any parameters in registers, in what order stack parameters should be pushed, and so on. That's the role played by a calling convention.

A calling convention defines how every aspect of a function call should be handled. When a function is compiled, the compiler determines which calling convention is associated with the function and generates the appropriate instructions to fetch parameters and return a value. When any code calling that function is compiled, the compiler must be made aware of the calling convention originally used to compile the function so that it can generate the appropriate instructions for the call.

By default, all functions in D are assumed to have the D calling convention. As I write, the D calling convention on non-Windows systems is documented to be the same as the C calling convention supported by the system C compiler. In practice, there are undocumented discrepancies, but this isn't an issue for general use. The convention for Windows is described at `http://dlang.org/abi.html`.

Putting it together

When binding to any C library from D, it's important to know exactly which calling convention the library uses. On non-Windows systems, this is almost always the C calling convention. On Windows, it is usually either the C calling convention or the system calling convention, `stdcall` (standard call). Often, the calling convention used is not described anywhere in a library's documentation and it's necessary to look at the headers. If you find `__stdcall` defined in any of the headers, such as something like this:

```
#define DLL_CALLCONV __stdcall
```

Then you know any functions annotated with `DLL_CALLCONV` have the standard call calling convention. The C calling convention might also be defined explicitly with a `__cdecl`. If no convention is declared, you can assume the C calling convention, which is the default for all C compilers.

Changing the default

Some C compilers allow changing the default calling convention through a command line switch. For people using Visual C++, this is easily done in a project's properties window. This is a potential issue when using precompiled libraries with bindings.

D allows you to specify both the name-mangling scheme of any symbol and the calling convention of any function by using a linkage attribute. Here's an example:

```
module linkage;
extern(C) int cint;
extern(D) int dint;
extern(C) int aFuncWithCLinkage() { return 1; }
extern(D) int aFuncWithDLinkage() { return 2; }
void main() {
  import std.stdio;
  writeln(cint.mangleof);
  writeln(dint.mangleof);
  writeln(aFuncWithCLinkage.mangleof);
  writeln(aFuncWithDLinkage.mangleof);
}
```

`extern(C)` is a linkage attribute that turns off name mangling (to match C) and specifies that a function has the C calling convention. `extern(D)` specifies the D name mangling and calling convention. The output looks like this:

cint

_D7linkage4dinti

aFuncWithCLinkage

_D7linkage17aFuncWithDLinkageFZi

That's a big difference. It's easy to forget that linkage attributes affect more than calling conventions. Of course, since D is the default name-mangling scheme and calling convention, the need to specify it in code is rare (in the previous example, `main` has D linkage). However, linkage attributes can be declared with a colon (`:`) and with braces (`{}`), so it may sometimes be needed. For example:

```
extern(C):
    // A bunch of stuff with C linkage
extern(D):
    // Enable D linkage again
```

In addition to `C` and `D`, there are also the `Windows`, `System`, and `Pascal` linkage attributes. `extern(Windows)` is used for functions that have the standard call calling convention. `extern(System)` defaults to `extern(Windows)` on Windows and `extern(C)` elsewhere. There are some cross-platform libraries out there that use the default C calling convention on most platforms, but use standard call on Windows. `extern(System)` eliminates the need to declare two sets of function declarations to match the different calling conventions. The need for `extern(Pascal)` is extremely rare, if not nonexistent. It was the system calling convention for Windows back in the 16-bit days.

Linkage attributes have no effect on type declarations. We can see that in this example:

```
module types;
extern(C) struct CStruct {
    int x, y;
}
struct DStruct {
    int x, y;
}
void main() {
    import std.stdio;
    writeln(CStruct.mangleof);
    writeln(DStruct.mangleof);
}
```

The output:

```
S5types7CStruct
S5types7DStruct
```

Some new D programmers think that types must always be declared as extern(C) when binding to C, but that's not the case. The types in D don't even need to have the same name as the C types, as the type names will never be emitted to the binary. All that matters is that the D types are binary compatible with the C types. More on this in the next section.

Another point of confusion comes from function implementations with C linkage. Functions in a C library binding have no implementation, only declarations. However, when using a binding, it is sometimes necessary to implement an extern(C) function to use as a callback. Sometimes, new D users have the impression that D features cannot be used in such a function. This is not the case. Remember, the linkage attribute only affects the mangling of the function's name and its calling convention. There are no restrictions on the features that can be used in the function body. On the other hand, there can be negative consequences when it comes to throwing exceptions and allocating GC memory, but that has nothing to do with the linkage attribute. We'll cover those issues later in the chapter when we talk about calling C from D.

Binding D to C

The first step that must be taken when implementing a binding to a C library is to decide whether it will be a static or dynamic binding. The former requires nothing more than the translation of all of the C types, global variables, and function signatures. The latter additionally requires a supporting API to load a shared library into memory. We'll cover both approaches in this section.

Once the type of binding has been settled, then begins the work of translating the C headers. This requires enough familiarity with C to understand not just the types and function signatures, but also the preprocessor definitions. While we'll cover some common preprocessor usage to look out for and how to translate it to D, there's not enough room here to provide a full tutorial on C preprocessor directives. Those readers unfamiliar with C are strongly advised to take the time to learn some of the basics before taking on the task of translating any C headers.

There are two tools in the D ecosystem that provide some amount of automated translation from C headers to D modules. `htod` is available at `http://dlang.org/htod.html`. It's built from the frontend of DMC, the Digital Mars C and C++ compiler. Another option is DStep, which uses `libclang`. It can be found at `https://github.com/jacob-carlborg/dstep`. Neither tool is perfect; it is often necessary to manually modify the output of both, which makes the information in this chapter relevant. Furthermore, both tools only generate static bindings.

Function prototypes

As we saw earlier, the declaration of function prototypes differs for static and dynamic bindings. The one trait they have in common is that they both need to be declared with a linkage attribute. Given that the functions are implemented in C, it's also normally safe to declare them with the `@nogc` and `nothrow` attributes. With that, in any module where the C function signatures are declared, you can first set aside a block like so:

```
extern(C) @nogc nothrow {
  // Function signatures go here
}
```

Replace `extern(C)` with `extern(System)` or `extern(Windows)` as required.

Now, consider the following hypothetical C function declaration in a C header:

```
extern int some_c_function(int a);
```

Let's put a declaration in our `extern(C)` block for a static binding:

```
extern(C) @nogc nothrow {
  int some_c_function(int a);
}
```

A key thing to remember in a static binding is that the function names on the D side must exactly match the function names on the C side. The linker will be doing the work of matching up the function symbols (either via static or dynamic linking) and it isn't smart enough to guess that `someCFunction` declared in D is the same as `some_c_function` declared in C. It doesn't know or care that they came from different languages. All it knows about is object files and symbols, so the symbols must be the same.

Another thing to consider is that the parameter names are optional. These only have meaning in the function implementation. In the function prototypes, only the types of the parameters matter. You can omit the parameter names completely, or change them to something else. Both of the following will happily link to the C side:

```
int some_c_function(int bugaloo);
int some_c_function(int);
```

If you intend to add Ddoc comments to your binding, it's a good idea to keep the parameter names to make the documentation more clear. It's also best practice to use the same parameter names as the original C library, though I doubt anyone would fault you for changing the names for clarity where appropriate. Additionally, keeping the parameter names makes it possible to use them with compile-time reflection.

If the original C library is well documented, it's reasonable to point users of your binding to the original documentation rather than providing your own. After all, implementing Ddoc comments for the C API means you have to make sure that you don't contradict the original documentation. Then you have to make sure it all stays in sync. That seems like a waste of effort when a perfectly good set of documentation already exists. Ideally, users of your binding would never need to look at its implementation to understand how to use it. They can get everything they need from the C library documentation and examples.

In a dynamic binding, the declaration might look like this:

```
extern(C) @nogc nothrow {
    int function(int) someCFunction;
}
```

Here, we've declared a function pointer instead of a function with no body. Again, the parameter name is not required and, in this case, we've left it out. Moreover, we don't need to use the original function name. In a dynamic binding, the linker plays no role in matching symbols. The programmer will load the shared library, fetch the function address, and assign it to the function pointer manually. That said, you really don't want to use the real function name in this case.

The problem is that the variable that holds the function pointer is also declared as extern(C), which means the symbols for the function pointer and the C function will be identical. It may work most of the time on most platforms, but there is potential for things to blow up. I can tell you from experience that with many libraries it will cause errors during application startup. on Linux If you want to keep the same name, use an alias:

```
extern(C) @nogc nothrow {
    alias p_some_c_function = int function(int);
}
__gshared p_some_c_function some_c_function;
```

We'll see why __gshared is used here shortly.

If we were making a static binding to this single-function C library, we would be finished. All we would need to do is import the module containing the function declaration and link with the C library, either statically or dynamically, when we build the program. For a dynamic binding, however, there's still more work to do.

Manually loading shared libraries

A function pointer is useless until it has been given the address of a function. In order to get the address, we have to use the system API to load the library into memory. On Windows, that means using the functions LoadLibrary, GetProcAddress, and FreeLibrary. On the other systems DMD supports, we need dlopen, dlsym, and dlclose. A barebones loader might look something like this, which you can save as $LEARNINGD/Chapter09/clib/loader.d (we'll make use of it shortly):

```
module loader;
import std.string;
version(Posix) {
    import core.sys.posix.dlfcn;
    alias SharedLibrary = void*;
    SharedLibrary loadSharedLibrary(string libName) {
        return dlopen(libName.toStringz(), RTLD_NOW);
    }
    void unload(SharedLibrary lib) {
        dlclose(lib);
    }
    void* getSymbol(SharedLibrary lib, string symbolName) {
        return dlsym(lib, symbolName.toStringz());
    }
}
else version(Windows) {
    import core.sys.windows.windows;
```

```
alias SharedLibrary = HMODULE;
SharedLibrary loadSharedLibrary(string libName) {
  import std.utf : toUTF16z;
  return LoadLibraryW(libName.toUTF16z());
}
void unload(SharedLibrary lib) {
  FreeLibrary(lib);
}
void* getSymbol(SharedLibrary lib, string symbolName) {
  return GetProcAddress(lib, symbolName.toStringz());
}
}
else static assert(0, "SharedLibrary unsupported on this
platform.");
```

Error handling

This implementation does no error handling, but a more robust implementation would throw exceptions with a system-generated error message as the exception message. See the functions `std.windows.syserror.sysErrorString` and `std.posix.dlfcn.dlerror`.

With that in hand, we can do something like this to load a library:

```
auto lib = loadSharedLibrary(libName);
if(!lib) throw new Error("Failed to load library " ~ libName);
```

To load a function pointer that is not aliased, such as `someCFunction` which we saw previously, we can't just call `getSymbol` and assign the return value directly to the function pointer. The return type is `void*`, but the compiler requires a cast to the function pointer type. However, the type used with the `cast` operator must include the linkage and function attributes used in the declaration of the function pointer. It's not possible to include all of that directly in the cast. There are different ways to handle it.

The simplest thing to do in our case is to call `typeof` on `someCFunction` and use the result as the type in the `cast`:

```
someCFunction =
cast(typeof(someCFunction))lib.loadSymbol("some_c_function");
```

Things are different when the aliased form is used:

```
extern(C) @nogc nothrow {
  alias p_some_c_function = int function(int);
}
__gshared p_some_c_function some_c_function;
```

With this, we can then load the function like so:

```
some_c_function =
cast(p_some_c_function))lib.loadSymbol("some_c_function");
```

One issue with this approach is that `some_c_function`, being a variable, has thread-local storage like any other variable in D. This means that in a multi-threaded app, every thread will have a copy of the pointer, but it will be `null` in all of them except for the one in which the library is loaded. There are two ways to solve this. The hard way is to make sure that `getSymbol` is called once in every thread. The easy way is to add `__gshared` to the declaration as we have done.

We'll dig into this a little more in *Chapter 11, Taking D to the Next Level*, but there are two ways to make a variable available across threads in D: `__gshared` and `shared`. The former has no guarantees. All it does is put the variable in global storage, making it just like any global variable in C or C++. The latter actually affects the type of the variable; the compiler is able to help prevent the variable from being used in ways it shouldn't be.

Trying it out

In the `$LEARNINGD/Chapter09/clib` directory of the book's sample source distribution, you'll find a C source file, `clib.c`, which looks like this:

```
#include <stdio.h>
#ifdef _MSC_VER
__declspec(dllexport)
#endif
int some_c_function(int a) {
  printf("Hello, D! From C! %d\n", a);
  return a + 20;
}
```

This is accompanied by four Windows-specific binaries: `clib32.lib`, `clib32.dll`, `clib64.lib`, and `clib64.dll`. The library files are import libraries, not static libraries, intended to be linked with the static binding. Because they are import libraries, each has a runtime dependency on its corresponding DLL.

If you are working on a platform other than Windows, you can use GCC (or clang, if it is your system compiler) to compile the corresponding version of the shared library for your system. The following command line should get the job done:

```
gcc -shared -o libclib.so -fPIC clib.c
```

You'll also find `loader.d`, the implementation of which we saw previously, and a D module named `dclib.d`. The top part of this module provides both a static and dynamic binding to `some_c_function`. The rest shows how to use the two versions of the binding. The implementation is:

```d
extern(C) @nogc nothrow {
  version(ClibDynamic)
  int function(int) some_c_function;
  else
    int some_c_function(int);
}
void main() {
  version(ClibDynamic)
  {
    import loader;
    version(Win64) enum libName = "clib64.dll";
    else version(Win32) enum libName = "clib32.dll";
    else enum libName = "libclib.so";

    auto lib = loadSharedLibrary(libName);
    if(!lib) throw new Exception("Failed to load library " ~
    libName);

    some_c_function =
    cast(typeof(some_c_function))lib.loadSymbol
    ("some_c_function");
    if(!some_c_function) throw new Exception("Failed to load
    some_c_function");
  }
  import std.stdio : writeln;
  writeln(some_c_function(10));
}
```

The command line used to compile all of this depends on the platform and linker you are using. Compiling to use the static binding in the default 32-bit mode on Windows:

```
dmd dclib.d clib32.lib -oftestStatic
```

This uses the static binding, links with `clib32.lib`, and creates an executable named `testStatic.exe`. To see the sort of error a user would get when the DLL is missing, temporarily rename `clib32.dll` and execute the program. To test the dynamic binding, use this command line:

```
dmd -version=ClibDynamic dclib.d loader.d -oftestDynamic
```

This time, we don't link to anything, but need to compile `loader.d` along with the main module. We specify the version `ClibDynamic` to trigger the correct code path and we output the binary as `testDynamic.exe` to avoid mixing it up with `testStatic`. Once again, temporarily rename `clib32.dll` and see what happens. When manually loading a shared library like this, the loader also needs to manually handle the case where loading fails. One benefit of this approach is that it provides the opportunity to display a message box with a user-friendly message instructing the user on how to solve the problem, or provide a link to a web page that does.

Compiling in 64-bit mode with the MS linker is similar:

```
dmd -m64 dclib.d clib64.lib -oftestStatic64
```

```
dmd -m64 -version=ClibDynamic dclib.d loader.d -oftestDynamic64
```

Again, we're using distinct file names to avoid overwriting the 32-bit binaries.

When compiling the static binding with GCC on other platforms, we need to tell the linker to look for the library in the current directory, as it is not on the library search path by default. `-L-L.` will make that happen. Then we can use `-L-lclib` to link the library:

```
dmd -L-L. -L-lclib dclib.d -oftestStatic
```

Compiling the dynamic binding is almost the same as on Windows, but on Linux (not Mac or the BSDs) we have to link with `libdl` to have access to `dlopen` and friends:

```
dmd -version=ClibDynamic -L-ldl dclib.d loader.d -oftestDynamic
```

When executing either version at this point, you will most likely see an error telling you that `libclib.so` can't be found. Unlike Windows, Unix-like systems are generally not configured to search for shared libraries in the executable's directory. In order for the library to be found, you can copy it to one of the system paths (such as `/usr/lib`) or, preferred for this simple test case, temporarily add the executable directory to the `LD_LIBRARY_PATH` environment variable. Assuming you are working in `~/LearningD/Chapter09/clib`, then the following command will do it:

```
export LD_LIBRARY_PATH=~/LearningD/Chapter09/clib:$LD_LIBRARY_PATH
```

With that, you should be able to execute `./testStatic` and `./testDynamic` just fine.

No matter the platform or linker, a successful run should print these lines to the console:

```
Hello, D! From C! 10
30
```

C types to D types

Getting from C to D in terms of types is rather simple. Most of the basic types are directly equivalent, as you can see from the following table:

C types	D types
void	void
signed char	byte
unsigned char	ubyte
short	short
unsigned short	ushort
int	int
unsigned int	uint
long	core.stdc.config.c_long
unsigned long	core.stdc.config.c_ulong
long long	long
unsigned long long	ulong
float	float
double	double
long double	core.stdc.config.c_long_double

There are a few entries in this table that warrant explanation. First, the translation of `signed char` and `unsigned char` to `byte` and `ubyte` applies when the C types are used to represent numbers rather than strings. However, it's rare to see C code with char types explicitly declared as `signed`. The reason it appears in this table is because the C specification does not specify that the default `char` type be signed or unsigned, but rather leaves it implementation defined. In practice, most C compilers implement the default `char` as a signed type, which matches the default for other types (`short`, `int`, and `long`), but it's still possible to encounter libraries that have been compiled with the default `char` type to be unsigned; GCC supports the `-funsigned-char` command line switch that does just that. So while it's generally safe to treat the default C `char` as signed, be on the lookout for corner cases.

The size of the C `long` and `unsigned long` types can differ among C compilers. Some implement them as 32-bit types and others as 64-bit. To account for that difference, it's best to import the DRuntime module `core.stdc.config` and use the `c_long` and `c_ulong` types, which match the size of the `long` and `unsigned long` types implemented by the backend. When it comes to `long double`, you may come across some documentation or an old forum post that recommends translating it to `real` in D. Once upon a time, that was the correct thing to do, but that has not been true since DMD gained support for the Microsoft toolchain. There, the size of `long double` is 64 bits, rather than 80. To translate this type, import `core.stdc.config` and use `c_long_double`. This list of special cases could grow as support is added for more compilers and platforms.

Don't define your own

If, for whatever reason, you're tempted to avoid importing `core.stdc.config` and declare your own alias for `c_long_double` to treat it as a `double` when using the MS backend, please don't. The compiler specially recognizes `c_long_double` when it's used with the MS backend and generates special name mangling for instances of that type. Using anything else could break ABI compatibility.

Strings and characters

There are two character types in C, `char` and `wchar_t`. Strings in C are represented as arrays of either type, most often referred to as `char*` and `wchar_t*` strings. The former can be translated to D directly as `char*`, although some prefer to translate it as `ubyte*` to reflect the fact that the D `char` type is always encoded as UTF-8, while there is no such guarantee on the C side. In practice, this is more of an issue for how the instances of the type are used, more than how they are translated.

The `wchar_t` type can't be directly translated. The issue is that the size and encoding of `wchar_t` is not consistent across platforms. On Windows, it is a 2-byte value encoded as UTF-16, while on other platforms it is a 4-byte value encoded as UTF-32. There is no wrapper type in `core.stdc.config`, but in this case it's easy to resolve:

```
version(Windows) alias wchar_t = wchar;
else alias wchar_t = dchar;
```

Special types

The types `size_t` and `ptrdiff_t` are often used in C. These are types that are not part of the language, but are defined in the standard library. D also provides aliases that correspond exactly to the type and size of each as defined in the relevant C compiler, so a direct translation is appropriate. They are always globally available, so no special import is required.

Complex types have been a part of C since C99. There are three types, `float _Complex`, `double _Complex`, and `long double _Complex`. In D, these translate to, respectively, `cfloat`, `cdouble`, and `creal`. The functions found in the C header file `complex.h` are translated to D in the DRuntime module `core.stdc.complex`. It's expected that these three complex types will be deprecated at some point in the future, to be replaced by the type `std.complex.Complex`, which is usable now.

C99 also specifies a Boolean type, `_Bool`, which is `typedefed` to `bool` in `stdbool.h`. The specification requires only that the type be large enough to hold the values `0` and `1`. The C compilers we need to worry about for DMD implement `_Bool` as a 1-byte type. As such, the C `_Bool` or `bool` can be translated directly to D `bool`. Older versions of GCC implemented it as a 4-byte type, so be on the lookout if you're ever forced to compile a D program against C libraries compiled with GCC 3.x.

C99 also introduced `stdint.h` to the C standard library. This provides a number of `typedef`s for integer types of a guaranteed size. For example, `int8_t`, `uint8_t`, `int16_t`, `uint16_t`, and so on. When you encounter these in a C header, you have two options for translation. One option is just to translate them to the D type of the same size. For example, `int8_t` and `uint8_t` would translate to `byte` and `ubyte`. The other option is to import `core.stdc.stdint` and use the C types directly.

Enumerations

The C `enum` and the D `enum` are equivalent, so that a direct translation is possible. An example:

```
// In C
enum {
  BB_ONE,
  BB_TWO,
  BB_TEN = 10
};
// In D
enum {
  BB_ONE,
  BB_TWO,
  BB_TEN = 10
}
```

Some thought needs to be given toward how to translate named enums. Consider the following:

```
typedef enum colors_t {
  COL_RED,
  COL_GREEN,
  COL_BLUE
}
```

It may seem that a direct translation to D would look like this:

```
enum colors_t {
  COL_RED,
  COL_GREEN,
  COL_BLUE
}
```

However, that isn't an accurate translation. There is no notion of `enum` namespaces in C, but to access the members of this `enum` in D would require using the `colors_t` namespace, for example, `colors_t.COL_RED`. The following would be more appropriately called a direct translation:

```
alias colors_t = int;
enum {
  COL_RED,
  COL_GREEN,
  COL_BLUE
}
```

Now this can be used exactly as the type is used on the C side, which is important when you want to maintain compatibility with existing C code. The following approach allows for both C and D styles:

```
enum Colors {
  red,
  green,
  blue,
}
alias colors_t = Colors;
enum {
  COL_RED = Colors.red,
  COL_GREEN = Colors.green,
  COL_BLUE = Colors.blue,
}
```

Structures

The D `struct` is binary compatible with the C `struct`, so here too, most translations are direct. An example is:

```
// In C
struct point {
  int x, y;
};
// In D
```

```
struct point {
   int x, y;
}
```

The only difference between these two types shows up in usage. In C, anywhere
the point type is to be used, the struct keyword must be included, for example, in
the declaration struct point p. Many C programmers prefer to use a typedef for
their struct types, which eliminates the need for the struct keyword in variable
declarations and function parameters by creating an alias for the type. This typically
takes one of two forms:

```
// Option 1
typedef struct point point_t;
struct point {
   int x, y;
};
// Option 2
typedef struct {
   int x, y;
} point_t;
```

Option 2 is shorthand for Option 1, with the caveat that point_t is not usable inside
the braces. A good example of where this comes into play is a linked list node:

```
typedef struct node_s node_t;
struct node_s {
    void *item;
    node_t *next;
};
typedef struct node_s {
    void *item;
    struct node_s *next;
} node_t;
```

Note that in the first version of node_s, the the typedefed name is used.. This is
perfectly legal when using an external typedef, but it isn't possible in the second
version. There, since node_t is not visible inside the braces, the struct keyword
cannot be omitted in the declaration of the member next. In D, the two types look
like this, regardless of which approach was used in their C declarations:

```
struct point_t {
   int x, y;
}
struct node_t {
   void* item;
   node_t* next;
}
```

When any C `struct` has a `typedef`ed alias, the alias should always be preferred in the D translation.

It's possible to have multiple type aliases on a single C `struct`. This is most often used to declare both a value type and a pointer type:

```
typedef struct {
    int x, y;
} point_t, *pointptr_t;
```

In D, we would translate this as:

```
struct point_t {
    int x, y;
}
alias pointptr_t = point_t*;
```

Sometimes, a C `struct` is aliased only to a pointer and without a `struct` name. In that case, only pointers to that type can be declared:

```
typedef struct {
    int i;
} *handle_t;
```

Most often, when this form is used, the members of the `struct` are only intended to be used internally. If that's the case, the `struct` can be declared like this on the D side:

```
struct _handle;
alias handle_t = _handle*;
```

We could declare _handle as an empty `struct`, but by omitting the braces we prevent anyone from declaring any variables of type _handle. Moreover, no `TypeInfo` is generated in this case, but it would be with an empty `struct`. These days, most C programmers would likely not implement a handle type like this. A more likely implementation today would look like this:

```
typedef struct handle_s handle_t;
```

In the public-facing API, there is no implementation of `handle_s`. It is hidden away inside one of the source modules. Given only the header file, the compiler assumes that `struct handle_s` is implemented somewhere and will let the linker sort it out. However, without the implementation handy, the compiler has no way of determining the size of a `handle_t`. As such, it will only allow the declaration of pointers. The C API will then contain a number of functions that look like this:

```
handle_t* create_handle(int some_arg);
void manipulate_handle(handle_t *handle, int some_arg);
void destroy_handle(handle_t *handle);
```

In D, we can declare `handle_t` the same way we declared `_handle` previously:

```
struct handle_t;
```

Another C idiom that isn't so common these days, but may still be encountered now and again, is the inclusion of an array declaration in the declaration of the `struct` type itself. For example:

```
struct point {
    int x, y;
} points[3] = {
    {10, 20},
    {30, 40},
    {50, 60}
};
```

D does not support this syntax. The array must be declared separately:

```
struct point {
    int x, y;
}
point[3] points = [
    point(10, 20),
    point(30, 40),
    point(50, 60)
];
```

Pointers

While C pointers are directly translatable to D, it pays to keep in mind the difference in declaration syntax. Consider the declarations of these two variables in C:

```
int* px, x;
```

This is not a declaration of two `int` pointers, but rather one `int` pointer, `px`, and one `int`. In a perfect world, all C programmers would conform to a style that brings a little clarity:

```
int *px, x;
```

Or, better still, declare the variables on separate lines. As it stands, there are a variety of styles that must be interpreted when reading C code. At any rate, the previous declarations in D must be separated:

```
int* px;
int x;
```

Always remember that a pointer in a variable declaration in D is associated with the type, not the variable.

Type aliases

It's not uncommon to see type aliases in C libraries. One common use is to define fixed-size integers. Since the C99 standard was released, such types have been available in `stdint.h`, but not all C compilers support C99. A great many C libraries are still written against the C89 standard for the widest possible platform support, so you will frequently encounter `typedef`ed and `#define`d aliases for integer types to hide any differences in type sizes across platforms. Here are a couple of examples:

```
typedef signed char Sint8;
typedef unsigned char Uint8;
```

Despite the name, the C `typedef` does not create a new type, only an alias. Whenever the compiler sees `Sint8`, it effectively replaces it with `signed char`. The following defines have the same effect, but are handled by the preprocessor rather than the compiler:

```
#define Sint8 signed char
#define Uint8 unsigned char
```

The preprocessor parses a source module before the compiler does, substituting every instance of `Sint8` and `Uint8` with `signed char` and `unsigned char`. The `typedef` approach is generally preferred and is much more common. Both approaches can be translated to D using `alias` declarations:

```
alias Sint8 = sbyte;
alias Uint8 = ubyte;
```

It is not strictly necessary to translate type aliases, as the actual types, `byte` and `ubyte` in this case, can be used directly. But again, maintaining conformance with the original C library should always be a priority. It also minimizes the risk of introducing bugs when translating function parameters, `struct` members, or global variables.

Function pointers

In C libraries, function pointers are often declared for use as callbacks and to simulate `struct` member functions. They might be aliased with a `typedef`, but sometimes they aren't. For example:

```
typedef struct {
  void* (*alloc)(size_t);
  void (*dealloc)(void*);
} allocator_t;
void set_allocator(allocator_t *allocator);
```

And using type aliases:

```
typedef void* (*AllocFunc)(size_t);
typedef void (*DeallocFunc)(void*);
typedef struct {
  AllocFunc alloc;
  DeallocFunc dealloc;
} allocator_t;
void set_allocator_funcs(AllocFunc alloc, DeallocFunc dealloc);
```

Sometimes, they are declared as function parameters:

```
void set_alloc_func(void* (*alloc)(size_t));
```

There are a couple of things to remember when translating these to D. First, callbacks should always follow the same calling convention they have in the C header, meaning they must be given the appropriate linkage attribute. Second, they should probably always be marked with the `nothrow` attribute for reasons that will be explained later in the chapter, but it isn't always quite so clear whether or not to use `@nogc`.

Function pointers intended for use as callbacks aren't intended to be called in D code. The pointers will be handed off to the C side and called from there. From that perspective, it doesn't matter whether they are marked `@nogc` or not, as the C side can call the function through the pointer either way. However, it makes a big difference for the user of the binding. `@nogc` means they won't be able to do something as common as calling `writeln` to log information from the callback. In our specific example, it's not a bad thing for the user to want the `AllocFunc` implementation to allocate GC memory (as long as he or she keeps track of it). Consider carefully before adding `@nogc` to a callback, but, as a general rule, it's best to lean toward omitting it.

Careful consideration should also be given to function pointers that aren't callbacks, but are intended for use as `struct` members. These may actually be called on the D side and may need to be called from `@nogc` functions. In this case, it might make sense to mark them as `@nogc`. Doing so prevents any GC allocations from taking place in the implementations, but not doing so prevents them from being called by other `@nogc` functions. Consider how the type is intended to be used, and what tasks the function pointers are intended to perform, and use that to help guide your decision. Of course, if the function pointers are set to point at functions on the C side, then go ahead and add `@nogc` and `nothrow` to your heart's content.

With that, we can translate each of the previous declarations. The first looks like this:

```
struct allocator_t {
extern(C):
  void* function(size_t) alloc;
  void function(void*) dealloc;
}
```

The function `set_allocator` can be translated directly. From the second snippet, `allocator_t` and `set_allocator_funcs` can be translated directly. `AllocFunc` and `DeallocFunc` become aliases:

```
extern(C) nothrow {
  alias AllocFunc = void* function(size_t);
  alias DeallocFunc = void function(void*);
}
```

Finally, the function `set_alloc_func` could be translated like this (using the form for a static binding):

```
extern(C) @nogc nothrow {
  void set_alloc_func(void* function(size_t));
}
```

In this situation, a function pointer declared as a function parameter picks up the `extern(C)` linkage, but does not pick up the two function attributes. If you want the callback implementation to be `nothrow`, you'll have to declare it like this:

```
extern(C) @nogc nothrow {
  void set_alloc_func(void* function(size_t) nothrow);
}
```

It may be preferable to go ahead and alias the callback anyway:

```
extern(C):
alias AllocFunc = void* function(size_t) nothrow;
void set_alloc_func(AllocFunc) @nogc nothrow;
```

Defined constants

Despite the presence of an `enum` type in C, it's not uncommon for C programmers to use the preprocessor to define constant values. A widely used library that does this is OpenGL. Just take a peek at any implementation of the OpenGL headers and you'll be greeted with a massive list of `#define` directives associating integer literals in hexadecimal with names such as `GL_TEXTURE_2D`. Such constants need not be in hexadecimal format, nor do they need to be integer literals. For example:

```
#define MAX_BUFFER 2048
#define INVALID_HANDLE 0xFFFFFFFF
#define UPDATE_INTERVAL (1.0/30.0)
#define ERROR_STRING "You did something stupid, didn't you?"
```

All of these can be translated to D as manifest constants:

```
enum MAX_BUFFER = 2048;
enum INVALID_HANDLE = 0xFFFFFFFF;
enum UPDATE_INTERVAL = 1.0/30.0;
enum ERROR_STRING = "You did something stupid, didn't you?";
```

Function parameters and return types

When translating function parameters and return types to D, everything that has been said about types so far in this chapter applies. An `int` is an `int`, a `float` is a `float`, and so on. As mentioned earlier, parameter names can be included or omitted as desired. The important part is that the D types match the C types. However, there is one type of parameter that needs special attention: the static array.

Consider the following C function prototype:

```
void add_three_elements(float array[3]);
```

In C, this signature does not cause three floats to be copied when this function is called. Any array passed to this function will still decay to a pointer. Moreover, it may contain fewer than or more than three elements. In short, it isn't different from this declaration:

```
void add_three_elements(float *array);
```

A little-known variation is to use the static keyword inside the array brackets:

```
void add_three_elements(float array[static 3]);
```

This tells the compiler that the array should contain *at least* three elements.

To translate the first function to D, we could get away with treating it as taking a `float` pointer parameter, but that would be misleading to anyone who looks at the source of the binding. The C code is telling us that the function expects three parameters, even though it isn't enforced. For the form that uses the `static` keyword, the `float*` approach is an even worse idea, as that would allow the caller to pass an array containing fewer elements than the function expects. In both cases, it's best to use a static array.

We can't just declare an `extern(C)` function in D that takes a static array and be done with it, though. Recall from *Chapter 2, Building a Foundation with D Fundamentals*, that a static array in D is passed by value, meaning all of its elements are copied. Try passing one to a C function that expects a C array, which decays to a pointer, and you'll corrupt the stack. The solution is to declare the static array parameter to have the `ref` storage class:

```
extern(C) @nogc nothrow void add_three_floats(ref float[3]);
```

Be careful with static arrays that are aliased. Take, for example, the following C declarations:

```
typedef float vec3[3];
void vec3_add(vec3 lhs, vec3 rhs, vec3 result);
```

When we translate the `vec3` to D, it's going to look like this:

```
alias vec3 = float[3];
```

Once that is done and work begins on translating the function signatures, it's easy to forget that `vec3` is actually a static array, especially if it's used in numerous functions. The parameters in `vec3_add` need to be declared as `ref`.

One more thing to consider is when `const` is applied to pointers used as function parameters and return types. For the parameters, the C side doesn't know or care anything about D `const`, so from that perspective it doesn't matter if the parameter is translated as `const` on the D side or not. But remember that `const` parameters serve as a bridge between unqualified, `const`, and `immutable` variables, allowing all three to be passed in the same parameter slot. If you don't add the `const` on the D side, you'll needlessly force callers to cast away `const` or `immutable` in some situations. This is particularly annoying when dealing with strings. The short of it is, always translate `const` function parameters as `const`.

It's also important to keep the const around when it is applied to return types. The C function is expecting that the contents of the pointer will not be modified. If const is not present on the D side, that contract is easily broken:

```
// In C
int const *;      // mutable pointer to const int
const int *;      // ditto
int * const;      // const pointer to mutable int
int const * const; // const pointer to const int
// In D
const(int)*       // The first two declarations above
const(int*)       // The second two -- const pointer to
                  // mutable int isn't possible in D.
```

Symbols

Function parameters, struct members, and type aliases need to be named according to the rules set out in *Chapter 2, Building a Foundation with D Fundamentals*. It's not uncommon to see names in C that are keywords in D. For example, the previous add_vec3 function could easily look like this:

```
void vec3_add(vec3 lhs, vec3 rhs, vec3 out);
```

Since out is a D keyword, it can't be used in the translation. The options are to drop the name entirely, or to use a different name. For struct members, dropping it is not an option, so the only choice is to change the name. For example, _out, out_, or anything that can distinguish it from the keyword. If you're trying to maintain conformance with the original C code, you'll want to make it as close to the original as possible.

That solution works for member variables and function parameters, but sometimes C functions might have a D keyword as a name. In this case, prepending an underscore isn't going to work if you're implementing a static binding. D defines a pragma, mangle, which solves the problem. Simply name the function anything you'd like and give the desired name to the pragma. Consider a C function named body. Translated to D:

```
pragma(mangle, "body") extern(C) void cbody();
```

We use cbody to avoid conflict with the D keyword body, but the pragma instructs the compiler to use body instead of cbody for its generated output.

Global variables

Just as a function in C is usually separated into a prototype in a header and an implementation in a source module, so is a global variable. This is because anything that is implemented in a header file will be copied directly into every source module that includes that header. In order to have only one global instance, the prototype and implementation must be separate. Here's what a global variable might look like:

```
// foo.h
extern int g_foo;
// foo.c
int g_foo = 0;
```

For a static binding, there are three things that need to be accounted for in the translation of g_foo. One is the linkage attribute, since it affects the mangling of the symbol. If the variable is declared to have D linkage, the linker will never be able to find it. Another is the `extern` keyword. Note that `extern(C)` indicates a linkage attribute, but `extern` by itself, with no parentheses, tells the compiler that the symbol is not implemented in the current compilation unit, so it can leave it to the linker to sort things out.

The last thing at issue is something we touched on earlier in this chapter. Recall that variables in D have thread-local storage by default. This is not the case in C. Any global variable declared in C is accessible to all threads. This can't be forgotten when translating. In this case, `shared` is not an option, since it actually affects the type of the variable. The type must be the same as it is in C. So, once again, we turn to __gshared.

With all of that in mind, the translation of g_foo from C to D should look like this:

```
__gshared extern extern(C) g_foo;
```

Substitute `System` or `Windows` for `C` as needed. If there are multiple global variables to declare, a colon or a pair of brackets could be used:

```
__gshared extern extern(C) {
  int g_foo;
}
__gshared extern extern(C):
  int g_foo;
```

For dynamic bindings, the variable must be declared as a pointer. In this case, the linkage attribute is not necessary. Since the symbol is going to be loaded manually, having D linkage isn't going to hurt. Also, `extern` does not apply here. Since the variable is a pointer, it really is implemented on the D side. We can use the same `getSymbol` implementation we used for loading function pointers to load the address of the actual `g_foo` into the pointer.

The `__gshared` attribute isn't a strict requirement in this case, but it ought to be used to make things easier and faster. Remember, space will be reserved for a thread-local pointer in each thread, but it will not be set automatically to point at anything. If you don't want the complexity of calling `getSymbol` every time a thread is launched, use `__gshared`. Bear in mind that if it is not used and the pointer is thread-local, that does not affect what the pointer actually points to. Implementing a bunch of thread-local pointers to a global C variable may very well be begging for trouble.

There's one last thing to consider with global variables in dynamic bindings. Because the variable is declared as a pointer, the user will inevitably have to take this into account when assigning a value to it. After all, to set the value of a pointer, the dereference operator has to be used: `*g_foo = 10`. Not only does this break compatibility with any existing C code, it's very easy to forget. One solution is to use two wrapper functions that can be used as properties. Another is to use a single function that returns a reference.

So, our global variable in a dynamic binding could look like this:

```
private __gshared int* _foo;
int g_foo() { return *_foo; }
void g_foo(int foo) { *_foo = foo; }
```

Users can then do:

```
g_foo = 20;
writeln(g_foo);
```

This also makes for consistency between the static and dynamic version of a binding, if both are implemented.

Macros

Macros are a common sight in C headers. Here's an example:

```
#define FOURCC(a,b,c,d) ((d)<<24) | ((c)<<16) | ((b)<<8) | (a)))
```

Technically, anything implemented with #define is referred to as a macro, but in this text I'm using the term to refer to any #defined bit of code that doesn't establish type aliases or constant values, simply to differentiate between the various types of usage.

There are two options for translating a macro like this: make it a function, or make it a function template. Which approach is taken often boils down to personal preference. The only issue to be wary of is whether the template can be instantiated without the instantiation operator. If not, then existing C code can't be copied verbatim into D. For most macros, like the previous one, that shouldn't be an issue.

Sometimes macros include a cast to a specific type so that it's obvious what the translated function should return. Other times, it must be deduced. It may be possible to derive hints by looking at the C source or examples, or by using existing tools (such as gcc -E), though frequently we are left to figure things out on our own. In this case, given that the macro makes use of the full range of a 32-bit integer, we should choose uint. Then the translated function becomes:

```
uint FOURCC(uint a, uint b, uint c, uint d) {
    return ((d)<<24) | ((c)<<16) | ((b)<<8) | (a)));
}
```

Note that a static binding that only includes type and function declarations does not need to be linked at compile time; its modules only need be present on the import path. Adding function bodies means the binding now becomes a link-time dependency. This would not happen if FOURCC were implemented as a template.

Not all macros are this straightforward. Sometimes you have to follow a chain of nested macros to figure out what's going on. That might mean implementing one function for each macro, or perhaps combining them all into one. It largely depends on how they are used on the C side. Sometimes, a macro is not intended to be used by users of the library, but is instead used only in other macros. Ultimately, this sort of thing is a judgment call.

Some macros can't be translated to functions easily. Consider the following:

```
#define STRINGIFY(s) #s
#define CASESTRING(c) case c: return STRINGIFY(c)
```

A hash (#) in front of a macro argument expands to the string form of whatever was given to the macro. Some C programmers would prefer to use return #c in the CASESTRING macro, but others would prefer to make it as clear as possible that a symbol is being converted into a string by using a helper such as STRINGIFY.

CASESTRING is a fairly common macro, the purpose of which is to take an enum member, use it in a `case` statement inside a `switch`, and return its string representation. Something like this:

```
switch(enumValue) {
  CASESTRING(BB_ONE);
  CASESTRING(BB_TWO);
  CASESTRING(BB_THREE);
  default: return "Undefined";
}
```

Macros such as CASESTRING and STRINGIFY are surely intended primarily for internal use in the C library. When they are in the public-facing headers, users of the library can make use of them, but they shouldn't be considered part of the library's API. Given that, and that they have no use in D, there's normally no need to try to translate them when creating a binding.

Sometimes macros are used to give a semblance of inheritance to C `struct` types:

```
#define OBJECTBASE \
  int type; \
  const char *name; \
  size_t size;
typedef struct {
  OBJECTBASE
} object_base_t;
typedef struct {
  OBJECTBASE
  int x, y, z;
} extended_object_t;
```

The backslash (\) at the end of the first three lines tells the compiler that the macro continues on the next line. We could choose not to implement an equivalent of OBJBASE on the D side and just manually add each field to every `struct` declaration that needs them, but that's error prone. It's better to go ahead and declare a template or string mixin and use that instead:

```
mixin template OBJBASE() {
  int type;
  const(char)* name;
  size_t size;
}
struct base_object_t {
  mixin OBJBASE;
}
```

```
struct extended_object_t {
    mixin OBJBASE;
    int x, y, z;
}
```

Sometimes, arguments to a macro are pasted together to form something new. This is akin to D's string mixins, though nowhere near as flexible. Most often, such macros are used for convenience, but sometimes they are used for a specific purpose, such as hiding implementation details. For example, the Win32 API makes use of many different types of object handles. Normally, these handles are aliased to `void*` with a `#define`, but when compiled with the preprocessor definition `STRICT`, they are aliased to something else completely:

```
#define DECLARE_HANDLE(n) typedef struct n##__{int i;}*n
```

When this macro is called with something like this:

```
DECLARE_HANDLE(HMODULE);
```

It expands to this:

```
typedef struct HMODULE__ {
    int i;
} *HMODULE;
```

The `__` is pasted on to the macro argument with `##` to form the `struct` name. Translating to D:

```
struct HMODULE__ {
    int i;
}
alias HMODULE = *HMODULE__;
```

Here, the `struct` name need not be `HMODULE__`. It can effectively be anything. The important bit is the `alias`. At any rate, whenever pasting with `##` is encountered in a macro, careful attention needs to be given to what the macro is doing in order to decide if and how it needs to be translated.

There are so many creative ways to use (or abuse) the C preprocessor that even someone who has been programming in C for more than 20 years can still learn new tricks. Thankfully, it's rare to encounter arcane preprocessor magic, so most of the macros you encounter will be fairly easy to translate. For those cases where you can't figure out quite what's going on, try looking up a tutorial on the C preprocessor or asking for help in the D forums.

Conditional compilation

In D we have `version` blocks and `static if`, but C programmers use the preprocessor for conditional compilation. This takes the form of `#if`, `#ifdef`, and `#if defined`. The `#if` directive is used to test the value of a defined constant:

```
#define DEBUG_MODE = 1
#if DEBUG_MODE
// Debug code
#else
// Non-debug code
#endif
```

In this specific case, we could likely get away with `debug {}` in the D translation, while in others we'd want to use a `version` block with the same name as the C code. The `#if` directive can also be used with the `>` and `<` operators:

```
#if DEBUG_MODE > 2
// Debug mode   code
#endif
```

This translates nicely to D as `debug(3) {}`.

The `#ifdef` directive tests whether something has been defined. It's frequently used to test for platform, CPU architecture, and even debug mode:

```
#ifdef _WIN32
// Windows code
#else
// Other platforms
#endif
```

`_WIN32` is predefined by most C compilers when compiling on Windows. It's easily translatable as `version(Windows)`. Keep in mind that `_WIN32` is defined by C compilers even when compiling in 64-bit mode on Windows, while `version(Win32)` in D means compilation is targeting 32-bit Windows specifically.

`#if defined` allows multiple checks to be combined into one:

```
#if defined(linux) || defined(__FreeBSD__)
// Code specific to Linux and FreeBSD
#endif
```

Recall from *Chapter 4, Running Code at Compile Time*, that D does not allow Boolean version blocks. There, we saw a way to use `static if` to achieve the same result, but using `version` blocks, the previous code would look like this:

```
// Add this to the top of every module that needs it
version(linux) version = LinuxOrFreeBSD;
else version(FreeBSD) version = LinuxOrFreeBSD;
// Then elsewhere in the module...
version(LinuxOrFreeBSD) { }
```

Alternatively, the code could be duplicated for each platform.

It's often obvious how to translate predefined preprocessor macros like these to D, but it still helps to familiarize yourself with the predefined macros found in DMC, GCC, and the Microsoft compiler. Tests for custom defines, such as ENABLE_LOGGING, or ALLOW_PNG, are always translated to use version blocks.

One potential source of trouble to be aware of is something like this:

```
typedef struct {
    float x, y;
#ifdef ENABLE_3D
    float z;
#endif
} vertex_t;
```

The D translation is straightforward:

```
struct vertex_t {
    float x, y;
    version(ENABLE_3D) float z;
}
```

With this type, anything compiled with ENABLE_3D is going to be binary incompatible with anything that isn't. For a C library you control, this is a non-issue. On Windows, it's easy to compile the C library exactly how you want it and, if linking dynamically or using a dynamic binding, ship the DLL with your app. With a widely distributed library, particularly on a system such as Linux where a number of libraries are preinstalled and users often compile their own versions, the potential for breakage is high. Especially when using a dynamic binding. The best thing to do in that scenario is to determine what the most common compile configuration is for the C library and use that as the default for your binding.

Calling C from D

Once a binding is complete, there are potential crash-inducing bugs to be on the lookout for. Incorrect linkage attributes, the wrong number of function parameters, or any given function parameter declared with the wrong size can all bring the house down when the problem function is called. These are issues on the implementation side. There are other potential problems on the user's side that can also cause crashes or unexpected behavior. That's the focus of this section.

D arrays and C arrays

The inherent difference between C arrays and D arrays is a potential source of both compile-time and runtime errors. Here, we'll see the major issues to be aware of.

Basic arrays

When a C function expects to take an array as an argument, the corresponding parameter is declared as a pointer. Take the following example:

```
#include <stdio.h>
void printThreeInts(int *ints) {
  int i;
  for(i=0; i<3; ++i)
    printf("%i\n", ints[i]);
}
```

It's common practice in C to require an array length to be passed along with the array pointer in functions that have array parameters. In this case, a length parameter is omitted since the expected length of the array is in the name of the function, a practice that, while dangerous and error-prone, isn't exactly uncommon.

C programmers really have to be on their toes, but that means D programmers also have to pay close attention when interacting with C. It's so easy to get used to the safety of D's arrays and forget that calling C functions often requires extra vigilance. Any array you pass to this function must have at least three elements. What happens when you pass a shorter array depends entirely on what exists in the memory locations beyond the end of the array at the time the function is called.

There are two ways to call `printThreeInts` that require no copying or conversions. One is to use a cast, something that is not recommended. The other, recommended, way is to use the `.ptr` property common to all arrays:

```
extern(C) @nogc nothrow void printThreeInts(int*);
void main() {
  int[] ints = [1, 2, 3];
  printThreeInts(cast(int*)ints);
  printThreeInts(ints.ptr);
}
```

Knowing that a D array is a data structure that contains a length and a pointer, it may appear baffling that we can legally cast it to a pointer. Consider this:

```
struct IntArray {
  size_t length;
  int* ptr;
}
auto ia = IntArray(ints.length, ints.ptr);
auto pi = cast(int*)ia;
```

If you were to insert this at the end of `main` and try to compile, the compiler would rightly complain that you can't cast `ia` of type `IntArray` to `int*`. But that's because your `IntArray` type doesn't have the privileges given to built-in arrays.

When we cast our `ints` array to `int*`, the compiler is smart enough to pick up on the fact that all we really want to do is substitute `ints.ptr` in place of the cast. That's essentially what it does. Often, new D programmers tend to use the cast, probably because that's the sort of thing they're used to in other languages, and there is some existing D code out there that does that. Veteran D programmers tend to prefer using the `.ptr` property directly. Not only is it fewer characters to type and makes it clear exactly what's going on, but there's no room for getting the type wrong. Using the cast, you could inadvertently do something like cast away `immutable` or `const`. Always prefer passing the `.ptr`.

If you save the previous C example as `$LEARNINGD/Chapter09/threeints/arrc.c` and the D example as `arr.d` in the same directory, you can compile with the following commands. Using DMD with the default Digital Mars linker:

dmc -c arrc.c

dmd arr.d arrc.obj

Using DMD with the Microsoft linker (be sure to use the x64 Native Tools Command Prompt shortcut in the Visual Studio installation directories):

```
cl /c arrc.c
dmd -m64 arr.d arrc.obj
```

Using DMD on platforms other than Windows:

```
gcc -c arrc.c
dmd arr.d arrc.o
```

Wrapping array functions

One way to avoid making mistakes in calling C functions such as `printThreeInts` is to use a wrapper function. The wrapper accepts a D array as a parameter and verifies it's of the correct length:

```
void printThreeInts(int[] arr) {
    assert(arr.length >= 3);
    printThreeInts(arr.ptr);
}
```

When a C function takes a pointer parameter to which it intends to write data, it's important that the destination array has enough space to hold all of the elements it will be assigned. For example, this function writes three integers to an `int` array:

```
void storeThreeInts(int *ints) {
  int i;
  for(i=0; i<3; ++i)
    ints[i] = i+100;
}
```

With the appropriate binding, we can call it like so:

```
auto threeInts = new int[3];
storeThreeInts(threeInts.ptr);
writeln(threeInts);
```

Here, we've used a dynamic array allocated to hold three elements, but it could be a static array as well. As long as the array has enough space allocated to hold *at least* three elements, we're good.

Arrays of arrays

Sometimes, a C function takes a pointer-to-a-pointer, such as int**, to represent either a single array or an array of arrays. How to handle this depends on the context. Let's first consider the case of a pointer to an array. The following C function takes an array of int arrays and prints the members of each:

```
void printIntArrays(size_t count, int **arrays, size_t *sizes) {
  size_t i, j;
  for(i=0; i<count; ++i) {
    printf("Array #%d:\n", i + 1);
      for(j=0; j<sizes[i]; ++j)
        printf("\t%i\n", arrays[i][j]);
  }
}
```

The first parameter, count, is necessary for the function to know how many arrays it has to work with. The second parameter is the array of arrays, and the third is an array containing the size of each int array. The prototype for a static D binding is:

```
extern(C) @nogc nothrow
void printIntArrays(size_t, int**,size_t*);
```

Though it may seem odd, it's possible to pass a single array to this function. Let's look at that case first, since less work needs to be done than when we pass an array of arrays:

```
auto fourInts = [10, 20, 30, 40];
auto fourIntsSize = fourInts.length;
auto pfi = fourInts.ptr;
printIntArrays(1, &pfi, &fourIntsSize);
```

The highlighted lines are important here. It's not possible to take the address of either .length or .ptr. The only way to get the pointers we need is to first assign them to temporary variables and take the addresses of those. Still, this is easy compared to what we have to do for an array of arrays:

```
auto intArrays = [[10, 20, 30], [1, 3, 5, 7, 9], [100, 101]];
auto ptrs = new int*[3];
auto sizes = new size_t[](intArrays.length);
foreach(i, ia; intArrays) {
  ptrs[i] = ia.ptr;
  sizes[i] = ia.length;
}
printIntArrays(intArrays.length, ptrs.ptr, sizes.ptr);
```

The two highlighted lines show that we have to allocate two arrays for this case. It's not possible to cast a D rectangular array to a C pointer-to-a-pointer.

In a different context, a function might always expect a pointer-to-a-pointer to actually be a pointer to a single array, rather than to multiple arrays, perhaps to assign the array variable a new address. For example, the following function takes an `int**` and reassigns the pointer to a local static array. It then returns the size of the local array so that the calling code knows how many elements it's pointing to:

```
size_t getIntList(int** parray) {
  static int localArray[3] = {10, 20, 30};
  *parray = localArray;
  return 3;
}
```

Given what we've seen so far, your first instinct might be to try this:

```
int*[] ipa = new int*[](1);
auto size = getIntList(ipa.ptr);
```

Since an array of pointers is just like any other array, it makes sense that we should be able to allocate an array of them large enough to hold the number of elements the function wants to write to it. This is no different than what we did for the `storeThreeInts` example. We know we're getting one array element, so we allocate space to hold one element.

If you think about it, the allocation is wasteful. There's no reason to allocate space on the GC heap to hold any C array pointers. If we're worried about the contents of the array changing out from under us on the C side, or perhaps the original array address becoming invalid, allocating space to store the pointer buys us nothing. We would need to allocate space for the elements, then copy them all over to guarantee we can hang on to them for as long as we want. So we can do away with the allocation and just do this:

```
int* pi;
auto size = getIntList(&pi);
```

Now we can take this pointer and slice it to get a D array:

```
auto intList = pi[0 .. size];
```

At this point, we still haven't allocated any GC memory. If we want, we can call `.dup` on the array to allocate space for a new array and copy all the elements over, or we can just work with the slice directly. If you don't want to modify the original elements, or to manually manage their lifetime, or if you're concerned about something happening to them on the C side, just go for the `.dup`.

Strings

We know that D strings are also D arrays, so it's reasonable to expect that they behave the same when interacting with C. To a large extent, they do. However, the compiler does give string literals some special treatment that normal arrays just don't get. Try to compile and run the following program and see what happens:

```
void main() {
    import core.stdc.stdio : puts;
    puts("Giving a D string literal to a C function.");
}
```

Here, we are calling the standard C library function `puts` with a D string literal as an argument. `puts` is not a D wrapper, but a direct binding to the C function. It takes a C string, `const char*`, as an argument. So, what gives? How does this compile and run?

The compiler treats string literals specially. A string literal is implicitly convertible to a `const` or `immutable` pointer to `char`. This is true of function parameters and variable declarations. The same does not hold for regular array literals, nor is it true of `string` variables:

```
void main() {
    import core.stdc.stdio : puts;
    auto str = "Giving a D string to a C function.";
    puts(str);
}
```

This will fail to compile. From what we've seen so far about passing D arrays to C, we know we can work around this:

```
puts(str.ptr);
```

In this particular case, this works and causes no harm, but it isn't a general-purpose solution. This is another point where D strings differ from other array types.

There's no getting around the fact that C strings are expected to be null-terminated, meaning the last character in the string should be `'\0'` (or `0`). The D compiler will let you pass D string literals directly to C functions because all string literals in D are null-terminated. This feature exists specifically to make them directly compatible with C. However, D does not require *all* strings to be null-terminated. Strings received from external sources, such as files or network packets, are not guaranteed to have a trailing `'\0'`; they will only have one if they've been initialized with a literal. For that reason, the compiler does not allow string variables to be implicitly converted to C-style strings, treating them just like any other array.

In this specific case, we know that `str` was assigned a literal, so we know that it is null-terminated. In the general case, however, when we cannot guarantee the original source of a string variable was a literal, we need to turn to the Phobos function `std.string.toStringz`.

We've already seen this function and its cousin, `std.utf.toUTF16z`, in the `loader` module presented earlier in the chapter. Given a string `str`, `toStringz` ensures that it is null-terminated. This usually means that a new string is allocated with space for the null-terminator. The UTF variations perform the same task, while also converting the input to the appropriately UTF-encoded string type.

Memory and toStringz

As I write, `str.ptr` is sometimes returned by `toStringz`, meaning no allocation is made if the null-terminator is already present. Unfortunately, bugs can arise in specific situations that create a false positive, so this is almost certain to change at some point unless D gains the ability to detect string literals through compile-time introspection.

When implementing a function that accepts a D string and hands it off to a C function, you should always use `toStringz` or, if the C API requires it, one of the UTF versions, before passing the string on to C. If you don't, then you've not only allowed the potential for a crash, you've also opened a pretty big security hole. Even if you think you're 100% sure that the function will only take literals, perhaps because it's private to the module and you completely control the types of strings it gets, you should still use `toStringz`.

Another thing to watch out for is what the C function does with any strings you give it. I have actually seen someone recommend that a C function declared to take a `char*` be translated to D to accept a `const(char)*` instead, solely to make it easier to pass a D string to it. When using a binding that you didn't create, always familiarize yourself with the original C API before you get started. You certainly don't want a C function to attempt to modify your `immutable(char)[]` strings in D. Nothing good can come of that. If you do need to pass a string to a C function that will be modified, just `dup` it to a variable of type `char[]` and then pass that on to the C function. Note that there's no guarantee that duping a string will preserve the null-terminator in the copy.

```
auto s = "Dup me!";
char[] cstr = s.dup ~ '\0';
modifyString(cstr.ptr);
```

If the C function is treating the string as a buffer and doesn't need to read it first, just do as you would with any array; allocate an array of characters large enough to hold the output, then pass it on:

```
auto cstr = new char[1024];
writeToBuffer(cstr.length, cstr.ptr);
```

Sometimes, such a function might be documented to require that the array contain the null-terminator, even though it's empty. In that case, keep in mind that the .init value of a char is 0xFF, not 0, so you'll have to set the value yourself.

Memory

When interacting with C, never forget that D has a garbage collector. The potential for nasty bugs is high here. Any memory allocated by the GC that is passed off to C could cause problems down the road. Consider this function:

```
void dFunction() {
   auto ints = [1, 2, 3];
   cFunction(ints);
}
```

ints is allocated on the GC heap from an array literal and then passed to a C function. Once dFunction returns, what happens depends on what cFunction does with the pointer. If it is stored in a stack variable, all is well as the GC knows how to scan the stack. If, on the other hand, it's stored somewhere in the C heap, such as in a struct instance allocated via malloc, all bets are off; the GC has no way of knowing that an active reference to the allocated memory still exists. At any point, the GC could collect the memory it allocated for ints. If a reference to it still exists in the C heap, then the next attempt to access it on the C side will be accessing an invalid memory location.

There are different options for ensuring that things don't blow up in this situation. The first that might come to mind is to keep a reference to the GC-allocated memory somewhere on the D side. Another option is to just use C's malloc to handle the allocation and forget about the GC issues completely. A third option is to inform the GC to always consider the memory block as live and never bother to collect it. This is done by importing std.memory and calling GC.addRoot, something we'll look at in *Chapter 11, Taking D to the Next Level*.

Unfortunately, it isn't always obvious when GC memory is being allocated. Sometimes, the allocation might be hidden. Earlier, we saw the function std.string.toStringz and learned that it sometimes allocates memory, but not always. You'll see a great deal of D code calling C functions like this:

```
some_c_function(myString.toStringz());
```

There's no way of knowing just by looking at this function call whether or not `toStringz` is allocating. That's perfectly fine as long as it's certain that `some_c_function` isn't going to keep a pointer to the string hanging around for later use (or even if it will call `realloc` or `free` on your pointer, which is just bad news for GC-allocated memory). If there's no way of knowing for sure what the C function is going to do, then it's best to be safe and store a reference to or call, `GC.addRoot` with, the return value of `toStringz`.

Thankfully, the majority of C functions that handle strings do not need to keep them locally. If they do, well-written functions will copy the string to a locally allocated buffer so that the calling code need not worry about it. It's the corner cases you have to watch out for. The same holds true for any pointer to GC-allocated memory that you pass to a C function. Always read the documentation for the C library first. If it isn't clear, check the source if it's available. Never pass GC-allocated memory into C blindly.

C callbacks and exceptions

Earlier in the chapter, I recommended that you annotate every C callback in a binding with `nothrow`. Now we're going to see why. To do so, save the following C file as `$LEARNINGD/Chapter09/exceptions/call.c`:

```
void callCallback(void (*callback)(void)) {
  callback();
}
```

Then, save the following as `except.d` in the same directory:

```
extern(C) @nogc nothrow void callCallback(void function());
extern(C) void callbackImpl() {
  throw new Exception("Testing!");
}
void main() {
  try {
    callCallback(&callbackImpl);
  }
  catch(Exception e) {
    import std.stdio : writeln;
    writeln("Caught it!");
  }
}
```

To compile, use the same command lines we used a few pages back with the array examples. For example, compiling with the DMC toolchain:

```
dmc -c call.c
dmd except.d call.obj
```

I compiled and executed the program on both Windows and Linux with the DMC, 64-bit Microsoft, and GCC linkers. I even tried it out with the 32-bit MinGW-backed and 64-bit Microsoft-backed versions of ldc2 on Windows. In every test run except for one, the exception was printed to the screen, meaning that it was never caught; it completely bypassed the exception handler. The odd man out was the 64-bit ldc2 version, which only managed to crash.

In effect, any exception thrown in a D implementation of a function that is called from C is either an unrecoverable exception or, potentially, the cause of a crash. If you are creating a binding to a C library that makes use of callbacks, marking the callbacks as nothrow will prevent users of the binding from unwittingly allowing recoverable exceptions to become unrecoverable.

As a user, whether the binding annotates the callbacks as nothrow or not, you should never throw, or allow to be thrown, an exception from a C callback. There's just no guarantee that it won't corrupt the program state. Neither is it a good idea to litter your callbacks with try...catch blocks which just swallow the exception and move on. Doing that could eventually cause your program to become unstable.

One way to work around this issue is to collect any exceptions thrown inside a callback and tuck them away in a variable that can be tested at a convenient time. This means every callback that does anything that could potentially throw will need a try...catch block that, in the catch, adds the caught exception to the array. Elsewhere in the program, at a point after the callbacks have run, the program can test for specific recoverable exceptions and continue if any of those are encountered. Otherwise, the first unrecoverable exception is thrown.

In this example, saved as $LEARNINGD/Chapter09/exceptions/except2.d, the exception is generated manually rather than caught. This is what you would need to do anyway if you wanted to throw from a callback. The exception is stored in an array, which is checked after the callback is called, where it is compared against a fictitious RecoverableLibraryException. Since it isn't an instance of that type, it is immediately thrown after a message is printed:

```
extern(C) nothrow alias CallbackFunc = void function();
extern(C) @nogc nothrow void callCallback(CallbackFunc);
extern(C) nothrow void callbackImpl() {
  _callbackExceptions ~= new Exception("Testing!");
}
```

```
class RecoverableLibraryException : Exception {
  this(string msg) {
    super(msg);
  }
}
Exception[] _callbackExceptions;
void main() {
  import std.stdio : writeln;
  callCallback(&callbackImpl);
  foreach(ex; _callbackExceptions) {
    if(auto arle = cast(RecoverableLibraryException)ex)
      writeln(arle.toString);
    else {
      writeln("Not recoverable!");
      throw ex;
    }
  }
}
```

A more sophisticated implementation would chain all caught exceptions together and forgo the array. For a real-world example, see an article I wrote on the topic at `http://www.gamedev.net/page/resources/_/technical/general-programming/d-exceptions-and-c-callbacks-r3323`. Note that the example there does not use `nothrow`, but really should.

Calling D from C

There's very little new to bring to the table when discussing how to call D from C. On the D side, any functions and global variables that should be available for C should be declared `extern(C)`. You could use `extern(Windows)` or `extern(System)` for special cases, but generally `extern(C)` is what you want. On the C side, all that needs to be done is to create a standard C header with the appropriate type declarations and function prototypes, or global variables. As long as the linkage attributes are correct, any C code linked with the D code will think it's talking to C.

At the time of writing, shared library support for DMD is not complete. It isn't implemented at all on OS X. Now and again, someone asks for help in the forums when having trouble compiling shared libraries on other platforms. In the interest of saving space, we won't cover how to build them here. You can find information on how to compile shared libraries with DMD on Windows at `http://wiki.dlang.org/Win32_DLLs_in_D` and instructions for Linux at `http://dlang.org/dll-linux.html#dso7`. If you run into trouble, please head to the forums for help.

Regardless of how a D library is used in C, through static or dynamic linking, or manual loading, it is critical that DRuntime be initialized somewhere. When linking with static D libraries, this can be done on the C side. The runtime exposes two C functions, `rt_init` and `rt_term`, which do what needs to be done. Simply declare prototypes for them in C and call them during initialization and shutdown:

```c
#include <stdlib.h>
#include <stdio.h>
extern int rt_init(void);
extern void rt_term(void);
void initialize() {
  // Initialize D runtime.
  if(rt_init() == 0) {
    fputs("Failed to initialize D runtime.", stderr);
    exit(EXIT_FAILURE);
  }
}
void terminate() {
  // Shutdown D runtime.
  rt_term();
}
```

When using D shared libraries on Linux, either through dynamic linking or manual loading, the C program can link with `libphobos2.so` and do the same thing. Multiple calls to `rt_init` are harmless, so don't worry about whether or not the shared libraries are doing the same.

When using D shared libraries on Windows, the responsibility to initialize the runtime lies with the DLLs, since they each have their own copy and there is no DLL version of Phobos. One way to do this is to give each DLL its own `initialize` and `terminate` functions, but it's probably easier just to do it in the `DLLMain` function. In this case, the D code has access to the `Runtime` struct, so it need not use `rt_init` or `rt_term`:

```d
import core.sys.windows.windows;
extern (Windows)
BOOL DllMain(HINSTANCE hInstance, ULONG ulReason, LPVOID pvReserved)
{
  import core.runtime : Runtime;
  switch (ulReason)
  {
    case DLL_PROCESS_ATTACH:
      dll_process_attach( hInstance, true );
      Runtime.initialize();
      break;
```

```
    case DLL_PROCESS_DETACH:
      Runtime.terminate();
      dll_process_detach( hInstance, true );
      break;

    case DLL_THREAD_ATTACH:
      dll_thread_attach( true, true );
      break;

    case DLL_THREAD_DETACH:
      dll_thread_detach( true, true );
      break;

    default:
  }
  return true;
}
```

As the highlighted lines demonstrate, the calls should happen when handling the DLL_PROCESS_ATTACH and DLL_PROCESS_DETACH events. We only need to call the functions once per process, not once per thread. Again, if you make a mistake and do it in the _THREAD_ cases, no harm will be done.

Aside from managing the runtime, the only other thing that you should be cognizant of on the D side is how you handle pointers to memory allocated on the GC heap. Don't try to free memory in C that was allocated in D; don't store pointers to GC memory for the life of the program unless it really needs to be around that long; and so on. Most of the work that needs to be done to prevent crashes and unexpected behavior has to happen on the D side.

Summary

In this chapter, we've defined the terminology that we should use when talking about how to get D and C to interact, we've examined some of the low-level details involved in getting bindings to work, we've seen how to translate C headers into D, and we've looked at how to call C functions from D and vice versa. With this chapter as a reference, you have all you need to create a binding to almost any C library.

In the next chapter, we're going to get back to writing D code and recreate MovieMan as a web application.

10
Taking D Online

Looking back at the version of `MovieMan` we developed over the course of the first seven chapters of this book, its console-based interface is far from user-friendly and its array-based database doesn't have much in the way of scalability. It serves its purpose as a playground for D language features, but if anyone wanted to seriously consider a more appealing application, they would want to provide a user-friendly GUI of one form or another. To support multiple users (or extremely large DVD collections), an actual database should replace the simple arrays in `db.d`. A web-based version of MovieMan would fit the bill nicely. That's quite convenient for us, given that this chapter is about web development with D.

This chapter presents a brief introduction to vibe.d, an asynchronous I/O framework often used to develop web applications in D. It begins with a look at what vibe.d offers, then demonstrates the basics by showing one way to implement MovieMan as a web app. The end result is much nicer than the primitive command line app presented in previous chapters and serves as a better foundation for expansion and exploration, ideas for which are presented at the end of the chapter. The flow of the chapter looks like this:

- Introduction: an overview of key vibe.d packages, the anatomy of a vibe.d web app, and a look at potential database APIs to use with MovieManWeb

- MovieManWeb: a step-by-step walkthrough showing one possible implementation of MovieMan as a vibe.d web app, and ideas for how to expand the project

The software

Although the web app framework provided by vibe.d is a major selling point of the project, it's not the only reason vibe.d exists. In this section, we'll explore some of the key features vibe.d offers for different types of client-server applications. We'll close with a quick look at d2sqlite3, the database library we'll use in the MovieManWeb example project.

vibe.d

The vibe.d project, located at `http://vibed.org/`, is billed as "Asynchronous I/O that doesn't get in your way". Strip away the web app and REST layers, the HTTP and database packages, plus all the accompanying utilities, and you're left with a fast, event-based, asynchronous I/O framework suitable for just about any sort of client-server application you can imagine. Here, we'll take a quick look at some of the key vibe.d packages to see how things break down, followed by a brief overview of what a vibe.d web app looks like.

Package overview

vibe.d contains several packages that provide a variety of functionality for different layers of web development. From low-level socket handling to the high-level web framework, the packages can be used as needed to meet the needs of a server application. Following is a brief introduction to some of the packages:

- The `vibe.core` package is the heart of vibe.d and the foundation upon which the rest of the framework is built. Here live the modules for fiber-aware concurrency, asynchronous event handling, file handling, TCP and UDP sockets, and logging. Any project that requires an asynchronous I/O framework can make use of this package in isolation.

- `vibe.http` provides HTTP 1.1/1.0 client and server implementations, an HTTP file server, web sockets, a URL router, session management, a form data handler, an HTTP-based logger, and more. Sitting on top of `vibe.core`, `vibe.http` is somewhat analogous to the Java Servlet API. It's a barebones web-app framework with a few bells and whistles. At this level, the user must explicitly verify HTTP POST and GET parameters, set the content type, throw exceptions on bad requests, and generally do all of the work that is handled internally by the higher-level `vibe.web` package.

- `vibe.web` is built atop `vibe.http` to allow for convenient declarative web and REST interfaces. It also has modules for validating HTTP parameters and handling internationalization. The MovieManWeb application makes uses of the declarative web interface to simplify the implementation.

- `vibe.mail` provides a single module that contains an SMTP client implementation. `vibe.db` contains interfaces for the Mongo and Redis database APIs. Most of the remaining packages are utilities used internally by the other framework packages. There are packages for cryptography, data serialization, data streams, text parsing, data structures, and more.

As a demonstration of a vibe.d based server that expands on what vibe.d provides, take a look at **vibenews** at `https://github.com/rejectedsoftware/vibenews`. The project includes a web forum, but also implements an NNTP server using the `vibe.core` and `vibe.stream` packages.

The anatomy of a vibe.d web app

Getting started with vibe.d is extremely easy with DUB. In fact, DUB began life as a tool for generating and building vibe.d projects and distributing vibe.d extensions. Only later did it morph into a more generic build tool and package manager. Its roots as a vibe.d specific tool live on in the `init` command that we first saw way back in *Chapter 1*, *How to Get a D in Programming*. It takes an optional argument, `-t`, to specify the type of project to create. There are three options:

- `minimal`: This is the default when `-t` is not specified. It creates a standard D application with a main function.

- `vibe.d`: This creates a vibe.d project that implements a minimal HTTP server.

- `deimos`: This generates a skeleton for a Deimos-like static binding to a C library.

To get a look at a simple vibe.d app, open up a command prompt to any directory and execute the following command:

```
dub init MyWebApp -t vibe.d
```

This creates a `MyWebApp` directory with the layout shown in the following screenshot:

```
08/23/2015  04:41 PM    <DIR>          .
08/23/2015  04:41 PM    <DIR>          ..
08/23/2015  04:41 PM                38 .gitignore
08/23/2015  04:41 PM               185 dub.sdl
08/23/2015  04:41 PM    <DIR>          public
08/23/2015  04:41 PM    <DIR>          source
08/23/2015  04:41 PM    <DIR>          views
              2 File(s)            223 bytes
              5 Dir(s)  36,033,839,104 bytes free
```

The first file in the list, `.gitignore`, is a convenience for those working with the git source control program. Quite a number of D projects live on GitHub and private git servers. `.gitignore` is a text file that contains a list of file patterns git should not consider when evaluating local changes. `dub.sdl` is the DUB project configuration we're already familiar with. For this vibe.d based project, it looks like this:

```
name "mywebapp"
description "A simple vibe.d server application."
copyright "Copyright © 2015, Mike Parker"
authors "Mike Parker"
dependency "vibe-d" version="~>0.7.23"
versions "VibeDefaultMain"
```

The only thing here that should warrant explanation at this point is the `VibeDefaultMain` version. When this version is specified, vibe.d apps need not implement a `main` function; the implementation in the `vibe.appmain` module will be used instead. This is a simple implementation that does some logging, runs the event loop, and catches all exceptions. It can be overridden by specifying `VibeCustomMain` as a version in the configuration file.

> As I write, an alpha version of vibe.d 0.7.26 is available for testing. In previous releases, if neither `VibeDefaultMain` nor `VibeCustomMain` were specified, the former would be the default. With the latest alpha, which will likely be released by the time this book is complete, the default is the latter. Regardless, DUB explicitly configures `VibeDefaultMain` in the generated `dub.sdl`.

The `public` folder is where publicly accessible files, such as static HTML pages and style sheets, should be saved. The `source` folder is for the source code and, just as with a normal DUB app, the tool looks for `source/app.d` by default. Finally, the `views` folder is for **Diet templates**, an HTML template engine based on **Jade** (much of the documentation at `http://jade-lang.com/` serves for Diet templates as well). We'll dig a bit into the details when we implement MovieManWeb.

Peek into the `source` directory and you'll find that DUB has generated a default `app.d`. It does everything necessary to set up a minimal HTTP server that accepts connections and perpetually serves a plain text document that says, `"Hello, World!"`. The unmodified output of that file follows:

```
import vibe.d;

shared static this()
{
  auto settings = new HTTPServerSettings;
```

```
    settings.port = 8080;
    settings.bindAddresses = ["::1", "127.0.0.1"];
    listenHTTP(settings, &hello);

    logInfo("Please open http://127.0.0.1:8080/ in your browser.");
}

void hello(HTTPServerRequest req, HTTPServerResponse res)
{
    res.writeBody("Hello, World!");
}
```

First off, notice the import of `vibe.d` at the top of the file. Although any D programmer should know that this indicates a file with the path `vibe/d.d`, it is all too easy for the human brain to subconsciously interpret it as a file named `vibe.d` (full disclosure: it happens to me every time I see it). Since the module does nothing more than publicly import `vibe.vibe`, then anyone bothered by `vibe.d` can directly import `vibe.vibe` instead.

The next thing to point out is that there is no `main` function in sight. We already know that vibe.d has its own implementation of main. When using the default main, all of the initialization the app requires should happen in a module constructor. As you can see, getting a minimal HTTP server up and running with vibe.d requires very little initialization. This generated implementation uses the low-level API from `vibe.http`. First, the connection settings for the server are set up in an `HTTPServerSettings` instance, then `listenHTTP` is called to start listening for active connections. The function is given a pointer to the `hello` function, which accepts `HTTPServerRequest` and `HTTPServerResponse` objects. Since this particular function isn't interested in any input from the request, it only concerns itself with the response by printing a plain text message, which is sent back to the browser.

There are more complex examples of how to use the low-level API in the project's source repository at `https://github.com/rejectedsoftware/vibe.d`, as well as in the documentation at the project home page.

The database library

There are a number of database options available for any vibe.d app. As shown previously, bindings for MongoDB and Redis ship with the project in the `vibe.db` package. More packages can be found in the DUB registry for other database distributions. Some of those libraries can automatically make use of the vibe.d networking layer when it is available. Some of them are native D APIs with no external dependencies, while others are bindings to C libraries.

A handful of database options were considered for the MovieManWeb project we'll develop in this chapter. The primary goal was to select a database that requires minimal effort to install and set up. The focus of this chapter is on programming a vibe.d app, not on setting up and managing database servers. A softer requirement was that the database have either a pure D interface, or an easy-to-use wrapper on top of a C binding. Dealing with a C API and translating from database types to D types would just be too distracting. Fortunately, one database and API combo was found that meets both requirements exceedingly well.

sqlite3 is a popular and easy-to-use library for embeddable databases that can exist in memory or on disk. There are no executables required and no server connections to configure and launch; it can be used just like any other C library. There is also no need to set up database users or create a database with SQL. Databases are created programmatically when the app launches. Tables still need to be created with SQL statements, but it is easy to do this during initialization.

d2sqlite3 (`http://code.dlang.org/packages/d2sqlite3`) is a library that provides both a binding and a wrapper for sqlite3. The wrapper provides a convenient interface over the C API, including a range-based interface to the result sets returned by database queries. It takes just a few lines to get a database created and ready for use, and queries can also be implemented concisely and cleanly.

Phobos ships with an sqlite3 binding in the `etc.c.sqlite3` module, but it is often a few releases behind the official sqlite3 distribution. The binding in d2sqlite3 is updated more frequently.

The only downside to d2sqlite3 is its unavoidable dependency on the sqlite3 C library. Linux and Mac users should be able to easily get the development version of the library through their system package manager and, if not, the sqlite3 download page at `https://www.sqlite.org/download.html` has binaries for multiple platforms. It's quite possible that your system package manager has an older version of the library that will not compile with MovieManWeb, in which case you'll need to download and install the binaries for your platform or compile from source yourself. The d2sqlite3 project configuration has a directive telling DUB to link with the sqlite3 library, so nothing need be done beyond installing the binaries where the linker can find them. On Windows, it's a different story entirely.

The sqlite3 download page provides a ZIP file with a precompiled 32-bit DLL. By itself, this isn't actually very useful for DMD users. Some work needs to be done to get an import library in the appropriate object file format. To make things easier, I've generated a 32-bit import library in OMF format for the default DMD linker, and have compiled 32-bit and 64-bit static libraries in COFF for those who want to compile with the `-m64` and `-m32mscoff` compiler switches. To hide all of this, a few version statements and a pragma can be added to one of the source modules. We're getting a bit ahead of ourselves here, though, as we haven't yet set up the MovieManWeb project. That's right around the corner in the next section, so let's get to it.

MovieManWeb

The purpose behind MovieManWeb as presented here is to provide an easy-to-follow example of how to use vibe.d. The focus should be largely on vibe.d itself, not on the vagaries of web development, aspects of good database design, or how to make the app as robust and feature-rich as possible. Toward that end, there are a few constraints we'll keep in mind as we go along that wouldn't apply to most vibe.d apps:

- The application is intended to run on the desktop for a single user. There is no need to handle login credentials, hash passwords, sanitize input, or implement any such security features an application intended for deployment on the web would normally require.

- The only data the application is concerned with are movie titles, case numbers, page numbers, disc numbers and, for television shows, season (or series) number. This constraint allows for a simple, single-table database, with no need to worry about efficient database design.

- The output of the application is pure HTML5, with no scripting or fancy effects. No attempt is made to accommodate older browsers. A stylesheet is provided with the downloadable source code to give the user interface a more pleasing appearance, but it is not covered in the chapter. Given the first constraint, the default stylesheet assumes a desktop monitor and does not apply any responsive web design techniques.

These constraints may make MovieManWeb sound like it isn't a web app, but it absolutely is. With the implementation of the proper security precautions, a more flexible stylesheet, more user-friendly features in the UI and, optionally, more data to store (such as movie directors, actors and actresses, and so on), MovieManWeb could serve as the core of a more feature-complete, multi-user web application. Here's a look at the finished product:

MovieMan Database

	ID	Title	Case	Page	Disc	Season	Action
Home	11	Snatch	1	11	0	0	Edit Delete
Add New Movie	12	12 Monkeys	1	12	0	0	Edit Delete
Find Movie(s)	13	Very Bad Things	1	13	0	0	Edit Delete
	14	True Romance	1	14	0	0	Edit Delete
	15	The Big Lebowski	1	15	0	0	Edit Delete
	16	Léon: The Professional	1	16	0	0	Edit Delete
	17	Romeo+Juliet	1	17	0	0	Edit Delete
	18	Moulin Rouge	1	18	1	0	Edit Delete
	19	Moulin Rouge	1	19	2	0	Edit Delete
	20	The Million Dollar Hotel	1	20	0	0	Edit Delete
		Next				Previous	

Getting started

Before generating the dub project, Linux and Mac users will have to go through some preliminary steps. On Linux, you'll probably need to install libevent through your package manager (`sudo apt-get install libevent libevent-dev` on Debian-based systems) if it isn't already installed. On Mac, you'll have to get the source from `https://github.com/libevent/libevent` and follow the instructions to build using autoconf in the README file. If you get compiler errors on Mac and have no access to a Windows or Linux system, an alternative is to install Linux on a VM and follow along that way.

The first step in setting up the project is to tell DUB to initialize a new vibe.d app. Navigate to `$LEARNINGD/Chapter10` and execute the following command:

```
dub init MovieManWeb -t vibe.d
```

That will create the `MovieManWeb` directory and populate it with the default contents we saw earlier. To make sure there aren't any networking issues on your system, `cd` into the `MovieManWeb` directory and execute `dub` with no arguments to compile and run the program (or `dub -ax86_64` for a 64-bit build). Then open up your preferred web browser and enter either `localhost:8080` or `127.0.0.1:8080` into the address bar. If you see the default `"Hello, World!"` output, then all is well.

Windows and the loopback address

`127.0.0.1`, or `localhost`, is known as the **loopback address**. In Windows 10, typing `127.0.0.1` into a browser address bar will work as expected, but typing `localhost` will not. This is because it is disabled by default. If you want to enable it, you'll need to open the file `C:\Windows\System32\drivers\etc\hosts` and uncomment one or both of these lines:

```
#   127.0.0.1          localhost
#   ::1                localhost
```

To uncomment, delete the hash tags (#) from the front of each line. Because this is a system file, you will need administrator privileges to save the changes. If you have an administrator account, you can right-click on the shortcut to a text editor and choose **Run as administrator**. Alternatively, you can drag a copy of the file from Windows Explorer to the desktop, edit the copy, and then drag it back to the original location. Windows will prompt you for administrative permission before completing the copy.

Next, open up `MovieManWeb/source/app.d` in your text editor. You'll want to replace the default low-level example function with the initial version of the high-level web interface we'll be using. Delete the following highlighted lines:

```
import vibe.d;

shared static this()
{
  auto settings = new HTTPServerSettings;
  settings.port = 8080;
  settings.bindAddresses = ["::1", "127.0.0.1"];
  listenHTTP(settings, &hello);

  logInfo("Please open http://127.0.0.1:8080/ in your browser.");
}

void hello(HTTPServerRequest req, HTTPServerResponse res)
{
  res.writeBody("Hello, World!");
}
```

Soon, we'll change `listenHTTP` to do something a bit different. Now it's time to create the web interface. Create a new directory, `MovieManWeb/source/mmweb`, and inside of it a new source file, `web.d`. The content of this file should look like this:

```
module mmweb.web;
import vibe.vibe;

final class MovieMan {
  void index() {
    render!("index.dt");
  }
}
```

Here, `index.dt` is the name of a diet template that we'll create in the `views` folder. We'll have an introduction to the mechanics of the web interface and diet templates shortly. For now, let's focus on getting something up and running. Create a new file and save it as `MovieManWeb/views/index.dt`. Implement the following:

```
doctype html
html
  head
    title MovieManWeb
  body
    h3 Hello, MovieManWeb!
```

That's much nicer to look at than raw HTML, isn't it?

We're almost ready to launch. To put the last pieces in place, go back to `app.d` and make the following highlighted changes:

```
shared static this()
{
  import mmweb.web : MovieMan;
  auto router = new URLRouter;
  router.registerWebInterface(new MovieMan);

  auto settings = new HTTPServerSettings;
  settings.port = 8080;
  settings.bindAddresses = ["::1", "127.0.0.1"];
  listenHTTP(settings, router);
}
```

Now you've got a customized minimal vibe.d HTTP web app. Execute `dub` in the MovieManWeb directory and reload `127.0.0.1:8080` to see the following result:

To stop the server, you'll need to go back to the console window and press the *Ctrl + C* key combination on your keyboard. The server will then cleanly shut down.

The basics of diet templates

Looking at the `index.dt` presented in the previous subsection, one thing stands out quite clearly. Each line begins with a tag that maps directly to an HTML tag, only there are no brackets and no corresponding closing tags. The template engine is able to understand how to properly generate HTML tags from the input through indentation and new lines. Add the following highlighted lines to `index.dt`, then recompile the app and reload the web page:

```
doctype html
html
  head
    title MovieManWeb
  body
    h3 Hello, World!
    p This is a paragraph.
    p This is a new paragraph with a link to
    a(href="http://google.com")Google
    | and more text following the link.
```

The reason we need to recompile before seeing the changes is because diet templates are parsed at compile time. The generated HTML is then loaded into memory when the application launches, so that nothing is ever loaded from disk at runtime. It's still possible to serve static files from disk, as we'll see a bit later in the chapter, but most, if not all, of the UI in a `vibe.d` app will usually be generated at compile time. The result of the two new lines can be seen in the following screenshot:

In this subsection, we're going to talk first about the interaction between tags and indentation, then we'll see how to combine multiple diet templates into a single generated HTML page. We'll finish off by setting up a common layout for every page MovieManWeb generates. Later in the chapter, when we actually have data to display, we'll look at another feature of Diet templates that allows us to generate output at runtime.

Tags and indentation

The parser uses indentation to determine when to insert a closing tag for any open tags that require them. Indentation can be via tabs or spaces and there is no required number of either; one space works equally as well as four, and two tabs work equally as well as one. When the parser first encounters an indented line, it will determine the type of indentation and will use that as the basis to understand the rest of the file. Whatever approach you choose for indentation, just be consistent. You can't use four spaces on one line and five on the next; the first indented line sets the pattern for each successive indented line and any deviation from the pattern will result in a compiler error.

Consider the very first line, `doctype html`. The parser understands that the equivalent HTML tag, `<!DOCTYPE html>`, has no corresponding closing tag and does not wrap any content. Therefore, the line following it need not be indented. However, the tag on the next line, `html`, corresponds to `<html>` and `</html>`, two tags between which all of the page content must exist. Every line following the second is indented, telling the parser that the content goes between those tags.

The third line is `head`, which corresponds to the HTML `<head>` and `</head>` tags. The parser sees that the fourth line, `title`, is indented, so it knows the output belongs between those two tags. It then encounters `body`, which is on the same indentation level as `head`. This is an indication to first insert the `</head>` tag in the generated content, followed by the opening `<body>` tag. The same logic is used when the `p` tags are on the same indentation as the `h3` tag. By the end of the file, the parser sees that the `body` and `html` tags are still open, so it generates the `</body>` and `</html>` closing tags automatically.

Only tags need to be indented. Text content intended for output can appear on the same line as any tags to which they correspond. We can see this with the `title` and `h3` tags, as well as the first `p` tag. The second paragraph contains a link to `http://www.google.com`. As such, the tag for the link needs to be indented. If you put it on the same line as the `p` tag, like so:

```
p Go to a(href="http://google.com")Google
```

Then the output will look like this:

The same thing applies to the paragraph text that follows the `a` tag. If it is on the same line as the tag, it will be included as part of the link, so we have to put it on the next line. However, if we just do this:

```
p This is a new paragraph with a link to
  a(href="http://google.com")Google
  and more text following the link.
```

The first word of the last line will not appear in the output. The parser treats the first word on every line as a tag. If it doesn't understand the tag, it just ignores it. In order to let the parser know that this is a line of text belonging to the preceding `p` tag and not a completely new tag, we have to use the pipe (|) character:

```
p This is a new paragraph with a link to
  a(href="http://google.com")Google
  | and more text following the link.
```

The indentation is also important. If the line is not one indentation level beyond the p tag, the parser will assume the paragraph should be closed, so it will generate a `</p>` HTML tag to make a new paragraph with the text. In effect, this...:

```
p This is a new paragraph with a link to
    a(href="http://google.com")Google
| and more text following the link.
```

...results in this:

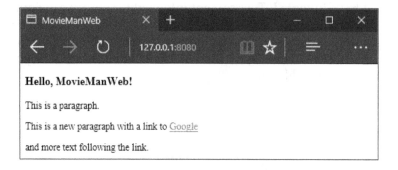

Including and extending templates

If it were necessary to rewrite the same common tags for every diet template in the program, then the benefits of using the templates would be dramatically reduced. There are two ways to combine multiple templates to generate a single web page: we can include one template in another, and one template can extend another.

To include one template in another, the `include` directive should be used at the point in which the included template should appear. For example, given the template `head.dt`:

```
head
    title MovieManWeb
```

We can insert it into any other template like so, perhaps one called `content.dt`:

```
doctype html
html
    include head.dt
    body
        h3 Hello, World!
```

Don't forget about indentation rules; the `include` should be at the same indentation level at which the content would appear if it were typed in directly. When using includes, the included template is not given to the parser. In this example, the program would tell vibe.d to render `content.dt`.

Extending a template is like including one in reverse. Given a module `sub.dt`, which extends `base.dt`, `sub.dt` is fed to the parser. The parser will then take the entire content of the `sub.dt` and include it in `base.dt` to generate the final output. This requires two steps to be taken. For one, the extending template must include an `extends` directive at the top of the file. For example, the very first line of `sub.dt` should be:

```
extends base.dt
```

Additionally, the parser must be told where to insert the content of `sub.dt` into `base.dt`. Doing so requires `block` directives in both files. This implementation of `base.dt` shows how to do it in the template that is being extended:

```
doctype html
  head
    block title
  body
    block body
```

Block names need not be the same as the tags they belong to, nor are they required to be lowercase, but it's a convention I prefer.

Any template that extends `base.dt` will now need to include two blocks, one implementing the content that will replace the `title` block in `base.dt`, and another that will replace the `body` block. These blocks must be named the same as those in `base.dt`. Our `sub.dt` implementation might look like this:

```
block title
  title MovieManWeb - Page One
block body
  h3 Hello, MovieManWeb!
```

Again, the indentation rules apply at the point where all content from `sub.dt` is pasted into `base.dt`.

The MovieManWeb layout

While it's possible to use one diet template to represent multiple pages by inserting D code to generate different content for each page (as we'll see later), it's more manageable to use multiple templates. This is the approach taken in `MovieManWeb`. We will have one template for each page, with an additional `layout.dt` template that all of the others will extend. We will not use any includes. The complete implementation of `layout.dt` follows:

```
doctype html
html
  head
    title MovieManWeb
    link(href='/reset.css', rel='stylesheet')
    link(href='/style.css', rel='stylesheet')
  body
    nav
      ul
        li
          a(href='/') Home
        li Add New Movie
        li Find Movie(s)
    article
      block article
```

The stylesheets referenced in the link tags are located in the `MovieManWeb/public` directory of the downloadable source package. `reset.css` is a file released in the public domain and is available at `http://meyerweb.com/eric/tools/css/reset/`. It sets the properties of all HTML tags to a common state, allowing for custom styles to have a more consistent appearance across browsers. The file `style.css` is where the custom properties for MovieManWeb are implemented. When creating your own styles for the application, that is the file you should edit.

We are using the HTML5 `nav` and `article` tags, which are not supported by older browsers. An alternative is to use `div` tags with unique IDs. These can be generated with the long form `div(id='nav')`, or using the shortcut `#nav`, which generates the same output. Alternatively, `div.nav` and `.nav` are the same as `div(class='nav')`. If you choose to use `div` tags, then `style.css` will need to be edited appropriately.

With this in place, we can change `index.dt` to look like this:

```
extends layout
block article
  h3 Hello, MovieManWeb!
```

This file is going to become bigger as we progress. In the end, it will be the most complex template in the program, but will still be easy to follow.

In order for the stylesheets to be applied to the page, vibe.d has to be told the location from which it should serve static content. There are two functions in the module vibe.http.fileserver that can help with this. Both return a delegate that can be passed to a URLRouter during startup. One, serveStaticFile, is for associating a specific file with a URL. The other, serveStaticFiles (note the 's' at the end), is for associating a directory. The latter function works for our purposes. Modify app.d to include the following highlighted line:

```
shared static this()
{
    import mmweb.web : MovieMan;
    auto router = new URLRouter;
    router.registerWebInterface(new MovieMan);
    router.get("*", serveStaticFiles("./public/"));

    auto settings = new HTTPServerSettings;
    settings.port = 8080;
    settings.bindAddresses = ["::1", "127.0.0.1"];
    listenHTTP(settings, router);
}
```

The asterisk (*) tells the router that any URLs not already associated with any web interfaces or delegates should be handed off to the delegate returned by serveStaticFiles. The argument to that function, "./public/", means that any files in a URL the delegate handles should be searched for in the public directory.

With these changes in place, you can compile and run the app again to see the effect. Make sure to copy reset.css and style.css from the downloadable source package and place them in the MovieManWeb/public directory. Once that is done, reloading 127.0.0.1:8080 in the browser will produce the following output:

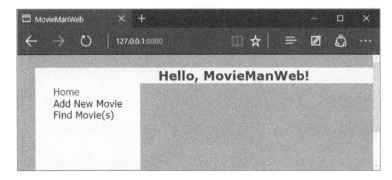

Setting up the database

Now that we've got the basic layout configured, it's time to turn our attention toward the database layer. We need two things before we can continue: a data structure that can hold all of the data associated with a given DVD when going to and from the database layer, and a database with a table in which to store the data.

We're going to be storing more data for each movie than we did in the console version of MovieMan. This means that if we choose to represent each movie as a `struct`, it's going to be a few bytes larger, which can have an impact on the efficiency of passing instances around by value. In a large application, it would force careful consideration of whether any given function argument of that type should be passed by value or reference. If we choose instead to use a `class`, we will be required to instantiate new instances for every movie we pull from the database. In an application with heavy database usage, that could add quite a bit of garbage for the GC to clean up.

Realistically, it doesn't matter which approach we take for our single-user desktop web app. The number of database queries will be measured per minute at most, rather than per second, meaning the likelihood of generating enough garbage to clog up the GC is near zero. For the same reason, we need not worry about passing around high numbers of large `struct` instances by value. Regardless, we still need to choose one or the other.

As a general rule of thumb, any aggregate type that is intended to be a **POD** (**Plain Old Data**) type is better suited to be a `struct` than a `class`. Our `Movie` type is most certainly a POD type; it will consist of a number of member variables, with no member functions at all, and serves the sole purpose of carrying data between the database and the UI.

Now we have enough to create `MovieManWeb/source/mmweb/db.d` and enter the following:

```
module mmweb.db;
import d2sqlite3;
struct Movie {
  long id;
  string title;
  int caseNumber;
  int pageNumber;
  int discNumber;
  int seasonNumber;
}
```

The sole database table will contain fields corresponding to each member of this structure. Notice that we're importing the d2sqlite3 module here so that we can use its symbols throughout the `db` module.

Creating the database is as easy as calling a class constructor. Here's how it's implemented:

```
_db = Database("./movieman.db");
```

`Database` is a `struct` type in d2sqlite3 that wraps a sqlite3 database handle. Creating the table for the database requires a bit of SQL. Since SQL is the focus of neither this chapter nor this book, we will not indulge in any explanations of the SQL statements we see. If you aren't familiar with SQL, the Kahn Academy tutorial is a good place to start. You can find it at `https://www.khanacademy.org/computing/computer-programming/sql`.

The SQL statements need to be strings. To make them more manageable and to keep the readability of `db.d` nice and clean, we'll declare a number of manifest constants in a separate module. Create a new module, `MovieManWeb/source/mmweb/sql.d`, and add the following:

```
module mmweb.sql;
package:
  enum createTableSQL =
  `CREATE TABLE IF NOT EXISTS movie (
    movieID INTEGER NOT NULL PRIMARY KEY,
   title TEXT NOT NULL,
    caseNum INTEGER NOT NULL,
    pageNum INTEGER NOT NULL,
    discNum INTEGER,
    seasonNum INTEGER
);`;
```

This is the SQL statement needed to create our database table. Because it spans multiple lines, note that it's implemented as a WYSISWYG string using backticks (`). We'll add more SQL statements to this module as we go along.

We'll implement a module constructor to do the work of creating both the database and the table. sqlite3 allows for database transactions, meaning that we can set things up such that any changes we make to the database can be rolled back on error. We will use transactions in every function that modifies the database to minimize the chance of database corruption. d2sqlite3 exposes the transaction API through the database object. The `begin`, `commit`, and `rollback` functions are what we are interested in. The first one starts a transaction, the latter two complete and abort it respectively. We can use `scope` statements to guarantee the appropriate functions are called.

With all of that in hand, we can add the following to `db.d`:

```
shared static this() {
  import mmweb.sql;

  // Create the database if it doesn't exist
  _db = Database("./movieman.db");

  // Begin a database transaction
  _db.begin();

  // Only commit the changes if no errors occur
  scope(success) _db.commit();

  // Abort on error
  scope(failure) _db.rollback();

  // Create the movie table if it doesn't exist
  _db.execute(createTableSQL);
}
```

Next, add the following to the bottom of the file:

```
private:
  Database _db;
```

There is at least one thing to do before this can compile, and more for those on Windows. First, we have to add the d2sqlite3 dependency to `dub.sdl`:

```
dependency "d2sqlite3" version="~>0.7.3"
```

This can go anywhere in the file, but I prefer to keep all dependencies grouped together, so I've inserted this right under the vibe.d dependency. If you are on any platform other than Windows, you can execute `dub build` now to make sure there are no errors and move on to the next subsection, *Fleshing out the index page*.

d2sqlite3 contains a line in its project configuration that will cause sqlite3 to automatically be linked in if it is on the system path. Under the hood, DUB will handle the compiler command line and make sure the appropriate naming convention is used. This is why users on Mac or Linux need not manually link with the library; no matter whether you're compiling for 32-bit or 64-bit architectures, the library will be installed to a location where the linker can find it. On Windows, the linker will be looking for `sqlite3.lib` on the system library path, but it's not going to be there unless you've put it there yourself (not recommended). The Windows ecosystem is not like that of other platforms.

To accommodate two different object file formats (COFF versus OMF) and two different architectures (32-bit and 64-bit), we need three different builds of the sqlite3 library on Windows. Windows users should open up app.d and add the following to the top of the file. It can go above or below the import statement:

```
version(Windows) {
  // When compiling with -m64
  version(Win64)
    enum sqliteLib = "lib\\sqlite3-ms64.lib";
    // When compiling with -m32mscoff
  else version(CRuntime_Microsoft)
    enum sqliteLib = "lib\\sqlite3-ms32.lib";
    // The default, or when compiling with -m32
  else
    enum sqliteLib = "lib\\sqlite3-dm-dll.lib";

    pragma(lib, sqliteLib);
}
```

This will allow you to link to the appropriate build of sqlite3, no matter the linker or architecture you are compiling for. The first two are static libraries, but sqlite3-dm-dll.lib is an import library. It's used when compiling with the default architecture (32-bit) and linker (OPTLINK). All three libraries can be found in the MovieManWeb/lib directory of the downloadable source package. Additionally, sqlite3.dll is in the root MovieManWeb directory. Copy all four files over to your own project into the same locations. Now you can execute dub build to ensure everything is set up correctly for OPTLINK.

There's one more thing Windows users need to be aware of. DMD will issue a warning about the lib directive in d2sqlite3's project configuration, saying that sqlite3.lib cannot be found. No problem. The MS linker, unfortunately, is more strict and will issue a linker error instead. We can work around that, though. d2sqlite3 ships with two project configurations, one that includes the lib directive (the default) and one that does not (called without-lib). To specify the latter, add this to MovieManWeb's dub.sdl:

```
subConfiguration "d2sqlite3" "without-lib"
```

Now, you'll see no warning from DMD and no error from the MS linker when compiling with dub build -ax86_64. As I write, there is no command line flag to tell DUB to use the -m32mscoff switch telling DMD to link with the 32-bit MS linker. Adding it to the project configuration manually only results in errors. It will certainly be supported in a future version of DUB, hopefully one released not too long after this book.

Fleshing out the index page

The index page is always going to be used to display a list of movies. If there are no movies available in the database, it will simply display a message to inform the user that there are no movies to display. In order to make this happen, we need to embed some D code into the diet template.

To tell the parser to treat a given line in the template as code, we prefix the line with a dash (-):

```
-if(movies.length == 0)
  p There are no movies to display.
```

This snippet will only output the header if the `movies` array is empty. That raises the question, where does the `movies` array come from? To answer that, let's go back to our `MovieMan` web interface in `web.d` and modify the index function:

```
final class MovieMan {
  void index() {
    Movie[] movies;
    render!("index.dt", movies)();
  }
}
```

We've added two things. First, we've declared an empty array of `Movie` instances. Next, we've given that array to the `render` function. For completeness, we'll need to add this line to the top of the file:

```
import mmweb.db;
```

We'll need all of the database API to be available in the `web` module before we're through. Now let's look at what's going on with the index function.

Mapping web interface functions to URLs

When we give an instance of `MovieMan` to the `registerWebInterface` function in `app.d`, vibe uses compile-time reflection to map each member function to a URL. Any `public` function named `index` is mapped to the root URL `/`. Other `public` functions are mapped according to the format of their names. The URL will be `/name`, and the type of HTTP request it is mapped to is dependent upon the presence of any prefixes or `@property` annotations:

- Functions annotated with `@property` that are getters (no parameters, return a value) are mapped to GET requests

- Functions annotated with `@property` that are setters (one parameter, no return value) are mapped to PUT requests

- Functions prefixed with `get` or `query` are mapped to GET requests
- Functions prefixed with `set` or `put` are mapped to PUT requests
- Functions prefixed with `add`, `create`, `post`, or no prefix at all are mapped to POST requests
- Functions prefixed with `remove`, `erase`, or `delete` are mapped to DELETE requests
- Functions prefixed with `update` or `patch` are mapped to PATCH requests

By far, the most common HTTP requests are GET and POST. The latter is normally used to submit form data, while the former is normally what is used when you type a URL in the browser's address bar or click on a link.

Be careful with case

In my testing, I was unable to determine how camel-cased function names, such as `addMovie` or `postAddMovie`, are mapped by default. The URLs `/addMovie`, `/addmovie`, and `/AddMovie` all resulted in 404 errors at runtime. However, `addmovie` and `postAddmovie` will map to `/addmovie`. In the end, I opted for one-word names in the web interface to keep it simple.

So, now we know that when `vibe.d` receives a request for the root page, it will call the `index` function on its instance of `MovieMan` to handle the request. In order for `index.dt` to have a movie array to work with, we need to pass one to the `render` template function.

Rendering diet templates

The `vibe.web.web.render` function template is a high-level wrapper of the lower level function template `vibe.http.server.render`. The latter requires an `HTTPServerResponse` as a parameter. When working with the low-level API, you have an `HTTPServerResponse` instance passed as a parameter to functions mapped to a URL. Using the web interface approach, the request and response objects are hidden behind the scenes, so `vibe.web.web.render` handles the response object for us.

Look again at the modifications to the `index` function:

```
Movie[] movies;
render!("index.dt", movies)();
```

Here, I've added empty parentheses to the end of the function call to make it as clear as possible that `"index.dt"` and `movies` are template arguments and not function arguments. Recall that the HTML output of `index.dt` is generated at compile time. Internally, vibe.d uses D's string mixins to take any lines of D code it finds in the template to turn it into compilable D code. All of this takes place when the compiler encounters this call to the `render` function and instantiates the template with the given parameters. Take this line out of the function, and the index page will never be generated.

Any variables that need to be handed off to the Diet template can be passed to the `render` function as template alias parameters after the filename. The name of the argument as it is passed to the function is the name that needs to be used in the Diet template. In this case, because the variable we are passing to `render` is named `movies`, then any D code in `index.dt` that needs to manipulate it must use the same name.

It's easy to forget during development what is and isn't visible inside a diet template. If you ever get confused, just keep two simple things in mind. First, if a variable is never passed to `render` together with the name of a Diet template, then that variable isn't visible in that template. Second, to make use of any D symbol, such as a function or an `enum`, a Diet template can import any module. For example:

```
-import std.string;
```

Rewriting index.dt

Now we've got almost all of the information we need to begin the real implementation of `index.dt`. As a first pass, it looks like this:

```
extends layout
block article
  h3 MovieMan Database
  -if(movies.length == 0)
    p There are no movies to display.
```

Note that the `p` tag is indented one level past that of the `-if` statement. Just as with everything else in a Diet template, indentation plays a major role in how the parser interprets lines of D code. If we did not indent the `p` line, the parser would assume it is not part of the `-if` statement, thereby including it in the final output no matter the state of the `movies` array.

To test this, go ahead and compile and run the server, then reload the page in the browser. The output looks like this:

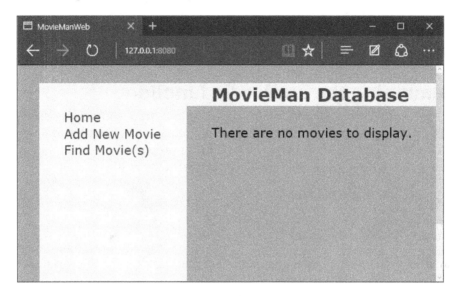

We're going to be using index.dt to display movies in multiple circumstances. For example, when simply accessing the root URL, we will pull the first ten movies from the database and display them without any input from the user, providing links to show the next ten and, when appropriate, the previous ten. We will also use it to show the result of search queries and to display the result of adding a new movie or updating an existing one. That will require more programming logic in the template and a little more information to pass to the render function. We'll keep coming back to index.dt as we add more features.

Adding movies

Every feature we add to MovieManWeb is going to be more interesting to test if we have some actual data to test it with, so the first feature we'll implement is adding movies to the database. This will consist of the following steps:

- Implement a function in db.d to add a movie to the database.
- Implement a function in web.d that can map to a POST request handling data from an input form.
- Implement a diet template that displays an input form where the user can enter movie data.

- Modify `index.dt` to display the new movie.
- Modify `app.d` to handle requests for the input form's URL.
- Add a link to the input form in `layout.dt`.

Let's get to work.

Implementing the addMovie function

The `addMovie` function we'll add to `db.d` is going to require some support. We'll need to add an SQL statement to `sql.d`. In order to make the database queries more efficient (and our code a bit cleaner), we'll be using prepared statements, so we need to implement one for adding a movie. Let's start with the SQL.

Open up `sql.d` and add the following line:

```
enum insertSQL = "INSERT INTO movie(title, caseNum, pageNum,
discNum, seasonNum) VALUES(?1, ?2, ?3, ?4, ?5);";
```

The numbers prefixed with question marks are placeholders for the variables we will insert into the prepared statement.

In d2sqlite3, prepared statements take the form of a `struct` type named `Statement`. `Statement`s are created by calling the `prepare` member function of a database instance and passing it a string containing an SQL statement. When the `Statement` is ready to be used, variables are bound to the placeholders via their `bind` function, then the SQL is executed with the execute function. When all this is done, the `Statement`'s `reset` function should be called before attempting to bind any variables to it again.

First, we need to declare a `Statement` instance in the private section of `db.d`. Add the highlighted line:

```
private:
  Database _db;
  Statement _insert;
```

Now we need to turn our attention to the module constructor in `db.d`. Here, we need to set `_insert` with a call to `_db.prepare`. Add the highlighted lines to the end of the module constructor:

```
// Create the movie table if it doesn't exist
_db.execute(createTableSQL);
// Create the prepared statements
_insert = _db.prepare(insertSQL);
```

Now we can implement the `addMovie` function. Because this function will modify the database, we'll want to use a database transaction. That calls for two `scope` statements. Here is the function in its entirety:

```
long addMovie(Movie movie) {
  _db.begin();
  scope(success) _db.commit();
  scope(failure) _db.rollback();

  _insert.reset();
  _insert.bind(1, movie.title);
  _insert.bind(2, movie.caseNumber);
  _insert.bind(3, movie.pageNumber);
  _insert.bind(4, movie.discNumber);
  _insert.bind(5, movie.seasonNumber);
  _insert.execute();

  return _db.lastInsertRowid();
}
```

The very first thing we do is begin the database transaction, then we set up the scope blocks just as we did in the module constructor. After that, the prepared statement is reset to prepare it for new values. Next, we bind the value of each member of `Movie`, excluding `id` (the database will generate one for us) to the corresponding placeholder in the prepared statement. After that, we execute the statement. Finally, we return the result of `_db.lastInsertRowid`. This will be used later in the web interface to fetch and display the newly added movie.

> Those familiar with SQL but not sqlite3 may have noticed in the `createTableSQL` constant that `AUTO INCREMENT` was missing from the declaration of the `movieID` field as a `PRIMARY KEY`. sqlite3 will automatically assign what it calls the `rowid` to any primary key field in a table if `AUTO INCREMENT` is not specified. If `AUTO INCREMENT` is specified, the database has to do a little more work. Therefore, it is recommended to only use `AUTO INCREMENT` when you absolutely cannot reuse any value as a primary key. Once an item is deleted from a table, its `rowid` may be recycled.

Implementing the postAdd function

The web interface function that handles the form for adding new movies is called
postAdd. This means that when we implement the form, we will need to configure
it to send its data to the /add URL using the POST method. It's a short function that
essentially performs two tasks: it calls addMovie, then renders the index page with
the appropriate information to display the newly added movie.

One of the conveniences of the web interface is that any form data or URL
parameters are automatically pulled from the request and mapped to function
parameters via compile-time reflection. This means that fields in the form should
have names that match the parameters of the function that will handle the data.
With that in mind, open up web.d and add the following to the MovieMan class:

```
void postAdd(string title, int caseNumber, int pageNumber,
int discNumber, int seasonNumber)
{
  auto id = addMovie(Movie(0, title, caseNumber, pageNumber,
    discNumber, seasonNumber));
}
```

By the time we're finished, index.dt is going to have a handful of variables it
needs to properly render the movie list. Each function that calls render with "index.
dt" as a template argument will need to pass all of those variables along. We can
save ourselves some annoyance by wrapping them all in a struct, which we'll
call ListInfo.

ListInfo contains four fields, only two of which we need to concern ourselves with
right now, and one convenience constructor. Its implementation follows. It should be
added to the top of web.d:

```
struct ListInfo {
  long offset;
  long limit = 10;
  Movie[] movies;
  ListType type;

  this(ListType type) { this(0, type); }

  this(long offset, ListType type) {
    this.offset = offset;
    this.type = type;
  }
}
```

We'll worry about the `offset` and `limit` fields later. For now, the two members of interest are `movies` and `type`. The former is the array from which `index.dt` will pull all of the movies it needs to display. The latter is an `enum` that tells `index.dt` why it is being called. The code in the template will use this value to display a context-specific header. `ListType`, which you can also add to the top of `web.d`, looks like this:

```
enum ListType {
  generic,
  addMovie,
  findMovie,
  updateMovie,
}
```

With these two types in place, we can now complete the `postAdd` function by adding the following highlighted lines:

```
void postAdd(string title, int caseNumber, int pageNumber,
  int discNumber, int seasonNumber)
{
  auto id = addMovie(Movie(0, title, caseNumber, pageNumber,
  discNumber, seasonNumber));
  auto info = ListInfo(ListType.addMovie);
  info.movies = [Movie(id, title, caseNumber, pageNumber,
  discNumber, seasonNumber)];
  render!("index.dt", info);
}
```

`info` is initialized with the single argument constructor to set the type of the list for `index.dt` to read. We give `info.movies` a `Movie` instance constructed with the same parameters we added to the database. Technically, that's cheating. While it lets the user verify the information was entered into the form correctly, it doesn't allow for any corruption of the data that may have occurred when it was handed off to `addMovies`. The proper thing to do here is to use `id` to fetch the newly added information from the database and send that to `index.dt` for rendering. Since we don't have that functionality yet, this will do. Later, once we've added the ability to find a movie by ID, we'll come back and make the change.

While we're here in `web.d`, we also will need to modify the `index` function. Recall that we adjusted it earlier to pass an array of `Movies` to the `render` function. Since `index.dt` is going to be modified to work with `ListInfo` instances instead, `index` will also need to send one. If we don't change it, we won't be able to compile. Here, the `ListType` we need is `ListType.generic`:

```
void index() {
  auto info = ListInfo(ListType.generic);
  render!("index.dt", info);
}
```

Implementing add.dt

The input form consists of five pairs of input fields and labels in a simple table, with a button at the bottom. Create a file `MovieManWeb/views/add.dt`. Here's the boilerplate that goes on top:

```
extends layout
block article
    h3 Add a New Movie
```

Every Diet template we create for this application will have the same three lines at the top, with the text in the `h3` tag being context specific. Next up is the `form` tag, which sits at the same indentation level as the `h3` tag. We need to specify the action and method properties to trigger the `postAdd` function that we implemented previously:

```
form(action='/add', method='post')
```

This is followed by the `table` tag, one indentation level beyond the `form` tag. For our implementation, we've given it a class called `Form` so that we can style it in `style.css`. In HTML, classes are specified as a property of the tag, such as `action` and `method` properties on the `form` tag, but in Diet templates we append classes to the tag name with a dot (`.`):

```
table.Form
```

Finally, we have a series of six table rows (`tr` tags). The first five rows contain two cells (`td` tags) each. The first of each pair of cells contains a label identifying the input field in the second cell. The first input field is a `text` field; the remainder are all `number` fields. Each input `field` is given a `size` property for aesthetics. The final row contains a single cell that spans two columns. This cell contains the form's `submit` button.

It's important when viewing the content of `add.dt` to make sense of the indentation, given that it directly affects how the template is parsed. Unfortunately, formatting such things in a book can distort the text to a degree that makes it difficult to follow the original formatting. So to make sure you get the full picture, the content of `add.dt` is displayed here as an image, rather than as copy-and-pasted text. Other Diet templates will be displayed this way as we work through the chapter, where necessary. If you want to copy the text yourself, refer to the downloadable source code:

```
add.dt                ×
1   extends layout
2   block article
3       h3 Add a New Movie
4       form(action='/add', method='post')
5           table.Form
6               tr
7                   td
8                       label(for='title') Movie Title
9                   td
10                      input(type='text', name='title', id='title', size='64')
11              tr
12                  td
13                      label(for='caseNumber') Case Number
14                  td
15                      input(type='number', name='caseNumber', id='caseNumber', size='4')
16              tr
17                  td
18                      label(for='pageNumber') Page Number
19                  td
20                      input(type='number', name='pageNumber', id='pageNumber', size='4')
21              tr
22                  td
23                      label(for='discNumber') Disc Number
24                  td
25                      input(type='number', name='discNumber', id='discNumber', size='4', value='0')
26              tr
27                  td
28                      label(for='seasonNumber') Season Number
29                  td
30                      input(type='number', name='seasonNumber', id='seasonNumber', size='4', value='0')
31              tr
32                  td(colspan='2')
33                      input(type='submit', value='Add Movie')
34
```

Note that each input field has an `id` property to match the `for` property of its corresponding label. This is a feature of HTML5 that allows focus to shift to an input when its corresponding label is clicked, but is also important for usability and accessibility, for example, screen readers.

Modifying index.dt

Now we need to add two pieces of functionality to `index.dt`. First, is a check for the `ListType` it is intended to display. This will allow it to show the appropriate header. Next, we'll need to implement the logic to set up a table in which all of the movie data will be displayed. First up is the header. The highlighted lines are new:

```
extends layout
block article
  -import mmweb.web;
  -if(info.type == ListType.addMovie)
    h3 Sucessfully Added Movie
  -else
```

```
     h3 MovieMan Database
-if(movies.length == 0)
   p There are no movies to display.
```

Note that the existing h3 tag, which reads MovieMan Database, has been indented one level past the else. Also note that we've imported mmweb.web. This is so we can have access to the members of the ListType enumeration.

The table we're going to implement has one column for each member of the Movie type and an additional column for the **Edit** and **Delete** links, for a total of seven columns. The first row consists of seven table headers (th tags), indicating the purpose of each column. We'll generate a new row for each Movie instance in the movies array via a foreach loop. For each instance, the value of each member is extracted and placed into the output via the !{} syntax, for example, to extract the value of the title field: !{movie.title}. Using the id field of each movie, links to the /edit and /delete URLs, the handlers for which we'll implement later, are generated and placed in the last cell of each row. All of the following highlighted code is new:

```
-if(info.movies.length == 0)
   p There are no movies to display.
-else
   table.MovieList
     tr
       th ID
       th Title
       th Case
       th Page
       th Disc
       th Season
       th Action
       -foreach(i, movie; info.movies)
         tr
           td !{movie.id}
           td.Title !{movie.title}
           td !{movie.caseNumber}
           td !{movie.pageNumber}
           td !{movie.discNumber}
           td !{movie.seasonNumber}
           td
             a(href='/edit?movieID=!{movie.id}') Edit
             br
             a(href='/delete?movieID=!{movie.id}') Delete
```

The first line, not highlighted since it isn't new, was modified so that the `-if` tests `info.movies.length` instead of `movies.length`. The `table` tag is given the `MovieList` class so that it can be styled to taste in `style.css`. Notice the second of the last three lines is a break (`br`) tag. Break tags should always be inserted at the same indentation level as the text they apply to. In this case, we want the **Edit** link to appear on one line and the **Delete** link to be on the next, so the `br` tag is at the same indentation level as both.

Modifying app.d

We've got everything in place to get the work done, but as yet the server has no idea how to display the input form. We don't have a function in the web interface to render it. The `postAdd` function is for handling the data from the form, not for displaying the form itself. We could add a new function to `MovieMan` to render `add.dt`, but there's another approach that works equally well and helps us keep `MovieMan` clear of functions that don't need any logic.

What we need to do is to tell the server how to associate a URL with a function that knows how to render `add.dt`. We can do that by registering a delegate with the `get` function of `URLRouter`, just like we did when we configured it to serve static files. The `vibe.http.server` module has a function, `staticTemplate`, which takes the name of a template and returns a delegate that will render it. So open up `app.d` and add the highlighted line:

```
router.registerWebInterface(new MovieMan);
router.get("/forms/add", staticTemplate!"add.dt");
router.get("*", serveStaticFiles("./public/"));
```

We could choose anything for the URL except `/` or `/add`, since those already map to the `index` and `postAdd` functions of `MovieMan`. However, since the form in `add.dt` is associated with the `postAdd` function that handles the `/add` URL, it's a good convention to keep `add` in the form URL so that we never lose track of how the related parts of the app match up. `/forms/add` allows us to do that.

Modifying layout.dt

Now the only step remaining is to give the user a way to access the input form. This requires one minor modification of `layout.dt`. We need to convert the second list item into a link that points at `/forms/add`. The following highlighted lines show the modifications:

```
ul
  li
    a(href='/') Home
```

```
li
  a(href='/forms/add') Add New Movie
li Find Movie(s)
```

All we've done is move the text of the second list item to a new line, add an anchor tag in front of it that points to the form URL, and indented it one level beyond the preceding `li` tag.

That's the last of the changes to add a movie to the database. Now you can launch the server, reload the page in the browser, click on the **Add New Movie** link, and add as many movies to the database as you like.

Invisible tables

If the table doesn't appear after adding a movie, try increasing the size of the browser window. If it still isn't visible, you'll probably need to tweak the stylesheet to be more flexible. Or, while testing, just remove the stylesheet links from `layout.dt`.

Listing movies

Recall that the intended default behavior of `index.dt` is to show a list of ten movies from the database. That's the `ListType.generic` flag. When the user loads the page for the first time, the index function in `MovieMan` should fetch the first ten movies from the database and hand them off to the `render` function. `index.dt` will display each movie and, depending on the context, add **Next** and/or **Previous** links to display more. To implement this functionality, the following steps are required:

- Implement a function in the database layer that can fetch a certain number of movies, given a row offset and a count
- Modify the `index` function to fetch movies from the database and pass them off to the `render` function
- Modify `index.dt` to display **Next** and **Previous** links when appropriate

Implementing the listMovies function

The first thing to do on the database side is to set up an SQL statement to fetch a number of movies from the DB. Open up `sql.d` and add the following:

```
enum listSQL = "SELECT * FROM movie LIMIT ?1 OFFSET ?2;";
```

Again, we're going to use a prepared statement for this query. We have two parameters that we'll need to bind. The first is the `limit`, which specified how many database rows to return in the result set; the second is the row offset, namely, which row to pull first. An offset of `0` is the first row, an offset of `10` the first 10 rows, and so on. Although we won't implement it in this book, the database layer, the `index` function, and the table logic in `index.d` support limits other than `10`. Adding the ability for the user to select the number of movies to display at once is a potential post-book exercise.

Next up, we need to get the prepared statement ready. Add the highlighted line to the `private` section of `db.d`:

```
Statement _insert;
Statement _list;
```

Then add a line to the module constructor to set it up:

```
// Create the prepared statements
_insert = _db.prepare(insertSQL);
_list = _db.prepare(listSQL);
```

Next, we're going to implement a helper function. `listMovies` isn't the only function in the DB layer that will need to return an array of `Movie`s. Extracting all of the data from a d2sqlite3 `ResultRange` into a `Movie` instance is repetitive. To make it easier to manage, add the `getResults` function to the private section of `db.d`:

```
Movie[] getResults(Statement statement) {
  auto results = statement.execute();
  Movie[] movies;

  if(!results.empty) {
    movies.reserve(10);
    foreach(row; results) {
      movies ~= Movie(
        row.peek!long(0),
        row.peek!string(1),
        row.peek!int(2),
        row.peek!int(3),
        row.peek!int(4),
        row.peek!int(5)
      );
    }
  }
  return movies;
}
```

The statement is executed and, if the result range is not empty, a new `Movie` instance is populated with data and added to an array. The `ResultRange` is a range that contains `Rows`. A `Row` is a range that contains `ColumnData`, and those contain the data we are interested in. The `Row` type has a convenience function, `peek`, which takes an index as a function argument and a type as a template argument. It grabs the data at that index and converts it to the desired D type. Without `peek`, this loop would be much uglier, as we'd have to iterate over every `Row` and manually extract the data.

Finally, add the `listMovies` function to the `public` section of `db.d`:

```
Movie[] listMovies(long limit, long offset) {
  _list.reset();
  _list.bind(1, limit);
  _list.bind(2, offset);
  return _list.getResults();
}
```

The helper function allows `listMovies` to be nice and compact.

Modifying the index function

Now that `listMovies` is implemented, we can go ahead and use it in the `index` function. We're going to need to do more than just call `listMovies`, though. The function will always need to know which row offset should be the starting point of the list. We can't just always start with the first row. This means the `index` function will need to have a parameter.

> For those not familiar with HTTP GET and POST methods, each can send parameters to the server. For POST methods, the parameters are part of the packet of data the browser sends to the server and are never seen by the user. For GET methods, the parameters are appended to the URL like so: `http://mysite.com?param1=2;x=3`.

The parameter for the root page should always be optional, so that when you browse to `http://127.0.0.1:8080` to see your app, you don't need to specify any parameters manually. To make that work, we can give the index function a parameter, which we'll call `offset`, and give it a default value of `0`. That way, if the URL contains no parameters, vibe.d will see that we have assigned a default value to the function parameter and won't error out on us. When a parameter with no default value is missing from the request, vibe.d will always throw an exception (when using the web interface API).

With that information, we can open up `web.d` and modify the index function to look like this:

```
void index(long offset=0, long limit = 10) {
    auto info = ListInfo(offset, ListType.generic);
    info.limit = limit;
    info.movies = listMovies(limit, offset);
    render!("index.dt", info);
}
```

Modifying index.dt

Now all that remains is to add the **Next** and **Previous** links to `index.dt`. The way it works is this: We first test whether the `ListType` is `ListType.generic`, as other list types (in this book's implementation of `MovieManWeb`) aren't concerned with limits or **Next** and **Previous** links. If it is a generic list, we'll add another row to the table with a total of five cells, two of which span two columns. Inside the two longer cells, we'll implement some logic to either display the links or display nothing. This time, I'll show both an image and the new code. The image is shown first, so you can get a frame of reference, as follows:

```
-foreach(i, movie; info.movies)
    tr
        td !{movie.id}
        td.Title !{movie.title}
        td !{movie.caseNumber}
        td !{movie.pageNumber}
        td !{movie.discNumber}
        td !{movie.seasonNumber}
        td
            a(href='/edit?movieID=!{movie.id}') Edit
            br
            a(href='/delete?movieID=!{movie.id}') Delete
-if(info.type == ListType.generic)
    tr
        td.NextPrev
        td.NextPrev
            -if(info.movies.length >= info.limit)
                a(href='/?offset=!{info.offset + info.limit}') Next
        td.NextPrev(colspan='3')
        td.NextPrev
            -if(info.offset >= info.limit)
                a(href='/?offset=!{info.offset - info.limit}') Previous
        td.NextPrev
```

And now for the code:

```
-if(info.type == ListType.generic)
  tr
    td.NextPrev
    td.NextPrev
    -if(info.movies.length == info.limit)
      a(href='/?offset=!{info.offset + info.limit}') Next
    td.NextPrev(colspan='3')
    td.NextPrev
      -if(info.offset >= info.limit)
        a(href='/?offset=!{info.offset - info.limit}') Previous
        td.NextPrev
```

The new addition begins immediately after the code for the loop. The `-if` is on the same indentation level as the `-foreach`, because it follows it and is not part of it. Just to be clear, in normal D code it would look as follows:

```
foreach(i, movie; info.movies) {
  ...
}
if(info.type == ListType.generic) {
  ...
}
```

Putting the `-if` one indentation level beyond the `-foreach` would be the same as putting the `if` statement inside the `foreach` block.

The `td` tags all have the `NextPrev` class applied. Like the other CSS classes we've seen so far, this is to allow styling that's specific to these cells. Again, if you aren't happy with the style, modify `style.css` as much as you like.

The part that does the work is in the two `-if` lines inside the cells. The first one checks whether `info.movies.length` is greater than or equal to `info.limit`. This is a fairly good indicator that the **Next** link can be shown. If the test passes, a link will be generated with `info.offset + info.limit` as the `offset` parameter for the `index` function. Similar logic is used to decide whether or not to show the **Previous** link, testing `info.offset` against `info.limit` rather than the length of the movie array.

With all of that completed, you can recompile and relaunch the server, then reload the browser at `127.0.0.1:8080` to see all of the movies you added to the database after completing the previous subsection.

Finding movies

There are a few different keys we might like to use to search for a movie in the database. Internally, it can be useful to search by ID (to edit or delete a movie, or fetch a movie that has just been added), though that probably isn't of much interest to the user. The user would be more interested to search by title, case number, or perhaps case and page number or case and title. We'll implement a search feature that accounts for all of these, following these steps:

- Implement a function in the web interface to handle the processing of form data containing the search criteria

- Implement a Diet template that displays an input form where the user can enter search criteria

- Modify index.dt to support the listing of search results

- Modify app.d to map the input form's URL to the new Diet template

- Modify layout.dt with a link to the new input form

- Implement support for multiple search criteria in the database layer

Notice that we're modifying the database layer last this time. This is because db.d is going to require a lot of new code, which we will implement a chunk at a time. By completing the other steps first, we can test each chunk as we add it.

Implementing the postFind function

The postFind function will receive three parameters from the input form: a movie title, a case number, and a page number. A page number can never be a search key by itself, but other than that any combination of the three form fields can be filled out to search for a movie. If the user only enters a title, the search is by title; if case number and page number are filled out, then the search is by case number and page number. The job of postFind is to figure out which fields have values and call findMovie in the database layer with the appropriate flag. So, for the first step, let's add the following enumeration to the top of db.d:

```
enum Find {
  none        = 0x0,
  byTitle     = 0x1,
  byCase      = 0x2,
  byTitleCase = 0x3,
  byCasePage  = 0x4,
  byAll       = byTitle | byCase | byCasePage,

}
```

One of `Find`'s members will be the first argument passed to `findMovie`. Now let's turn to `web.d` and add `postFind` to `MovieMan`.

The first line initializes a local variable, `params`. After that, the function tests each parameter to determine which of the `Find` flags apply. If a title was provided, `Find.byTitle` is set. If there is a case number but no page number, `Find.byCase` is set, otherwise if there is both a case number and a page number, `Find.byCasePage` is set:

```
void postFind(string title, int caseNumber, int pageNumber) {
  Find params;
  if(title !is null && title != "N/A")
    params |= Find.byTitle;
  if(caseNumber && !pageNumber) params |= Find.byCase;
  else if(caseNumber && pageNumber) params |= Find.byCasePage;

  auto info = ListInfo(ListType.findMovie);
  info.movies = findMovie(params, title, caseNumber, pageNumber);
  render!("index.dt", info);
}
```

These few lines cover all the cases we are interested in. Finally, if `params` is still equal to the default value after the checks, then the `index` method is called to render the index page with the default parameters. Otherwise, `findMovie` is called to perform the search and the resulting array is stored in a `ListInfo` instance, which is then handed off to the render function to list all of the movies on the index page. Notice that `info.type` is set to `ListType.findMovie`.

Implementing find.dt

The diet template `find.dt` looks very much like the `add.dt` we implemented earlier. The only difference is that it has three input fields and posts its data to `/find`. Once again, here's a screenshot of the code:

```
find.dt                    x
 1  extends layout
 2  block article
 3      h3 Find a Movie
 4      form(action='/find', method='post')
 5          table.Form
 6              tr
 7                  td
 8                      label(for='title') Movie Title
 9                  td
10                      input(type='text', name='title', id='title', size='64', value='N/A')
11              tr
12                  td
13                      label(for='caseNumber') Case Number
14                  td
15                      input(type='number', name='caseNumber', id='caseNumber', size='4', value='0')
16              tr
17                  td
18                      label(for='pageNumber') Page Number
19                  td
20                      input(type='number', name='pageNumber', id='pageNumber', size='4', value='0')
21              tr
22                  td(colspan='2')
23                      input(type='submit', value='Find Movie(s)')
```

Modifying index.dt

We only need to do a little work in `index.dt`. First, add two lines to check for
`ListType.findMovie` and display a context-specific header:

```
-if(info.type == ListType.addMovie)
  h3 Sucessfully Added Movie
-else if(info.type == ListType.findMovie)
  h3 The Following Movies Were Found
-else
  h3 MovieMan Database
```

Next, we want to also display a context-specific message if the movie array is empty.
The default message looks like this already:

```
-if
  p There are no movies in the database.
```

Let's change it to this:

```
-if(info.movies.length == 0 && info.type == ListType.findMovie)
  p No movies match your search criteria.
-else if(info.movies.length == 0)
  p There are no movies in the database.
```

Modifying app.d and layout.dt

Let's kill two birds with one stone. First, a new line in `app.d`:

```
router.get("/forms/add", staticTemplate!"add.dt");
router.get("/forms/find", staticTemplate!"find.dt");
router.get("*", serveStaticFiles("./public/"));
```

And second, the addition of a link to the form in `layout.dt`:

```
ul
  li
    a(href='/') Home
  li
    a(href='/forms/add') Add New Movie
  li
    a(href='/forms/find') Find Movie(s)
```

Now we're ready to try out all the pieces we'll add to `db.d` as we add them.

Implementing the findMovie functions

We're going to implement two versions of the `findMovie` function. One simply takes an ID to search for; the other takes four parameters, one to indicate which of the other three to use as search criteria. Since the former is shorter and easier to implement, that's where we'll begin.

findMovie the first

Here's the SQL that needs to be added to `sql.d`:

```
enum byIDSQL = "SELECT * FROM movie WHERE movieID=?1";
```

In the interests of saving space, I'll trust that you know by now where and how to add and initialize a `Statement` named `_findByID` in `db.d`. Once you've done that, you can add the following version of `findMovie`:

```
Movie[] findMovie(long id) {
  _findByID.reset();
  _findByID.bind(1, id);
  return _findByID.getResults();
}
```

Even though we're only looking for a single movie here, we're still returning an array. Given that everything else deals with an array of Movies, it fits right in. Now let's go back to web.d and modify postAdd as shown by the highlighted line:

```
void postAdd(string title, int caseNumber, int pageNumber,
int discNumber, int seasonNumber)
{
  auto id = addMovie(Movie(0, title, caseNumber, pageNumber,
  discNumber, seasonNumber));
  auto info = ListInfo(-1, ListType.addMovie);
  info.movies = findMovie(id);
  render!("index.dt", info);
}
```

findMovie the second

The second function for db.d is a little long to show all at once. So what we'll do is look at the basic skeleton first, then we'll implement it one case at a time in the switch statement:

```
Movie[] findMovie(Find by, string title, int caseNumber,
int pageNumber)
{
  Statement sql;
  scope(exit) sql.reset();
  final switch(by) with(Find) {
    case byTitle:
      break;
    case byCase:
      break;
    case byTitleCase:
      break;
    case byCasePage:
      break;
    case byAll:
      break;
    case none:
      return [];
  }
  return sql.getResults;
}
```

Since we're going to have multiple prepared statements for the different search criteria, we start off by declaring a `Statement` instance to which we will assign the `Statement` we need in the `switch`. For convenience, we'll call `reset` on it when the function exits. We're using a `final switch` to guarantee we cover every member of `Find`, and a `with` statement to save some keystrokes. Finally, we call `getResults` on the instance we've assigned to `sql`.

Each case in the `switch` will first assign the appropriate `Statement` to `sql`, bind the appropriate parameters, then `break`. The tedious bit is setting up the prepared statements. Again, I'll show you the SQL each statement requires and give you a variable name, then you can add the necessary lines to `db.d` for each `Statement`. The first one we'll need is `_selectTitleStmt`, the SQL for which is:

```
enum byTitleSQL= "SELECT * FROM movie WHERE title=?1 ORDER BY
caseNum, pageNum;";
```

Following is the case statement to search by title:

```
case byTitle:
  sql = _findByTitle;
  sql.bind(1, title);
  break;
```

At this point, you can compile and launch, then click on the `Find Movie(s)` link to test out searching by title. Next up, we'll need a statement called `_findByCase`, which requires this SQL:

```
enum byCaseSQL = "SELECT * FROM movie WHERE caseNum=?1 ORDER BY
pageNum";
```

And the `case` statement:

```
case byCase:
  sql = _findByCase;
  sql.bind(1, caseNumber);
  break;
```

Run DUB again and perform a couple of searches based on case number. Next in line are the `_findByTitleCase` and the following SQL:

```
enum byTitleCaseSQL= "SELECT * FROM movie WHERE title=?1 AND
caseNum=?2 ORDER BY caseNum, pageNum;";
```

The implementation:

```
case byTitleCase:
  sql = _findByTitleCase;
  sql.bind(1, title);
  sql.bind(2, caseNumber);
  break;
```

There are only two case statements left. Once you've tried searching by title and case number, go ahead and get them both implemented. We'll need two statements, _findByCasePage and _findByAll. The SQL for each:

```
enum byCasePageSQL = "SELECT * FROM movie WHERE caseNum=?1 AND
pageNum=?2 ORDER BY pageNum;";
enum byAllSQL = "SELECT * FROM movie WHERE title=?1 AND caseNum=?2
AND pageNum=?3";
```

And the code:

```
case byCasePage:
  sql = _findByCasePage;
  sql.bind(1, caseNumber);
  sql.bind(2, pageNumber);
  break;
case byAll:
  sql = _findByAll;
  sql.bind(1, title);
  sql.bind(2, caseNumber);
  sql.bind(3, pageNumber);
  break;
```

Editing and deleting movies

In order for this book version of MovieManWeb to become feature complete, it needs to have support for editing and deleting movies. The links to the appropriate URLs are already configured in index.dt and are displayed alongside each movie in the table. We're not going to implement them together, however. Should you choose to do so, adding support for both features is a good first target for expanding on the program. I will outline the necessary steps and show the required SQL here (it is also present in sql.d in the downloadable source package), but other than that, you're on your own.

For edit functionality, you'll need to complete the following steps:

- Implement a function, `updateMovie`, in `db.d` to update the fields of a database entry, given a `Movie` instance.

- Implement a function, `postEdit`, in `web.d` to take the data from a form, construct a `Movie` instance, and call the `updateMovie` function.

- Implement a function, `getEdit`, in `web.d` to call `findMovie` with an ID, then pass call the `render` function with `edit.dt` and the result of the find as template arguments.

- Implement a Diet template, `edit.dt`, which contains an input form with fields corresponding to each member of a `Movie` instance. The default values of each field should be taken from the `Movie` instance that was given to the `render` function.

- Modify `index.dt` to show a context-specific header after the update.

Notice that using `URLRouter` to map `edit.dt` to a URL such as `/forms/edit` isn't going to work this time. In `index.dt`, the link to edit a movie looks like this:

```
a(href='/edit?movieID=!{movie.id}') Edit
```

The ID of the movie to be edited is added to the URL as a `movieID` parameter, which means we need to implement a `getEdit` function that takes a single parameter named `movieID`. The server will make sure that GET requests made when clicking on the link go to `getEdit`, and POST requests made from the form in `edit.dt` go to `postEdit` (assuming you properly configure the form properties). The SQL for the edit feature is:

```
enum updateSQL = `UPDATE movie
SET title = ?1, caseNum=?2, pageNum=?3, discNum=?4, seasonNum=?5
WHERE movieID=?6;`;
```

To support deleting a movie from the database, follow these steps:

- Implement a function, `deleteMovie`, in `db.d` to delete a movie from the database

- Implement a function, `getDelete`, in `web.d` to call `deleteMovie`

That's all that's needed to delete a movie. How you handle the implementation is entirely up to you, but `getDelete` must take a `movieID` parameter to match up with the **Delete** link in `layout.dt`. You might first call `findMovie` with the ID and, if it doesn't exist, render `index.dt` with an empty array. Otherwise, call `deleteMovie` and then use the result of `findMovie` to display the data that was deleted. Don't forget to make use of `ListType` in both cases.

Expanding on MovieManWeb

Once you've implemented the edit and delete features, there are a number of ways to expand and enhance the program. Perhaps two of the most important are data validation and error handling. To see why, try entering text in a number field, or leaving it empty. What you'll end up with is a page showing you the backtrace of an exception because `std.conv.to` couldn't convert the text to a number.

The cost of the convenience of the web interface API is that you lose all of the low-level control over data conversion and error handling. There is an attribute with which you can annotate any function in `MovieMan`, `@errorDisplay`, which can be given a function that will be called when an exception is thrown during execution of the annotated function (see `http://vibed.org/api/vibe.web.web/errorDisplay`), but if you want any control over form input validation, you'll need to do it client side with JavaScript. Alternatively, you could implement a new version of the program using the low-level API to get a feel for how it works. That would also give you complete control over how to handle invalid parameters and form data.

vibe.d has support for localization. Adding support to display the UI in multiple languages would be a nice little project to work on. Other ideas include expanding the database to allow for movie directors, actors and actresses, producers, release dates, notes, or any other data you'd like to support. This sort of project would touch every aspect of the code base, requiring more SQL statements, more D code and more Diet templates. You could also add support for music CDs.

If you want to take MovieManWeb (or anything you derive from it) online, you'll need to take steps for security first. At a minimum you'll want to add support for user accounts and input sanitization. Rather than worrying about storing salted and hashed passwords and user IDs, it might be a better idea to use something such as Google Sign-in (`https://developers.google.com/identity/sign-in/web/sign-in`) or other APIs to allow logging in with using credentials from popular social media websites.

Whatever you decide to do with the code presented here, have fun. The D programming language is always a pleasure to use, but using it together with vibe.d is quite sublime.

Summary

In this chapter, we have taken an all-too-brief tour of vibe.d by implementing an example application, MovieManWeb. We learned a little about what vibe.d provides, how to use the web interface API, how to implement Diet templates and, as a bonus, how to work with the d2sqlite3 library.

In the next chapter, we'll introduce some more advanced language and library features in order to point you in the right direction to continue your journey with D.

11
Taking D to the Next Level

The previous ten chapters cover enough of D, its standard library, and the ecosystem for any programmer to use as a guide in implementing a variety of applications and libraries in D. The language and library features that were covered were either fundamental, such as those discussed in *Chapter 2*, *Building a Foundation with D Fundamentals*, and *Chapter 3*, *Programming Objects the D Way*, or used so frequently that they are encountered on a regular basis in D libraries, tutorials, and example code. A number of features were not covered, either because they do not fit into the categories of fundamental and frequently used, or because they aren't quite ready for prime time.

This chapter introduces several of the language and library features that were not covered elsewhere in the book. None of the features here are given in-depth coverage, only enough to provide a general overview of each. Consider this chapter a platform from which to launch further exploration of the D programming language to improve your knowledge and experience. Here are the things we'll be looking at in this chapter, which are organized in no particular order:

- Concurrency: D's support for different multithreaded programming models in the language, the runtime, and the standard library

- SafeD: an introduction to the language features that help guarantee memory safety

- Functional purity: a brief introduction to D's support for pure functions

- The garbage collector: a look at the garbage collector API, which can be used to gain more control over when and how the GC does its work

- Connecting with C++: A quick look at binding D with C++ libraries

- The Future of D: a few optimistic words about D's future

Concurrency

Once upon a time, multithreaded programming was the exclusive realm of people with pointy hats who uttered strange incantations. Mere mortals fell victim to the evils of race conditions and deadlocks too easily. Yet, in this age of multi-core processors, the arcane is on the verge of becoming the mundane. D's multifaceted support of concurrency is oriented toward giving programmers the tools to make it so.

The traditional model of multithreaded programming, lock-based synchronization and data sharing, began to fall out of favor even before multicore processors came along. Such code is difficult to properly implement, test, and maintain. Other models, such as thread-per-system, thread-per-task, and message passing, improved the situation, making it easier to design frameworks that hide the nasty details behind an interface that appears single-threaded. Recently, it has become easier to implement loops that operate on data in parallel in some languages through built-in support, libraries, and compiler extensions. As software gains access to more and more cores, both on the CPU and the GPU, this latter model becomes more important. D comes with support for each of these models, spread across the language, the runtime, and the standard library. This section presents a brief introduction to all of the support for concurrent programming in D, with suggestions on where to go to learn more.

Threads and fibers

The heart of any concurrent programming model in D is the `Thread` class found in the DRuntime package `core.thread`. D's threads are heavyweight, meaning they map to kernel threads managed by the operating system. They carry all the baggage that comes from each thread having its own context that needs to be activated when a thread is given its time slice. A more lightweight option is the `Fiber` class. Not only do fibers carry around less baggage, their execution is managed by the program rather than the operating system.

Threads

You may use the `Thread` class to spawn new threads. Even in single-threaded programs, its static methods, such as `sleep` or `yield`, can be called to affect the execution of the current thread. New threads can be created either by subclassing `Thread`, or by instantiating a `Thread` instance directly. In both cases, a function that returns `void` and takes no arguments can be passed to the `Thread` constructor in the form of a delegate or function pointer.

```
import core.thread;
import std.stdio;
```

```
class MyThread : Thread {
  this() {
    super(&run);
  }
  private void run() {
    writeln("MyThread is running.");
  }
}
void myThreadFunc() {
  writeln("myThreadFunc is running.");
}
void main() {
  auto myThread1 = new MyThread;
  auto myThread2 = new Thread(&myThreadFunc);
  myThread1.start();
  myThread2.start();
}
```

There are C libraries and frameworks that provide a platform-agnostic way to create threads. Sometimes, such as when the C library requires the use of a custom thread handle for certain functions, it is necessary to use the foreign API to create new threads. This usually requires a pointer to a function that the new thread will call when it is executed. Any such threads should usually be registered with DRuntime inside the thread function by calling `thread_attachThis`.

```
extern(C) void threadFunc(void* data) {
  import core.thread : thread_attachThis, thread_detachThis;
  thread_attachThis();
  scope(exit) thread_detachThis();
}
```

Registering foreign threads with DRuntime is necessary to ensure that all required thread-local initialization is done. It's also important if the thread touches GC-managed memory. Before the GC scans any particular block of memory, it pauses the execution of all active threads. If a thread has not been registered with DRuntime, then the GC can't pause it. For this reason, you should always prefer to use the `Thread` class to create new threads in D, even when using C libraries. Threads should be created through third-party APIs only in the rare cases when it is unavoidable. Foreign threads should always be registered with DRuntime if they touch anything on the D side.

Fibers

A `Fiber`, an alternative implementation of a coroutine, can be spawned in the same manner as a `Thread`, by subclassing or by instantiation with a function pointer.

The delegate or function pointer associated with a fiber is executed when the `call` member function is called. Execution happens in the calling thread, which is blocked until the `yield` function is called, as shown in the following example:

```
import core.thread;
import std.stdio;
void myFiberFunc() {
  writeln("Execution begun.");
  Fiber.yield();
  writeln("Execution resumed.");
}
void main() {
  auto fiber = new Fiber(&myFiberFunc);
  fiber.call();
  writeln("Execution paused.");
  fiber.call();
}
```

Always keep in mind the difference between a fiber and a thread. A `Thread` instance represents a system resource. Each system thread has its own copies of thread-local data, so any mutations of such data through the `run` member function of a `Thread` instance happen on local copies and will not be visible in other threads. Non thread-local mutable data should be protected through synchronization primitives. A `Fiber` instance does not represent a system resource, meaning it does not have its own copies of thread-local data. If there is any possibility that multiple threads can run the `call` function on a `Fiber` instance, then care must be taken to synchronize access to all data that can be accessed through that function. As long as the same thread executes the function every time, synchronization is only an issue with data that is not thread-local. We'll see a bit about synchronization in D shortly.

Data sharing

As we know from *Chapter 2, Building a Foundation with D Fundamentals*, all variables declared in D are thread-local by default, meaning each thread has its own copy of each variable. We've also seen brief mentions of the `shared` and `__gshared` attributes. Fundamentally, they both achieve the same end in that they flag a variable as being outside of thread-local storage, meaning it is shared by all threads. Other than that, they are quite different, each coming with its own guarantees and consequences.

__gshared

Applying __gshared to a module-scope variable in D is essentially the same as declaring any variable in C. It is entirely up to the programmer to ensure that access to the variable by multiple threads is properly guarded. The same holds true for member variables of aggregate types, with the added side effect that such variables are also static. For example, the declarations of shared1 and shared2 in the following snippet are equivalent:

```
class SharedMembers {
  __gshared static int shared1;
  __gshared int shared2;
}
```

__gshared is a necessity when declaring variables in C library bindings, but it should otherwise be a rarity in normal D code.

Shared

There are a few things to be aware of when applying the shared attribute to a variable. First, it must be understood that shared modifies the type.

```
int tlsVar;              // type == int
shared int sharedVar;    // type == shared(int)
```

This has consequences in how shared variables are used as function arguments and assigned to other variables. While value types can convert just fine, this does not hold with reference types or pointers, for example, a shared(int) * does not implicitly convert to int*.

Second, shared is transitive. Applying shared to an instance of an aggregate type means all of its members are also shared.

```
struct ShareMe {
  int* intPtr;
}
shared ShareMe sm;
int x;
sm.intPtr = &x; // Error!
```

Here, sm.inPtr = &x fails because &x yields int*, not shared(int*), which is the type of sm.intptr thanks to the declaration of sm as shared.

Third, the compiler prohibits any unprotected, non-atomic modification of a shared variable. In the following snippet, the second line is illegal:

```
shared int sharedInt;
++sharedInt;
```

In this case, the error can be avoided using a template function from the `core.atomic` module in DRuntime.

```
import core.atomic : atomicOp;
atomicOp!"+="(sharedInt, 1);
```

> As I write, `++sharedInt` does not result in a compiler error. Instead, the compiler outputs the following message: **Deprecation: read-modify-write operations are not allowed for shared variables. Use core.atomic.atomicOp!"+="(sharedInt, 1) instead**. The code will still compile and the program will execute, but there's a good chance for a race condition to appear. At some point, this will become a compiler error. For now, it's necessary to pay attention to the compiler output to ensure that this sort of thing doesn't slip into any code using `shared` variables.

Synchronization and atomics

Synchronization goes hand-in-hand with data sharing. Without the means to protect a variable from simultaneous access by multiple threads, strange things can happen (note that there is no need to protect data from multiple fibers; `Fiber` instances are no different from any other class instance in that regard). Another option, as seen in the previous section, is to perform modifications of variables atomically; in one step, where possible. D has support for synchronization both in the language and in the runtime and for atomic operations in the runtime.

Automatic synchronization

The `synchronized` statement creates a scope in which all variable accesses are protected by a **mutex**. When the scope is entered, the mutex is acquired (locked). When the scope is exited, the mutex is released.

```
private int _someInt;
void setSomeInt(int newVal) {
  synchronized {
    _someInt = newVal;
  }
}
```

The compiler will allocate a new mutex object specifically for each `synchronized` blocks. This behavior can be overridden by providing any expression that yields a class or interface instance for the `synchronized` statement to use. Every class instance has its own mutex which the compiler will use instead of allocating a new one. That said, it's considered good practice to use an instance of `std.mutex.Mutex`.

```
import std.mutex;
auto mutex = new Mutex;
synchronized(mutex) {
    ...
}
```

`synchronized` can be applied to `class` (but never `struct`) declarations. Doing so makes every member function of that class `synchronized` and causes the mutex associated with each instance of the class to be used as the monitor, meaning that it's equivalent to adding a `synchronized(this)` statement inside every function in the class. With this, only shared instances of the class can be instantiated and all member function calls will be serialized.

As I write, there are two issues to watch out for regarding synchronized classes. One is public member variables. Right now, it's possible to declare them in a synchronized class, but this can be problematic if they are mutable as it allows for non-synchronized mutation. It is expected that this will be deprecated at some point.

The second is the documentation at `http://dlang.org/class.html#synchronized-classes` says the following:

> *"Member functions of non-synchronized classes cannot be individually marked as synchronized. The synchronized attribute must be applied to the class declaration itself."*

In practice, the compiler actually does allow `synchronized` to be applied to individual member functions. Again, instances of the class must be declared as `shared`. It is unlikely that this will change, as it is certain to break code in active projects. One such project is DWT, a port to D of the SWT library for Java (see `https://github.com/d-widget-toolkit/dwt`).

Manual synchronization

The DRuntime package `core.sync` contains several modules that expose primitives that can be used to manually implement synchronization for different behaviors. The package includes two types of mutexes, a generic recursive mutex in the `mutex` module, and a mutex that allows for shared read access and exclusive write access in the `rwmutex` module. Additionally, the modules `condition`, `semaphore`, and `barrier` provide eponymous primitives. If you're looking to implement lock-based data sharing yourself, this is a good place to start.

Atomics

An **atomic** operation is one that appears to happen instantaneously. Such operations are safe in multithreaded programming because there is an inherent guarantee that only one thread can perform the operation at a time, meaning that no locks are required. The `core.atomic` module in DRuntime provides a handful of functions that allow for lock-free concurrency. Earlier, we observed how to use the template function `atomicOp` to convert the non-atomic operation of adding 1 to a `shared(int)` into an atomic one. Other functions in the module allow for atomic loads and stores, atomic **compare and swap** (**cas**), and atomic **memory barriers** (**memory fences**).

When using atomic operations, it's important to have a good grasp of memory ordering. Members of the enumeration `core.atomic.MemoryOrder` can be used with the `atomicLoad` and `atomicStore` functions to specify the type of memory barrier instruction the CPU should use in carrying out the operation. Although it's a talk related to C++, a good place to start is Herb Sutter's two-part talk from *C++ and Beyond 2012*, titled, *atomic<> Weapons: The C++ Memory Model and Modern Hardware* at https://isocpp.org/blog/2013/02/atomic-weapons-the-c-memory-model-and-modern-hardware-herb-sutter.

Message passing

Phobos provides foundational support for the message passing model of concurrent programming in the `std.concurrency` module. This is the preferred way of handling concurrency in D; you should only turn to other models if `std.concurrency` doesn't meet your needs. This module hides most of the raw details of concurrent programming behind a simplified API; rather than manipulating the `Thread` class directly, programs call `std.concurrency.spawn` and get a `Tid` (thread ID) in return that is then used as a marker to identify messages sent and received between threads.

```
import std.concurrency;
import std.stdio;
void myThreadFunc(Tid owner) {
```

```
    receive(
       (string s) { writefln("Message to thread %s: %s", owner, s); }
    );
}
void main() {
   auto child1 = spawn(&myThreadFunc, thisTid);
   auto child2 = spawn(&myThreadFunc, thisTid);
   send(child1, "Message for child1.");
   send(child2, "Message for child2.");
}
```

Here, two new threads are created by passing a pointer to myThreadFunc and the result of thisTid, which returns the Tid of the current thread, to spawn. Then the parent thread sends a message to each child. The send function takes a Tid followed by any number of parameters of any type. The receive function is a template that takes any number of delegates as parameters, each of which can itself have different parameters and return types. The delegates are registered with the owning thread as message handlers; when a message is received, all of the registered delegates are searched to see if any have a parameter list that matches the parameters sent via the send function. In this example, one handler that accepts a string is registered for each child thread.

It's notable that std.concurrency deals in **logical threads**. In other words, a Tid may represent an actual Thread, or it may represent a Fiber. By default, spawn creates new kernel threads, but it's possible to implement a Scheduler, such as the example std.concurrency.FiberScheduler, that causes spawn to create new fibers instead.

std.concurrency contains variations of spawn, send, and receive, as well as utility functions and types, which can be used as a foundation for a higher-level message passing API.

Parallelism

When processing large amounts of data, one way to utilize the power of multi-core processers is to break the data into chunks and process each chunk in parallel. D has support for this in the form of the Phobos module std.parallelism.

The module is built around the `Task` and `TaskPool` types, with a few helper functions to make things more convenient to use. A `Task` represents a unit of work. A `TaskPool` maintains a queue of tasks and a number of worker threads. Member functions of `TaskPool` can be called to process and apply algorithms to the data in the task queue. For example, the member functions `map` and `reduce` perform the same operations as their `std.algorithm` counterparts, but do so across multiple threads in parallel. Another interesting member function of `TaskPool` is `parallel`, which allows the execution of a parallel `foreach` loop. There is a convenience function, also called `parallel`, which uses the default `TaskPool` instance. The following example scales 100 million two-dimensional vectors. When compiled with `–version=SingleThread`, it all happens on one thread.

```
struct Vec2 {
  float x = 1.0f, y = 2.0f;
}
void main() {
  import std.stdio : writeln;
  import std.datetime : MonoTime;
  auto vecs = new Vec2[](100_000_000);
  auto before = MonoTime.currTime;
  version(SingleThread) {
    foreach(ref vec; vecs) {
      vec.x *= 2.0f;
      vec.y *= 2.0f;
    }
  }
  else {
    import std.parallelism : parallel;
    foreach(ref vec; parallel(vecs)) {
      vec.x *= 2.0f;
      vec.y *= 2.0f;
    }
  }
  writeln(MonoTime.currTime - before);
}
```

Given that there are only two multiplications and assignments per vector, there isn't enough work for a parallel `foreach` loop to be beneficial with lower numbers of vector instances. Change the `100_000_000` to `100_000`, for example, and you may find that the parallel version is slower. It was for me. But with 100 million instances, the parallel version won out in multiple runs on my machine. If you need to process large datasets, particularly by performing complex operations, `std.parallelism` makes it quite simple to take advantage of multiple cores and process the data in parallel.

More information

The Phobos documentation at `http://dlang.org/phobos/index.html` is a source of more detailed information for most of the topics we've covered in this section. Additionally, the concurrency chapter of Andrei Alexandrescu's book *The D Programming Language* is available online at `http://www.informit.com/articles/printerfriendly/1609144`. The article *Getting More Fiber in Your Diet* at `http://octarineparrot.com/article/view/getting-more-fiber-in-your-diet` contains a more complex fiber example that is compared against an implementation using threads.

SafeD

Memory safety is an important issue in software development. Systems languages like C, C++ and D offer a number of opportunities for programmer mistakes to open the door to memory corruption during program execution, possibly leading to critical system failures, or making it easier for those with nefarious intent to achieve their goals. Other languages, such as Java and C#, have built-in features intended to minimize this risk and increase memory safety.

While D is a systems language, it includes some features by default that aim to increase memory safety. Arrays all carry around their length, meaning it's always easy to determine exactly how many elements an array contains. This is further enhanced through the bounds-checking of all array accesses, though this can be disabled on the command line; a systems programming language needs to allow performance to be a priority when it has to be. Still, D gives you that same proverbial gun that C and C++ do; you're less likely to blow off your entire foot with it, but that's not the whole story.

There is a subset of D that allows for a high degree of memory safety. This subset, commonly referred to as **SafeD**, allows programmers to opt-in in order to avoid common mistakes that can lead to memory corruption. This is achieved by annotating code with the attributes `@safe`, `@trusted`, and `@system`.

By default, all D code is `@system`. This means it is possible for the programmer to take advantage of the full power of the language. Memory safety is enforced by applying the `@safe` attribute. Like other attributes, it can be applied directly to functions, or to entire blocks of code using colons or braces.

```
module my_safe_module;
// Enable SafeD
@safe:
void thisFunctionIsSafe() {}
```

```
// Go back to the default
@system:
void thisFunctionIsNotSafe() {}
void anotherSafeFunction() @safe {}
```

@safe functions come with a few restrictions on the sort of code they can contain. For example, pointer arithmetic is forbidden, casts from pointers to non-pointers are forbidden, taking the address of a local variable is not allowed, const, immutable, and shared cannot be cast away, all array accesses are bounds-checked even when the command line switch -release is given to the compiler (though -boundscheck=off will disable it completely), and more. Another important component of SafeD is that @safe functions can only call other functions that are annotated with @safe or @trusted.

The @trusted attribute presents a safe interface, but the compiler does not attempt to verify that the implementation meets the restrictions of @safe. In other words, functions marked as @trusted can serve as a bridge between safe and unsafe code. It is incumbent upon the programmer to verify that @trusted code isn't doing anything that can corrupt memory. For example, taking the address of a local variable isn't an unsafe operation in and of itself; @safe prohibits it solely because it's the easiest and cheapest way to prevent local addresses from escaping, so any function where it is necessary to do this can be safely marked with @trusted (as long as the programmer verifies that the address doesn't escape). The same can be said of pointer arithmetic; as long as the programmer verifies that it stays within the bounds of the block of memory to which the pointer points, the code can be considered @trusted. Ultimately, @trusted serves as a marker indicating that maintainers need to pay extra attention when modifying this code and clients can trust that nothing untoward is going on.

Fully understanding and responsibly using SafeD requires an intimate knowledge of D and any peripheral libraries used in a project. Moreover, not all D programmers make use of these features, so there are a number of libraries in the D ecosystem where no consideration has been given to the SafeD subset, limiting the range of libraries available for those who do choose to use it. That said, as more D programmers take the plunge to understand and use it, it will become less of an issue. That makes it worthwhile to explore at some point during your journey with D. For more about SafeD, refer to http://dlang.org/function.html#function-safety.

Functional purity

The concept of functional purity was discussed briefly back in *Chapter 7, Composing Functional Pipelines with Algorithms and Ranges*. Now it's time for a quick introduction to functional purity as it is implemented in D. Consider the following function:

```
Vec2 add(Vec2 a, Vec2 b) pure {
   return Vec2(a.x + b.x, a.y + b.y);
}
```

Assuming that `Vec2` is a `struct` and not a `class`, then this function is as pure as a function can be. No global state is mutated, no parameters are mutated, and given multiple calls with the same arguments, the result will be the same every time. Note that it has been marked with the `pure` attribute. With this, the compiler will produce an error if the function tries to modify any mutable static data (such as a module-scope variable) or if it calls any function not marked `pure`.

What the compiler does not do is prevent the modification of any reference variables, such as class instances, arrays or ref parameters. This, for example, is legal:

```
Vec2 add(ref Vec2 a, Vec2 b) pure {
   a.x = 1.0f;
   return Vec2(a.x + b.x, a.y + b.y);
}
```

In a functional programming language, this sort of thing isn't going to fly. There, only functions like the first version of `add` are considered pure. In D, such a function is informally referred to as *strongly pure*, whereas the second version of `add` would be called *weakly pure*. The first pass at purity in D did not include the notion of weak purity. The relaxation of the rules came only after experience showed it was necessary. D is not, after all, a functional language, but a language with an imperative core and other paradigms built on top.

For a more in-depth introduction to functional purity in D, and to learn how weak purity actually helps the language better support strong purity, David Nadlinger's blog post *Purity in D* at `http://klickverbot.at/blog/2012/05/purity-in-d/` is a good place to start.

The garbage collector

The GC has been a background presence throughout this book, occasionally coming to the fore when we discussed specific language and library features. For a large number of D programs, it is never necessary to interact directly with the GC. A programmer needs to be aware of when collection cycles may occur, how to write GC-free code with `@nogc`, and how to avoid the potential issues that may arise when using GC-managed memory with C libraries, but the need to get down and dirty with the GC API is rare. When those times do arise, the `core.memory` module comes into play.

In this module, you'll find a single structure, `GC`, which contains a number of `static` member functions. Automatic garbage collection can be turned off with `GC.disable`. This doesn't turn off the GC completely—it will still run when the system is out of memory—but it does prevent it from running during normal usage. Collection can be forced by calling `GC.collect`. There have been reports of significant performance increases for some applications when turning off automatic collection in favor of manual collection. Automatic collection can be turned on again at any time with `GC.enable`.

Now and again, it's necessary to ensure that a block of memory hangs around indefinitely, or until the programmer determines it's no longer needed. One such scenario was presented in *Chapter 9, Connecting D with C*; when a block of memory allocated by the GC on the D side is handed off for a C library to make use of, bad things can happen if the GC collects the memory before the C code is finished with it. Passing a pointer to the memory to `GC.addRoot` will guarantee the memory block remains alive indefinitely. When `GC.removeRoot` is called, the GC will then be free to collect the memory block at any time.

Normally, GC memory is allocated indirectly though the `new` operator, expanding the capacity of dynamic arrays, or other language features. However, it's possible to allocate memory from the GC directly via `GC.malloc`. With this function, flags from the `GC.BlkAttr` enumeration can be used to control how the GC treats the memory, giving the programmer more fine-tuned control; when you know a block of memory contains no pointers to GC-managed memory, it's a waste of cycles for the GC to scan it again and again.

Sometimes, it's necessary to allocate memory outside of the GC, such as through a third-party C library or one of the standard C library allocators (such as `malloc`), that will be used to store pointers to memory allocated through the GC, such as class references or dynamic arrays. In this case, the memory block can be registered with the GC via the `GC.addRange` function. This will add the block to the list of memory locations the GC will scan. When the memory is no longer needed, `GC.removeRange` can be called to remove it from the GC's list.

As an aid in tuning the GC usage of a D application, DMD provides the `-vgc` command-line switch, which lists all of the GC allocations that can occur in a program. This includes hidden allocations, such as those that happen under the hood with dynamic arrays or inside Phobos functions. When the garbage collector starts to become a performance issue in a D program, as it sometimes may, this switch can be used to help guide manual optimizations, such as the addition of `@nogc` where appropriate and the use of GC member functions like `disable` and `collect`. For more on D's garbage collector, refer to `http://dlang.org/phobos/core_memory.html` and `http://dlang.org/garbage.html`.

Connecting with C++

This book devoted an entire chapter to connecting D and C, yet there's only this small section here in the last chapter to discuss interfacing with C++. The reason is that this feature of D is, as I write, under active development. Interfacing with C is rather easy, as most C compilers conform to well-defined, standard ABIs. The story is different with C++, where there is no standard ABI. This is particularly an issue when it comes to name-mangling, where compilers have traditionally followed their own schemes. Additionally, there is no such one-to-one correspondence between C++-specific features and D features as there is when C is compared with D. There are also key differences in the languages to consider. For example, C++ supports multiple inheritance, D does not; classes in C++ are value types, while D classes are reference types; D `const` is transitive, C++ `const` is not; and so on. Most of these issues as yet have no solutions.

Despite all the caveats, there is a significant amount of interoperability between the two languages. There is much common ground in their shared compatibility with C. Additionally, progress has been made on interacting with several C++-specific features. It all starts with the linkage attribute `extern(C++)`. This is important in getting the name-mangling correct and is highly dependent on the linker being used. Libraries generated with the Microsoft tools, whether they are static or dynamic, will have different name-mangling than those generated by the Digital Mars C++ compiler (DMC) or with GCC.

Namespaces are neatly handled as an extension to the linkage attribute. Consider the following C++ declaration:

```
namespace mylib {
  void MyFunction(int a);
}
```

This can be directly translated to D as:

```
extern(C++, mylib) {
```

```
        void MyFunction(int a);
    }
```

A C++ `struct`, when used as a POD type with no inheritance, can be translated directly to a D `struct`. It's also possible to translate some C++ aggregate types directly to D classes or interfaces, though things get complicated when templates or multiple inheritance are involved.

If you are interested in pursuing D and C++ interoperability, a great place to begin is with a presentation Walter Bright gave at a meeting of the Northwest C++ Users' Group, titled *Interfacing D to Legacy C++ Code*. A video of the talk can be found on YouTube at `https://www.youtube.com/watch?v=IkwaV6k6BmM`. Alternatively, there is a fork of LDC called Calypso that takes a different approach to getting the two languages to work together. You can find it at `https://github.com/Syniurge/Calypso`. There are a few members of the D community taking the time to explore this topic, so more current information can usually be found in the #D IRC channel or the D forums.

More on Phobos

We have only touched the surface of what's available in Phobos, D's standard library. We've seen a handful of functions scattered throughout the book, with the most detail being given in *Chapter 7, Composing Functional Pipelines with Algorithms and Ranges*, where we discussed the library's algorithms and other range-based functions. In this section, we'll take a quick hop around some of the more notable modules and packages in Phobos.

std.container

The `std.container` package contains modules in a collection of data structures, such as linked lists and a red-black tree. All of the containers share a similar, range-based API. Though the containers are usable now, the state of the package has been in a sort of limbo for some time, awaiting the arrival of a `std.allocator` package so that custom allocators can be used with each of the containers. At the time of writing, `std.allocator` has been approved by community review for inclusion in the `std.experimental` Phobos package. It was once expected that this event would trigger more work on the modules in `std.container`. However, much has been learned about ranges and collections in the years since `std.container` was first introduced, so it is more likely that a new package will be added to Phobos, using the new allocators, to replace it. Still, `std.container` is usable today. Refer to `http://dlang.org/phobos/std_container.html`.

An alternative to `std.container` is the third-party `containers` package. Developed and maintained by a company called **EMSI (Economic Modeling Specialists, Intl.)**, this company uses D in production and the `containers` package is battle-tested there. The containers in this library do not use the GC and are already making use of the future `std.allocator` package. Visit `https://github.com/economicmodeling/containers` for details.

std.datetime

`std.datetime` provides a variety of date and time functions and objects. Here, you'll find a number of ways to represent points in time, intervals of time, ranges over intervals of time, and time zones. There are also function templates that take any number of functions to execute for benchmarking. There's also the `MonoTime` type, which we saw earlier in this chapter, providing high-precision timing. In all, there are a lot of things in this module to dig through, but it's all well-documented and none of it is difficult to use. Refer to the documentation at `http://dlang.org/phobos/std_datetime.html` for details.

std.digest

This package contains modules that provide implementations of various hashing functions. At the time of writing, implementations exist for CRC, MD5, RIPEMD-160, SHA1 and SHA2. The base API can be found in the `std.digest.digest` module. All implementations follow this API. You can read more about this at `http://dlang.org/phobos/std_digest_digest.html`.

std.experimental

This package serves as a staging ground for new Phobos modules and packages. The idea is that each proposed module (or package) goes through a brief review period in the forums, where community members can vote whether it is suitable for inclusion in `std.experimental`. If approved, it remains in the package, while users put it through the paces, find the weaknesses, and look for ways to improve it. At some point, the package goes up for review again in the forums, where users will voice their opinions, before coming up for a vote on final inclusion into Phobos proper.

std.getopt

This entire module is geared around doing one thing: processing command-line options. For such a seemingly small task, it's quite a popular module. There's little reason for anyone writing a D program to manually process command line options these days, except for special-case needs not covered by this module. This example shows how easy it is:

```d
void main(string[] args) {
  import std.getopt;
  import std.stdio : writeln;
  bool printMeaning;
  int repeatCount = 1;
  auto helpInfo = getopt(
  args, "print-meaning", "Print the meaning of life.",
  &printMeaning, "repeat-count", "Number of times to repeat the
  meaning of life.", &repeatCount
  );
  if(helpInfo.helpWanted) {
    defaultGetoptPrinter(
    "This program can show you the meaning of life, if you tell it
    to.", helpInfo.options
    );
    return;
  }
  if(printMeaning && repeatCount > 0) {
    for(int i=0; i<repeatCount; ++i)
      writeln("The meaning of life is 42.");
  }
  else {
    writeln("You have opted not to learn the meaning of life.");
  }
}
```

Executing this program with `-h` or `-help` will print the help message, `This program can show you the meaning of life, if you tell it to,` along with each option and its description. To see the meaning of life, execute it with the `--print-meaning` switch. To print the message ten times, execute the following (assuming the executable is named `options`):

`options --print-meaning --repeat-count=10`

Refer to `http://dlang.org/phobos/std_getopt.html` for more information.

std.process

This module provides the means to launch new processes and pipe data between them, with a number of different options for doing so. For example, `spawnProcess` launches a new process, with the option of assigning it standard input, output, and error streams, then returns immediately, allowing the child process to continue running. The `execute` function launches a new process, but blocks until the process is finished. Similarly-named functions, such as `spawnShell` and `executeShell`, behave in the same way, except that they accept arbitrary string commands, which they run through the system's default command shell. For all the details on `std.process`, refer to `http://dlang.org/phobos/std_process.html`.

std.socket

There are certain types of networked applications for which a dependency on vibe.d might be overkill. Sometimes, a simple thread-per-client or selector model of networking is more appropriate. For those situations, `std.socket` provides types analogous to those found in the well-known Berkeley Sockets API, which is the basis for Posix Sockets and a version of which exists in the WinSock API for Windows. Anyone familiar with Berkeley Sockets, or the venerable `java.net` API, should feel right at home with `std.socket`. There you'll find a base `Socket` type, with subclasses called `TcpSocket` and `UdpSocket` for communicating via the TCP and UDP protocols. `Socket` provides member functions for setting socket options, and there are several enumerations to assist. There is also a `SocketSet` type that allows using the selector model of connection management. You can read more about `std.socket` at `http://dlang.org/phobos/std_socket.html`.

Modules for Unicode and other encodings

There are four modules in Phobos related to character encodings: `std.ascii`, `std.encoding`, `std.uni`, and `std.utf`.

The `std.ascii` module consists of a number of functions that work with ASCII characters. Some examples are `toUpper`, `toLower`, `isUpper`, `isWhite`, and so on. All of the functions accept Unicode characters, but the `is*` functions will return `false` upon encountering them and the `to*` functions will do nothing. Unicode-enabled counterparts to the functions in this module are found in `std.uni`, along with several other Unicode algorithms and data structures. Refer to `http://dlang.org/phobos/std_ascii.html` and `http://dlang.org/phobos/std_uni.html`.

`std.utf` exposes functions for encoding and decoding strings to and from the three Unicode encodings, UTF-8, UTF-16, and UTF-32. `std.encoding` is where you can find functions for transcoding between UTF-8, UTF-16, UTF-32, ASCII, ISO-8869-1, and WINDOWS-1252. Visit `http://dlang.org/phobos/std_utf.html` and `http://dlang.org/phobos/std_encoding.html` for more.

System bindings

In addition to bindings for the C standard library, there are some system-specific bindings living in DRuntime under the `core.sys` package. There, you'll find the following subpackages: `freebsd`, `linux`, `osx`, `posix`, `solaris`, and `windows`. With these, you should have everything you need for programming on each supported system. The `windows` package for years was woefully inadequate, but at the time of this writing, a third-party Windows API binding project has been merged into the DRuntime repository and should be released with DMD 2.069. This is a fairly complete binding that allows you to develop Win32 GUI applications with D. Now, you should be able to pick up Petzold's *Programming Windows* or Stevens's *Advanced Programming in the Unix Environment* and write all of the examples in D. If you find anything missing, submit a bug report at `https://issues.dlang.org/` or a pull request at `https://github.com/D-Programming-Language/DRuntime`.

Game development with D

Chapter 8, *Exploring the Wide World of D*, introduced the Derelict and Diemos bindings projects. While Deimos includes bindings for C libraries that are useful for game development, Derelict was created with games in mind. Between them, you can find dynamic and/or static bindings for several C and C++ libraries that are commonly used in game development, such as:

- **SDL2**: The Simple Directmedia Layer is a library that abstracts window and input handling on several platforms. It allows creating OpenGL-capable windows and ships with a hardware-accelerated 2D renderer that has backends for OpenGL, OpenGL ES, and Direct3D. It is available at `http://libsdl.org/`.

- **SFML2**: The Simple and Fast Multimedia Library is a C++ library similar to SDL2. It can be used solely to create OpenGL-enabled windows on mulitple platforms, but also ships with a 2D renderer built on top of OpenGL. Its home page is at `http://www.sfml-dev.org/`. There is an alternative static binding available at `http://www.dsfml.com/`.

- **GLFW3**: GLFW is a small, simple library aimed at one thing: abstracting the window and event handling for OpenGL applications on multiple platforms. Unlike SDL2 or SFML2, it does not come with any bells and whistles for rendering, image loading, or anything other than window and event handling. Refer to `http://www.glfw.org/`.

Derelict includes bindings for OpenGL, OpenAL, OpenCL, OpenIL, FreeImage, FreeType, and other libraries useful for game development. There is also a binding in Derelict for the Allegro library (`http://liballeg.org/`). A static binding for Allegro, maintained by one of the Allegro developers, can be found at `https://github.com/SiegeLord/DAllegro5`.

If you're looking for libraries to help make a game engine, GFM is a project that has a number of convenience wrappers to several of the libraries mentioned above and more. It's available at `https://github.com/d-gamedev-team/gfm`. To handle all of the vectors, matrixes, quaternions, and other math constructs you may need, there's the gl3n library at `https://github.com/Dav1dde/gl3n`.

If you aren't looking for C library bindings and aren't planning to make your own game engine, you may want to turn to DGame, a simple but popular 2D game framework at `https://github.com/Dgame/Dgame`. If you're looking to move into 3D, Circular Studios maintains the Dash engine at `https://github.com/Circular-Studios/Dash`. For anyone looking to integrate D into an existing game engine, Manu Evans gave a presentation at DConf 2013 on how Remedy Games did just that for one of their projects (refer to `http://dconf.org/2013/talks/evans_1.html`).

There are a number of hobbyist game developers in the D community, and some who work in the industry. At the time of writing, a couple of D games have been released on Steam and there are quite a few projects scattered around the internet. Game development is one of the areas where there is ample opportunity for anyone developing D-specific tools and libraries. If it's an area of interest for you, I encourage you to reach out to others on the #D IRC channel and in the forums.

The future of D

In the years I have been involved with the D community, I have watched it grow from a handful of programmers posting on an obscure newsgroup to a large, vibrant community of users, contributors, and an annual conference. The language has changed and improved dramatically over that same period. As someone who enjoys using the language and who keeps abreast of D-related news and discussions in several different online communities, I'm quite optimistic about D's staying power.

On August 24, 2015, Andrei Alexandrescu announced in the D forums that he was resigning from his position as a researcher at Facebook to work full time on "pushing D forward." On October 16, 2015, he announced the incorporation of a D Foundation to promote and develop the D programming language. One of D's greatest strengths is that anyone in the community can contribute toward its development, but that has also been one of its greatest weaknesses; contributors tend to focus on the aspects of the language and its ecosystem that they enjoy or need themselves. This has led to a number of holes that contributors have not yet filled. The establishment of a D Foundation is expected to help alleviate that situation.

Another optimistic sign is that D is being used now by companies in production, including in scenarios where high-performance is a critical requirement. The success of these companies has proven that D is a serious contender in different arenas. It has also resulted in some direct contributions back to the D community, such as the containers library released by EMSI. As more companies find success with D, more will begin to adopt it, ultimately benefitting all D users.

It is my hope that you find the same enjoyment in the language that I have found, and go on to develop new software with D, whether open source or closed. I've always viewed the D ecosystem much like the Wild West; there are so many unexplored possibilities out there that anything goes. If you have an itch that existing D tools and libraries can't scratch, I encourage you to put your new D skills to use and develop something that does. I also hope that this book provides some help along the way.

Summary

This chapter has provided short introductions to a few topics not covered elsewhere in the book. We've seen the different forms of support for concurrent programming that D provides in the language, the runtime, and the standard library. We've had brief overviews of memory safety with SafeD, the garbage collector API, and binding D to C++. We've also taken a quick look at a handful of useful Phobos modules. In short, this chapter serves as a starting point for further exploration of the D programming language. Good luck!

Index

isInfinite 222
URL 223
output range 220

P

packages, vibe.d
  about 4, 21
  vibe.core 354
  Vibe.http 354
  vibe.mail 355
  vibe.web 354
padding 150
parameters, template
  alias parameters 171
  this parameters 172
  value parameters 169
Phobos
  about 416
  modules, for other encodings 419
  modules, for Unicode 419
  navigating 239
  range-based functions, searching 259
  std.algorithm package 247
  std.array package 257
  std.ascii module 419
  std.container package 416, 417
  std.datetime package 417
  std.digest package 417
  std.experimental package 417
  std.getopt package 418
  std.process module 419
  std.range package 239
  std.socket 419
  system bindings 420
Plain Old Data (POD) 202, 370
Planet D
  about 270
  URL 270
pointers
  about 46-48
  void pointers 47
polymorphism 110-113
port 300-302
pragma
  about 132
  inline pragma 134

lib pragma 132, 133msg pragma 133
  URL 132
process function 232
properties
  .init 41
  .sizeof property 41
  about 41-43
  URL 41
public imports 30

R

random-access range
  about 219
  obtaining, from char[] 220
  obtaining, from wchar[] 220
ranges
  about 223
  custom algorithms 229, 230
  custom ranges 224
  defining 207
  in use 223
  solutions, to problems 210
  used, for solving problems 207-209
RDMD 286, 287
real ranges
  about 216
  bidirectional ranges 219
  forward ranges 218
  input ranges 216
  optional range primitives 221
  output ranges 220
  random-access range 219
receive function 409
reddit 270, 271

S

SafeD
  about 411, 412
  URL 412
scope
  about 27
  block scopes 27
  function scope 27
  global scope 27
  module scope 27

synchronization
about 406
automatic synchronization 406, 407
manual synchronization 408

T

template
as code blocks 160-163
basics 160
class template 163-165
constraints 177, 178
enum template 166
function templates 166-168
mixins 178, 179
parameters 169
specializations 173, 174
struct template 163-165
using 173
variadic templates 180-182
templated operator overloads
about 192
binary overloads 193
cast overloads 195
operator assignment overloads 195, 196
slice operator overloads 196-198
unary overloads 192
template specializations
about 173, 174
on pointers and arrays 175, 176
ternary operator 69
textadept
about 274
URL 274
text editors
about 274
Emacs 274
Sublime Text 275
textadept 274
Vim 274
this parameters 172
Thread class 402, 403
tools and utilities
about 277
D Completion Daemon (DCD) 289
DMD 277
DustMite 287, 288

DVM 289
GDC 285
LDC 285
RDMD 286
toStringz 345
type qualifiers
const 72
immutable 72

U

Unicode
algorithms and data structures,
references 419
Uniform Function Call Syntax (UFCS) 6
unit tests 122-125
Universal Character Names (UCN) 26
updateMovie function 398
user-defined attributes (UDAs) 154-156
user-defined types
about 93
enumerations 93, 94
structs and classes 95-97
unions 95

V

value parameters 169
value range propagation 40
variadic functions 78
variadic template
about 180-182
expression tuple 182, 183
template tuple parameter 182
type tuple 182, 183
usages 184, 185
version condition
about 134-137
URL 135
vibe.d
about 354
database library 357, 358
packages 354, 355
URL 354, 357
web app anatomy 355
Vim
references 274
URL 274

Visual D
about 276
URL 276
Voldemort type 102

W

web app anatomy, vibe.d
about 355-357
deimos option 355
minimal option 355
vibe.d option 355
wrapper function
about 300
using 341
writeln function 27

Thank you for buying
Learning D

About Packt Publishing

Packt, pronounced 'packed', published its first book, *Mastering phpMyAdmin for Effective MySQL Management*, in April 2004, and subsequently continued to specialize in publishing highly focused books on specific technologies and solutions.

Our books and publications share the experiences of your fellow IT professionals in adapting and customizing today's systems, applications, and frameworks. Our solution-based books give you the knowledge and power to customize the software and technologies you're using to get the job done. Packt books are more specific and less general than the IT books you have seen in the past. Our unique business model allows us to bring you more focused information, giving you more of what you need to know, and less of what you don't.

Packt is a modern yet unique publishing company that focuses on producing quality, cutting-edge books for communities of developers, administrators, and newbies alike. For more information, please visit our website at www.packtpub.com.

About Packt Open Source

In 2010, Packt launched two new brands, Packt Open Source and Packt Enterprise, in order to continue its focus on specialization. This book is part of the Packt Open Source brand, home to books published on software built around open source licenses, and offering information to anybody from advanced developers to budding web designers. The Open Source brand also runs Packt's Open Source Royalty Scheme, by which Packt gives a royalty to each open source project about whose software a book is sold.

Writing for Packt

We welcome all inquiries from people who are interested in authoring. Book proposals should be sent to author@packtpub.com. If your book idea is still at an early stage and you would like to discuss it first before writing a formal book proposal, then please contact us; one of our commissioning editors will get in touch with you.

We're not just looking for published authors; if you have strong technical skills but no writing experience, our experienced editors can help you develop a writing career, or simply get some additional reward for your expertise.

open source *
community experience distilled
PUBLISHING

D Cookbook

ISBN: 978-1-78328-721-5   Paperback: 362 pages

Discover the advantages of programming in D with over 100 incredibly effective recipes

1. Leverage D to write efficient and correct programs with minimum code.

2. Learn advanced code generation techniques to automate programming tasks.

3. See how to apply D idioms to real-world problems and understand how it can benefit you.

Mastering D3.js

ISBN: 978-1-78328-627-0   Paperback: 352 pages

Bring your data to life by creating and deploying complex data visualizations with D3.js

1. Create custom charts as reusable components to be integrated with existing projects.

2. Design data-driven applications with several charts interacting between them.

3. Create an analytics dashboard to display real-time data using Node and D3 with real world examples.

Please check **www.PacktPub.com** for information on our titles

Objective-C Memory Management Essentials

ISBN: 978-1-84969-712-5   Paperback: 200 pages

Learn and put into practice various memory management techniques in Objective-C to create robust iOS applications

1. Learn about the concepts of memory management in Objective-C.

2. Get introduced to Swift, an innovative new programming language for Cocoa and Cocoa Touch.

3. A step-by-step approach to various memory management techniques with lots of sample code and Xcode projects for your reference.

C# Multithreaded and Parallel Programming

ISBN: 978-1-84968-832-1   Paperback: 344 pages

Develop powerful C# applications to take advantage of today's multicore hardware

1. Make use of the latest Visual Studio debugging tools, to manage and debug multiple threads running simultaneously.

2. Learn how to use the Thread, Task, and Parallel libraries in your C# applications.

3. Explore the evolution of multithreaded development in C#, starting with BackgroundWorker classes and moving on to threads and tasks and finally covering Async.

Please check **www.PacktPub.com** for information on our titles

www.ingramcontent.com/pod-product-compliance
Lightning Source LLC
Chambersburg PA
CBHW081457050326
40690CB00015B/2833